SPELLING

'Nothing short of a complete spelling-book will serve the turn of a really weak speller.'

H.W.Fowler, *Modern English Usage*

TEACH YOURSELF BOOKS

'Recommendation of steadiness and uniformity does not proceed from an opinion that particular combinations of letters have much influence on human happiness, or that truth may not be successfully taught by modes of spelling fanciful and erroneous.... Language is only the instrument of science [knowledge], and words are but the signs of ideas: I wish, however, that the instrument might be less apt to decay, and that signs might be permanent, like the things which they denote.'

Samuel Johnson, *A Dictionary of the English Language*

SPELLING

Patrick Thornhill

TEACH YOURSELF BOOKS
Hodder and Stoughton

First published 1976
Second edition 1983
Third impression 1987

ISBN 0 340 28764 0

Printed and bound in Great Britain
for Hodder and Stoughton Educational,
a division of Hodder and Stoughton Ltd,
Mill Road, Dunton Green Sevenoaks, Kent,
by Richard Clay Ltd, Bungay, Suffolk
Photoset by Memo Typography Ltd
Nicosia, Cyprus

Preface

If you follow the instructions given on page x, they should lead you quickly to the spelling of any English word you are likely to need for everyday purposes.

Looking up words in a dictionary, unless you already know how to spell them, can waste much time. If, for instance, you cannot spell the four words that sound like 'newclear', 'newmatic', 'newrotic', 'newsance', you should be able to track them down more speedily here than in a dictionary. Most pocket-dictionaries, moreover, are unable to find room for the many and various endings of a particular word — a favourite haunt of spelling mistakes — so a list of common word-endings has been added to the end of this book, together with some general guide-lines which follow the Introduction.

P.T.

Introduction

1 **Headings** are in strict alphabetical order, but within the word-lists this order is sometimes modified so that related words are kept together.

2 **Changes in stress** may occur, for example: abdom/en-inal *means* ābdomen, abdōminal.

3 **One spelling** may cover more than one meaning, for example: ground (earth, did grind).

4 **Meanings** – Where the meaning of a word is indicated in brackets its sole purpose is to avoid confusion between that word and another, for example: cue (drama, billiards), queue (line up). These indications should not be regarded as true definitions of meaning. For definitions refer to a dictionary.

5 **Prefixes** are standard word-openings, such as anti- de- ex- im- in- pro- un-. They are used in two ways:
  (i) to precede complete words, as in: antiseptic, decipher, immature, invertebrate, unpleasant;
  (ii) as an integral part of the word, as in: antipodean, decision, extort, imply, invoke, progress, ungainly.

In the latter type the removal of the prefix would leave an incomplete word, so such words are given in full in the lists, but the inclusion of all words of the former type would greatly lengthen this book, so such words are starred (*) and a footnote asks the reader to omit the prefix and look for the rest of the word.

6 **Initial capital letters.** While the names of people and places are always spelt with a capital letter (Darwin, Cheddar), there is no fixed rule about words derived from them, for example, Darwinism or darwinism, Cheddar cheese or cheddar. Generally, the small letter prevails as the use of the word increases, as with hamburger, hoover, marxism and demerara sugar.

7 **Hyphens** are used less than formerly: day-time has become daytime.

8 **Words ending in -ise or -ize.** In America, -ise is often used, but in British English most words of this type have in the past used -ize, though with exceptions (e.g., surprise). In this book we use -ise but mark with (z) those words in which the use of -ize is permissible.

9 **Apostrophes** are used in more than one way:

(i) With 's' to show possession, as in:

the dog's dinner	*meaning*	the dinner of the dog
the dogs' dinner	"	the dinner of the dogs
a woman's rights	"	the rights of a woman
women's rights	"	the rights of women
the boss's car	"	the car of the boss
the bosses' cars	"	the cars of the bosses

(ii) to shorten 'not' to 'n't', as in:
aren't can't didn't doesn't hadn't hasn't haven't isn't oughtn't shan't shouldn't wasn't won't wouldn't (and, in Ireland, amn't)

(iii) in these combinations:

	am	are	have	is, has	will	had, would
I	I'm		I've		I'll	I'd
he				he's	he'll	he'd
she				she's	she'll	she'd
it				it's[1]	it'll	
we		we're[2]	we've		we'll	we'd
you		you're[3]	you've		you'll	you'd
they		they're[4]	they've		they'll	they'd
that				that's	that'll	
there				there's[5]	there'll	there'd
where				where's		
who				who's[6]	who'll	who'd

1 *not* its (See that sheep? *It's* lost *its* lamb)
2 *not* were *or* where (*We're* not *where* we *were* yesterday)
3 *not* your (*You're* trailing *your* coat)
4 *not* their (*They're* eating *their* lunch)
5 *not* theirs (*There's* nothing of ours and little of *theirs*)
6 *not* whose (*Who's* the man *whose* horse won the race?)

(iv) to show the dropping of initial h, in conversation. ('I 'adn't the 'eart to tell 'im.')

(v) to shorten words in various ways, for example:
e'er (ever) 'twas (it was) 'twixt (betwixt), and in such conversational situations as, 'What's yours?' 'Mine's a...'

Note: There is no apostrophe in the words: hers, ours, theirs, yours
There is an apostrophe in 'its' only when it means 'it is' or 'it has'.

10 **Common word-endings** appear in a separate section at the end of this book.

Guidelines

Only simple 'rules', subject to few exceptions, are of practical use. Those given here refer mainly to word-endings.

Terms used:

> *singular* referring to one only (cat, mouse)
> *plural* referring to more than one (cats, mice)
> *vowels* the sounds of the letters a e i o u and y
> *consonants* the sounds of the other twenty letters
> *prefix* an addition at the beginning of a word (arm, *dis*arm; dear, *en*dear)
> *suffix* an addition at the end of a word (arm, arm*ed;* dear, dear*ly)*
> *soft* c when sounded like s; g when sounded like j
> *hard* c when sounded like k; g as in go

1 **Plurals.** The plural of most words is formed by adding -s (chair, chairs; desk, desks).

Words ending in -s -sh -ch -x and -z make the plural by adding -es (passes, wishes, churches, boxes, buzzes).

Words ending in -y after a consonant (baby, story) change the -y into -ies (babies, stories), but after a vowel they simply add -s (days, greys, boys, guys).

Some words ending in -o add -s (pianos), others add -es (potatoes); refer to main list.

Some words ending in a single -f change it to -ves in the plural (calf, calves; leaf, leaves); refer to main list.

2 **Silent -e.** A silent -e at the end of a word affects the sound of the previous vowel (hat, hate; din, dine; not, note; tub, tube). When you add a suffix that begins with a vowel, such as -ing -able -age -ular, you omit the silent -e (hate, hating; note, notable; mile, milage; tube, tubular).

When you add a suffix that begins with a consonant, such as -ly -ful, you keep the silent -e (love, lovely; sincere, sincerely; hope, hopeful). Exceptions: truly, duly, awful.

3 **Doubling the final consonant.** When a word ends in a single consonant after a single vowel (hot, big, map, bed) double the consonant before a suffix that begins with a vowel, such as -er -est -ing -ed -y (hotter, biggest, mapping, bedded).

4 **Adding -ing to words ending in -ie.** When -ing is added to a word ending in -ie, the -ie is changed to -y (die, dying; lie, lying).

5 **-ie or -ei?** An old rhyme says:
'I before e, except after c
Or when sounded as ay, as in neighbour and weigh.'
'I before e': (pie, brief, niece).
'Except after c': There are, in fact, very few *cei* words (ceiling, conceit, conceive, deceit, deceive, perceive, receipt, receive) and there are several exceptions (ancient, conscience, science, specie, species).
'Sounded as ay' words include deign, feign, heinous, heir, reign, rein, their, veil, vein.
Other exceptions to 'i before e' include either, height, heifer, leisure, neither, seize, weird.

6 **-able or -ible?** There is no simple way of being certain, though there are more words ending in -able than in -ible, and -able is always used in newly coined words. As both of these suffixes start with a vowel, the silent -e rule (see 2) applies (like, likable; sense, sensible) except when -able follows ce or ge (chargeable, enforceable).

7 **-ant (-ance -ancy) or -ent (-ence -ency)?** Use -ant after hard c and g (applicant, elegant); use -ent after soft c and g (innocent, diligent). Otherwise, there are no easy guidelines. In a few instances both forms are used, though with a difference in meaning (dependent, dependant).

8 **-ful, -fully.** Words such as harmful, wonderful, hopeful can add -ly (harmfully, wonderfully, hopefully).
Terms such as 'a cupful' when used in the plural can be either 'cupfuls' or 'cupsful'; or you can use 'full' as a separate word and ask for 'a cup full of tea'.

9 **-cede, -ceed or -sede?** It is best to memorise the following words: cede, concede, intercede, precede, recede; exceed, proceed, succeed; supersede.

How To Find The Word You Want

1   Think of, or guess, the first 3 or 4 letters of the word you want and find the heading with that group of letters, e.g. **ABA**

2   Scan the words listed under that heading.

3   If the word you want is not there, try the most likely of any word-openings suggested at the end of the list, e.g. (ABB ABE OBE)

4   Word-endings are shown in two ways, for example:
   (i)   abandon -ed -ing -ment *means* abandon abandoned abandoning abandonment;

   (ii) abat/e -ed -ing -ement *means* abate abated abating abatement; that is, the stroke (/) marks the place at which the ending can be joined to the main part of the word.

5   When 's' alone is added to form the plural of a word, it is shown only if there is likely to be doubt about it, e.g. contralto-s.

Abbreviations

Am	American	*Jap*	Japanese
Arab	Arabic	*L*	Latin
Aus	Australian	*NZ*	New Zealand
F	French	*Nor*	Norwegian
Ger	German	*Russ*	Russian
Gr	Greek	*Sc*	Scottish
Heb	Hebrew	*Sp*	Spanish
Hind	Indian languages	*Sw*	Swedish
Ir	Irish	*W*	Welsh
It	Italian		

A

ABA
aback
abac/us - i
abaft
abandon - ed - ing - ment
abas/e - ed - ing - ement
abash - ed
abat/e - ed - ing - ement
abattoir
(ABB ABE OBE)

ABB
abbess - es
abbey - s
abbot
abbreviat/e - ed - ing - ion
(AB)

ABD
abdicat/e - ed - ing - ion
abdom/en - inal - inally
abduct - ed - ing - ion

ABE
abeam
abed
abedient? *No*, obedient
abel? *No*, able
aberration
abet - ted - ting - tor
abeyance
(ABB HAB OBE)

ABH
abhor - red - ring - rence - rent

ABI
abid/e - ing; abode
abilit/y - ies
(ABY HAB OBI)

ABJ - ABN
abject (degraded) - ion; *not*
object
abjur/e (renounce) - ed - ing

-ation; *not* adjure
ablaze
abl/e - er - est - y
ablution
abnegat/e - ion - ory
abnormal - ly - ity - ities
(OBJ OBL OBN)

ABO
aboard
abode
abolish - ed - ing; abolition
abomin/able - ably - ate - ation
aborigin/e - es - al
abort - ed - ing - ion - ionist - ive
abound - ed - ing; *but*
abundance
about
above
(ABB ABH)

ABR
abra/de (chafe) - ded - ding
- sion; *not* upbraid
abreast
abreviate? *No*, abbreviate
abridg/e - ed - ing - ment *or*
- ement
abroad
abrogat/e - ed - ing - ion
abrupt - ly - ness
(ABB)

ABS
abscess - es - ed
abscissa - e
abscond - ed - ing - er
abseil - ed - ing - er
absence
absent - ed - ing - ly - ee
absolut/e - ely - eness - ion
absolv/e - ed - ing
absorb - ed - ing - ent - ently

1

-able -ability
absorpt/ion -ive -iveness
abstain -ed -ing -er
abstemious -ly -ness
abst/ention -inence
abstract -ed -ing -ion
abstruse -ly -ness
absurd -er -est -ly -ity
(OBS)

ABT
(OBT)

ABU
abundan/t -tly -ce
abus/e -ed -ing -ive -ively
-iveness
abut -ted -ting -ment
(EBU)

ABY
abys/s -mal -mally -ses
Abyssinia -n
(ABI)

ACA
acacia
academ/y -ies -ic -ical -ically
(ECA OCC)

ACCE ACCI
acced/e (consent) -ed
-ing; not exceed
accelerat/e -ed -ing -ion -or
accent (in words) -ed -ing;
not ascent, assent
accentuat/e -ed -ing -ion
accept (admit) -ed -ing
-ance; not except
acceptab/le -ly -ility
access (entry) -ion -ible -ibly
-ibility; not assess, excess
accessor/y -ies
accident -al -ally
(AX ECC EX)

ACCL
acclaim -ed -ing
acclamation
acclimatis/e -ed -ing -ation
(z)
(ECC ECL OCC)

ACCO
accommodat/e -ed -ing -ion
accompan/y -ies -ied -ying
-ist

accomplice
accomplish -ed -ing -ment
accord -ed -ing -ingly -ance
accordion -ist
accost -ed -ing
account -ed -ing -ant -ancy
accountab/le -ly -ility
(ACO ECO)

ACCR
accredit -ed -ing -ation
accretion
accru/e -ed -ing
(ACR)

ACCU
accumulat/e -ed -ing -ion -or
accura/te -tely -cy
accus/e -ed -ing -ation -ative
-atory
accustom -ed -ing
(ACQU ACU ECU OCCU)

ACE
ace
acerbity
acetic (acid); not ascetic,
aseptic
acet/one -ous -ate -ylene
acetif/y -ied -ying -ication
(ASC ASE ASS)

ACH
ach/e -ed -ing
achiev/e -ed -ing -ement
(ACK AK ECH)

ACI
acid -ly -ity -ify -ified
-ification
acidul/ated -ous
acidosis
(ASI ASS ASY)

ACK
ack-ack
ackmy? No, acme
acknowledg/e -ed -ing -ment
or -ement
ackney? No, acne or hackney
ackward? No, awkward
(ACC ACH ACQU AK AQU
HAC)

ACL
(ACCL ECL)

2

ACM ACN

acme (highest point)
acne (pimples)
acnowledge? *No,*
acknowledge

ACO

acorn
acoustic - al - ally
(ACCO ECHO ECO)

ACQU

acquaint - ed - ing - ance
-anceship
acquiesc/e - ed - ing - ent
-ence
acquir/e - ed - ing
acquisit/ion - ive - ively
-iveness
acquit - ted - ting - tal
(AQU EQU)

ACR

acre - age
acrid
acril/an - ic
acrimon/y - ious - iously
acrobat - ic - ically
acronym
across
acrostic
(ACCR)

ACS

(ACC AX EX)

ACT

act - ed - ing - able - or - ress
action - able - ably
activ/e - ely - ity - ities - ist
activat/e - ed - ing - ion
actual - ly - ity
actuar/y - ies - ial - ially
actuat/e - ed - ing - ion

ACU

acuity
acupuncture
acumen
acute - ly - ness
(ACCU ACQU ECU)

AD ADA

ad, *for* advertisement
A.D., *for* anno domini (*L*)
adage
adagio (*It*)

adamant - ly - ine
adapt (alter) - ed - ing - ation
adaptab/le - ly - ility
(ADD ADO HAD)

ADD

add - ed - ing
addend/um - a
adder
addict - ed - ing - ion
addit/ion (put on) - ional
-ionally - ive - ively; *not*
edition
addl/e - ed
address - es - ed - ing - ee - or
or- er
addressograph - ed - ing
adduc/e - ed - ing - ible
(AD HAD)

ADE

adenoids
adept (skilled); *not* adapt
adequa/te - tely - cy
(ADD ADI HAD)

ADG

(AG ADJ)

ADH

adher/e - ed - ing - ent
adhes/ion - ive - ively
ad hoc (*L*)

ADI

adieu - s *or* - x
adipos/e - ity
adit (tunnel); *not* edit
(ADDI ADE EDI)

ADJ

adjacent
adjar? *No,* ajar
adjectiv/e - al - ally
adjoin - ed - ing
adjourn - ed - ing - ment
adjudicat/e - ed - ing - ion - or
adjunct
adjur/e (request) - ed - ing
-ation; *not* abjure
adjust - ed - ing - ment - able
adjutant
(AGE AJ)

ADL

ad lib, *for* ad libitum (*L*)
(ADD)

ADM

admass
administer - ed - ing
administrat/ion - ive - ively - or
admirab/le - ly
admiral - ty
admir/e - ed - ing - ation
admiss/ion - ible - ibility
admit - ted - ting - tance
admonish - ed - ing
admonition

ADO

ado (fuss); *not* adieu
adolesc/ent - ence
adopt - ed - ing - ion - ive; *not*
  adapt, adept
ador/e - ed - ing - ation - able
adorn - ed - ing - ment
  (ADU)

ADR

adrenalin
adrift
  (ADDR)

ADU

aduce? *No*, adduce
adue? *No*, adieu
adulat/e - ed - ing - ion - or - ory
adult - hood
adulterat/e - ed - ing - ion
adulter/y - ies - er - ess
adumbrat/e - ed - ing - ion
  (ADD EDU)

ADV

advanc/e - ed - ing - ement
advantage - ous - ously
advent
adventitious - ly
adventur/e - ed - ing - er - ess
adventurous - ly - ness
adverb - ial - ially
adversar/y - ies
advers/e - ely - ity
advert (refer to) - ed - ing
advertis/e - ed - ing - ement
  -er (*not* z)
advice
advis/e - ed - ing - er - ory - edly

advisab/le - ly - ility
advoca/te - ted - ting - tory - cy

ADZ

adze (a tool)

AEG

aegis
  (AGE EJ)

AEO

aeolian
aeon *or* eon
  (EO IO YO)

AER

aerat/e - ed - ing - ion
aerial - ly
aero-*, *prefix meaning*
  related to air
aero/batic - naut - nautics - sol
aero/drome - foil - plane - lite
  (AIR)

AES

aesthet/e - ic - ical
  (ES EAS)

AFA-AFF

afar
affab/le - ly - ility
affair
affect (influence) - ed - ing;
  not effect (result,
  accomplish)
affectation
affection - ate - ately
affidavit
affiliat/e - ed - ing - ion
affinit/y - ies
affirm - ed - ing - ation
affirmative - ly
affix - ed - ing
afflict - ed - ing - ion
affluen/t (wealthy) - tly - ce
afford - ed - ing
afforest - ed - ing - ation
affront - ed - ing
  (AF- APH EFF OFF)

AFG-AFR

Afghan - istan
afire
aflame

---

* If the word you wish to spell is not in this list, omit the prefix
and look for the rest of the word.

afloat
afoot
aforesaid
afraid
afresh
Africa - n
Afrikaans
Afrikaner
(AFF APH EFF)

AFT
aft
after - wards - noon
after - math - thought
(HAFT)

AGA
again
against
agast? *No,* aghast
agate
(EGA)

AGE
age, aged, ageing *or* aging
agenc/y - ies
agenda
agent
(ADJ AJ EJ)

AGG
agglomerat/e - ion
aggrandise - ment
aggravat/e - ed - ing - ion - or
aggregat/e - ed - ing - ion
aggrieve - d
aggress/ion - ive - ively
 - iveness - or
aggro
(AGR EGR)

AGH
aghast

AGI
agil/e - ity
agitat/e - ed - ing - ion - edly
 - or
(ADJ HAG)

AGN AGO
agnostic - ally - ism
ago
agog

agon/y - ies - ise - ised - ising
(z)
agoraphobia
(EGO)

AGR
agree - d - ing - able - ment
agricultur/e - al - ist *or* alist
aground
(AGGR EGR)

AGU
ague (fever); *not* argue

AH
ah! aha! ahoy!
ahead

AI
aid - ed - ing
aide - de - camp
aik? *No,* ache
ail (to be ill) - ed - ing - ment
aileron
aim - ed - ing - less - lessly
ain't (am not, is not)
air (atmosphere) - ed - ing - y
 - less; *not* hair *or* heir
air - *, *prefix to* - borne - craft
 - man - way, etc.
Airedale
airial? *No,* aerial
airo - ? *No,* aero-
aisle (in church) - d; *not* isle
ait *or* eyot (island); *not* ate (did
eat) *or* eight (8)
aitch (H) - bone
(AE AY EI EY HAI)

AJ
ajar
(ADJ AGE EJ)

AK
ake - ake (*NZ*)
akimbo
akin
(AC HAC HAK)

ALA
à la carte (*F*)
alacrity
alaminium? *No,* aluminium
alarm - ed - ing - ist

* If the word you wish to spell is not in this list, omit the prefix
and look for the rest of the word.

alarum
alas!
(ALLA HALA ELA ILLA)
ALB
alb
albacore
albatross
albin/o -os -ism
album
album/en -inous -inoid
albuminuria
alburn? *No*, auburn
(HALB AUB)
ALC
alchem/y -ist -ical
alcheringa (*Aus*)
alcohol -ic -ism
alcove
(ALK)
ALD
alder/man -men -manry
(AUD ELD ORD)
ALE
ale (beer); *not* ail, hail, hale
alert -ed -ing -ness
(AIL ALLE ELE HAIL HALE)
ALF
alfalfa
al fresco
(ALPH ELF HALF)
ALG
algebra -ic -ically
alga -e
Algeria -n
ALI
alias -es
alibi -s
alienab/le -ly -ility
alien -ate -ating -ated -ation
alight -ed -ing
align -ed -ing -ment
alike
aliment (food) -ary -ation
alimony
aline? *No*, align
alive
(ALLI ELI HALI)
ALK
alkali -s *or* -es -ne
(ALC)

ALL ALLA
all (every one)
Allah
allay -ed -ing
(ALA ELA HALA)
ALLE
alleg/e -ed -ing -ation
allegiance
allegor/y -ies -ical -ically
alleluia! *or* hallelujah!
allerg/y -ies -ic
alleviat/e -ed -ing -ion
alley (narrow way); *not* ally
(ALE ALLI ELE)
ALLI
alli/es -ed -ance; *but* ally -ing
alligator
alliterat/ion -ive
(ALLE ALI ELI ELL ILLI)
ALLO
allocat/e -ed -ing -ion
allot -ted -ting -ment
allow -ed -ing -ance -able
alloy -ed -ing
(ALO ELO HALLO ILLO)
ALLR-ALLT
allready? *No*, already
allright? *No*, all right
allso? *No*, also
allthough? *No*, although
alltogether? *No*, altogether *or*
  all together
allways? *No*, always
ALLU
allud/e (refer) -ed -ing; *not*
  elude (avoid)
allur/e -ed -ing -ement
allurgic? *No*, allergic
allusion (reference) -ive; *not*
  illusion, elusion
alluvi/um -al -ation
ally -ing (*see* allies)
(ALU ELU HALLU ILLU)
ALM
almanac
almighty
almond
almoner
almost
alms (gift); *not* arms

(ARM HALM HARM)

ALO
aloe
aloft
alone
along - side
aloof
aloud; *not* allowed
(ALLO ELO HALO)

ALP-ALS
alp - ine - inist
alpaca
alpenstock
alpha (*Gr*)
alphabet - ic - ical - ically
already
alright? *No*, all right
also

ALT
altar (in church); *not* halter
alter (change) - ed - ing - ation
altercation
alternat/e - ed - ing - ion - ely
alternative - ly
although
altitude
alto - s
altogether
altru/ism - ist - istic
(HALT ULT)

ALU
alum - ina
aluminium (*Am*, aluminum)
alumn - us - i
alurgic? *No*, allergic
(ALLU ELU ILLU HALLU)

ALV
alveol/e - us - ar - ate
(HALV)

ALW
always

AM AMA
am
amalgam - ate - ating - ation
amarous? *No*, amorous
amass - ed - ing
amateur - ism - ish
amat/ive - ory - orial
amaz/e - ed - ing - ment
(AMM EMA HAM)

AMB
ambassador - ial, *but*
  embassy
amber
ambergris
ambidext/rous - erity
ambien/t - ce
ambigu/ity - ities - ous - ously
ambit
ambit/ion - ious - iously
ambivalen/ce - t - tly
ambl/e - ed - ing - er
ambrosia - l
ambulance
ambush - ed - ing, ambuscade
(EMB HAMB UMB)

AME
ameba (*Am*.) *see* amoeba
ameliorat/e - ed - ing - ion
amen
amen/able - ability
amend (improve) - ed - ing;
  not emend (correct)
amenit/y - ies
America - n - nism
amerous? *No*, amorous
ameture? *No*, amateur
amethyst - ine
(AIM AMA AMME EME)

AMF
(AMPH)

AMI
ami/able - ably - ability - ty
amic/able - ably - ability
amid - st
amidships
amino- acid
amiss
amit? *No*, omit (leave out),
  emit (give out)
(EMI OMI)

AMM
ammeter (electric); *not*
  amateur (unprofessional)
ammick? *No*, hammock
ammonia - ted
ammunition *or* ammo
(AM- HAM)

AMN
amnesia

7

amnest/y -ies
amni/on -otic
AMO
amoeb/a -ic
amok *or* amuck
among -st
amontillado (*Sp*)
amoral -ity
amorous -ly, -ness
amorphous -ly, -ness
amortis/e -ation (z)
amount -ed -ing
amour
  (AMA AMMO EMO
  HAMM)
AMP
amp, *for* ampere, amperage
ampersand
amphetamine
amphibi/an -ous -ously
amphitheatre
ampl/e -y -itude
amplif/y -ies -ied -ier -ying
 -ication
ampoule
amputat/e -ed -ing -ion
  (EMP HAMP)
AMU
amuck *or* amok
amulet
amus/e -ed -ing -ement
  (AMMU EMUL)
AN ANA
an
anabatic
anabranch (*Aus*)
anachron/ism -istic
anaconda
anaem/ia -ic
anaesthe/sia -tic -tist
anaesthetis/e -ed -ing -ation
 (z)
anagram -matic
anal -ly
analgesic
analine? *No*, aniline
analogue (*Am*, analog)
analog/y -ies -ous
analys/e -ed -ing -is -es -t
analytic -al -ally

anarch/y -ic -ical -ist
anathema
anatom/y -ical -ist
  (ANNA ANO ENA)
ANC
ancest/or -ry -ral
anchor -ed -ing -age
anchov/y -ies
ancient
ancillar/y -ies
anctious? *No*, anxious
  (ANK ENC HAN)
AND
and
andante (*It*)
andiron
andro/gen -gyny -gynous
  (END HAND)
ANE
anecdot/e -al -age
anemic *or* anaemic
anemometer
anemone (*not* -y)
anent
aneroid
anesthetic *or* anaesthetic
aneur/in -ism
  (ANNE)
ANG
angel (spirit) -ic; *not* angle
  (corner, to fish)
angelica
angelus
anger -ed; *but* angry
angina
angl/e -ed -ing -er; *not* angel
Anglican
Anglo -Saxon
Anglo/phile -phobe -phobia
angora
angostura
angr/y -ily
angsiety? *No*, anxiety
anguish -ed
angular -ity -ities
  (ENG HANG)
ANH
anhydrous
  (ENH)

ANI

anialate? *No*, annihilate
anigma? *No*, enigma
aniline
animadver/t - ted - ting - sion
animal - ity
animat/e - ed - ing - ion
anim/ism /ist
animosit/y - ies
aniseed
anisthetic? *No*, anaesthetic
(ANNI ENI)

ANJ

(ANG ENJ)

ANK

anker? *No*, anchor
ankle
(ANC ANX HANK)

ANN

annals
anneal - ed - ing
annex - ed - ing - ation
annexe (building)
annihilat/e - ed - ing - ion
anniversar/y - ies
anno domini (A.D.)
annotat/e - ed - ing - ion
announc/e - ed - ing - ement
annoy - ed - ing - ance
annual - ly
annuit/y - ies - ant
annul - led - ling - ment
annular
annum
annunciation; *not*
  enunciation (pronouncing)
  (AN -)

ANO

anode
anodyne
anoint - ed - ing
anomal/y - ous
anon (soon)
anonym/ous (*short form*,
  anon.) - ously - ity
anopheles
anorak

another
  (ANA ANNO ENO)

ANS

answer - ed - ing - able
  (ANC ENS HANS)

ANT ANTA

ant (insect); *not* aunt
antagon/ist - ism - istic
antagonis/e - ed - ing
Antarctic
  (ENT)

ANTE

ante*, *prefix meaning*
  before; *not* anti - (against)
anteceden/ce - t - tly
antediluvian
antelope
ante meridiem (a.m.)
antenn/a - ae *or* - s - al - ary
antepenultimate
ante - post
anterior (front) - *not* interior
  (ANTI ENTE)

ANTH

anthem
anther
antholog/y - ies - ist
anthracite
anthrax
anthropoid
anthropolog/y - ical - ically - ist
anthropomorph/ic - ous - ism
anthropophag/i - y - ous
  (ANS ENTH)

ANTI

anti*, *prefix* meaning
  against; *not* ante- (before)
antibiotic - ally
antic
anticipat/e - ed - ing - ion - or
  - ory
anticlin/e - al
antidote
antimacassar
antimony
antipath/y - ies - etic
antipod/es - ean

---

* If the word you wish to spell is not in this list, omit the prefix
and look for the rest of the word.

antiqu/e -ated -arian
antiquit/y -ies
antirrhinum
antiseptic -ally
antithes/is -es
 (ANTE ENTI UNTI)
ANTL
antler
ANTO
antonomasia
antonym -ous
 (ENTO)
ANU-ANZ
anurism? *No*, aneurism
anus, anal
anvil
anxiet/y -ies
anxious -ly
any -body -one -how -thing
 -way -where
Anzac
 (EN)
AO
aorta
 (AEO EO)
APA
apace
apache -s
apart -ment
apartheid (*Af*)
apath/y -etic -etically
 (APE APPA OPA)
APE
ape -d -ing
aperient
aperitif
aperture
apex -es *or* apices
 (APA API APPE)
APH
aphasia
aphi/s -des
aphorism
aphrodisiac
 (AF EFF EPH HAPH UPH)
API
apiar/y -ies -ian
apiece
 (EPI OPI)

APL
aplomb
 (APPL)
APO
apocalyp/se -tic
apocrypha -l
apologis/e -ed -ing (z)
apolog/y -ies -etic -etically
apolster? *No,* upholster
apopl/exy -ectic
aposta/te -sy
apost/le -olic
apostrophe -s
apothecar/y -ies
 (APPO EPO OPO OPPO)
APPA
appal -led -ling
apparatus -es
apparel -led -ling
apparent -ly
apparition
 (APA APPE)
APPE
appeal -ed -ing
appear -ed -ing -ance
appeas/e -ed -ing -ement
appell/ation -able -ability
append -ed -ing -age
appendicitis
appendi/x -ces (to books)
appendix -es (medical)
appertain -ed -ing
appetis/er -ing (z)
appetite
 (APE HAP)
APPL
applaud -ed -ing
applause
apple
appliance
applic/ant -able -ation
appl/y -ies -ied -ying
APPO
appoint -ed -ing -ment
apportion (share) -ed -ing
 -ment; *not* abortion
apposit/e (appropriate) -ly
 -ness -ion; *not* opposite
 (APO OPO OPPO)

APPR

 apprais/e (judge) - ed - ing - al;
   not apprise (inform)
 appreciab/le - ly
 appreciat/e - ed - ing - ion
 apprehen/d - ded - ding - sion
 apprentic/e - ed - ing - eship
 appris/e (inform) - ed - ing;
   not appraise (judge)
 appro, *for* approval
 approach - ed - ing - able
   - ability
 approbation
 appropriat/e - ed - ing - ion - ely
 approv/e - ed - ing - al
 approximat/e - ed - ing - ion
   - ely
   (APR OPPR)

APPU

 appurtenance
   (APE APPE)

APR

 apricot
 April
 apron
 apropos
   (APPR)

APS

 apse
 apsidal
   (ABS)

APT

 apt - ly - itude
 apteryx
   (ABD OBT)

AQU

 aqua -*, *prefix meaning*
   water, *with* - lung - marine,
   etc.
 aquar/ium - ia
 Aquari/us - an
 aquatic - ally
 aqueduct
 aqueous
 aquiline
   (ACQ EQU)

ARA

 Arab - ia - ian - ic - y
 arabesque
 arable
   (ARRA ERA ERRA HARA)

ARB

 arbit/er - rary - rarily
 arbitrat/e - ed - ing - ion - or
 arboreal
 arbour (bower); (*Am* arbor)
 arbutus
   (HARB)

ARC

 arc (of circle); *not* Noah's ark.
 arcade
 arcad/y - ian
 arch -*, *prefix meaning*
   super-, *with* - bishop, - fiend,
   etc.
 archaeolog/y - ical - ist
 archaic - ally
 archangel - ic
 archer - y
 archipelago - s
 architect- ure - ural - onic
 architrave
 archiv/e - al - ist
 Arctic
   (ARK HARK)

ARD

 ardent
 ardour (*Am*, ardor)
 arduous/ly
   (HARD)

ARE

 are
 area (space); *not* aria (music)
 arena
 aren't, *for* are not
   (AER AIR ARRE ERE HARE)

ARF

   (AF HAF HALF)

ARG

 argent
 Argentin/a - e - ian
 argle - bargle
 argon

---

* If the word you wish to spell is not in this list, omit the prefix
and look for the rest of the word.

argos/y - ies
argu/e - ed - ing - able - ably
argument - ation - ative

ARI
aria (music); *not* area (space)
arid - ity
arigh? *No* , awry
aris/e - en - ing
aristocra/t - tic - cy
arithmetic - al
   (ARE ARRI ARY AURI
   HARR)

ARK
ark (Noah's); *not* arc

ARM
arm - ed - ing - let - ful - pit
armada
armadillo - s
Armageddon
armament
armature (electric); *not*
   amateur
Armenia - n
armistice
armorial
armour - ed - er - y (*Am* armor)
arms (limbs, weapons); *not*
   alms (gifts)
army, army's, armies
   armies'
   (ALM HARM)

ARN
arnica (plant)
   (HARN)

ARO
aroma - tic
arose
around
arous/e - ed - ing
   (ARRO ERO)

ARP
arpeggio - s
   (HARP)

ARR
arrack
arraign (accuse) - ed - ing
   - ment
arrang/e (put in order) - ed
   - ing - ement
arrant (notorious); *not* errant

(wandering)
array - ed - ing
arrear
arrest - ed - ing
arriv/e - ed - ing - al
arrog/ant - ate - ated - ating
   - ation
arrow (bow and); *not* harrow
   (agric., etc.)
   (AR- HAR)

ARS
arse; *not* ass (donkey)
arsenal
arsenic - al
arson - ist
   (ASK HARS)

ART
art - ist - iste - istic - istically
artefact *or* artifact
arter/y - ial - ially
artesian
artful - ly - ness
arthrit/is - ic
arthur (writer)? *No*, author
artichoke
artic? *No*, arctic
article
articulat/e - ed - ing - ion
artific/e - er
artificial - ly - ity
artillery
artisan
artless - ly; *not* heartless
arty (artistic); *not* hearty
   (genial)
   (HART HEART)

ARU
arum (lily);
   (ERU)

ARY
aryan
arye? *No*, awry
   (ARI)

AS
as; *not* has (to have)
   (ASS AZ)

ASB
asbestos
   (ASP)

ASCE

ascend - ed - ing - ant
ascension
ascent (rise); *not* assent
  (agree); *not* accent (in
  speech)
ascertain - ed - ing - ment
ascetic (austere); *not* acetic
  (acid); *not* aseptic (sterile)
  (ASE ASSE)

ASCR

ascrib/e - ed - ing; *not* escribe
  (math.)
ascription
  (ESCR)

ASE

asepsis
aseptic - ally
asexual - ly - ity
  (ACE ASCE ASSE)

ASF

  (ASPH)

ASH

ash - es - er y
ashamed
ashet (*NZ*)
ashfelt? *No,* asphalt
ashlar
ashore (on land); *not* assure
  (ASSU HASH)

ASI

Asia - n - tic
aside
asinin/e - ity
  (ACI ASSI ASY)

ASK

ask - ed - ing
askance
askari
askew
  (ASC ESC ESK)

ASL

aslant
asleep

ASM

asma? *No,* asthma

ASP

asp (serpent); *not* hasp
  (fastening)
asparagus

aspect
aspen
asperit/y - ies
aspersion
asphalt
asphodel
asphyxia - te - ted - ting - tion
aspic
aspidistra
aspirant
aspirat/e - ed - ing - ion
aspir/e - ed - ing - ant
aspirin
  (ESP)

ASS ASSA

ass (donkey) -'s (donkey's)
  - es (donkeys)
assagai *or* assegai
assail - ed - ing - ant
assassin - ate - ated - ating
  - ation - ator
assault - ed - ing
assay (test) - ed - ing; *not*
  essay
  (ESS)

ASSE

assemblage
assembl/e - ed - ing - y
assent (agree) - ed - ing; *not*
  ascent (rise); *not* accent (in
  speech)
assert - ed - ing - ion
assess (estimate) - ed - ing
  - ment; *not* access (entry)
asset
  (ACE ASC ASE)

ASSI

assidu/ity - ous - ously
assign - ed - ing - ment
assignation
assimilat/e - ed - ing - ion
assist - ed - ing - ance - ant
assize
  (ACI ASI ASY)

ASSO

associat/e - ed - ing - ion
assort - ed - ing - ment
  (HASS ESO)

ASSU

assuag/e - ed - ing

assum/e -ed -ing -ption
assunder? *No,* asunder
assure/ -ed -ing -ance
(ASU AZU)
AST
aster (flower)
asterisk
astern
asteroid
asthma -tic
astigmat/ism -ic
astir (stirring)
astonish -ed -ing -ment
astound -ed -ing
astral
astray
astride
astringent
astrolog/y -er -ist -ical -ically
astronaut -ic -ical -ically
astronom/y -ic -ical -ically -er
astute -ly -ness
(EST)
ASU
asunder
(ASSU AZU)
ASY
asylum
asymmetr/y -ical
(ASSI)
AT ATE
at
ate (did eat); *not* eight (8)
(ATT HAT)
ATH
athe/ism -ist -istic -istically
athirst
athlet/e -ic -icism
athritis? *No,* arthritis
athwart
(ETH HATH)
ATI
(ATTI ATY)
ATL
Atlantic
atlas
ATM
atmosphere
ATO
atoll

atom -ic -ise -ised -ising
-isation (z)
atonal -ity
aton/e -ed -ing -ement
(ATTO)
ATR
atrabilious
atrip
atrocious -ly
atrocit/y -ies
atroph/y -ies -ied -ying
atropine
(ATTR HATR)
ATTA-ATTI
attaboy!
attach -ed -ing -ment
attaché
attack -ed -ing -er
attain -ed -ing -ment
attar
attempt -ed -ing
attend -ed -ing -ance -ant
attent/ion -ive -ively
attenuat/e -ed -ing -ion
attest -ed -ing -ation
attic
attir/e -ed -ing
attitud/e -inise (z)
ATTO
attorney
(ATO)
ATTR
attract -ed -ing -ive -ion
attribut/e -ed -ing -ive -ion
attrition
(ATR)
ATTU
attun/e -ed -ing
atturney? *No,* attorney
ATY
atypical
(ATTI ETY)
AUB
aubergine
aubrietia
auburn
(HAUB ORB)
AUC
auckward? *No,* awkward
auction -ed -ing -eer

(HAWK ORC)

AUD
audaci/ty - ous - ously
audib/le - ility
audience
audio -*, *prefix meaning*
  hearing
audit - ed - ing - or
audit/ory - orium - ion
(ALD ORD)

AUF
aufull? *No*, awful
(OFF ORPH)

AUG
Augean
auger (tool)
aught (anything); *not* ought
augment - ed - ing - ation
augur (foretell) - y - ed - ing
August
(HAU ORG)

AUK
auk (sea bird); *not* hawk
aukward? *No*, awkward
(ORC)

AUN
aunt (relation); *not* ant
  (insect), *or* aren't (are not)
(AWN HAU ORN)

AUP
au pair
(ORP)

AUR
aura
aural (by ear) - ly; *not* oral (by
  mouth)
aureole
au revoir
auricula (flower)
auricular (related to hearing)
auriferous
aurist (ear doctor)
aurora -/- borealis - australis
(AR HOR HOA OR WHO)

AUS
auspic/e - es - ious - iously
Aussie, *for* Australian

auster/e - ity - ities
austral - oid
Australasia - n
Australia - n
australite
(HOS OS)

AUTH
authentic - ally - ity - ate - ated
  - ating - ation
author - ship
author/ise - ised - isation (z)
authorit/y - ies - ative - arian
(ORTH)

AUTI
aut/ism - istic
  (self - absorbed); *not* artistic
(HAU HOR)

AUTO
auto -*, *prefix meaning* self
auto, *for* automobile
autobahn
autobiograph/y - ies - ical - er
autocra/cy - cies - tic - tically
autograph - ed - ing
automat/ic - ion
automobile
autonom/y - ous - ously
autopsy
autostrada
(ORT)

AUTU
autumn - al

AUX
auxiliar/y - ies
(OX)

AV
avail - ed - ing - able - ability
avalanche
avaric/e - ious - iously
avast!
aveng/e - ed - ing - er
avenue
aver - red - ring
averag/e - ed - ing
avers/e - ion
avert (ward off) - ed - ing; *not*
  evert

---

* If the word you wish to spell is not in this list, omit the prefix
and look for the rest of the word.

avian
aviar/y - ies
aviat/ion - or
avid - ity - ly
avocado - s
avocation
avocet
avoid - ed - ing - able - ance
avow - ed - ing - edly
avuncular - ity
(EV HAV)

AW

await - ed - ing
awak/e - en - ened *or* awoken
award - ed - ing
aware - ness
awash
away
awe, awed
awful - ly - ness
awhile
awkward - ly - ness
awl (tool); *not* all (everyone)
awn (husk); *not* horn
awning
awoke - n
awry, *pronounced* arye
(AU HAW HOR OR)

AX

axe, axes, axed, axing
axes (more than one axis)
axil - lary
axiom - atic - atically
axis, axes, axial - ly
axle
(ACC EX)

AY

ay (yes), ayes
ayatollah
aye (always)
(AI HAI HAY)

AZ

azalea
azimuth - al
azure
(AS HAS HAZ)

B

BAA

baa (bleat) - ed - ing

baal - im
baas (boss)
(BAR)

BAB

babbl/e - ed - ing - er
babe
baboon
babtise? *No*, baptise
babu
baby - ish

BAC

baccarat
bacchanalia - n
baccy, *for* tobacco
bach, *for* bachelor (*Aus, NZ*)
bachelor - dom
bacill/us - i
back - ed - ing - er
backside
backslid/e - ing
backward - s - ness
backwoods - man - men
bacon
bacteri/um - a
bacteriolog/y - ist - ical - ically
(BAK BEC)

BAD-BAG

bad - ly - ness - dy - dies
bade (asked)
badge
badger - ed - ing
badinage
badminton
baffl/e - ed - ing
baffy
bag - ged - ging - gy - gier
- giest
bagatelle
baggage
bagnio - s
bagpipe

BAI

baige? *No*, beige
bail (legal, cricket); *not* bale
(bundle, empty)
bailey
bailie (*Sc*)
bail/iff - or (legal)
bailiwick
bain? *No*, bane

16

bairn
baist? *No*, baste
bait - ed - ing; *not* bated
   (breath)
baize (woollen stuff); *not*
   bays
   (BAY)
BAK
bak/e - ed - ing - er - ery
bakelite
   (BAC)
BAL
balaclava
balalaika
balanc/e - ed - ing - er
balcon/y - ies
bald - ing - er - est - ly - ness
balderdash
baldric
bal/e (bundle) - ed - ing; *not*
   bail (empty out water)
baleen
balk *or* baulk - ed - ing
balkan
   (BALL BEL BOL)
BALL
ball (globe); *not* bawl (shout)
ballad
ballast - ed - ing
ballerina
ballet
ballistic
balloon - ed - ing - ist
ballot - ed - ing
ballyhoo
   (BAL-BAWL)
BALM-BALU
balm/y - ier - iest
baloney? *No*, boloney
balsa
balsam
Baluchi - stan - stani
balustrade
   (BALL)
BAM
bambin/o - i
bamboo
bamboozle
   (BOM)

BAN-BAND
ban - ned - ning; *not* banns (of
   marriage), *not* band
banal - ity
banana
banausic
banbur/y - ies
band - ed - ing
bandag/e - ed - ing
bandana
bandeau
bandicoot (*Aus*)
bandit - ry
bandolier
band/y - ied - ying
BANE-BANK
bane - ful - fully
bang - ed - ing - er
bangalow (palm); *not*
   bungalow (house)
bangle
bangtail (*Aus*)
banish - ed - ing - ment
banister
banjo
bank - ed - ing - er
bankrupt - ed - ing - cy
banksia (*Aus*)
BANN-BANZ
banner
bannock
banns (of marriage)
banquet - ed - ing
banshee
bantam
banter - ing
Bantu - stan
banyan
Banzai! (*Jap*)
BAO
baobab
   (BOW)
BAP
bap
baptis/e - ed - ing - able (z)
bapt/ism - ist - istry - ismal
BAR-BARB
bar - red - ring
barathea
barb - ed

barbar/ian -ic -ism -ity -ous
  -ously
Barbary
barbecu/e -ed -ing
barbel
barber
barberry
barbette
barbican
barbiturate
barbola

BARC-BARG
Barcoo rot (*Aus*)
bard -ic -olatry
bard/y -ies (*Aus*)
bare (naked) -ness; *not* bear
  (animal, carry)
bar/ely -est
bargain -ed -ing
barg/e -ed -ing -ee

BARI
baritone
barium
  (BARR BARY)

BARK
bark -ed -ing -er
  (BARC BARQ)

BARL-BARN
barley
barm (yeast); *not* balm
barmy (mad); *not* balmy
barn
barnacle
barney

BARO
barograph
baromet/er -ric -rically
baron (lord) -ess -y -age -ial;
  not barren -ness
baronet -cy -age
baroque
barouche
  (BARR)

BARQ
barque (boat); *not* bark (of
  tree, of dog)
barquentine

BARR
barrack -ed -ing -er
barracuda *or* barracouta

barrage
barramundi (*Aus*)
barratry
barrel -led -ling
barren (unproductive) -ness
barricad/e -ed -ing
barrier
barrister
barrow
  (BAR-)

BART
bart, *for* baronet
barter -ed -ing
barton

BARY
barytes
  (BARI)

BAS-BASH
basal
basalt
bascule
bas/e -ed -ing -eless; *not*
  bass (voice)
bases (more than one base);
  not basis (foundation)
basement
bash -ed -ing -er
bashful -ly; *but* abash
  (BAZ)

BASI-BASR
basic -ally
basil
basilica
basilicon
basilisk
basin -ful
bas/is (foundation) -es
bask (get warm) -ed -ing; *not*
  Basque (language)
basket -ry
bason, *old spelling of* basin
basoon? *No*, bassoon
Basque (language)
bas relief
  (BAZ)

BASS-BAST
bass (fish)
bass (voice), *pronounced*
  'base'
basset

18

bassinet
bassoon
bast *or* bass (fibre)
bastard -y -ise -ised (z)
bast/e -ed -ing
bastinade
bastion

BAT-BATO

bat -ted -ting
batch
bat/e, *for* abate -ed -ing; *not*
  bait (food to catch prey)
bath -ed -ing
bath/e -ed -ing -er
bath/os -etic
bathymetric
bathysphere
batik
batiste
batman
baton
  (BATT)

BATT

battalion
batten -ed -ing
batter -ed -ing
batter/y -ies
battl/e -ed -ing -er
battledore
battlement
  (BAT-)

BAU BAW

bauble
baught? *No,* bought
bauld? *No,* bald
baulk *or* balk
bauxite
bawbee (*Sc*)
bawd -y -ier -iest -iness
bawl (shout) -ed -ing; *not* ball
  (BOR)

BAY

bay -ed -ing; *not* bey (Turkish
  title)
bayonet
bayou
  (BAI BEI)

BAZ

bazaar (market); *not* bizarre
  (fantastic)

baze? *No,* baize
bazooka
  (BAS BES BEZ)

BE-BEAT

be, been, being
beach (shore) -es -ed -ing;
  not beech (tree)
beacon
bead -ed -ing -y
beagl/e -ing
beaker
beam; *also* abeam (on the
  beam)
bean (vegetable); *not* been
  (used to be)
beano -s
bear (animal); *not* bare
  (naked)
bear (carry) -ing -er; *but* bore
  (did bear)
beard -ed -ing
beast -ly -liness
beastings (milk)? *No,*
  beestings
beat -en -ing -er
beatif/y -ic -ically -ication
beatitude
beatle? *No,* beetle
  (BEE BEI)

BEAU

beau -x
Beaufort (scale)
Beaune (wine)
beauteous
beaut -y -iful -ifully -ify -ified
  -ifying
  (BO BURE)

BEAV

beaver
  (BEV)

BEC

becalm -ed -ing
became
because
beck
becket
beckon -ed -ing
becloud -ed -ing
becom/e -ing; *but* became

19

BED

bed - ded - ding; *also* abed (in bed)
bedaub - ed - ing
bedeck - ed - ing
bedevil - led - ling - ment
bedew - ed - ing
bedizen - ed - ing
bedlam - ite
bedouin
bedraggled

BEE

bee (insect); *not* be (exist)
beech (tree); *but* beach (shore)
beef - y - ed - ing - eater - burger
beeing? *No,* being
been (used to be); *not* bean (vegetable)
beer (drink); *not* bier (for corpse)
beestings (milk)
beet - root
beetl/e - ed - ing
beezer
  (BEA BEI)

BEF

befall - en - ing; *but* befell
befit - ted - ting
befog - ged - ging
before - hand
befoul - ed - ing
befriend - ed - ing

BEG

beg - ged - ging
began
beget - ting - ter; *but* begot
beggar - ed - ing - ly - y
begile? *No,* beguile
begin - ning - ner
begone
begonia
begot - ten
begrudg/e - ed - ing - ingly
beguil/e - ed - ing
begum
begun

BEH

behalf

BEHAV

behav/e - ed - ing - iour
behead - ed - ing
beheld
behest
behind
behold - ing - er - en
behove - s

BEI

beige
being
  (BEA BEE)

BELA-BELI

belabour - ed - ing
belah (*Aus*)
belated
belay - ed - ing
belch - ed - ing
beleaguer - ed - ing
belfr/y - ies
Belgi/um - an
bel/ie - ied - ying; *not* belly (paunch)
belief - s
believ/e - ed - ing - er
Belisha beacon
belittl/e - ed - ing
  (BELL)

BELL

bell
belladonna
belle (a female beauty)
belles - lettres
bellic/ose - osity
belliger/ent - ently - ency
bellow - ed - ing; *not* below (under)
bell/y - ies - ied - ying - yache - yful
  (BEL-)

BELO-BELY

belong - ed - ing - ings
beloved
below (under); *not* bellow
belt - ed - ing
belvedere
belying (belie); *not* bellying (bulging)
  (BELL)

BEM

bemir/e - ed - ing

bemoan -ed -ing
bemus/e -ed -ing
  (BAM)

BEN-BENE
ben
benana? *No,* banana
bench -es -er
bend -ing; bent
beneath
benedicite
benedick
benedictine
benedict/ion -ory -us
benefact/or -ion
benefic/e -ed -ial -iary -ent
  -ence
benefit -ed -ing
benevol/ence -ent -ently
  (BAN BON)

BENG-BENZ
Bengal -i
benighted
benign
benign/ant -ancy -ity
benison
bent
ben trovato (*It*)
benumb -ed -ing
benzedrine
benzene *or* benzine
benzoin
benzol -ine

BEQU
bequeath -ed -ing
bequest

BER
berat/e -ed -ing
Berber
bereav/e -ed -ing -ement *or*
  bereft
beret
berg
bergamot
bergschrund (*Ger*)
beri -beri
berm
Bermud/a -ian
berry (fruit); *not* bury (inter)
berserk -er
berth (mooring -place) -ed

-ing
beryl -lium
  (BAR BIR BUR)

BES
beseech -ing -ingly; *but*
  besought
beset -ting
beshrew
beside (by the side of)
besides (also)
besieg/e -ed -ing -er
besmear -ed -ing
besmirch -ed -ing
besom
besot -ted -ting
besought (did beseech)
bespatter -ed -ing
bespeak -ing
bespoke -n
besprinkl/e -ed -ing
bessemer
best -ed
bestial -ly -ity -ise -ised (z)
  (BAS BIS BEZ)

BET
bet -ting; *not* abet (help)
betted? *No,* bet
beta (*Gr*)
betak/e -en
betatron
bethel
bethink
betide
betimes
betoken -ed -ing
betony
betook
betray -ed -ing -al -er
betroth -ed -ing -al
better -ed -ing -ment
bettong (*Aus*)
between
betwixt
  (BAT BIT)

BEU
  (BEAU)

BEV
bevel -led -ling
beverage
bev/y -ies

BEW

bewail - ed - ing
beware
bewilder - ed - ing
bewitch - ed - ing
(BEAU BU)

BEY

bey (Turkish title)
beyond
(BAY)

BEZ

bezel (of chisel)
bezique
(BES)

BI-BIB

bi-*, *prefix meaning* two *or*
twice; *not* by (*as in* by-pass,
etc.)
bias - sed - sing
biathlon
biaxial
bib
bibcock
bibelot
bibl/e - ical
bibliograph/y - ic - ical - er
bibliophile
bibulous - ly - ness
(BY BUY)

BIC

bicameral
bicarbonate
bice
bicentenary
bicephalous
biceps
bichloride
bichromate
bicker - ed - ing
bicuspid
bicycle
(BEC BIK BIS)

BID

bid (command) - den - ding;
(*but* bade, *not* bidded)
bid (at auction, etc.) - ding
- der (bid, *not* bidded)

biddable
bide, *for* abide
bidet
(BED)

BIE

biennial - ly
bier (for corpse); *not* beer
(drink)
(BEA BEE BY)

BIF-BIK

biff - ed - ing
bifid
bifocal
bifoliate
bifurcat/e - ed - ing - ion
big - ger - gest - ness
bigam/y - ous - ously - ist
bight (bay, loop); *not* bite
bigot - ry - ed
bijou - terie
bike, *for* bicycle
bikini - s
(BY)

BIL

bilateral - ly
bilberry
bilboes
bilb/y - ies (*Aus*)
bild? *No,* build, *or* billed
bil/e - ious
bilge
bilharzia
bilingual
bilk - ed - ing
(BEL BILL)

BILL

bill - ed - ing
billabong (*Aus*)
billet
billet - doux (*F*)
billiards
billion (number); *not* bullion
(gold, etc.)
billow - ed - ing
bill/y - ies
billycock
billy - goat

* If the word you wish to spell is not in this list, omit the prefix
and look for the rest of the word.

billy-o
(BIL-)
BILO BILT
bilobate
bilt? *No*, built
biltong (*Aus*)
(BEL)
BIM
bimetal/lism -lic -list
(BEM)
BIN
bin (receptacle); *not* been
binary
binaural
bind -ing -er -ery
bindi-eye (*Aus*)
bindweed
binge
binghi (brother, *Aus*)
bingy (stomach, *Aus*)
bingo
binnacle
binocular
binomial
(BEN)
BIO
bio-*, *prefix meaning* life
biochemistry
biogenesis
biograph/y -ies -ic -ical -ically
-er
biolog/y -ies -ic -ical -ically
-ist
biophysic/s -al -ally -ist
bioplasm
biops/y -ies
bioscope
(BAY BEY BIA)
BIP
biped -al
bipinnate
biplane
bipolar -ity
BIR
birch -ed -ing
bird -ie -ies
bireme

biretta
birth (nativity); *not* berth
(mooring-place)
(BER BUR)
BIS
bis (twice, repeat)
biscuit
bisect -ed -ing -ion -or
biseps? *No*, biceps
bisexual -ly -ity
bishop -ric
bisk (soup)
bismuth
bisness? *No*, business
bison
bisque (extra turn, etc;
unglazed china)
bistort
bistoury
bistre
bisy? *No*, busy
(BIZ BES)
BIT
bit
bitch -es -y
bit/e -ten -ing -er; *not* bight
(bay, loop)
bitter -ly -ness -est
bittern
bitts (for securing cables)
bitum/en -inous
(BET)
BIV
bivalent
bivalv/e -ed -ular
bivouac -ked -king
BIZ
biz, *for* business
bizarre (fantastic); *not* bazaar
(market)
bizy? *No*, busy
(BIS BEZ)
BLAB-BLAM
blab -bed -bing -ber
black -er -est -ed -ing
blacken -ed -ing -er
blackfellow

* If the word you wish to spell is not in this list, omit the prefix
and look for the rest of the word.

blackguard
blackmail -ed -ing -er
bladder -ed
blad/e -ed
blaeberry
blagard? *No*, blackguard
blah
blain
blam/e -ed -ing -eless
blamonge? *No*, blancmange

BLAN

blanch (whiten) -ed -ing; *not*
  blench (flinch)
blancmange
bland -er -est -ly -ness
blandishment
blank -ly -ness
blanket -ed -ing
blanquette (in cookery)
  (PLAN)

BLAR

blar/e -ed -ing
blarney -ed -ing

BLAS

blasé
blasphem/e -ed -ing -er -ous
  -ously
blast -ed -ing
blastoderm
  (BLAZ PLAS)

BLAT

blatant -ly
blather *or* blether
  (PLAT)

BLAZ

blaz/e -ed -ing; *also* ablaze
blazay? *No*, blaeberry
bleach -ed -ing -er
bleak -ly -ness
blear -y -iness
bleat -ed -ing
  (BLEE PLEA)

BLEB BLED

bleb
bled (did bleed)

BLEE

bleed -ing -er; *but* bled (did
  bleed)
bleep -ed -ing -er
  (BLEA PLEA)

BLEM-BLEW

blemish -ed -ing
blench (flinch) -ed -ing; *not*
  blanch (whiten)
blend -ed -ing
blende (zinc sulphide)
blenn/y -ies
bless -ed -ing -edness
blether *or* blather
blew (did blow); *not* blue
  (colour)

BLI

blight -ed -ing
Blighty (England)
blimey!
blimp -ish
blind -ed -ing -ness -ly
blindfold -ed -ing
blink -ed -ing -ers
bliss -ful -fully -fulness
blister -ed -ing
blithe -ly
blithering
blitz -ed -ing -krieg
blizzard

BLOA-BLON

bloat -ed -ing
bloater
blob
bloc (group)
block -ed -ing
blockad/e -ed -ing
bloke
blond (fair)
blonde (fair lady)

BLOO

blood -y -ier -iest -iness
  -less
bloom -ed -ing
bloomer
bloomery
  (BLEW BLU)

BLOS-BLOW

blossom -ed -ing
blot -ted -ting -ter
blotch -ed
blottesque
blotto
blouse
blow -ing -er -n

blowed *only in exclamation,*
e.g., 'Well, I'm blowed!'
blowy
blowzy (dishevelled); *not*
blousy
BLU
blubber -ed -ing
blud? *No,* blood
bludg/e -ed -ing -er
bludgeon
blu/e -er -est -ey -eness -ish
bluff -ed -ing -er
blunder -ing -er
blunt -er -est -ed -ing -ly
-ness
blur -red -ring
blur
blurt -ed -ing
blush -ed -ing -er
bluster -ed -ing -er
(BLOO)
BOA
boa
boar (pig); *not* bore *or* Boer
board -ed -ing -er; *also*
aboard (on board)
boast -ed -ing -er
boat -ing -er
boatswain *or* bosun
(BOW)
BOB-BOD
bob -bed -bing
bobin
bobbinet
bobby
bobby-soxer
bobcat
bobsl/ed -edge -eigh
bobstay
bobsy-die (*Aus*)
bobtail
Boche
bock
bod/e -ing
bodega
bodger (*Aus*)
bodgie (*Aus*)
bodice
bodkin
bod/y -ies -ied -ily -iless

BOE-BOH
Boer
boffin
bofors
bog -gy -giness
bogey (golf)
boggl/e -ed -ing
bogie (wheels)
bogong (*Aus*)
bogus
Bohemia -n
BOI
boil -ed -ing -er
boisterous -ly -ness
(BOY BUOY)
BOL
bolas
bold -er -est -ly -ness
bole (tree-trunk); *not* bowl *or*
boll
bolero
boll (seed vessel)
bollard
bolly gum (*Aus*)
bolometer
boloney
boshev/ik -ism -ist; bolshie
bolster -ed -ing
bolt -ed -ing
bolus
(BOWL BUL)
BOMB
bomb -ed -ing -er
bombard -ed -ing -ment
bombardier
bombardon
bombasine
bombast -ic -ically
bombe (cookery)
bombora (*Aus*)
(BUM)
BONA-BOND
bona fide
bonanza
bon-bon
bond -ed -ing -age
bondsman
BONE-BONZ
bon/e -ed -ing -y -eless; *not*
Beaune (wine)

bonfire
bongo
bonhomie (F)
bonito
bon mot (F)
bonne bouche (F)
bonnet
bonn/y - ier - iest - ily
bonus - es
bonze
bonzer (Aus)
 (BUN)

BOO

boo - ed - ing - er
boo - ay (NZ)
boob - y - ies
boobook or mopoke (Aus)
boodie - rat (Aus)
boodle
boogie - woogie
book - ed - ing - ish
book/maker - ie
boom - ed - ing - er
boomerang
boon
boong (Aus)
boongary (Aus)
boor (ill - bred) - ish - ishness;
 not bore
boost - ed - ing - er
boot - ed - ing - less - ee
booteek? No, boutique
booth
bootleg - ged - ging - ger
booty (plunder); not beauty
booz/e - ed - ing - er - eroo
 (BOU)

BOR

bora (wind)
boracic
borak (Aus)
borage
borax
Bordeaux
bordello - s
border (edge) - ed - ing - er;
 not boarder (lodger)
bor/e (hole) - ed - ing - er; not
 boar or boor
bor/e (weary) - ed - ing - edom

boreal
borecole
boree (Aus)
boric
born (birth)
borne (did bear; put up with)
boron
borough (town); not burrow
borrow - ed - ing - er
borsch
borstal
bort? No, bought
borzoi
 (BAU BAW BOOR BOUR)

BOS

bosh
bosky
bosie or bosey (cricket)
bosom - ed - y
boss - es - ed - ing - y
bosun or boatswain

BOT

bot (worm)
botan/y - ist - ic - ical - ically
botargo
botch - ed - ing
both
bother - ed - ing - ation - some
both/y - ies
bottl/e - ed - ing - er
bottom - ed - ing - less
bottomry
botulism

BOUC-BOUQ

bouclé
boudoir
bougainvillea
bough (branch); not bow
bought (did buy)
bouillabaisse (F)
boulli (F)
bouillon (F)
boulder
boulevard (F)
boulter (sieve)
bounc/e - ed - ing - er - y
bound - ed - ing - er - less
boundar/y - ies
bount/y - ies - iful - eous
 - eously

26

bouquet
  (BOW BOO)
BOUR
  bourbon
  bourdon
  bourgeois -e -ie
  bourn or bourne
  bourse
  (BOOR BOR)
BOUT
  bout
  boutique
  (BOAT BOOT)
BOV
  bovver-boots
  bovine
BOW
  bow (knot, archery, etc.)
  bow (bend) -ed -ing
  bow -s (front of ship); not
    bough (branch)
  bowdleris/e -ed -ing -ation
  bowel (intestine); not bowl
  bower
  bowl -ed -ing -er; not boll
    (seed vessel)
  bowls (game)
  bowline
  bowman
  bowser
  bowsprit
  (BOU BEAU)
BOX
  box -ed -ing -er
BOY
  boy -ish -hood; not buoy
    (float)
  boyang
  boycott -ed -ing
  (BOI BUOY)
BRA-BRAH
  bra, for brassière
  brac/e -es -ed -ing
  bracelet
  brachiate
  brachycephal/y -ic -ous
  bracken
  bracket -ed -ing
  brackish
  bract

brad -awl
brae (bank); not bray (ass's
  cry)
brag -ged -ging -gart
braggadocio
brahmin
BRAI
  braid -ed -ing
  brail -ed -ing
  braille (writing for blind)
  brain -ed -ing -y -ier -iest
  brais/e (stew) -ed -ing; not
    braze (brass)
  (BRAY BREA)
BRAK-BRAN
  brak/e (slow down) -ed -ing;
    not break (snap)
  bramble
  Bramley
  bran (husks); not brand
  branch -ed -ing
  brand -ed -ing
  brandish -ed -ing
  brandling
  brand-new or bran-new
  brandreth
  brand/y -ies
BRAS-BRAV
  brase? No, braise (cook) or
    braze (brass)
  brash -er -est
  brass -y -ily -iness
  brassard (worn on arm)
  brasserie (beer saloon, F)
  brassière (worn on chest)
  brat
  brattic/e -ed -ing
  bravado
  brav/e -er -est -ely -ery
  bravo
  bravura
BRAW
  braw (Sc)
  brawl -ed -ing -er
  brawn -y -ier -iest
  (BROA BROU)
BRAY
  bray -ed -ing
  (BRAI)

BRAZ

braz/e (brass) - ed - ing - en
- ier; *not* braise (stew)
Brazil - ian

BREA

breach (break) - ed - ing
bread (food); *not* bred (did
  breed)
breadth
break (snap) - ing - able - age;
  but broke; *not* brake
break/down - through
breaker
breakfast - ed - ing - er
breakneck
break - up
breakwater
bream
breast - ed - ing; *also* abreast
  (level with)
breath - less - lessly
breathalys/e - ed - ing - er
breath/e - ed - ing - er
  (BRAI BREE)

BREC BRED

breccia
bred (did breed); *not* bread

BREE

bree? *No*, Brie (cheese)
breech (garment) - es - ed;
  not breach
breed - ing - er; *but* bred (did
  breed)
breez/e - es - y
breeze - block
  (BRIE BREA)

BREN-BREV

bren (gun)
brest? *No*, breast
brethren
Breton
breve (music)
brevet
breviar/y - ies
brevity
  (BRA)

BREW

brew - ed - ing - er - ery - ster
brewis
brews? *No*, bruise

(contusion)
  (BROO BRU)

BRIA-BRID

briar *or* brier
brib/e - ed - ing - ery - able
bric - a - brac
brick - ed - ing
bricole
bridal (belonging to bride); *not*
  bridle
bride
bridegroom
bridesmaid
bridewell
bridge - ed - ing; *but* abridge
  (shorten)
bridl/e (harness) - ed - ing

BRIE

Brie (cheese)
brief (short) - er - est - ly
brief (instruction) - ed - ing
  - less
brier *or* briar
  (BREE BREA BRY)

BRIG

brig - antine
brigad/e - ier
brigalow (*Aus*)
brigand - age
bright - er - est - en - ening - ly
  - ness

BRIL-BRIN

brill
brilliant - ly
brillian/ce - cy
brilliantine
brim - med - ming - mer
brimstone
brindle - d
brin/e - y
bring - ing
brink - manship

BRIO-BRIT

brio
briony? *No*, bryony
briquette
brisk - er - ly
brisket
brisling
bristl/e - ed - ing

28

Bristol -ian
Britain (country)
Britannia
British -er
Briton (person)
Brittany (in France)
brittle
BROA
broach (open) -ed -ing; *not*
  brooch (pin)
broad -er -est -en -ening -ly;
  but abroad (away)
broadcast -ing -er
  (BRAW BRO-)
BROB-BROM
Brobdingnag -ian
brocade
broccoli
broch (*Sc*)
broché (fabric)
brochure
brock
brocket
broderie (*F*)
brogue
broil -ed -ing -er
brok/e -en -enly
brok/er -ing -ery
brolga (*Aus*)
brolly, *for* umbrella, -ies
brom/ine -ide -al -ate
BRON
bronch/i -ial -itis
broncho-pneumonia
bronco (horse) (*Am*)
brontosaurus
bronz/e -ed -ing
BROO
brooch (pin)
brood -ed -ing -er -y
brook -ed
broom -ie
  (BREW BRU)
BROT
broth
brothel
brother -ly -liness -hood
BROU BROW
brought (did bring)
brouhaha (*F*)

brow -ed
browbeat -ing -en
brown -er -est -ed -ing -ish
brownie
brows/e -ed -ing -er
  (BREW BROO BRU)
BRU
brucellosis
bruin (bear); *not* brewing
bruis/e -ed -ing -er
brumb/y -ies (*Aus*)
brummagem
brunette
brunt
brush -ed -ing -y
brusque
Brussels
brutal -ity -ise -ising -ised
  -isation (z)
brut/e -ish
  (BREW BROO BROU)
BRY
bryony
  (BRI)
BUB
bubbl/e -ed -ing -y
bubo -es -nic
BUC
buccaneer -ing
buccinator
buck -ed -ing
bucket -ed -ing -ful- fuls
buckl/e -ed -ing -er
buckram
buckshee
bucksome? *No*, buxom
buckwheat
bucolic
BUD
bud -ded -ding
budda (*Aus*)
Buddh/a -ism -ist
buddleia
budd/y -ies
budg/e -ed -ing -er -eree
budget -ed -ing -ary
budgie, *for* budgerigar
BUF
buff
buffalo -es

buffer
buffet -ed -ing
buffet (*F*, sideboard)
buffoon -ery
BUG
bug -ged -ging
bugaboo
bugbear
bugger -ed -ing -y
bugl/e -ing -er
BUI
buil/d -t -ding -der
buisness? *No*, business
  (BI)
BUL
bulb -ous -ously
bulbul
bulg/e -ed -ing -y -iness
bulk -ed -ing -y -ier -iest
bulkhead
bull -ish -ishly -ishness
bullace
bullate
bulldog
bulldoz/e -ed -ing -er
bullet
bulletin
bullion (gold, etc.)
bullock -y
bull/y -ied -ying
bulrush -es
bulwark
  (BOL)
BUM
bum
bumble -bee
bummaree
bummer
bump -ed -ing -er -y -ier
  -iest
bumpkin
bumptious -ly -ness
  (BOM)
BUN
bun
bunch -ed -ing
buncombe *or* bunkum
bundl/e -ed -ing
bung -ed -ing
bungal/ow (house) -ows

-oid; *not* bangalow (palm)
bungl/e -ed -ing -er
bunion (swelling); *not* banyan
  (tree)
bunk -ed -ing
bunker -ed -ing
bunkum *or* buncombe
bunn/y -ies
bunsen
bunt -ed -ing
bunya (*Aus*)
bunyip (*Aus*)
BUO
buoy (float) -ed -ing; *not* boy
buoy/ant -ancy -antly
  (BOI BOY)
BURB-BURE
burb/le -led -ling
burbot
burden -ed -ing -some
burdock
bureau -x
bureaucra/cy -cies -t -tic
  -tically
burette
  (BER BIR)
BURG
burgee
burgeon -ed -ing
burgess
burgh (*Sc*) -er
burglar -y -ious
burgl/e -ed -ing
burgomaster
Burgund/y -ies -ian
  (BERG)
BURI-BURN
buri/al -ed
burin
burk/e -ed -ing
burl
burlap
burlesque
burl/y -ier -iest
burley (humbug)
Burm/a -ese
burn -t -ed -ing -er
burnish -ed -ing
  (BER)

BURP-BURY

burp - ed - ing
burr
burrawong (*Aus*)
burrow - ed - ing
bursar - y - ial
burst - ing
burthen *or* burden
Burton
bur/y (inter) - ied - ying; *not*
  berry (fruit)
  (BER)

BUS

bus - sed - sing - es
busb/y - ies
bush - es - y - ier - iest - iness
bushie (*Aus*)
bushel
bushido (*Jap*)
bushrang/er - ing
bushveld
business - es - like
busk
busker
buskin
bust
bustard
bustl/e - ed - ing - er
bus/y - ied - ying - ier - iest
busyness (being busy); *not*
  business
  (BUZ)

BUT-BUZ

but
butane
buther - ed - ing - y
butler
butt - ed - ing; *but* abut
  (border on)
butte (land form)
butter - ed - ing - y
buttock
button - ed - ing
buttress - es - ed - ing
butt/y - ies
buty? *No,* beauty
butyrate
buxom
buy (purchase) - ing - er; *not*
  by (near)

buzz - ed - ing - er
buzzard

BY

by (near); *not* buy (purchase)
bye (subordinate)
bycicle? *No,* bicycle
bygone - s
byo-? *No,* bio-
byre
Byzant/ium - ine
  (BI)

C

CAB

cab - by - bies
cabal (clique); *not* cable
caballero (*Sp*)
cabaret
cabbage
cabbal/a - istic
caber
cabin - ed
cabinet
cabl/e - ed - ing
cablegram
cabochon
caboodle
caboose
cabriolet

CAC

cacao (cocoa tree)
cachalot
cache (hiding place); *not*
  cash
cachet
cachinnat/e - ion
cachou
cachuca
cackl/e - ed - ing - er
cacophon/y - ies - ous
cact/us - i *or* - uses

CAD

cad - dish
cadastral
cadaver - ous
caddie (golf)
caddis - es
cadd/y (tea) - ies
cadence
cadenza

cadet
cadg/e - ed - ing - er
cadgole? *No* cajole
cadmium
cadre
(KAD)

CAE
caec/um - a
Caesar
caesar/ean *or* ian
caesium
caesura
(CEA CEI SEA SEE)

CAF
café, cafeteria
caffeine
caftan
(KAF)

CAG
cag/e - ed - ing; *not* cadge
cag/ey - ier - iest
(CADG)

CAH
cahoots
(KAH)

CAI CAJ
cainozoic
cair? *No,* care
cairn
cairngorm
caisson
caitiff
cajol/e - ed - ing - ery
(CAY KAI KAY)

CAK
cak/e - ed - ing
(CAC KAK)

CALA
calabash
calamander
calamine
calamint
calamit/y - ies - ous
(CALL CALO COLLA)

CALC
calcareous
calceolaria
calci/fy - fied - fying - fication
calcin/e - ed - ing - ation
calcite

calcium
calcul/able - ably - ability
calculat/e - ed - ing - ion - or
calcul/us - i *or* - uses
(CAUL)

CALD
cald? *No,* called (did call)
caldron *or* cauldron
caldera

CALE
Caledonia - n
calendar (dates)
calender (press) - ed - ing
calends
calenture
(CALI CALLI CHALY COLLE
KALE)

CALF
cal/f - ves

CALI
calibr/e - ate - ated - ating
- ation
calicle
calico - es
caliper *or* calliper
caliph - ate
cali/x (anatomy) - ces; *not*
calyx (botany)
(CALE CALLI CALY CHALY
COLLI KALE)

CALL CALLI
call - ed - ing - er
calligraph/y - ic - er
calliope
calliper *or* caliper
callisthenic
(CALE CALI CALY CHALY
COLI KALE)

CALLO
callos/ity - ities
callous (hard) - es - ly - ness
callow (inexperienced)
(CALO COLLO COLO)

CALM
calm - er - est - ed - ing - ly;
also becalm
calmative
(CARM KALM)

CALO
calomel

32

calor/ie - ic - ific - ify
calorimet/ry - er
calotte
  (CALA COLL COLO)
CALS
  (CALC)
CALU
calumet
calumn/y - ies - iate - iator
  - ious
  (COLLU)
CALV CALX
calvary
calv/e (bear a calf) - ed - ing;
  not carve (slice)
Calvin - ism - ist - istic
calx, calces
CALY
caly? *No*, ceilidh (*Gaelic*)
calypso
caly/x (botany) - xes *or* ces,
  - cinal; *not* calix
  (CALI CALLI CHALY)
CAM
cam
camaraderie (*F*)
camber - ed - ing
cambium
cambrel
Cambria - n
cambric
Cambridge
  (KAM COMB)
CAME-CAMO
came
camel
camellia
camembert
cameo - s
camera
Cameron - ian
camisole
camomile
camouflag/e - ed - ing
  (COM)
CAMP
camp - ed - ing - er
campaign - ed - ing - er
campan/ile - ology - ologist
campanul/a - ate - aceous

camphor - ated
campion
campus - es
  (COMP)
CANA
can - ned - ning - ner - nery - ful
Canaan - ite
Canad/a - ian
canal (waterway) - ise (z); *not*
  cannel
canapé
canard
canar/y - ies
canasta
  (CANN CONA KANA)
CANC
cancan (*F*)
cancel - led - ling - lation
cancer - ed - ous; *not* canker
  (CONC)
CAND
candelabr/um - a
candid (frank) - ly - ness
candida/te - ture - cy
candied (sugary)
candle - light - wick
Candlemas
candour
cand/y - ies
candytuft
  (COND)
CANE-CANK
can/e - ed - ing
canine
canister
canker - ed; *not* cancer
  (CANN CON KAN)
CANN
canna (plant)
cannabis
cannel (coal); *not* canal
  (waterway)
cannibal - ism - istic - ise - ised
  - ising (z)
cannon (gun) - ade; *not* canon
  (clergy)
cannot
cannula
cann/y - ier - iest - ily - iness
  (CAN- CONN KEN)

CANO

canoe -s -d -ing -ist
canon -ical -ically -ise -ised
-isation (z)
canoodl/e -ed -ing -er
canop/y -ies -ied
(CONNO)

CANS

(CONS)

CANT

cant (hypocrisy) -ing
can't (cannot)
cantaloup
cantankerous -ly -ness
cantata
canteen
canter -ed -ing
cantharides
canthus
canticle
cantilever -ed
cantle
canto -s
canton
cantonment; *not* -toon-
cantor -ial
cantrip
(CONT KANT KENT)

CANV-CANZ

canvas (fabric)
canvass (solicit votes) -ed
-ing -er
canyon
canzonet
(CONV)

CAO

caocao? *No,* cocoa *or* cacao
caos? *No,* chaos

CAP CAPI

cap -ped -ping -ful
capab/le -ly -ility -ilities
capacious -ly
capacit/ance -or
capacit/y -ies -ate
cap-à-pie
caparison -ed
cape
caper -ed -ing -er
capercaillie *or* capercailzie
capillar/y -ies -ity

capital -ly -ise -ised -ising
-isation (z)
capital/ism -ist -istic
capitat/e -ed -ing -ion
capitol (building)
capitulat/e -ed -ing -ion

CAPO-CAPS

capo, *see* da capo (music)
capok? *No,* kapok
capon
caponier
capric/e -ious -iously
-iousness
Capricorn
capriole
caps, *for* capital letters
capsicum
capsiz/e -ed -ing
capstan
capsule
(COP)

CAPT-CAPY

captain -ed -ing
caption -ed
captious -ly -ness
captivat/e -ed -ing -ion
captiv/e -ity
captor
captur/e -ed -ing
capuchin
caput? *No,* kaput
capybara

CAR CARA

car
carabineer
caracal (lynx); *not* coracle
(boat)
caracol/e (horse movement)
-ed -ing
caracter? *No,* character
carafe
caramel
carat (gold); *not* caret, carrot
caravan -ned -ning
caravanserai
caravel
caraway
(CARR CORR KAR)

CARB

carbide

34

carbine
carbohydrate
carbolic
carbon -ic -ate
carboniferous
carbonis/e -ed -ing -ation (z)
carborundum
carboy
carbuncle
carburett/or or -er

CARC CARD

carcase -s or carcass -es
carcin/oma -ogen -ogenous
card
cardamom
cardiac
Cardigan
cardinal
cardio -*, prefix meaning
  heart

CARE-CARG

car/e -ed -ing
care/ful -fully -fulness -less
  -lessly -lessness
careen -ed -ing -age
career -ed -ing -ist
caress -es -ed -ing
caret (omission mark, Λ);
  not carat or carrot
carf? No, calf
cargo -es
  (CARR CORR)

CARI

Carib -bean
caribou
caricatur/e -ed -ing
caracter? No, character
cari/es (dental) -ous; not
  carries
carillon
carinate
carisma? No, charisma
  (CARR CURR KARR)

CARM

carmagnole (F)
Carmelite
carminative

carmine
  (CALM KARM)

CARN

carnage
carnal -ly -ity
carnation
carnelian or corn -
carnival
carnivor/e -ous
carnt? No, can't or cannot

CARO

carob
carol -led -ling -ler
carot/ene -id
carous/e -ed -ing -al
  (CARR CORO CORR KAR)

CARP

carp -ed -ing
carpel
carpent/er -ry
carpet -ed -ing
carpus (wrist -bone); not
  corpus
  (CORP)

CARR

carrel (cubicle, etc.); not carol
  (song)
carriage
carrick -bend
carrion
carronade; not cannonade
carrot (vegetable) -y; not
  carat
carr/y -ies -ied -ying -ier
  (CAR- CURR KAR)

CARS

  (CAS CARC)

CART

cart -ed -ing -er -age -ful
carte blanche (F)
cartel
cartesian
Carthusian
cartilag/e -inous
cartograph/y -ic -ical -er
carton
cartoon -ist

* If the word you wish to spell is not in this list, omit the prefix
and look for the rest of the word.

cartouche
cartridge
cartulary
(KART)

CARV
carv/e - ed - ing - er
carvel

CARY
caryatid
(CARI CARR KARR)

CASC-CASE
cascad/e - ed - ing
cascara
cas/e - ed - ing
casein
casemate
casement
casette? *No*, cassette
(CASS)

CASH
cash - ed - ing - ier - iered
cashew
cashmere (fabric); *but*
Kashmir (country)
(CACH)

CASI CASQ
casino - s
cask
casket
casm? *No*, chasm
caslon
casque (ancient helmet)

CASS
cassava
casserole
cassette
cassock
cassoon? *No*, caisson
cassowar/y - ies
(CAS-)

CAST
cast - ing - er
caster *or* castor (sugar)
castanet
castaway
caste (hereditary class)
castellated
castigat/e - ed - ing - ion - or
Castil/e - ian
castl/e - ed - ing

castor (oil); castor *or* caster
(sugar)
castrat/e - ed - ing - ion
(CUST)

CASU
casual (careless) - ly - ness;
not causal (due to a cause)
casual/ty - ties
casuarina
casuist - ic - ical - ically - ry
(CASH)

CAT CATA
cat - ty - tier - tiest - tish
catabolism *or* kata-
cataclysm - ic
catacomb
catafalque
Catal/onia - an
catalep/sy - tic
catalogu/e - ed - ing - er (*Am:*
catalog)
catalpa
catalys/e - ed - ing - ation (*not*
z)
cataly/sis - st - tic
catamaran
catamite
catapillar? *No*, cater-
cataplasm
catapult - ed - ing
cataract
catarrh (mucus) - al; *not*
guitar
catastroph/e - ic - ically
(KATA)

CATCH
catch - ing - er - ment - y - ier
- iest
catchup? *No*, ketchup
(CACH)

CATE-CATT
catech/ism - ist - umen
catech/ise - ised - ising (z)
categor/y - ic - ical - ically
catenary
catenat/e - ed - ing - ion
cater - ed - ing - er
caterpillar
caterwaul - ed - ing
catgut

cathar/sis - tic
cathedral
Catherine - wheel
catheter
cathode or kath -
catholic - ism - ity
catholicis/e - ed - ing - ation (z)
cation (cathode ion)
catkin
catling
catoptric
catt/y (see cat)
cattle

CAU

caucus - es
caudal (of a tail)
caudillo (Sp)
caudle (gruel)
caught (did catch); not court
caul (membrane); not call
cauldron
cauliflower
caulk (stop up ship's seams);
 - ed - ing; not cork
causal (due to a cause); not
 casual (careless)
causality; not casualty
caus/e - ed - ing - ation - eless;
 also because
causerie (F)
causeway
caustic - ally
cauteris/e - ed - ing - able
 - ation (z)
cautery
caution - ed - ing - ary
cautious - ly
 (CAW COR KAU)

CAV

cavalcade
cavalier - ly
cavalry
cavatina
cav/e - ed - ing - er
caveat
cavern - ous
cavesson
caviare
cavil - led - ling - ler
cavit/y - ies

cavort - ed - ing
cavy

CAW

caw - ed - ing
 (CAU COR KAU)

CAY

cayenne
cayman
cayuse
 (CAI KAI KAY)

CEA

ceanothus
ceas/e - ed - ing - less - lessly;
 but cessation
 (CAE CEI SEA SEE)

CED

cedar
ced/e (give up) - ed - ing; not
 seed
cedilla (mark under c, thus:
 ç); not sedilia
 (SED)

CEI

ceiling
ceilidh (Gaelic)
 (CAE CEA SEA SEE)

CEL

celacanth or coel -
celadon
celandine
celanese
celebr/ate - ated - ating - ant
celebrit/y - ies
celeriac
celerity
celery (vegetable); not salary
celeste
celestial - ly
celib/acy - ate
cell (small room); not sell
cellar - age - er
cellaret
cello, for violoncello; cellist
cellophane
cellul/e - ar - arity
cellul/ose - oid
celsius
Celt or Kelt - ic
 (SEL)

CEM
cement - ed - ing
cemeter/y - ies
  (SEM)

CENO
cenobite *or* coenobite
cenotaph
  (SENA)

CENS
censer (for incense)
censor (suppress) - ed - ing
  - ious
censur/e (reprimand) - ed - ing
cens/us (counting) - al; *but*
  consensus
  (SENS)

CENT
cent (money); *not* scent *or*
  sent
centaur
centaury
centavo
centen/ary - aries - arian - nial
centesimal
centi-*, *prefix meaning*
  hundred
centigrade
centipede
central - ly - ity - ist - ism
centralis/e - ed - ing - ation (z)
Centralia - n
centr/e - ed - ing (*Am:* center)
centrifug/e - al - ally
centripetal
centupl/e - icate
centurion
centur/y - ies
  (SCEN SENT)

CEPH
cephal/y - ic - ous
cephalopod
  (PSEPH SYPH)

CER
ceram/ic - ist
cereal (food); *not* serial (in
  series)
cerebellum

cerebr/um - al
cerebration (brain work); *not*
  celebration
ceremon/y - ies - ious - iously
cerise
cerium
cert, *for* certainty *or*
  certificate
certain - ly - ty
certificat/e - ed - ion
certif/y - ies - ied - ying - iable
  - ier
certitude
cerulean
ceruse
cervical
  (CIR SER SIR SUR)

CES
Cesarewitch
cessation (ceasing)
cession (ceding); *not* session
  (sitting)
cesspit
cesspool
  (CAES SES)

CET
cetacean
cetaline? *No,* acetylene
  (SET KET)

CHAF
chaf/e - ed - ing - er
chaff - ed - ing
chaffer - ed - ing - er
chaffinch - es
  (SHAF)

CHAG
chagrin - ed
  (SHAG)

CHAI
chain - ed - ing
chair - ed - ing - man - manship
chaise (carriage)
chaise - longue (*F,* sofa)
  (SHA)

CHAL
Chald/ea - ean - ees
chaldron

* If the word you wish to spell is not in this list, omit the prefix
and look for the rest of the word.

chalet
chalice (goblet)
chalk -ed -ing -y -ier -iest
challeng/e -ed -ing -er -eable
challis (fabric)
chalybeate
 (CAL SHAL)

CHAM
chamber -ed -ing
chamberlain
chameleon
chamfer -ed -ing
chamois
champ -ed -ing
champagne (wine)
champaign (open country)
champerty
champion -ed -ing -ship
 (CAM JAM SHAM)

CHAN
chanc/e -ed -ing -y
chancel
chancell/or -ery
chancery
chancre
chandelier
chandler -y
chang/e -ed -ing -eable
 -eability
changeling
channel -led -ling
chant -ed -ing -er -ress -ry
chanterelle
chanticleer
chant/y or shant/y (sea-song)
 -ies
 (CAN JAN SHAN)

CHAO
chao/s -tic -tically
 (KAO)

CHAP
chap -ped -ping -pie
chaps, for chaparejos
 (cowboy leggings)
chaparral (Am)
chapel -ry
chaperon -ed -ing -age
chaplain -cy
chaplet
chapman

chapter
 (JAP)

CHAR
char -red -ring -woman -lady
char-à-banc
character -istic -istically -less
character/ise -ised -ising (z)
charade
charcoal
charg/e -ed -ing -er -eable
chargé d'affaires
chariot -eer
charisma -tic -tically
charit/y -ies -able -ably
 -ability
charivari
charlatan -ry -ism
charlock
charlotte
charm -ed -ing -er -ingly
charnel-house
chart -ed -ing
charter -ed -ing
Chart/ism -ist
Chartreuse
char/y -ily -iness
 (CAR CHER JAR SHAR)

CHAS
chas/e -ed -ing -er
chasm
chassis
chast/e -er -est -ity
chasten -ed -ing -er
chastis -e -ed -ing -ement
 -er (not z)
chasuble
 (JAZZ)

CHAT
chat -ted -ting
chateau -x
chatelaine
chattel
chatter (talk) -ed -ing -er; not
 shatter (smash)

CHAU
chauffeu/r -se
chauvin/ism -ist -istic
 (CHO SHOW)

CHEA-CHEE
cheap -er -est -en -ly -ness

-ish
cheat -ed -ing
cheater; *not* cheetah
  (leopard)
check -ed -ing -er; *not*
  cheque (order on bank),
  Czech (nation)
checkers
checkmat/e -ed -ing
Cheddar
cheer -ed -ing -y -iness
cheerful -ly -ness
cheerio!
cheerless -ly -ness
chees/e -y -iness
cheesed off
cheetah (leopard)
  (CHIE SHE)

CHEF
chef
chef -d'oeuvre

CHEL
chela
chello? *No,* cello *or*
  violoncello
Chelsea
  (SHEL JEL GEL)

CHEM
chemical -ly
chemin -de -fer
chemis/e -ette
chemist -ry
chemotherap/y -ist
  (GEM JEM KEM SHEM)

CHEN CHEO
chenille
cheong -sam

CHEQ
cheque (*Am:* check)
chequer -ed -ing -wise
  (CHEC CZECH SHEK)

CHER
cherish -ed -ing
cheroot
cherr/y -ies
chert
cherub -s *or* -im -ic
chervil
  (CHAR CHIR CHUR GER
  JER SHER)

CHES
Cheshire
chess
chest -y
chesterfield
chestnut
  (GES JES)

CHEV
cheval -glass
chevalier
cheviot
chevron

CHEW
chew -ed -ing -er -y
  (CHOO SHO TEU TU)

CHIA
chianti
chiaroscuro
  (KIA)

CHIC CHID
chic (*F*)
chicane -ry -ries
chichi
chick -en
chickling
chicle
chicory *or* succory
chid/e -ing -den; chid (did
  chide) *or* chided

CHIE
chief -ly
chieftain -cy -ship
  (CHEA CHEE SHEA SHE)

CHIF-CHIL
chiff -chaff
chiffon -ier
chignon
chigoe *or* chigger *or* jigger
chihuahua
chi -hik/e -ed -ing
chilblain -ed
child -ren -ish -ishly -ishness
child/hood, -like -less
childermas
Chile -an
chill -ed -ing -y -ier -iest
chilli (spice)
  (GI JI SHI)

CHIM-CHIP
chim/e -ed -ing

40

chimer/a -ical
chimney - s
chimp - anzee
chin
Chin/a - ese
chinchilla
chin - chin
chine
chink
chinoiserie (F)
chinook
chintz
chip - ped - ping - per - py
chipmunk
chippendale
(GI JI SHI)

CHIR
chi - rho (early Christian
emblem)
chiropod/y - ist
chiropractic
chirp - ed - ing - y
chirrup - ed - ing
(CHER CHUR GYR SHER
SHIR)

CHIS-CHIV
chisel - led - ling - ler
chit
chitin - ous
chitterling
chival/ry - rous - rously
chive
chiv/y or chivv/y or chev/y
(chase) - ied - ying
(GY JI SHI)

CHLOR
chloral
chloride
chlorin/e - ate - ation
chloroform - ed - ing
chloro/phyll - plast
chlorosis
(CLAU CLAW CLO)

CHO
chock
chocolate
choice - ly
choir (singers); not quire
(paper) or coir (fibre)
chok/e - ed - ing - er

choko (Aus)
choler - ic
cholera
cholesterol
(CO JO SHO)

CHOO
choos/e - y - iness; but chose
(did choose)
(CHEW TEU TUI)

CHOP
chop - ped - ping - per
chop - suey
(SHOP)

CHOR
choral - ly - ist; not coral (reef)
chorale (hymn)
chord (music, math); not
cord (string)
chore
chorea (St Vitus' dance); not
Korea
choreograph/y - er - ic
chor/ion - oid
chorister
chortl/e - ed - ing
chorus - es - ed - ing
(CAU COR KOR)

CHOS-CHOW
chos/e - en
chough (crow)
chow (dog)
chowchilla (Aus)
chowder
(SHO)

CHRIS
chrism (sacred oil)
chrisom (baby's baptismal
robe)
Christ - ian - ianity
christen - ed - ing
Christendom
Christian/ise - ised - ising (z)
christiania
Christmas - tide
Christolog/y - ist - ical
(CHRYS CRIS KRIS)

CHRO
chromat/e - in - ic - ically; not
cremate (burn)
chrome

41

chrom/ium - ic - ate
chromograph - y
chromolithograph - y
chromosome
chronic - ally
chronicity
chronicl/e - ed - ing - er
chronolog/y - ical - ically
chronomet/er - ric - rically
(CRO KRO)

CHRYS
chrysal/is - id
chrysanthemum
chryselephantine
chrysolite
chrysoprase
(CHRIS CRIS CRYS KRIS)

CHU
chub
chubb/y - ier - iest - iness
chuck - ed - ing - er
chuckl/e - ed - ing
chug - chug - ged - ging
chukker (polo)
chum - my - mier - miest - mily
chump
chunk - y
chupatty
church - ed - ing - y
churinga (*Aus*)
churl - ish - ishly - ishness
churn - ed - ing
chuse? *No,* choose
chute (channel); *not* shoot
chutney - s
(CHEW SHU TU)

CHY
chyle (fluid formed from
  chyme)
chyme (food pulp in
  intestines)
(CHI SHI)

CIB-CIM
ciborium
cicada
cicatr/ice - ise - ised - isation
  (z)

cicerone
cider *or* cyder
cigar
cigarette
cilia
cimmerian
  (CY SCI SI)

CIN
cinch
cinchona
cincture
cinder
cinema - tic
cinematograph - y - er
cineraria
cinnabar
cinnamon
cinque *or* cinq (5)
  (CYN SCIN SIN SYN)

CIPH
cipher *or* cypher - ed - ing; *not*
  sypher (join)
  (SIF SIPH SYPH)

CIRC
circa (*L*, about)
circl/e - ed - ing
circlet
circs, *for* circumstances
circuit - ous - ously - ousness
circular - ity
circular/ise - ised - ising
  - isation (z)
circulat/e - ed - ing - ion - or
  - ory
circum -* *prefix meaning*
  around
circumcis/e - ed - ing - ion (*not*
  z)
circumferen/ce - tial
circumflex
circumjacent
circumlocu/tion - tory
circumspect - ly - ness
circumstan/ce - ced - tial
  - tially
circumvent - ed - ing - ion
circus

* If the word you wish to spell is not in this list, omit the prefix
and look for the rest of the word.

(SURC)
CIRQ CIRR
cirque
cirrhosis
cirr/us -ous -ose
(CYR SER SIR SUR)
CIS
cissy
cist (prehistoric); *not* cyst
(med)
Cistercian
cistern
cistus
(CYS SCIS SIS SYS)
CIT
citadel
cit/e (quote) -ed -ing; *not* site
or sight
citizen -ry -ship
citr/us -ic -ine -on
citronella
cit/y -ies
(CYT PSIT SIT)
CIV
civet
civic -ally
civil -ly -ity
civilian
civilis/e -ed -ing -ation (z)
civvies, *for* civilian clothes
(SIEV SEV)
CLAC-CLAN
clack (clatter) -ed -ing; *not*
claque (hired applauders)
clad -ding
claim -ed -ing -able -ant
clairvoyan/t -ce
clam
clamant
clamber -ed -ing
clamm/y -iness
clam/our -oured -ouring
-orous -orously
clamp -ed -ing
clan -nish -nishness -sman
clandestin/e -ely
clang -ed -ing -er
clang/our (continued
clanging) -orous -orously
clank -ed -ing

(KLA)
CLAP CLAQ
clap -ped -ping -per
clapboard
claptrap
claque (hired applauders)
CLAR
clarendon (type)
claret
clarif/y -ies -ied -ying -ication
clarinet *or* clarionet -tist
clarity
clarkia
(CLER)
CLAS
clash -ed -ing
clasp -ed -ing -er
class -es -ed -ing -y -ier -iest
classic -al -ally -ist -ism
classif/y -ies -ied -ying -iable
-ication
clastic
(GLAC GLAS)
CLAT
clatter -ed -ing
CLAU
Claus (Santa)
clause (grammar); *not* claws
claustral
claustrophobia
(CLAW CHLOR)
CLAV
clavate
clavi/chord -form
clavic/le -ular
CLAW
claw -ed -ing
(CLAU)
CLAY
clay -ey -eyness
claymore
(CLAI)
CLEA CLEE
clean -er -est -ed -ing -able
cleanl/y -ier -iest -iness
cleans/e -ed -ing -er
clear -er -est -ed -ing -ly
-ness
clearance
cleat

cleav/e (hold together) - ed
  (or clave) - ing
cleav/e (split) - ing - able - age;
  but cleft or cloven (did
  cleave)
cleek (golf)
CLEF-CLEP
clef (music)
cleft (split, did cleave)
cleg
clem
clematis
clemen/t - cy
clench or clinch - ed - ing - er
clepsydra
  (KL)
CLER CLEV
clerestory
clergy - man
cleric - al -ally
clerihew
clerk - ship
clever - er - est - ly - ness
clevis
  (CLEA)
CLEW
clew (naut) - ed - ing; not clue
  (CLU)
CLI
clianthus
cliché (F)
click - ed - ing - er
client - ele
cliff
climacteric
climat/e - ic -ically
climatolog/y - ical - ist
clima/x - xes - ctic
climb - ed - ing - er - able
clime (region)
clinch or clench - ed - ing - er
cling - ing - er
clinic - al -ally
clink - ed - ing - er
clinometer
clip - ped - ping - per - py
cliqu/e -ish - ishness - ey
clitor/is - al
  (CLY KLI)

CLOA-CLOG
cloaca - l
cloak (garment) - ed; not
  cloke (hide)
clobber - ed - ing
cloche
clock - ed - ing
clod - dish - dishness
clog - ged - ging - ger - gy
CLOI
cloisonné (F)
cloist/er - ered - ral
  (CLOY)
CLOK-CLOT
clok/e (hide) - ed - ing
clon/e - al
clor -? No, chlor-
clos/e - er - est - ely - eness
clos/e - ed - ing; not clothes
closet - ed - ing
closure
clot - ted - ting
cloth - s
cloth/e - es - ed - ing
clothier
CLOU
cloud - let - ed - less - lessly;
  also becloud
cloud/y - ier - iest
clough
clout - ed - ing
  (CLOW KLOO)
CLOV
clove (spice); not clothe
clov/e (did cleave) - en
clover
CLOW
clown - ed - ing
  (CLOU)
CLOY
cloy - ed - ing
  (CLOI)
CLU
club - bed - bing
clubbable
cluck - ed - ing
clu/e (guide) - ed - eless; not
  clew (naut)
clumber
clump - ed - ing

clums/y -ier -iest -ily -iness
clunch
clung
cluster -ed -ing
clutch -ed -ing
clutter -ed -ing
CLY
Clydesdale
clyster
(CLI)
CO
co -*, *prefix meaning* with,
jointly; *see also* com -, con -
CO*A
coach -ed -ing
coadjutor
coadunate
coagulat/e -ed -ing -ion
coal -ed -ing
coala? *No,* koala
coalesc/e -ed -ing -ent
-escence
coalition
coal -tit
coaming (naut); *not* combing
coan? *No,* cone
coars/e (unrefined) -er -est
-en -ely -eness; *not* course
(run)
coast -ed -ing -er -ward
-wise -al
coat -ed -ing -ee
coati (zoo)
coax -ed -ing -er
coaxial
(KOA KOH)
CO*B
cob
cobalt -ic -iferous
cobber (*Aus*)
cobbl/e -ed -ing -er
coble (boat)
cobra
cobweb -bed
(CAB KOB)
CO*CA-CO*CH
coca (shrub); *not* cocoa

coca-cola (drink)
cocaine (drug made from
coca)
coccy/x -geal
cochineal
cochlea
(CAC COK COX CUC)
COCK
cock -ed -ing -y
cockade (rosette); *not*
cock-eyed
cock -a -hoop
cockat/eel -oo
cockatrice
cockchafer
cocker (spaniel)
cockerel
cock-eyed
cockle
Cockney -s
cockpit
cockroach
cock -sure -ness
cocktail
cocky-leeky
(COX CUC)
CO*CO
cocoa
coconut *or* cokernut
cocoon -ed
cocotte (*F*); *not* coquette
(CAC CUC)
CO*D
cod (fish) -ling
cod (hoax) -ded -ding
coda (mus)
coddl/e -ed -ing; *not* codling
cod/e -ed -ing -er -ify -efied
-ifying -ification
codeine
cod/ex -ices
codger
codicil
codling (fish); *not* coddling
codpiece
(KOD)

* If the word you wish to spell is not in this list, omit the prefix
and look for the rest of the word.

CO*E

co - education - al - ally
coefficient
coelacanth *or* cela -
coeliac
coenobite *or* ceno -
coerc/e - ed - ing - ion - ionary
 - ible
coercive - ly - ness
coeval - ly - ity

CO*F

coffee
coffer
coffin - ed
(COUGH)

CO*G

cog - ged
cogen/t - tly - cy
cogitable
cogitat/e - ed - ing - ion - ive
cognac
cognate - ness
cognit/ion - ive
cognis/ance - ant
cognomen
cognoscent/e - i
cognovit

CO*H

cohabit - ed - ing - ation
coheir - ess
coher/e - ed - ing - ent - ently
 - ence
cohes/ion - ive - ively - iveness
cohort
(CAH KOH)

CO*I

coif
coiff/ure - eur - euse
coign (of vantage); *not* coin
 or quoin
coil - ed - ing
coincid/e - ed - ing
coinciden/t - tal - tally - ce
coin (money) - ed - ing - er
 - age
coir (fibre); *not* choir (singers)
coition

(COY)

CO*K

cok/e - ed - ing
cokernut *or* coconut
(COC CORK COX)

CO*L-CO*LI

col
cola *or* kola
colander *or* cullender
colchicum
cold - er - est - ly - ish - ness
cole? *No,* coal
cole - slaw
colic - ky
coliflower? *No,* cauli -
coliseum
colitis
(CAL CAUL CHOL COAL
COLL KO)

COLLA

collaborat/e - ed - ing - ion - or
collage (scraps made into
 picture); *not* college
collaps/e - ed - ing - ible *or*
 - able
collar - ed - ing - less - ette
collat/e - ed - ing - ion - or
collateral - ly
(CALA COLA CHOL COLLO
COLO)

COLLE

colleague
collect - ed - ing - ion - or - able
collectiv/e - ely - ism - ist - ity
collectivis/e - ed - ing - ation (z)
colleen
colleg/e - er - ian - iate; *not*
 collage (scrap picture)
collet
(CHOL COLLI)

COLLI

collid/e - ed - ing
collie
collier - y - ies
colliflower? *No,* cauli -
collimat/e - ed - ing - ion - or
collinear

* If the word you wish to spell is not in this list, omit the prefix
and look for the rest of the word.

collision
(CALLI CALY COLI COLLE)
COLLO
colloc/ate - ation
collocutor
collodion
colloid - al
collop
colloquial - ly - ism
colloqu/y - ies
collotype
(CALLO COLLA COLO)
COLLU
collud/e - ed - ing
collus/ion - ive - ively
(COLU)
COLLY
collyrium
collywobbles
(COLI COLLI)
CO*LO
colon - ic
colonel (army) - cy - ship; *not*
kernel (of nuts)
colonial - ist - ism
colonnad/e - ed
colon/y - ies - ist - ise - ised
- ising - isation (z)
colophon - y - ate
Colorado
coloration *or* colouration
color - ificatura
colorific
colossal - ly
colossus
colostom/y - ies
colour - ed - ing - less
(COLLA COLLO)
COLP COLT
colporteur
colt - ish
colter *or* coulter
CO*LU
columbari/um - a
columbine
column - ed - ar
colure

(COLLA COLLU)
COLZ
colza - oil
COM
com - * *prefix meaning* with
COMA
coma (stupor) - tose; *not*
comma (,)
COMB
comb - ed - ing - er
combat - ed - ing - ant
combative - ly - ness
combe *or* coomb *or* cwm (*W*)
combin/e - ed - ing - ation
- ative
combo (*Aus*)
combust/ion - ible - ibility
(CUMB)
COME
com/e - ing - ers ('all comers')
comedy/y - ies - ian - ienne
come - ly - lier - liest - liness
comestible
comet
come - uppance
(CAME COMME)
COMF
comfit
comfort - ed - ing - er - able
- ably - less
comfrey
COMI
comic - al - ally
Comintern
comity (courtesy); *not*
committee
(COMMI)
COMMA
comma (,); *not* coma (stupor)
command - ed - ing - ment - er
commandant
commandeer - ed - ing
commando - s
(COMA COMMO)
COMME
comme il faut (*F*)
commemorat/e - ed - ing - ion

* If the word you wish to spell is not in this list, omit the prefix
and look for the rest of the word.

-ive -or
commenc/e -ed -ing -ement
commend -ed -ing -able
 -ably -ation -atory
commensal -ity
commensurab/le -ly -ility
commensurate -ly -ness
comment -ed -ing -ary -ation
commentator
commerce
commercial -ly -ism -ist -ise
 -ised -ising -isation (z)
 (CAME COME CUMM)

COMMI

commie, for communist
comminat/ion -ory
comminut/e (reduce to
 fragments) -ed -ing -ion
commiserat/e -ed -ing -ion
 -ive
commissar
commissariat
commissar/y -ies -iat
commission -ed -ing -er -aire
commissur/e -al
commit -ted -ting -tal -table
 -ment
committee
 (COMI)

COMMO

commode
commodious -ly -ness
commodit/y -ies
commodore
common -er -est -ly
common -age -able
common/er -alty
commons
commonwealth
commotion
 (COMMA)

COMMU

commun/e -al -ally
communic/able -ability -ably
communicant
communicat/e -ed -ing -ion
 -or
communicativ/e -ely -eness
communion
communique

commun/ism -ist -istic
communis/e -ed -ing -ation
 (z)
communit/y -ies
commut/e -ed -ing -er -able
 -ability
commutator (electric)

COMPA

compact -ly -ness
companion -able -ably
 -ableness -ship
compan/y -ies
compar/able -ably
compar/e -ed -ing; not
 compère (introducer)
comparative -ly -ness
comparison
compartment
compass -es -ed -ing
compassion -ate -ately
compatib/le -ly -ility
compatriot
 (CAMP)

COMPE

compeer
compel -led -ling
compendi/um -a -ous -ously
 -ousness
compensat/e -ed -ing -ion
 -ory
compèr/e -ed -ing
compet/e -ed -ing
compet/ent -ence -ency
competit/ion -ive -ively -or

COMPI

compil/e -ed -ing -ation

COMPL

complac/ent (self-satisfied)
 -ently -ency; not
 complaisant
complain -ed -ing -t; not
 compliant (obedient)
complais/ant (yielding) -ance
complement (completion)
 -ed -ing -ary; not
 compliment
complet/e -ed -ing -er -est
 -ely -eness -ion
complex -ity -ly
complexion -ed

48

complian/t (obedient) - ce - tly
complicat/e - ed - ing - ion
complicity
compliment (praise) - ary; *not*
  complement
compline (relig). *not* complain
compl/y - ied - ying

COMPO
component
comport - ed - ing
compos/e - ed - ing - edly - er
composure
composit/e - ely - eness
composit/or - ion
compos mentis (*L*, sane)
compost - ed - ing
compote
compound - ed - ing

COMPR
comprehend - ed - ing
comprehens/ion - ible - ibly
  - ibility
comprehensive - ly - ness
compress - ed - ing - ible - ibly
  - ibility - ion - or
compris/e - ed - ing
compromis/e - ed - ing

COMPU
compuls/ion - ive - ively
compulsor/y - ily - iness
compunct/ion - ious - iously
compurgat/ion - or - ory
comput/e - ed - ing - able
  - ative - ation
computer - ise - ised - ising
  - isation (z)

COMR
comrade - ship

COMU
  (COMMU)

CON
con -* *prefix,meaning* with
con - ned - ning
  (CONN)

CONA
con amore (*It*)
conat/ion - ive

CONCA
concatenat/e - ed - ing - ion
concav/e - ity - ities - ely
  (CONQ)

CONCE
conceal - ed - ing - ment
conced/e - ed - ing
conceit - ed - edly
conceiv/e - ed - ing - able - ably
  - ability
concensus? *No,* consensus
concentrat/e - ed - ing - ion
concentric - ally - ity
concept - ual - ually - ive - ively
conception - al
concern - ed - ing - ment
concert - ed - ing
concertina
concerto - s
concession - aire *or* ary
concessive
  (CONSE)

CONCH
conch - iferous
concholog/y - ist - ical
conch/y - ies, *for*
  conscientious objector - s
  (CONK CONQ)

CONCI
concierge (*F*)
conciliar
conciliat/e - ed - ing - ive - or
  - ory - ion
concise - ly - ness
concision
  (CONSI)

CONCL
conclave
conclud/e - ed - ing
conclus/ion - ive - ively
  - iveness

CONCO
concoct - ed - ing - ion
concomit/ance - ant - antly
concord - ant - antly
concordance
concordat

* If the word you wish to spell is not in this list, omit the prefix
and look for the rest of the word.

concourse

CONCR
concrete -ly -ness
concretion

CONCU
concubin/e -age -ary
concupisc/ence -ent
concur -red -ring -rence
  -rent -rently
concuss -ed -ion

COND
condemn -ed -ing -ation
  -atory
condens/e -ed -ing -er -ation
  -able -ability
condescend -ed -ing -ingly
condescension
condign -ly
condiment
condition -ed -ing -al -ally
condol/e -ed -ing -ence
condom
condominium
condon/e -ed -ing -ation
condor
conduc/e -ed -ing -ive
conduct -ed -ing -or -ress
conduct -ion -ance -ible -ivity
conduit
condyl/e -oid

CONE
con/e -ic -ical -ally
coney or cony

CONFA-CONFL
confabulat/e -ed -ing -ion
  -ory
confection -er -ery
confeder/ate -ated -ating
  -ation
confer -red -ring -ence
confess -ed -ing -ion -ional
  -or
confetti
confidant (a trusted
  person); not confident
confid/e -ed -ing
confid/ence -ent -ently
confidential -ly -ity
configur/e -ed -ing -ation
confine -ed -ing -ement

confirm -ed -ing -ative
  -atively
confirm/ation -and; not
  conformation (form)
confiscat/e -ed -ing -ion -ory
conflagration
conflat/e -ion
conflict -ed -ing -ion
conflu/ence -ent
conflux

CONFO-CONFU
conform -ed -ing -ance
conformab/le -ly -ility
conformation (form); not
  confirmation
conform/ity -ist
confound -ed -ing -edly
confrere
confront -ed -ing -ation
Confuci/us -an
confus/e -ed -ing -ion -edly
confut/e -ed -ing -ation

CONG
congeal -ed -ing -able
congelation (congealing)
congenial -ly -ity
congenital -ly
conger-eel
congeries
congest -ed -ing -ion
conglomerat/e -ed -ing -ion
congratulat/e -ed -ing -ion
  -ory
congregat/e -ed -ing -ion
  -ional
congregational/ism -ist
congress -ional
congru/ence -ent -ity
congruous -ly -ness
  (CONJ)

CONI
coniac? No, cognac
conic -al -ally
conifer -ous (cone-bearing);
  not carnivorous
coniform
conine
  (CONE CONNI)

CONJ
conjectur/e -ed -ing -al -ally

conjoin -ed -t
conjugal -ly -ity
conjugat/e -ed -ing -ion
conjunct -ly -ure
conjunct/ion -ive -ively
conjunctiv/a -itis
conjur/e -ed -ing -ation
conjurer *or* conjuror
  (CONGE)

CONK
conk -ed -ing
conkers, *formerly*
  conquerors
  (CONC CONQ)

CONN
connat/e -ural
connect -ed -ing -ive -ively
connection *or* connexion
conniv/e -ed -ing -ance
conning -tower
connoisseur
connot/e -ed -ing -ation
  -ative
connubial -ly -ity
  (CANO CON-)

CONQ
conquer -ed -ing -able -or
conquest
  (CONK CONCU)

CONR
conrod, *for* connecting rod

CONSA CONSC
consanguin/e -eous -ity
conscience -less
conscientious -ly -ness
conscious -ly -ness
conscrib/e -ed -ing
conscript -ed -ing -ion

CONSE
consecrat/e -ed -ing -ion -or
  -ory
consecutive -ly -ness
consens/us -ual
consent -ed -ing
consequen/ce -t -tly
consequential -ly -ity
conservanc/y -ies
conservat/ion -ionist -or
conservativ/e -ely -ism
conservator/y -ies

conserv/e -ed -ing
  (CONCE)

CONSI
consider -ed -ing -able -ably
  -ation
considerate -ly -ness
consign -ed -ing -ee -or
  -ment -ation
consist -ed -ing -ent -ently
  -ence -ency
consistor/y -ial
  (CONCI)

CONSO
consol/e -ed -ing -ation
  -atory
consolidat/e -ed -ing -ion
consols, *for* consolidated
  loans
consommé (*F*)
consonance
consonant -al -ly
consort -ed -ing -ium -ia

CONSP
conspectus
conspicuous -ly -ness
conspir/e -ed -ing -acy -acies
  -ator

CONST
constab/le -ulary
constan/t -tly -cy
constellation
consternation
constipat/e -ed -ing -ion
constituen/t -cy -cies
constitut/e -ed -ing -ive -or
constitution -al -ally -alism
  -alist
constrain -ed -ing -edly
constraint
constrict -ion -ive -or
constring/e -ed -ent -ency
construct -ed -ing -ion -ional
  -ive -ively -or
constru/e -ed -ing

CONSU
consubstant/ial -ially -iality
  -iate -iation
consul -ar -ate
consult -ed -ing -ative -ation
  -ant

consum/e -ed -ing -er -edly
consummat/e -ed -ing -ion
  -ive -or -ely
consumption
consumptive -ly -ness

CONTA
contact -ed -ing
contadin/o -i (*It*)
contagi/on -ous -ously
  -ousness
contain -ed -ing -able -ment
container -ise -ised -ising
  -isation (z)
contaminat/e -ed -ing -ion
contango -s

CONTE
contemn (despise) -ed -ing
contemplat/e -ed -ing -ion
  -ive -ively -or
contemporane/ous -ously
  -ity
contemporar/y -ies
contempt -ible -ibly
contemptuous -ly
contend -ed -ing -er
content -ed -edly -edness
  -ment
contenti/ous -ously -ousness
contermin/al -ous -ously
contest -ed -ing -able -ant
context -ual -ually
contexture

CONTI
contigu/ity -ous -ously
continent -al -ally
continen/ce -t -tly
contingen/cy -t -tly
continual -ly
continu/e -ed -ing -ation
  -ative -ator -ity
continuous -ly -ness
continuum

CONTO
contort -ed -ing -ion -ionist
contour -ed -ing

CONTRA
contra-* *prefix meaning*

against
contraband
contracept/ion -ive
contract -ed -ing -ion -ile
  -ility
contract/or -ual -ually
contradict -ed -ing -or -ory
  -oriness
contrairy? *No*, contrary
contralto -s
contraprop
contraption
contrapuntal -ly
contrar/y -ily -iness -iwise
contrast -ed -ing -y
contrate (wheel); *not* contrite
  (repentant)
contratemps? *No*, contre-
contraven/e -ed -ing -tion

CONTRE-CONTRO
contretemps (*F*)
contribut/e -ed -ing -ion -or
  -ory
contrit/e -ely -ion
contriv/e -ed -ing -er -able
  -ance
control -led -ling -lable -ler
controvers/y -ies -ial -ially
  -ialist
controvert -ed -ing -ible

CONTU
contumacious -ly -ness
contume/ly -lious
contusion

CONU
conundrum
conurbation
  (CONNU)

CONVA
convalesc/e -ed -ing -ent
  -ence

CONVE
convect/ion -ional -or
conven/e -ed -ing -able -er
conveni/ence -ent -ently
convent -ual
conventicle

* If the word you wish to spell is not in this list, omit the prefix
and look for the rest of the word.

convention - al - ally - ality
converg/e - ed - ing - ent - ence
 - ency
converlescent? *No*, conval -
convers/ant - ance - ancy
conversation - al - ally
conversazione (*It*)
convers/e - ed - ing - ion - ely
convert - ed - ing - ible - ibly
 - ibility
convex - ity - ly
convey - ed - ing - able - er *or*
 - or
conveyanc/e - ing - er

CONVI-CONVU

convict - ed - ing - ion - ive
convinc/e - ed - ing - ingly - ible
convivial - ly - ity
convocation
convok/e - ed - ing
convolut/e -ed -ing -ion
convolvulus
convoy -ed -ing
convuls/e -ed -ing -ion -ive
 -ively

COO

coo (dove's note) - ed - ing;
 not coup (sudden move)
cooee!
cook - ed - ing - er - ery
cookie
cool - er - est - ish - ly - ness
coolabah (*Aus*)
coolamon (*Aus*)
coolie (labourer); *not* coolly
coomb *or* combe *or* cwm (*W*)
coon
coop (fowl - run) - ed; *not*
cope, coup
co - op, *for* co - operative
cooper *or* coper - age
co - operat/e - ed - ing - ion - ive
 - ively
co - opt - ed - ing - ation; *not*
 'co - option'
co - ordinat - e - ed - ing - ion
 -ely
coot
 (COU KOO)

COP

cop - ped - ping - per; *not*
 cope, coop
copal
copartner
cop/e - ed - ing
copeck
coper *or* cooper
coping
copious - ly - ness
copper - y - ish
copperas
coppic/e *or* cops/e - ed - ing
copra
copro/lite - litic - logy
copro/phily - philous - phagy
 - phagous
coprosma
cops/e *or* coppic/e - ed - ing
Copt - ic
copula
copulat/e - ed - ing - ion - ive
 - ively
cop/y - ies - ied - ying - ier - yist
copyright - ed - ing
 (CAP KOP)

COQ

coquet - ry - ries
coquett/e - ish - ishly; *not*
 cocotte (prostitute)
 (COC)

CORA-CORB

coracle
coral - line - loid; *not* choral
 (music), corral (cattle - pen)
cor anglais
corbel - led - ling
corbie (*Sc*)
 (CAR CHOR KOR)

CORD

cord - ed - ing - age
cordate
cordial - ly - ity
cordillera (*Sp*)
cordite
cordon - ed - ing
corduroy
cordwainer
 (CAUD CHORD)

53

CORE
core (centre) -d -less; *not*
caw, corps
corella
coreopsis
co-respondent; *not* corresp-
(CARE CAU CHOR CORRE)

CORF
corf (basket); *not* cough

CORG
corgi *or* corgy

CORI
coriaceous
coriander
Corinth -ian
(CHOR CORRE CORRI
CORY)

CORK
cork -ed -ing -er; *not* caulk
(stop up ship's seams)
corkage
corky
(COKE)

CORM
corm
cormorant
(CALM)

CORN
corn -ed
cornbrash
cornea -l
cornel
cornelian *or* carnelian
corneous
corner -ed -ing
cornet -ist
cornice -d
Cornish
cornucopia
cornuted
corn/y -ier -iest

CORO
corolla
corollar/y -ies
corona -te -ted
coronach
coronal
coronar/y -ies
coronation
coroner

coronet -ed
coronoid
(CARO CORRO)

CORP
corporal -ly -ity
corporat/e -ion -ely -ive; *not*
co-operate
corporeal -ly -ity
corps (army); *not* core
corpse (dead body)
corpul/ence -ency -ent -ently
corpus
corpusc/le *or* -ule -ular

CORR
corral (cattle-pen) -led -ling;
not coral, choral -e
correct -ed -ing -ion -or -ive
-ness -itude
correlat/e -ed -ing -ion -ive
correspond -ed -ing -ingly
correspond/ence -ent; *not*
co-resp-
corridor
corrie *or* coire (*Sc*)
corriedale (*NZ*)
corrigend/um -a
corrigibl/e -y
corroborat/e -ed -ing -ion -ive
-or -ory
corroboree (*Aus*)
corrod/e -ed -ing
corros/ion -ive -iveness
corrugat/e -ed -ing -ion
corrupt -ed -ing -ion -ly -ive
corruptib/le -ly -ility
(COR-)

CORS
corsage
corsair
corset -ed
corslet *or* corselet
(CAUS COARS COURS)

CORT
cortège (*F*)
cortes (*Sp*)
cort/ex -ices
cortic/al -ate -ated
cortisone
(CAU COURT)

54

CORU
corundum
corus? No, chorus
coruscat/e -ed -ing -ion
(CORA CORO CORRU)
CORV
corvette
corvine
CORY
corybantic
coryphee
coryza
(CORE CORI CORRI)
COS
cos (lettuce)
cos, for cosine
cosecant
coseismal
cosh -ed -ing -er; not kosher
(Jewish food)
cosine
cosiness
cosmesis
cosmetic -ally
cosmic -ally
cosmo/s -geny -logy -logist
-logical -graphy
cosmopoli/s -tan -te
cossack
cost -ed -ing -ly -lier -liest
-liness
costal (of the ribs); not
coastal
costermonger
costive -ly -ness
costum/e -ed -ing -ier
cos/y or coz/y -ies -ily -iness
-ier -iest
(CAS KOS)
COT
cot
cot, for cotangent
cote (shelter); not coat
coterie
cotillion or cotillon
cotoneaster
cottag/e -er

cotter
cotton -ed -ing -y
cotyledon -ous
cotyloid
(CAT)
COUB-COUL
coubah (Aus)
couch -ed -ing
couchant
cougar
cough -ed -ing
could (was able to); not
cooled
coulisse
coulomb
coulter or colter
(COO COW KOW)
COUN
council (assembly) -lor
counsel (advise) -led -ling
-lor
count -ed -ing -er -less
countenanc/e -ed -ing
counter-*, prefix meaning
against
counteract -ed -ing -ion -ive
counterfeit -ed -ing -er
counterfoil
countermand -ed -ing
counterpane
countervail -ed -ing
countess
countr/y -ies -yman -ified
count/y -ies
COUP
coup (sudden successful
move); not coop
coup d'état, coup de grace,
coup de main
coupé
coupl/e -ed -ing -er
couplet
coupon
(COOP CUP)
COUR
courage -ous -ously
courgette

* If the word you wish to spell is not in this list, omit the prefix
and look for the rest of the word.

courier (messenger); *not*
  currier
courlene
cours/e - ed - ing; *not* coarse
court - ed - ing - ship
courtelle
courteous - ly - ness
courtesan
courtes/y - ies
courtier
courtl/y - ier - iest - iness
  (COR CUR KUR)

COUS COUT
  cousin (relation); *not* cozen
  coustics? *No,* acoustics
  coutur/e - ier - ière

COV
  cove
  coven
  covenant - ed - ing - er
  cover - ed - ing - age
  coverlet
  covert - ly
  coverture
  covet - ed - ing - ous - ously
    - ousness
  covey - s
    (CAV)

COW
  cow - ed
  coward - ly - ice
  cower - ed - ing
  cowl - ed
  cowrie
  cowslip
    (COU)

COX
  cox, *for* coxswain
  coxa - l
  coxcomb
    (COCC COCK)

COY
  coy - ly - ness
  coyote
  coypu
    (COI)

COZ
  cozen (cheat) - ed - ing; *not*
    cousin
  coz/y *or* cos/y - ily - iness - ier

  - iest
    (COS)

CRAB-CRAM
  crab - bed - bing
  crack - ed - ing - er
  crackl/e - ed - ing
  cracknel
  cracksman
  cracky
  cradl/e - ed - ing
  craft - y - ier - iest - ily - iness
  craftsman - ship
  crag - ged - gy - gier - giest
    - giness
  craish? *No,* crèche
  crake
  cram - med - ming - mer
  crambo
  cramp - ed - ing - ness
  crampon
    (CRE KRA)

CRAN-CRAT
  cran
  cranberr/y - ies
  cran/e - ed - ing
  crani/um - a - al
  crank - ed - ing - y - ier - iest - ily
    - iness
  crankl/e - ed - ing
  crann/y - ies - ied
  crape *or* crêpe
  craps
  crapul/ent - ence - ous
  crash - ed - ing
  crass - ly - est - ness
  cratch
  crat/e - ed - ing
  crater
    (KRA)

CRAV-CRAZ
  cravat
  crav/e - ed - ing
  craven
  crawfish *or* crayfish
  crawl - ed - ing - y - er
  crayon - ed - ing
  craz/e - ed - ing - y - ier - iest
    - ily - iness

CREA-CRED
  creak - ed - ing

cream -ed -ing -er -ery; *but*
   crème de menthe
creas/e -ed -ing -y
creat/e -ed -ing -ion -ive
   -ively -iveness
creat/or -ress
creature
crèche
credence
credential
credib/le -ly -ility
credit -ed -ing -able -ably -or
credo
credul/ity -ous -ousness
   -ously
   (CREE KRI)

CREE
creed
creek (inlet); *not* creak
creel
creep -ing -er -y -iest; crept
creese *or* kris (Malay dagger)
   (CREA KRI)

CREM CREN
cremat/e -ed -ing -ion -or
   -orium -oria
crème de menthe
crenat/e (notched) -ed -ion
   -ure
crenel -late -lated -lation
   (CRI)

CREO-CREV
creole
creoso/l -te
crêpe, crêpe de chine (*F*)
crepitat/e -ed -ing -ion
crept (did creep)
crepuscular
crescendo -s
crescent -ic
cress
cresset
crest -ed -ing
cretaceous
cretin -ous -ism
cretonne
crevasse (chasm)
crevice (crack)

CREW
crew (of ship); *not* Krooman

   (Liberian seaman)
crew (did crow)
crewel (yarn); *not* cruel
   (unkind)
   (CROO CROU CRU)

CRIB-CRIM
crib -bed -bing -ber
cribbage
crick -ed -ing
cricket -ing -er
cricoid
cried (did cry)
crier
crime
criminal -ly -ity
criminat/ -ed -ing -ion -ive
   -ory
criminolog/y -ist
crimp -ed -ing
crimson
   (KRI)

CRIN
cring/e -ed -ing
cringle
crinite
crinkl/e -ed -ing -y
crinoid -al
crinoline

CRIO
   (CRYO)

CRIP
crippl -e -ed -ing
   (CRYP KRYP)

CRIS
cris/is -es
crisp -er -est -ly -ness -y
crispat/e -ion
criss-cross
   (CHRIS CHRYS CRYS KRIS)

CRIT
criteri/on -a
critic -al -ism
criticis/e -ed -ing -able (z)
critique

CROA
croak -ed -ing -er
croaky (hoarse); *not* croquet
   (game)
Croat -ia -ian
   (CROW)

57

CROC

crochet -ed -ing
(needlework); *not* crotchet
(music)
crock -ery
crocket
crocodile
crocus -es
(CROQ)

CROF-CRON

croft -er
cromlech
crone
cronk
cron/y -ies
(CHRO KRO)

CROO

crook -ed -edly -edness
croon -ed -ing -er
(CREW CROU CRU KROO)

CROP

crop -ped -ping -per

CROQ

croquet (a game) -ed -ing
croquette (meat ball)
(CROA CROC)

CROS CROT

crosier
cross -es -er -est -wise
cross -ed -ing -ly
crosse (lacrosse racquet)
cross -eyed
cross -section
cross -stitch
crotch
crotchet (music); *not* crochet
(needlework)

CROU

crouch -ed -ing -er
croup
croupier
crouton
(CREW CROO CROW CRU)

CROW

crow -ed -ing
crowd -ed -ing
crown -ed -ing

crowner, *old form of* coroner
(CROA CROU)

CRUC

crucial -ly
cruci/form -ate
crucible
cruciferous
crucifix -ion
crucif/y -ies -ied -ying
crucks? *No*, crux
(CRUS)

CRUD-CRUI

crud/e -er -est -ely -eness
-ity
cruel -ler -lest -ly -ty; *not*
crewel (yarn)
cruet
cruis/e -ed -ing -er
(CREW CROO CROU)

CRUM-CRUP

crumb -y
crumbl/e -ed -ing -y
crumpet
crumpl/e -ed -ing
crunch -ed -ing -y -ier -iest
crupper

CRUS

crusad/e -ed -ing -er
cruse (jar); *not* cruise (travel)
crush -ed -ing -er
crust -ed -y -ier -iest
crustace/a -an -ous
(CRUC)

CRUT-CRUX

crutch -es -ed
crux

CRY

cry -ing; cried
crylor
cryogen
cryolite
cryosurgery
crypt
cryptaesthesia
cryptic -ally
crypto -* *prefix meaning*
hidden

* If the word you wish to spell is not in this list, omit the prefix
and look for the rest of the word.

cryptogam (botany) -ic -ous -ist -y
cryptogram (cipher)
cryptograph -y -ic -er
cryptomeria
crystal -line -loid -lise -lised -lisation (z)
crystallograph -y -er -ic
(CHRI CHRY CRI KRI)

CUB
cub -bed -bing -bish
cubbard? *No,* cupboard
cubby -hole
cub/e -ic -ical -ically -iform -oid
cubicle (bed -place); *not* cubical
cub/ism -ist
cubit -al

CUC
cuckold -ed -ing -ry -ries
cuckoo -ed -ing
cucullat/e -ed
cucumber

CUD
cud; *not* could
cuddl/e -ed -ing -er -y -esome
cudd/y -ies
cudgel -led -ling -ler
cudgerie (*Aus*)
cudweed
(KUD)

CUE CUF
cue (drama, billiards); *not* queue (line up)
cued
cuff -ed -ing

CUI
cuirass -ier
cuisine
(QUI)

CUL
culack? *No,* kulak (*Russ*)
cul -de -sac
culinary
cull -ed -ing
cullender *or* colander
cullet
culm

culmin/ate -ated -ating -ation -ant
culpab/le -ly -ility
culprit
cult
cultivat/e -ed -ing -ion -or
cultivable
cultur/e -ed -al
culverin
culvert
(CAL COL)

CUM
cumber -ed -ing -some
Cumb/erland -rian
cumbrous -ly -ness
cummin *or* cumin (botany)
cummerbund
cumquat
cumulat/e -ed -ing -ation -ive -ively; *see also* accum-
cumulus
cumulo -nimbus
(COM KUM)

CUN
cuneate
cuneiform
cunjevoi (*Aus*)
cunjuror? *No,* conj-
cunning -ly
(CON)

CUP
cup -ped -ping -ful -fuls
cupboard
cupid
cupidity
cupola
cuppa, *for* cup of tea
cupr/ic -ous -eous
cupro -*prefix for* copper
cupule
(COUP)

CUR CURA
cur -rish
curaçoa *or* -çao
curar/e *or* -i
cura/te -cy
curative -ly
curator -ial -ship
(CURR)

CURB-CURD

curb (check) -ed -ing; *not*
  kerb (-stone)
curcuma
curd -y
curdl/e -ed -ing
  (KER KUR)

CURE-CURM

cur/e -ed -ing -able -ability
curett/e -age
curfew
curi/a -al
curio -s
curiosit/y -ies
curious -ly -ness
curium
curl -y -ier -iest -ed -ing -er
  -iness
curlew
curmudgeon
  (CURR KER)

CURR

currant (fruit)
currawong (*Aus*)
currenc/y -ies
current (movement) -ly
curricul/um -a
currier (leather-worker); *not*
  courier
curr/y -ies -ied -ying

CURS

curs/e -ed -ing -er -edly
cursive
cursor
cursorial
cursor/y -ily -iness
cursus
  (KURS)

CURT

curt -ly -ness
curtail -ed -ing -ment
curtain -ed -ing
curtsey -ed -ing, *or* curts/y
  -ied -ying
  (COUR KIR)

CURV

curv/e -ed -ing -aceous
  -ature
curvet -ted -ting
curvilinear -ly

CUS

cuscus
cushat
cushion -ed -ing
cush/y -ier -iest
cusp -ed -idal -ate
cuspidor
cuss, *form of* curse
cussed -ness
custard
custo/dy -dian -dial
custom -ary -er; see *also*
  accus-
custos (*L*)
  (CAS)

CUT

cut -ting -tingly -ter
cutaneous
cute -ly -ness; *see also*
  acute
cuticle
cutlass -es
cutler -y
cutlet
cutthroat
cuttle-fish
cutty
  (CAT KAT)

CWM

cwm (*W*) *or* coomb *or* combe

CYAN

cyan/ogen -ic -ide -osis
  -ometer

CYB-CYL

cybernetics
cycad
cyclamate
cyclamen
cycl/e -ed -ing -ist
cyclic -al
cycloid -al
cyclon/e -ic
cyclopean
cyclostyl/e -ed -ing
cyclotron
cyder *or* cider
cygnet (young swan); *not*
  signet (seal)
cylind/er -rical -roid
  (CI PSY SCI SI SY)

CYM-CYT

cymbal (music); *not* symbol
cymballon
Cymric
cynic - al - ally - ism
cynosure (centre of
  attraction); *not* sinecure
cypher *or* cipher
cypress (tree)
Cypr/us - iot - ian
cyrillic
cyst - ic - iform - oscope - itis
  - otomy
cyto - blast - plasm - logy
  - logist
  (CI SCI SI SY)

CZ

czar *or* tsar - ist - ism
Czech
Czechoslovak - ia
  (CH Z)

D

DAB-DAH

dab - bed - bing - ber - ster
dabbl/e - ed - ing - er
dabchick
da capo (music)
dace
dachshund
dacoit - y
dacron
dactyl - ic
dad - da - dy - dies
dado - s
daffodil
dafne? *No*, daphne
daft - er - est - ness
dag - ged - ging - gy (*Aus*)
dagger
dago - s *or* - es
daguerrotype
dahlia

DAI

dail (*Ir*)
dail/y - ies; *but* day
daint/y - ies - ier - iest - ily
  - iness
daiquiri - s
dair/y (milk) - ies; *not* diary

(journal)
dais
dais/y - ies
  (DAY)

DAL

dale
dalek
dall/y - ies - ied - ying - iance
Dalmatia - n
daltonism

DAM

dam (stop up) - med - ming;
  not damn
damag/e - ed - ing - eable
damas/k - cene
dame
damn (condemn) - ed - ing
  - ation - able - ably - atory
damnif/y - ies - ied - ying
  - ication
damp - er - est - ed - ing - ly
  - ness - en - ened - ening
damsel
damson
  (DEM DOM)

DAN

dan - buoy
danc/e - ed - ing - er
dandelion
dander
dandie dinmont
dandl/e - ed - ing
dandruff
dand/y - ies - ier - iest - yish
Dan/e - ish; *not* deign
  (condescend)
danger - ous - ously
dangl/e - ed - ing
dank
danthonia
  (DEN DON)

DAP

dap - ped - ping
daphne
dapper
dappl/e - ed - ing
  (DEP)

DAR

Darby? *No*, Derby - shire
dar/e - ed - ing - ingly

daresay? *Strictly*, (I) dare say
dark - er - est - ly
darken - ed - ing
darling
darn - ed - ing
darnel
dart - ed - ing - er; *not*
 daughter
Darwin - ism - ist - ian
dary? *No*, dairy

DAS
dash - ed - ing - er
dastard - ly
 (DAZ)

DAT
data, datum
dat/e - ed - ing - able - eless
dative
 (DET)

DAU
daub - ed - ing - er; *also*
bedaub
daughter - ly
daunt - ed - ing - less - lessly
dauphin - ess (*F*)
 (DAW DOR)

DAV
davenport
davit
davy, *for* affidavit
davy lamp
 (DEV)

DAW
daw, *for* jackdaw; *not* door
dawdl/e - ed - ing
dawn - ed - ing
 (DAU DOR)

DAY
day, *but* daily
 (DAI)

DAZ
daz/e - ed - ing
dazzl/e - ed - ing - ingly - er
 - ement

DE* DEA
de-*, *prefix that reverses the
 sense of the word it*

precedes
deacon - ess
dead - ly - liness - lock - pan
deaden - ed - ing
deaf - er - est - ly - ness
deafen - ed - ing
deal - t - ing - er
dean - ery
dear - er - est - ly - ness
dearie *or* deary
death - ly - like - less - lessly
deazle? *No*, diesel (engine)
 (DEE DIA)

DE* B
debacle
debar - red - ring
debark *or* disembark - ed - ing
 - ation
debas/e - ed - ing - ement
debat/e - ed - ing - er - able
debauch - ed - ing - er - ee - ery
debenture
debilit/y - ate - ated - ating
debit - ed - ing
debonair
deboo? *No*, debut
debouch - ed - ing - ment
debris
debt - or
debunk - ed - ing - er
debut - ant - ante

DE*CA
deca -*, *prefix meaning* ten
decade (ten years); *not*
 decayed
decad/ence - ent
decagon - al
decahedron
decalogue
decamp - ed - ing
decanal (of a dean)
decani
decant - ed - ing - er
decapitat/e - ed - ing - ion
decapod
decarbonis/e - ed - ing (z)
decathlon

* If the word you wish to spell is not in this list, omit the prefix
and look for the rest of the word.

decay - ed - ing

DE*CE

deceas/e (death) - ed; *not*
  disease (illness)
deceit - ful - fulness - fully
deceiv/e - ed - ing - er - able
decelerat/e - ed - ing - ion
December
decen/t - tly - cy - cies; *not*
  descent *or* dissent
decenni/um - al
decept/ion - ive - ively
  (DESC DESE DESI)

DE*CI

deci -, *prefix meaning*
  one - tenth
decibel
decid/e - ed - ing - er - able
deciduous - ly
decimal - ise - ised - ising
  - isation (z)
decimat/e - ed - ing - ion
decipher - ed - ing
decis/ion - ive - ively - eness
  (DESI)

DECK

deck - ed - ing; *also* bedeck
deckle
decko? *No,* dekko

DE*CL

declaim (speak) - ed - ing; *not*
  disclaim
declamat/ion - ory
declar/e - ed - ing - ation - atory
  - atively
déclassé (*F*)
declension
declin/e - ed - ing - ation
declivit/y - ies - ous

DE*CO

decoction
decollet/é - ée - age
decolouris/e - ed - ing - er (z)
décor (*F*)
decorat/e - ed - ing - ion - or
  - ive - ively
decorous - ly

decorticat/e - ed - ing - ion
decorum
decoy - ed - ing

DE*CR

decreas/e - ed - ing - ingly
decree - d - ing
decrement
decrepit - ude
decrepitat/e - ed - ing - ion
decretal
decr/y - ied - ying

DE*CU

decumbent
decuple (tenfold)
decussat/e - ion

DE*D

dedicat/e - ed - ing - ion - or
  - ory - ive
deduc/e - ed - ing - tion - ible
deduct - ed - ing - ion - ive
  - ively - able
  (DEAD DID)

DEE

dee (D - shaped)
deed
deem - ed - ing
deep - er - est - ly - ness; *but*
  depth
deepen - ed - ing
deer (animal); *not* dear
  (DEA DEI)

DE*FA

defac/e - ed - ing - ement
de facto (*L*)
defaecat/e *or* defecate - ed
  - ing - ion
defalcat/e - ed - ing - ion
defam/e - ed - ing - ation
  - atory
default - ed - ing - er
  (DIF)

DE*FE

defeas/ance - ible - ibility
defecat/e *or* defaecate - ed
  - ing - ion; *not* defect
defect - ed - ing - ion - ive - ively
  - iveness

---

* If the word you wish to spell is not in this list, omit the prefix
and look for the rest of the word.

defence -less -lessness
(*Am:* defense)
defend -ed -ing -er -ant
defens/ive -ively -ible -ibly
 -ibility
defer -red -ring -ment
deferen/ce -tial -tially
 (DIF)
DE*FI
defian/ce -t -tly
deficien/cy -cies -t -tly
deficit
defied (did defy); *not* deify
 (make a god)
defil/e -ed -ing
defin/e -ed -ing -able -ition
definite -ly -ness
 (DEFY DIF)
DE*FL
deflagrat/e -ed -ing -ion -or
deflat/e -ed -ing -ion
deflect -ed -ing -or
deflexion *or* deflection
defloration
DE*FO-DE*FY
deform -ed -ing -ation -ity
 -ities
defraud -ed -ing
defray -ed -ing
deft -ly -ness
defunct
defus/e (remove fuse) -ed
 -ing; *not* diffuse
def/y -ied -ying
DE*G
degauss
degenerat/e -ed -ing -ion
degeneracy
degrad/e -ed -ing -ation
degree
 (DAG DEJ DIG)
DE*H
de haut en bas (*F*)
dehisc/e -ence -ent
dehydrat/e -ed -ing -ion
DE*I
de -ic/e -ed -ing -er

deif/y -ies -ied -ying -ication
deign -ed -ing
design -ed -ing
deisel? *No,* diesel
de/ism -ist
deit/y -ies
DE*J
deject -ed -edly -ion -a
déjeuner (*F*)
de jure (*L*)
 (DEGE)
DE*K
dekko (*Hind*)
 (DEC)
DE*LA
delaine
delat/e (report) -ed -ing -ion
 -or; *not* dilate *or* delight
delay -ed -ing
 (DIL)
DE*LE
delect/able -ably -ation
delegac/y -ies
delegat/e -ed -ing -ion
delet/e -ed -ing -ion
deleterious -ly
 (DELI DIL)
DELF
delf *or* delft
 (DELPH)
DE*LI
deliberat/e -ed -ing -ion -ive
 -ively -ely -eness
deliberate -ly -ness
delica/te -tely -cy -cies
delicatessen
delicious -ly -ness
delict
delight -ed -ing -ful -fully;
 not delate
delineat/e -ed -ing -ion
delinquen/t -cy -cies
deliquesc/e -ed -ing -ent
 -ence
deliri/um -ous -ously
deliver -ed -ing -y -er -ance
 -able

* If the word you wish to spell is not in this list, omit the prefix
and look for the rest of the word.

(DELE DIL)
DELL-DELT
dell
delous/e - ed - ing
delph? *No,* delf *or* delft
Delphi - c - an
delphinium
delphinoid
delt? *No,* dealt
delta - ic
deltoid
(DEAL)
DE*LU DELV
delud/e - ed - ing
delug/e - ed - ing
delus/ion - ional - ive - ively
de luxe (*F*)
delv/e - ed - ing
(DIL)
DE*MA
demagog/ue - ic
demand - ed - ing
demarc/ate - ating - ation
démarche (*F*)
DE*ME
demean - ed - ing
demeanour
demented - ly
dementi (*F*)
dementia
Demerara
demerit
demesne *or* domain
(DOMI DIM DOME)
DE*MI
demi - *, prefix meaning* half
demi - mond/e - aine (*F*)
demise (*not* z)
demission
demit - ted - ting
(DEME DIMI)
DE*MO
demo, *for* demonstration
demob - bed - bing, *for*
  demobilise (z)
demobilis/e - ed - ing - ation (z)
democra/cy - cies - t - tic

- tically
democratis/e - ed - ing - ation
  (z)
démodé (*F*)
demograph/y - ic - er
demolish - ed - ing - er
demolition
demon - ic - ism - ology - olatry
demonetis/e - ed - ing - ation
  (z)
demoniac - al
demonstrab/le - ly - ility
demonstrat/e - ed - ing - ion
  - or
demonstrat/ive - ively
  - iveness
demoralis/e - ed - ing - ation (z)
demot/e - ed - ing - ion
demotic
DE*MU
demulcent
demur - red - ring - rant - rer
  - rable - rage
demure - ly - ness
DE*N-DE*NI
den
denary (decimal); *not*
  deanery
denatur/e - ed - ant
dendriform
dendrit/e - ic
dendro/logy - logist - phobe
  - id
dengue
deni/al - er - able; *but* deny
denier (silk or rayon measure)
denigrat/e - ed - ing - ion - or
denim
denizen
DE*NO
denominat/e - ed - ing - ion - or
  - ive
denot/e - ed - ing - ation - ative
dénouement (*F*)
denounc/e - ed - ing; *but*
  denunciation
de nouveau (*F*)

* If the word you wish to spell is not in this list, omit the prefix
and look for the rest of the word.

de novo (L)

DENS DENT

dens/e - er - est - ely - eness
densit/y - ies
dent - ed - ing
dent/al - ate
dentifrice
dentil
dentist - ry
dentition
denture

DE*NU

denud/e - ed - ing - ation
denunciat/ion - or - ory - ive;
  but denounce

DE*NY

den/y - ied - ying - ial
  (DENI)

DE*O

deodar
deodoris/e - ed - ing - er - ation
  (z)
Deo volente *or* D.V. (L)
  (DIO)

DE*PA-DE*PL

depart - ed - ing - ure
department - al - ally
depend - ed - ing - able
dependant (person who
  depends on another)
dependent (depending)
dependen/ce - cy - cies
depict - ed - ing - ion - er - or
depilat/e - ed - ing - ion - or
  - ory
deplet/e - ed - ing - ion - ory
deplor/e - ed - ing - able - ably
deploy - ed - ing - ment
  (DIP)

DE*PO

deponent
deport - ed - ing - ation - ee
deportment
depos/e - ed - ing - ition
deposit - ed - ing - ion - or
depositary (trustee)
depository (store)

depot

DE*PR-DE*PU

deprav/e - ed - ing - ity
deprecat/e (disapprove of)
  - ed - ing - ion - ory - ingly
depreciat/e (lower value) - ed
  - ing - ion
depredat/ion - or - ory
depress - ed - ing - ion - ible
  - ant - or
depriv/e - ed - ing - ation
de profundis (L)
depth
depurat/e - ed - ing - ion - ive
  - or
deput/e - ed - ing - ation
deputis/e - ed - ing (z)
deput/y - ies

DE*RA

deracinat/e - ed - ing - ion
derail - ed - ing
derang/e - ed - ing - ement
  (DERO)

DERB

derbar? *No,* durbar
derb/y (hat) - ies
Derby - shire

DE*RE DE*RI

derelict
derid/e - ed - ing
derigible? *No,* dirigible
de rigueur (F)
deris/ion - ive - ively - ory
deriv/e - ed - ing - ation - ative
  - altively
  (DERR DIR)

DERM

derm - al - atology - atologist
  - atitis
  (DURM)

DE*RO

derogat/e - ed - ing - ion
derogatory

DERR

derrick
derring - do
derringer

* If the word you wish to spell is not in this list, omit the prefix
and look for the rest of the word.

derris
derry
(DERE DERI)

DERV

derv
dervish - es

DE*SC

descant - ed - ing
descend - ed - ing - ant - able
or - ible
descent (way down); *not*
decent *or* dissent
describ/e - ed - ing - able
descript/ion - ive - ively
(DECE DESE DESQ DISC)

DE*SE-DE*SI

desecrate/e (profane) - ed
- ing - ion; *not* dessicate
desert (wilderness); *not*
dessert (food)
desert - ed - ing - ion - er
deserv/e - ed - ing - edly
desiccat/e (dry up) - ed - ing
- ion; *not* desecrate
desiderat/um - a
design - ed - ing - edly - er
designat/e - ed - ing - ion
desir/e - ed - ing - ous - able
- ably - ability
desist - ed - ing
(DECE DECI DESC DESS
DISE DISS)

DE*SK

desk
(DESC DESQ)

DE*SO

desolat/e - ed - ing - ion - or
- ely - eness
(DISS)

DE*SP

despair - ed - ing - ingly
despatch - ed - ing, *or* disp-
desperado - es
desperat/e - ely - ion - eness
despicab/le - ly
despis/e - ed - ing (*not* z)
despite

despoil - ed - ing - er
despoliation
despond/ency - ent - ently
despot - ism - ic - ically
(DISP)

DE*SQ-DE*SU

desquamat/e - ion - ive - ory
dessert (food); *not* desert
(wilderness)
dessicate? No, desiccate
destin/e - ed - ing - ation
destin/y - ies
destitut/e - ion
destroy - ed - ing - er - able (*or*
destructible)
destruct/ion - or - ive - ively
- iveness
destructib/le - ility
desuetude
desultor/y - ily - iness
(DIS)

DE*TA-DE*TE

detach - ed - ing - ment - able
- edly - edness
detail - ed - ing
detain - ed - ing - ee
detect - ed - ing - ion - or - ive
- able - ably
detent (in clockwork)
détente (*F*, improvement of
relations)
detention
deter - red - ring - rence - rent
detergent
deteriorat/e - ed - ing - ion - ive
determin/e - ed - ing - ation
- ism - ist - able
determin/ate - ant - ative
detest - ed - ing - ation - able
- ably - ableness

DE*TH

dethron/e - ed - ing - ement
(DEA)

DE*TO-DE*TR

detonat/e - ed - ing - ion
detour
detract - ed - ing - ion - or - ive

* If the word you wish to spell is not in this list, omit the prefix
and look for the rest of the word.

detriment - al - ally
detritus
de trop (*F*)

DE*U
deuce - ed - dly; *not* juice (fluid)
deus ex machina (*L*)
deuterium
deuteron
Deuteronomy
(DEW DUE DU)

DE*V
devastat/e - ed - ing - ion - or
develop - ed - ing - ment - mental - er
deviat/e - ed - ing - ion - ionist
device
devil - led - ling
devil - ish - ishly - ment - ry *or* - try; *also* bedevil
devious - ly - ness
devis/e - ed - ing - or - ee - able; (*not* z)
devoid
devol/ve - ved - ving - ution
Devon - ian
devot/e - ed - ing - ion - ee - edly
devotional - ly - ism - ist
devour - ed - ing - er
devout - ly - ness
(DIV)

DE*W
dew (moisture) - y; *also* bedew; *not* due (owing)
dewlap
(DEU DUE DU)

DEX
dexter - ity
dexterous *or* dextrous
dextr/in - ose
(DECK DIX)

DH
dharma
dhobi
dhoti
dhow

DIAB-DIAG
diabet/es - ic
diabol/ism - ic - ical - ically - ist
diabolo
diacon/al - ally - ate; *but* deacon
diacritical
diactinic
diadem - ed
diaeresis
diagnose/e - ed - ing - is - tic - tically - tician
diagonal - ly
diagram - matic - matically
diagraph (used in drawing); *not* digraph
(DYA)

DIAL
dial - led - ling
dialect - al - ology - ologist
dialectic (debate) - al - ally - ian; *not* dielectric
dialogue
dialy/sis - tic
(DIL)

DIAM-DIAPH
diamanté (*F*)
diamet/er - ric - rical - rically
diamond - iferous
diapason
diaper
diaphanous
diaphoretic
diaphragm - atic

DIAR
diarchy *or* dyarchy
diarrhoea - l
diar/y (journal) - ies - ist; *not* dairy (milk)
(DIRE DYA)

DIAS
diaspora
diasta/se - tic *or* - sic
diastole

DIAT
diatherm/y - ic - ancy - anous
diathes/is - es

diatom -ic -aceous
diatonic
diatribe
(DIET)

DIB
dibasic
dibber
dibbl/e -ed -ing -er
(DEB)

DIC
dic/e -ed -ing -er
dichloride
dichotom/y -ies -ic -ous
 -ously -ise (z)
dichroic
dichromat/e -ic
dick
dickens
dicker
dickey *or* dicky
dicotyledon
dictaphone
dictat/e -ed -ing -ion -or
 -ress
dictatorial -ly
diction (style of speaking);
 not dictation
dictionar/y -ies
dictograph
dict/um -a *or* -ums
(DEC DIK)

DID
did, didst, didn't
didactic -ism -ally
diddl/e -ed -ing
didgeridoo *or* -ydoo (*Aus*)
didynium
(DED)

DIE
die (death), died, dying; *not*
 dye (colour)
dielectric; *not* dialectic
diesel
diet -etic -ary -ician
(DY)

DIF
differ -ed -ing -ent -ence
 -ently
differentia -e
differenti/al -ate -ated -ation

difficult -y -ies
diffiden/t -ce
diffract -ed -ing -ion -ive
 -ively
diffus/e (spread about) -ed
 -ing -ion -eness; *not* defuse
(DIPH DEF)

DIG
dig -ging -ger
digastric
digest -ed -ing -ion -er -ive
 -ible -ibly -ibility
dight
digit -al -age -ated -ation
 -alis
digitalis
dignif/y -ied -ying
dignit/y -ies -ary -aries
digraph (two-letter sound)
digress -ed -ing -ion -ive
(DEG)

DIH
dihedral
(DEH)

DIK
dike *or* dyke
(DIC)

DIL
dilapidat/e -ed -ing -ion
dilat/e -ed -ing -or -ion *or*
 -ation
dilator/y -ily -iness
dilemma
dilettant/e -ism -ish
diligen/ce -t -tly
dill
dilly-dally -ed -ing
diluent
dilut/e -ed -ing -ion
diluvial
(DEL)

DIM
dim -mer -mest -ness -ly
 -mish
dim, *for* diminuendo
dime
dimension -al
diminish -ed -ing -ingly
diminuendo -s
diminut/ion -ive -ively

69

-iveness
dimissory; *but* dismiss
dimity
dimorph/ic -ous -ism
dimpl/e -ed -ing
(DEM)

DIN

din -ned -ning
dinar
dingbat
din/e -ed -ing -er; *not* dyne
(unit of force)
ding -dong
dingh/y (boat) -ies
dingle
dingo -es
ding/y (dirty -looking) -ier
-iest -ily -iness
dink
dinkum
dink/y -ier -iest
dinner
dinoceras
dinornis
dinosaur -ian
dinothere
dint
(DEN DYN)

DIO

dioces/e -an
diode
Dionys/us -ian -iac
diopt/er -ric -rically
dioram/a -ic
dioxide
(DEO)

DIP DIPH

dip -ped -ping -per -py
diphther/ia -ic -ial -oid
diphthong -al
(DEP DIF)

DIPL-DIPT

diplodocus
diploma -'d
diploma/cy -t -tist -tic -tically
diplomatis/e -ed -ing (z)
dipole/e -ar

dipper
dipsomani/a -ac
dipter/al -ous
diptych
(DEP)

DIRE-DIRT

dir/e -er -est -ely -eful
direct -ed -ing -ion -ive -ly
-ness
directoire (*F*)
direct/or -ress -orial
director/y -ies
dirge
dirigible
dirk
dirndl
dirt -y -ier -iest -ily -iness
(DER)

DIS*-DIS*B

dis -*, *a negative prefix*
disappoint -ed -ing -ment
-edly -ingly
disast/er -rous -rously
disburs/e (pay out) -ed -ing;
not disperse (scatter)

DIS*C-DIS*CI

disc *or* disk
discard -ed -ing
discarnate
discern -ed -ing -ment -ible
-ibly
discerpt/ion -ible -ibility
discip/le -ular -leship
disciplin/e -ed -ing -al -ary
-arian
(DESC DISS)

DIS*CO

disco, *for* discotheque
discography
discoid
discomfit -ted -ting -ure
discommod/e -ed -ing
disconsolate -ly
discord/ant -antly -ance
discount -ed -ing -able
discourag/e -ed -ing -ement
-ingly

---

* If the word you wish to spell is not in this list, omit the prefix
and look for the rest of the word.

discours/e - ed - ing
discover - ed - ing - y - ies - er
 - able

DIS*CR-DIS*CU

discreet (prudent) - ly
discrep/ancy - ant
discrete (separate) - ness
discretion - ary
discriminat/e - ed - ing - ion - or
discursive - ly - ness
discus (disc)
discuss - ed - ing - ion - ible
 (DESC)

DIS*D-DIS*K

disdain - ed - ing - ful - fully
 - fulness
disease - d
disect? *No*, dissect
disembowel - led - ling - ment
diseu/r - se
disgorg/e - ed - ing
disgrac/e - ed - ing - ful - fully
disgruntled
disguis/e - ed - ing (*not* z)
disgust - ed - ing - edly - ingly
dish - es - ed - ing
dishabille
dishevel/led - ment
disk *or* disc
 (DES DISS DYS)

DIS*L-DIS*M

dislexia? *No*, dyslexia
dislik/e - ed - ing
dislocat/e - ed - ing - ion
dismal - ly - ness
dismantl/e - ed - ing - ement
dismay - ed - ing
dismember - ed - ing - ment
dismiss - ed - ing - al - ible

DIS*P-DIS*R

disparag/e - ed - ing - ingly
disparate (different) - ly
 - ness; *not* desperate
disparit/y - ies
dispatch *or* despatch - ed - ing
dispel - led - ling
dispens/e - ed - ing - er - ary

 - able - ation
dispepsia? *No*, dyspepsia
dispers/e - ed - ing - ion - al
 - edly - ive
dispirit - ed - ing - edly
dispiteous - ly
display - ed - ing
disport - ed - ing
dispos/e - ed - ing - er - al - able
 - ability - ition
disput/e - ed - ing - ant - able
 - ably
disputat/ion - ious - iously
 - iousness
disquisition - al
disrupt - ed - ing - ion - ive
 (DES DYS)

DIS*S

dissapear? *No*, disappear
dissapoint? *No*, disappoint
dissect - ed - ing - ion - or
disseise *or* disseize (oust)
 - ed - ing; *not* disease
dissembl/e - ed - ing - er
disseminat/e - ed - ing - ion
 - ator
dissension
dissent - ed - ing - ingly - er
 - ient
dissertation
dissiden/t - ce
dissipat/e - ed - ing - ion - ive
dissociat/e - ed - ing - ion
 - ative
dissociable
dissolut/e - ely - eness - ion
dissolv/e - ed - ing - ent
dissonan/ce - t - tly
dissua/de - ded - ding - sion
 - sive
dissymmetr/y - ical
 (DESS DYS)

DIS*T

distaff
distal
distan/ce - t - tly
distend - ed - ing

* If the word you wish to spell is not in this list, omit the prefix and look for the rest of the word.

distens/ion -ible -ibility
distich -ous
distil -led -ling -late -lation
  -ler -lery
distinct -ly -ness -ion -ive
  -ively -iveness
distinguish -ed -ing -able
  -ably
distort -ed -ing -ion -ional
  -edly
distract -ed -ing -ion -edly
  -ingly
distrain -ed -ing -t -er -ee
  -ment
distrait -e (F)
distraught
distress -ed -ing -ingly -ful
  -fully
distribut/e -ed -ing -ion -or
  -ive -ively
district
distrophy? No, dystrophy
disturb -ed -ing -ance
  (DEST)

DIS*U DIS*Y

disuria? No, dysuria
disyllab/le or dissyllab/le -ic
  -ically

DIT

ditch -ed -ing -er
dither -ed -ing -er
dithyramb -ic
dittany
ditto -s
ditt/y -ies
  (DET)

DIU

diuretic
diurnal -ly
  (DEU DIA DIO)

DIV

divagat/e -ed -ing -ion
divalent
divan
divaricat/e -ion
div/e -ed -ing -er
diverg/e -ed -ing -ence -ency

-ent -ently
diverse -ly
diversif/y -ies -ied -ying
  -ication
divers/ion -ity -ities
divert/ed -ing -ible
divest -ed -ing -ment
divi or divvy, for dividend
divid/e -ed -ing -end -er
divin/e -ed -ing -ation
divin/e -er -est -ely
divinit/y -ies
divis/ion -ional
divis/or -ible -ibly -ibility -ive
divorc/e -ed -ing -ment -ee
divot
divulg/e -ed -ing -ence
  -ement
  (DEV)

DIX

Dixie -land
dixie dix/y -ies
  (DEX)

DIZ

dizz/y -ier -iest -ily -iness
  (DIS)

DJI

djibbah or jibbah

DO-DOD

do, does, did, done
do or doh (music); not dough
  (pastry)
do., for ditto
doat or dot/e -ed -ing -ingly
  -age
doch -an -doris
docil/e -ely -ity
dock -ed -ing -er
docket -ed -ing
doctor -ed -ing -ate -hood
  -ial
doctrin/e -al -ally -aire -airian
document -ed -ing -ary
  -aries -ation
dodder -ed -ing -er
dodeca-*, prefix meaning
  twelve

* If the word you wish to spell is not in this list, omit the prefix
and look for the rest of the word.

dodeca/gon - hedron - hedral
dodg/e - ed - ing - er - y
dodo - s

DOE-DOH

doe (deer) - s
doer (one who does things)
does (is doing)
doff - ed - ing
dog - gish - gy - giness
dog - ged - ging
doge (Venice)
dogger
doggerel
doggie (little dog)
doggo
dogma - tic - tically
dogmatis/e - ed - ing (z)
do - gooder
doh *or* do (music)
  (DOO)

DOI

doil/y - ies, *or* doyley - s
doing - s
  (DOY)

DOL

doldrums
dol/e - ed - ing - eful - efully
dolerite
dolichocephal/y - ic - ous
doll - y - ies - ish - ishly
 - ishness
dollar
dollop
dolman (robe)
dolmen (prehistory)
dolomit/e - ic
dolorous - ly
dolphin
dolt - ish - ishness

DOM

Dom (*Port*, title)
domain *or* demesne
dom/e - ed
Domesday book
domestic - ate - ated - ating
 - ation - ity - ally
domicil/e - ed - iary - iate
dominan/t - tly - ce

dominat/e - ed - ing - ion
domineer - ed - ing - ingly
dominical
Dominican
dominie
dominion
domino - es

DON

Don (*Sp*, title)
don (university) - nish
 - nishness
don (put on) - ned - ning
donah
donat/e - ed - ing †
donation (gift)
done (do); *not* dun (colour)
donee (recipient)
Donegal
donkey - s
donna (*It*)
donor (giver)
don't (do not)

DOO

doodl/e - ed - ing
doom - ed - ing
door
  (DOU)

DOP

dop/e - ed - ing - y *or* - ey
doppler

DOR

dor (insect)
doric
dorman/t - cy
dormer
dormitor/y - ies
dor/mouse - mice
dormy (golf)
dorothy bag
dorsal - ly
dorter (where monks sleep);
  not daughter
  (DAU DAW)

DOS

dosage
dos/e (medicine) - ed - ing;
  not doze (sleep)
doss - ed - ing

†*But to* give *is better than to* donate

73

dossier

DOT

dot - ted - ting
dot (*F*, dowry)
dot/e *or* doat, - ed - ing - ingly
 - age
doth, *old form of* does
dotterel *or* dottrel
dottle
dott/y - ier - iest

DOUB

doubl/e - ed - ing - y
double entendre (*F*)
doublet
doubloon
doubt - ed - ing - er - ful - fully
 - fulness - less
 (DAU DOW DUB)

DOUC-DOUS

douch/e - ed - ing
dough - y iness; *not* doe
 (deer), doh (music)
dought/y - ier - iest - ily - iness
dour - ly - ness
dous/e *or* dows/e - ed - ing - er
 (DOO DOW)

DOV

dove
dovetail - ed - ing
 (DUV)

DOW

dowager
dowd/y - ier - iest - ily - iness
dowel
dower *or* dowry
dowlas
down - ed - ing
down - y - ier - iest
downpour
downright
downstairs
downtrodden
dowry *or* dower
dows/ing - er (water divining)
 (DAU DOU)

DOX

doxolog/y - ies
dox/y - ies
 (DOC)

DOY

doyen - ne (*F*)
doyley - s, *or* doil/y - ies
 (DOI)

DOZ

doz/e - ed - ing
dozen
 (DOES DOS)

DRAB-DRAG

drab - ber - best
drabbet
drabble - ed - ing
drachma
draconian
draff
draft - ed - ing
drag - ged - ging
dragee
draggl/e - ed - ing; *also*
 bedraggle
dragoman
dragon
dragoon
dragster

DRAI

drail
drain - ed - ing - age - er
 (DRAY)

DRAK-DRAW

drake
dram
drama - tic - tically - tist
dramatis/e - ed - ing - ation (z)
drank
drap/e - ed - ing - er - ery - eries
drastic - ally
drat - ted
draught† - ed - ing - y - iness
Dravidian
draw - n - ing - er - ee; *but*
 drew
drawl - ed - ing - ingly - er

† *Use* draft for rough copy, military detachment; *use* draught for
air-current, game, drink, pulling, depth of water for ship; *use either*
for written order for money.

74

'draw-well
DRAY
dray (cart); *not* drey
 (squirrels' nest)
 (DRAI)
DRE
dread-ed-ing-ful-fully
dream-ed *or*-t-ing-er-y-ier
 -iest
drear/y-ier-ily-iness
dredge/e-ed-ing-er
dreg-gy
'drench-ed-ing-er
Dresden
dress-ed-ing-er-y-ier-iest
 -iness
dressage
drew
drey (squirrels' nest); *not* dray
 (cart)
 (DRA)
DRI
dribbl/e-ed-ing-er
driblet
dried
drier, driest
drift-ed-ing-er-age
drill-ed-ing-er
drily *or* dryly
drink-ing-er-able; *but*
 drank, drunk
drip-ped-ping-py
driv/e-en-ing-er; *but* drove
drivel-led-ling-ler
drizzl/e-ed-ing-y
 (DRY)
DRO
drogue
droll-er-est-ness-ery-y
dromedar/y-ies
dron/e-ed-ing-ingly-er
drongo (*Aus*)
drool-ed-ing-er
droop (bend)-ed-ing-ingly
 -y-ier-iest; *not* drupe (fruit)
drop-ped-ping-per
drops/y-ical-ically
drosky *or* droshky
drosophila
dross

drought-y
drov/e-ing-er
drown-ed-ing-er
drows/e-ed-ing-y-ier-iest
 -iness-ily
DRU
drub-bed-bing
drudg/e-ed-ing-ery
drug-ged-ging-gist-gy
drugget
druid-ic-ical-ess-ism
drum-med-ming-mer
drumlin
drunk-en-er-est-ard
drup/e (fruit)-el-elet
 -aceous; *not* droop (bend)
druse
 (DREW DROO)
DRY
dry-ing-ness-ish
dryly *or* drily
dryer *or* drier
dryad
 (DRI)
DUA-DUD
dual (twofold)-ly-ity-ism
 -ist-istic; *not* duel (fight)
dub-bed-bing
dubbin *or* dubbing (grease)
dubi/ous-ously-ety
ducal
ducat
duch/y-ies-ess
duck-ed-ing-er-ie
duct-ile-ility
dud
dude
dudgeon
DUE
due; *but* duly
duel (fight)-led-ling-list-ler;
 not dual (twofold)
duenna
duet-tist
 (DEU DEW JEW JU)
DUF-DUL
duff-ed-ing-er
duffel *or* duffle
dug
dugong

duke -dom; *but* ducal, duchy,
  duchess
dulcet
dulcif/y -ied -ication
dulcimer
dull -er -est -y -ish -ard
dullness *or* dulness
duly (fitly); *not* dully

DUM
dumb -er -est -ly -ness
dumbfound/ed -ing
dumm/y -ies
dump -ed -ing -er -iness -y
  -ier -iest
dumpling
  (DOM)

DUN
dun (colour); *not* done
dun (demand payment) -ned
  -ning
dunce
dunderhead -ed
dundrear/y -ies
dune
dung -ed -ing -hill
dungaree
dungeon
dunk -ed -ing
dunlin
dunnage
dunnock
dunn/y -ies
dunt -ed -ing
  (DON)

DUO
duo -*, *prefix meaning* pair,
  two
duodecim/o -al
duoden/um -al -ary -itis
duologue

DUP
dup/e -ed -ing
duple
duplex
duplicat/e -ed -ing -ion -or
duplicit/y -ies
  (JUP)

DUR
durab/le -ly -ility -leness
duralumin
durance
duration
durbar
duress
durge? *No,* dirge
durian
during
durmast
durra *or* dhurra
durst *or* dared
  (DER DIR JUR)

DUS
dusk -y -ily -iness
dust -ed -ing -er
dust/y -ier -iest -ily -iness

DUT
Dutch (Holland); *but* duchy,
  duchess
duteous -ly -ness
dut/y -iful -ifully
dut/y -iable
  (DEUT)

DUV
duvet (*F*)
  (DOV JUV)

DW
dwarf -s -ish -ishness; *not*
  dwarves
dwell -ing -er; dwelt
dwindl/e -ed -ing

DY
dyad -ic
Dyak
dyarchy *or* diarchy
dy/e (colour) -ed -eing -er
dying (death)
dyke *or* dike
dymond? *No,* diamond
dynam/ic -ism -ist
dynamic/s -al -ally
dynamit/e -ed -ing -er
dynamo -s -meter
dynast -y -ies -ic -ically
dyne (unit of force); *not* dine

* If the word you wish to spell is not in this list, omit the prefix
and look for the rest of the word.

dynel (fabric)
dysenter/y - ic
dysgenic - ally
dyslex/ia - ic
dyspep/sia - tic
dystrophy
dysuria
(DI)

E

EAC-EAP
each
eager - ly - ness
eag/le - let
eak? *No,* eke
(EE HEA HEE)

EAR
ear - ed - less; *not* ere
(before)
earing (sail - rope); *not*
ear - ring, hearing
earl - dom
earl/y - ier - iest - iness
earn - ed - ing - er; *not* erne
(eagle), urn (pot)
earnest - ly - ness
ear - ring
earth - ward - y - iness - ly
- liness
earthen - ware
earthquake
earwig
(EER ER HEAR HER UR)

EAS
ease - ful - fully - ment
easel
east - ern - erly - ward - ing
Easter
easthete? *No,* aesthete
eas/y - ier - iest - ily - iness

EAT
eat - en - ing - er - able; *but* ate
(did eat)
(ETE HEAT)

EAU
eau - de- (*F,* water of)
Cologne - Nil - vie

EAV
eaves - dropping - dropper
(EV HEAV)

EB
ebb - ed - ing
ebon - y - ite - ise (z)
ebullien - t - tly - ce - cy
ebullition
(AB HEB)

EC
écarté (*F*)
eccentric - ity - ities - ally
ecclesiastic - al - ally
ecclesiolog/y - ist - ical
ecdys/is - es
echelon
echidna
echin/us - ite - oderm
echo - es - ed - ing - ism
éclair (long cream bun)
éclat (applause)
eclectic - ally - ism
eclip/se - sed - sing - tic
eclogue
ecolog/y - ist
econom/y - ies - ic - ical - ically
- ist
economis/e - ed - ing (z)
ecsta/sy - sies - tic - tically
ecto/blast - derm - plasm
ecumenical - ly
eczema
(AC HEC)

ED
Edam
edd/y - ies - ied - ying
edelweiss (*Ger*)
edema *or* oedema
edentate
edg/e - ed - ing - y - eways
- ewise
edib/le - ility
edict
edifice
edif/y - ies - ied - ying - ication
edit - ed - ing - or - orial
edition (of book); *not* addition
educab/le - ility
educat/e - ed - ing - ion - ional
- ionally - ive - or
educ/e - ed - ing - tion - ible
Edward - ian
(AD HEAD HED)

77

EE

eek? *No,* eke
eel (fish); *not* heal *or* heel
e'en, *for* even
e'er, *for* ever; *not* ere
 (before)
eerie - er - est - ly - ness
 (EA HE)

EF

effac/e - ed - ing - ement
 - eable
effect (result, accomplish)
 - ed - ing - ive - ively - ual
 - ually; *not* affect (influence)
effemin/ate - ately - acy
efferent
effervesc/e - ed - ing - ence
 - ent
effete - ness
efficac/y - ious - iously
 - iousness
efficien/t - tly - cy
effig/y - ies
effloresc/e - ed - ing - ence
 - ent
effluen/t (ouflow) - ce; *not*
 affluent (wealthy)
effluvi/um - a
efflux - ion
effort - less - lessly
effronter/y - ies
effulgen/t - tly - ce
effus/e - ed - ing - ion - ive
 - ively - iveness
eft
 (AF APH EPH)

EG

e.g. (*L,* for example)
egad
egalitarian
egg - ed - ing - y
egis? *No,* aegis
eglantine
ego
egois/m *or* egotis/m †- t - tic
 - tically
egregious - ly - ness

egress - ion (way out)
egret
Egypt - ian - ology - ologist
 (AG EAG EJ EX HEG IG)

EH

eh?

EI

eider - duck - down
eidograph
eidolon
eigh/t (8) - th - thly
eighteen (18) - th
eight/some - fold - sided
eight/y (80) - ies - ieth - yfold
Eir/e - ann
eisteddfod - au *or* - s (*W*)
either
 (AI EY I)

EJ

ejaculat/e - ed - ing - ion - ory
eject - ed - ing - ion - ive - or
 (AEG EG)

EK

ek/e - ed - ing
 (EC)

ELA-ELD

elaborat/e - ed - ing - ion - ely
 - eness - ive
élan (*F*)
eland
elaps/e - ed - ing
elastic - ity - ally
elat/e - ed - ing - ion
elbow - ed - ing
elce? *No,* else
elder - ly
eldest
El Dorado - s
eldritch
 (AL IL)

ELEC

elecampane
elect - ed - ing - ive
election - eer - eering
elector - ate - al
electress
electric - ity - al - ally - ian

---

† For difference, if any, refer to dictionary, or use 'selfish'.

electro-*, *prefix relating* to
  electricity
electrocut/e -ed -ing -ion
electrode
electroly/sis -te -tic -tically
electrolys/e -ed -ing -ation (z)
electron -ic -ics -ically
electrum
electuary

ELEE-ELEV

eleemosynary
elegan/ce -t -tly
elegiac
eleg/y -ies
element -al -ary; *not* aliment
  (food) -ary
elephant -ine -oid -iasis
elevat/e -ed -ing -ion -or -ory
eleven -th -ses -fold
  (ALE ALI ALLE ELI ILLE)

ELF

elf -in -ish; elves, elvish
  (ALPH)

ELI

elicit (draw out) -ed -ing; *not*
  illicit (illegal)
eli/de -ded -ding -sion
eligib/le (suitable) -ly -ility;
  not illegible (unreadable)
eliminat/e -ed -ng -ion -or
elision
élite (*F*)
elixir
Elizabeth -an
  (ALI ALLI ELE ELL ELY ILLI)

ELK

elk -hound
  (ALC ALK)

ELL

ell (measure); *not* hell
ellip/se -soid -tic -tical -tically
  -ticity
ellip/sis -tical -tically
  (ELI ILLI)

ELM

elm (tree); *not* helm
  (ALM)

ELO

elocution -ary -ist
elongat/e -ed -ing -ion
elop/e -ed -ing -ement
eloquen/ce -t -tly
  (ALLO ALO ILLO)

ELS

else -where

ELU

elucidat/e -ed -ing -ion -ive
  -ory
elud/e (avoid) -ed -ing; *not*
  allude (refer)
elus/ion (avoidance) -ive
  -ively -iveness; *not* allusion
  (reference)
  (ALLU ALU HALLU ILLU)

ELV

elvan
elver
elves, elvish; *but* elf

ELY

elysian
elytron
  (ELI)

EM EMA

em
emaciat/e -ed -ing -ion
emanat/e -ed -ing -ion
emancipat/e -ed -ing -ion -or
  -ory
emancipist
emasculat/e -ed -ing -ion
  -ive -ory
  (AMA IMA IMMA)

EMBA

embalm -ed -ing -er -ment
  (-mm-)
embank -ed -ing -ment
emgargo -es
embark -ed -ing -ation
embarras de richesse (*F*)
embarrass -ed -ing -ingly
  -ment
embass/y -ies; *but*
  ambassador
embattl/e -ed

---

* If the word you wish to spell is not in this list, omit the prefix
and look for the rest of the word.

embay - ed - ing - ment
EMBE-EMBL
embed or imbed - ed - ding
embellish - ed - ing - ment
ember
embezzl/e - ed - ing - er
embitter - ed - ing - ment
emblazon - ed - ing - ment - ry
emblem - atic - atically
(AMB IMB)
EMBO
embod/y - ies - ied - ying
 - iment
embolden - ed
embolism
embonpoint (F)
embosom - ed - ing
emboss - es - ed - ing - ment
embower - ed
EMBR EMBU
embrac/e - ed - ing - eable
 - ement
embrangl/e - ed - ing - ement;
 or imb -
embrasure
embrocat/e - ed - ing - ion
embroider - ed - ing - y - er
embroil - ed - ing - ment
embryo - s - nic - logy - tomy
 - genesis
embus - sed - sing - sment
(IMB)
EME
emend (remove mistakes)
 - ed - ing - ation - ator - atory;
 not amend (improve)
emerald - ine
emerg/e - d - ing - ence - ent
emergenc/y - ies
emeritus (L)
emerods or haemorrhoids
emery
emetic
(AME IMME)
EMI
emigrant (leaver); not
 immigrant (arriver)
emigrat/e - ed - ing - ion - ory
emigré (F)
eminen/t (outstanding) - tly

 - ce; not immanent or
 imminent
emir - ate
emissar/y - ies
emiss/ion (giving off) - ive;
 not omission (leaving out)
emit (give off) - ted - ting; not
 omit (leave out)
 (AMI HEMI IMI IMMI)
EMM
emmet or ant
 (HEM)
EMO
emollient
emolument
emot/ion - ive - ively
emotional - ly - ism - ist
 (AMMO AMO IMMO)
EMP
empanel or impanel - led - ling
empathy
emp/eror - ress
emphas/is - es - ise - ised
 - ising (z)
emphatic - ally
emphysema
empire; but imperial
empiric - al - ally - ism - ist
emplacement
emplan/e - ed - ing
employ - ed - ing - ment - er
 - ee - able
empori/um - a
empower - ed - ing
empress
empt/y - ies - ier - iest - ied
 - ying - iness
empurple
empyrean
 (HEMP IMP)
EMU
emu - s
emulat/e - ed - ing - ion - or
 - ive
emulous - ly
emulsif/y - ied - ying
emuls/ion - ive
 (AMU IMMU)
ENA
enabl/e - ed - ing

80

enact -ed -ing -ment
enamel -led -ling -ler
enamour -ed -ing
enantio/morph -pathy
(ANA HENNA INA)

ENB
en bloc (*F*)
en brosse (*F*)

ENCA-ENCH
encag/e *or* incag/e -ed -ing;
 not engage
encamp -ed -ing -ment
encapsulat/e -ed -ing -ion
encas/e *or* incas/e -ed -ing;
 not in case (if)
encash -ed -ing -ment
encaustic
encaphal/ic -itis -ogram
 -ograph -otomy
enceinte (*F*)
enchain -ed -ing
enchant -ed -ing -ingly -ment
 -er -ress
 (HENC INC)

ENCI
encircl/e -ed -ing
 (ENCY ENSI INCE INCI)

ENCL-ENCU
en clair (*F*)
enclave
enclitic -ally
enclos/e *or* inclos/e -ed -ing
 -ure
encod/e -ed -ing
encomium
encompass -es -ed -ing
 -ment
encore
encounter -ed -ing
encourag/e -ed -ing -ingly
 -ement
encroach -ed -ing -ment
encrust *or* incrust -ed -ing
encumb/er -ered -ering
 -rance
 (INC)

ENCY
encyclic -al
encycloped/ia *or* -aed/ia -ic
 -ist
encyst -ed -ation; *not* insist
 (emphasise)
 (ENSI INCI INSI)

END
end -ed -ing -less -lessly
 -lessness
endanger -ed -ing
endear -ed -ing -ingly -ment
endeavour -ed -ing
endemic -ally
endive
endo -*, *prefix meaning*
 within
endocard/ium -ial -itis
endo/carp -derm
endocrin/e -ology
endogam/y -ic -ous -ously
endogen -ous
endo/morph -plasm
endors/e *or* indors/e -ed -ing
 -ement
endosmo/sis -tic
endothelium
endow -ed -ing -ment
endu/e *or* indu/e -ed -ing
endur/e -ed -ing -ingly -ance
endways *or* endwise
 (IND)

ENE
enema
enem/y -ies; *but* enmity
energ/y -ies -etic -etically
 -ise -ised (z)
enervat/e -ed -ing -ion
 (ANE ENA ENI ENN INE)

ENF
en famille (*F*)
enfant terrible (*F*)
enfeebl/e -ed -ing -ement
enfeoff -ment
en fête (*F*)
enfilad/e -ed -ing
enfold -ed -ing

* If the word you wish to spell is not in this list, omit the prefix
and look for the rest of the word.

enforc/e -ed -ing -ement
 -eable
enfranchis/e -ed -ing -ement
 (*not* z)
 (EMPH INF)

ENG
engag/e -ed -ing -ement
 -ingly
engender -ed -ing
engine
engineer -ed -ing
England, English
engorge -ment
engraft -ed -ing
engrail -ed -ing
engrain -ing; *but* ingrained
engrav/e -ed -ing -er
engross -ed -ing -ment
engulf -ed -ing -ment
 (ENJ ING)

ENH
enhanc/e -ed -ing -ement
enharmonic -ally
 (ANH INH)

ENI
enigma -tic -itcal -tically
 (ANY ENE INI)

ENJ
enjoin -ed -ing
enjoy -ed -ing -ment -able
 -ably
 (ENG INJ INGE)

ENL
enlac/e -ed -ing -ement
enlarg/e -ed -ing -ement -er
enlighten -ed -ing -ment
enlist -ed -ing -ment
enliven -ed -ing -ment
 (INL)

ENM
en masse (*F*)
enmesh -ed -ing
enmit/y -ies; *but* enemy
 (INM)

ENN
ennui (*F*)
ennobl/e -ed -ing
 (ANN INN)

ENO
enormit/y -ies

enormous -ly -ness
enosis (*Gr*)
enough
 (ANNO ANO ENN INO
 INNO)

ENP
en passant (*F*)
en pension (*F*)

ENQ
enquir/e *or* inquir/e -ed -ing
 -y -ies
 (INQ)

ENR
enrag/e -ed -ing
en rapport (*F*)
enraptur/e -ed -ing
enrich -ed -ing -ment
enrol -led -ling -ment, *or*
 enroll -ment
en route (*F*)
 (INR)

ENS
ensconc/e -ed -ing
ensemble (*F*)
enshrin/e -ed -ing -ement
ensign
ensilag/e -ed -ing
enslav/e -ed -ing -ement
ensnar/e -ed -ing -ement
ensu/e -ed -ing
ensur/e (make sure) -ed -ing;
 not insure
 (ENCI ENZ INS)

ENTA
entablature
entablement
entail -ed -ing -ment
entangl/e -ed -ing -ement
entasis
 (ANTA INTA)

ENTE
entelechy
entente (*F*)
enter -ed -ing -able; *but*
entrance, entry
enter/ic -itis -olite -otomy
enterpris/e -ing -ingly (*not* z)
entertain -ed -ing -ingly
 -ment -er
 (ANTE ANTI INTE)

ENTH

enthral -led -ling, or enthrall
  -ed -ing
enthron/e -ed -ing -ement
enthus/e -ed -ing
enthusi/asm -ast -astic
  -astically
  (ANTH)

ENTI

entic/e -ed -ing -ingly
  -ement
entire -ly -ty
entitl/e -ed -ing -ement
entit/y -ies
  (ANTI INTI)

ENTO

entomb -ed -ing -ment
entomolog/y -ical -ist
entourage (F)
en -tout -cas (F)
  (INTO)

ENTR

entr'acte (F)
entrails
entrain -ed -ing -ment
entrammel -led -ling
entran/ce (way in) -t
entranc/e (fascinate) -ed -ing
  -ement
entrap -ped -ping
entreat -ed -ing -ingly -y
entrechat (F, in dancing)
entrecôte (F, steak)
entrée (F)
entrench or intrench -ed -ing
  -ment
entre nous (F)
entrepôt (F)
entrepreneur (F) -ial
entropy
entrust -ed -ing
entr/y -ies; but enter
  (INTR)

ENTW

entwin/e or intwin/e -ed -ing

ENU

enucleat/e -ed -ing -ion
enumerat/e -ed -ing -ion -or

  -ive
enunciat/e (pronounce) -ed
  -ing -ion -or -ive; not ann -
enure? No, inure
enuresis
  (ENOU INNU INU)

ENV

envelop -ed -ing -ment
envelope
envenom -ed
envi/able -ably -ous -ously;
  but envy
environ -ment -mental
  -mentally
envisag/e -ed -ing -ement
envoy -s
env/y -ies -ied -ying
  (INV)

ENZ

Enzed -der, for New Zealand
  -er
enzootic
enzyme
  (ENS)

EO

Eocene
eolith -ic
eon or aeon
eosin
eozoic
  (AEO IO YO)

EPA

epacrid (Aus)
epact
eparchy
epaulement
epaulet -te
  (APA EPO HEPA)

EPE

epée (F)
epeirogen/y -esis
epergne
  (APE APPE)

EPH

ephemer/a -on -al -is -ides
ephod (vestment)
ephor (overseer)
  (AFF APH EFF HEF)

EPI*

epi-*, *prefix meaning* upon, in addition, etc.
epic-al-ally
epicene
epicur/e-ean-ism
epicycl/e-ic-oid
epidem/ic-ically-iology
epiderm-is-al-ic-oid
epidiascope
epigastrium
epigen/e-esis
epigram-matic-matically -matist
epigraph-y-ic-ist
epilep/sy-tic
epilogue
epiphan/y-ies
epiphyt/e-al-ic
episcop/acy-ate-al-alian
episod/e-ic-ically
epistemolog/y-ical
epist/le-olary
epitaph
epithalam/ium-ic
epithet
epitom/e-ise-ised-ising (z)
(APE API)

EPO

epoch-al
epode
eponym-ous
epoxide
(APO APPO)

EQUA EQUE

equab/le-ly-ility
equal-led-ling-ity-ly
equanimity
equat/e-ed-ing
equation-al-ally
equator-ial-ially
equerr/y-ies
equestri/an-enne
(ACQU AQU EQUI)

EQUI

equi-*, *prefix meaning* equal
equilibr/ium-ate-ation-ist

equine
equino/x-ctial
equip-ped-ping-ment
equipage
equipoll/ent-ence-ency
equitation
equit/y-ies-able-ably
equival/ent-ently-ence -ency
equivocal-ly
equivocat/e-ed-ing-ion
(ACQU AQU EQUE)

ERA

era (period); *not* error (mistake)
eradicat/e-ed-ing-ion
eradicab/le-ly
eras/e-ed-ing-er-ure-able
Erastian-ism
(ERRA IRA IRRA)

ERB

(URB)

ERE

ere (before); *not* e'er (ever), 'ere (here), air
erect-ed-ing-ion-ile-or-ly -ness
(ARE ARRE EAR HERE)

ERG

erg-on
ergent? *No*, urgent
ergo (L)
ergonomic
ergot-ism
(URG)

ERI

ericaceous
Erin
(ARI EARI ERY HERI IRE IRR)

ERL

erl-king
(EARL HURL)

ERM

ermine
(HERM)

* If the word you wish to spell is not in this list, omit the prefix and look for the rest of the word.

ERN
erne (eagle)
(EARN HERN)

ERO
erod/e - ed - ing
eros/ion - ive
Eros
erot/ic - icism - omania
(ARO ERRO HERO)

ERR
err - ed - ing - or
errand (message)
erran/t (roaming) - try - cy
erratic - ally
erratum - a
erroneous - ly - ness
error
(AER ARR EAR HER IRR
UR)

ERS
ersatz (Ger)
Erse
erstwhile
(URS)

ERU
eruct - ed - ing - ation
erudit/e - ely - ion
erupt (volcano) - ed - ing - ion
- ive; not irruption (invasion)

ERY
erysipelas
erythema
(ARI ERI)

ESC
escalat/e - ed - ing - ion - or
escallonia
escallop or scallop
escapade
escap/e - ed - ing - ism - ist
- ology - ologist
escapement (clock)
escarpment or scarp (steep
side of hill)
eschatolog/y - ical
escheat
eschew - ed - ing
eschscholtzia
escort - ed - ing
escribe (math.); not ascribe
escritoire

escro
escudo (Port)
esculent
escuctcheon
(ASC ASK ESK ESQ)

ESK
esker
Eskimo - s
(ASC ASK ESC ESQ)

ESO
esophagus or oesophagus
esoteric - al - ally
(ASSO)

ESP
espalier
esparto grass
especial - ly
Esperanto
espionage
esplanade
espous/e - ed - ing - al
espresso
esprit de corps (F)
esp/y - ied - ying - ial
(ASP)

ESQ
esq. for esquire
(ESC ESK)

ESS
essay (attempt) - ed - ing; not
assay (test)
essence
essential - ly - ity
(ASC ASS HESS)

EST
establish - ed - ing - ment
- mentarian
estaminet (F)
estate
esteem - ed - ing
ester
estimab/le - ly
estimat/e - ed - ing - ion - or
- ive
estival or aestival
estivat/e or aestivat/e - ed - ing
- ion
estop - page - pel
estovers
estrang/e - ed - ing - ement

estrogen *or* oestrogen
estreat
estuar/y -ies -ine
  (AST AEST EAST)

ETC

etc. *for* et cetera (*L*)
etch -ed -ing -er
  (ECH)

ETE

eternal -ly
eternit/y -ies
  (EAT)

ETH

ethane
ether -ise -ised -ising
  -isation (z)
ethereal -ly -ity -ise -ised
  -ising -isation (z)
ethic -al -ally
Ethiopia -n
ethmoid
ethnic -al -ally
ethno/logy -graphy -graphic
  -grapher
etho/s -logy -logical
ethyl -ene
  (ATH ITH)

ETI

etiolat/e -ed -ing -ion
etiquette
  (ETY)

ETO ETR

Eton -ian
Etru/ria -scan

ETY

etymolog/y -ical -ically -ise
  -ising (z)
  (ETI)

EU

eucalaly? *No*, ukulele
eucalypt -us -uses
eucharist -ic
euchre
Euclid -ian
eudiomet/er -ry -ric; *not*
  udometer (rain gauge)
eugenic -ally
eulog/y -ies -ist -istic
  -istically
eulogis/e -ed -ing (z)

eunuch
euonymus
eupeptic
euphem/ism (putting it mildly)
  -istic -istically; *not*
  euphuism
euphon/y -ic -ious -ically
  -iously -ium
euphorbia (plant); *not*
  euphoria
euphor/ia (well-being) -ic
euphu/ism (high-flown
  writing) -istic; *not*
  euphemism
Eurasia -n
eureka!
eurhythmic -al -ally
euro (kangaroo)
Europ/e -ean -eanise
  -eanised (z)
eustachian
eutectic
euthanasia
  (HU U YEW YOU YU)

EVA

evacuat/e -ed -ing -ion
evacu/ee -ant
evad/e -ed -ing -able
evaginat/e -ed -ing -ion
evaluat/e -ed -ing -ion
evanesc/e -ed -ing -ence
  -ent -ently
evangel -ic -ical -ically -ism
  -ist -istic
evangelis/e -ed -ing (z)
evaporat/e -ed -ing -ion -ive
  -or
evas/ion -ive -ively -iveness
  (AVA)

EVE

eve (day before, or evening)
even (level) -ed -ing
evening (poet.: even)
event
eventful -ly
eventu/al -ally -ality -ate
ever
everlasting -ly
ever/t (turn inside out) -ted
  -ting -sion; *not* avert

every
  (AVE)

EVI

evict -ed -ing -ion -or
evidence
evident -ly -ial -ally
evil -ly
evinc/e -ed -ing
eviscerat/e -ed -ing -ion

EVO

evocat/ion -ive -ively -ory
evok/e -ed -ing
evolute
evolution -ary -ist -ism
evolv/e -ed -ing
  (AVO)

EW

ewe (sheep)
ewer (jug)
  (EU HEW HU U YOU YU)

EX*

ex -* *prefix; where ex-
  simply means* formerly,
  *refer to the stem word, e.g.,
  for ex-president refer to*
  president

EX*A

exacerbat/e -ed -ing -ion
exact -ed -ing -ion -or -able
exact -ly -ness -itude
exaggerat/e -ed -ing -ion -or
  -edly -ive -ively
exalt -ed -ing -ation
exam *for* examination
examin/e -ed -ing -ation -er
  -ee -atorial
example; *but* exemplary
exasperat/e -ed -ing -ion
  -ingly
  (EXHA)

EX*CA

excape? *No,* escape
excavat/e -ed -ing -ion -or

EX*CE

exceed -ed -ing -ingly
excel -led -ling
excell/ent -ently -ence -ency

excentric? *No,* ecce-
except (omit) -ed -ing; *not*
  accept (agree to)
exception -al -ally
excercise? *No,* exercise
excess -es -ive -ively -ed
excerpt -ible
  (ACCE EXE)

EX*CH

exchang/e -ed -ing -eable
exchequer

EX*CI

excis/e (duty, or cut out) -ed
  -ing -able -ion (*not* z)
excit/e -ed -ing -ement -edly
  -able -ability
excit/ant -ation -ative -atory
  (ACCI EXHI EXI)

EX*CL-EX*CR

exclaim -ed -ing
exclam/ation -atory
exclud-e -ed -ing
exclus/ion -ive -ively
  -iveness
excogitat/e -ed -ing -ion
excommunicat/e -ed -ing
  -ion -ive -ory
excoriat/e -ed -ing -ion
excrement -al -itious
excrescen/ce -t
excret/e -ed -ing -ion -ive
  -ory -a
excruciat/e -ed -ing -ingly
  -ion

EX*CU

exculpat/e -ed -ing -ion -ory
excursion -ary -ist
excursive -ly -ness
excus/e -ed -ing -able -ably
  -atory
  (EXECU EXQU)

EX*E

exeat (*L*)
execrab/le -ly
execrat/e -ed -ing -ion -ive
  -ory
execut/ant -able

---

* If the word you wish to spell is not in this list, omit the prefix
and look for the rest of the word.

execut/e - ed - ing - ion - ioner
executiv/e - ely
execut/or - rix - orial - orship
exege/sis - tic - tically
exema? *No,* eczema
exemplar - y - ily - iness
exemplif/y - ies - ied - ying
 - ication
exempt - ed - ing - ion
exercis/e - ed - ing - able (*not*
 z); *not* exorcise (expel evil)
exert - ed - ing - ion
 (ECCE EXA EXCE EXI)

EX*F-EX*H
exfoliat/e - ed - ing - ion - or
ex gratia (*L*)
exhal/e - ed - ing - ation
exhaust - ed - ing - ion - ible
 - ibility
exhaustive - ly - ness
exhibit - ed - ing - or - ory
exhibition - er - ist - ism
exhilarat/e - ed - ing - ion - ive
exhorbitant? *No,* exorb -
exhort - ed - ing - ation - ative
 - atory
exhum/e - ed - ing - ation

EX*I
exig/ence - ency - ent - ible
exigu/ous - ously - ousness
 - ity
exil/e - ed - ing
exist - ed - ing - ence - ent
existential - ly - ism - ist
exit
 (EXCI EXE EXHI)

EX*L
ex libris (*L*)

EX*O
exoderm
exodus
ex officio (*L*)
exogam/y - ous - ously
exogen - ous
exoplasm
exosmosis
exonerat/e - ed - ing - ion

exophthalm/us - ic
exorbitan/t - tly - ce
exorcis/e (expel evil) - ed - ing
 (z); *not* exercise
exorc/ism - ist
exordi/um - a *or* ums
exotic - ally
 (EXHO)

EX*PA
expand - ed - ing
expans/e - ion - ile - ible - ibility
expansiv/e - ity - eness - ely
ex parte (*L*)
expatiate/(hold forth) - ed - ing
 - ion - ory
expatriat/e (banish) - ed - ing
 - ion

EX*PE
expect - ed - ing - ation - ative
 - ant - ancy
expector/ate - ated - ating
 - ation - ant
expedien/ce - cy - t - tly
expedit/e - ed - ing - ion
 - ionary
expeditious - ly - ness
expel - led - ling; *but*
 expulsion
expend - ed - ing - able - iture
expens/e - ive - ively - iveness
experien/ce - ced - cing - tial
 - tially - tialist
experiment - ed - ing - ation
 - al - ally
expert - ly - ness - ise

EX*PI
expiat/e - ed - ing - ion - or
 - ory; expiable
expir/e - ed - ing - ation - atory
 - y

EX*PL
explain - ed - ing - able *or*
 explicable
explanat/ion - ory - orily
expletive
explicat/e - ed - ing - ion - ive
 - ory

---

* If the word you wish to spell is not in this list, omit the prefix
and look for the rest of the word.

explicab/le - ly
explicit - ly - ness
explod/e - ed - ing
exploit - ed - ing - er - ation
explor/e - ed - ing - ation - er
 - ative - atory
explos/ion - ive - ively
 - iveness

EX*PO-EX*PU

exponent - ial - ially
export - ed - ing - ation - er
 - able
expos/e - ed - ing - ure
exposit/ion - ive - or - ory
ex post facto (*L*)
expostulat/e - ed - ing - ion
 - ory
expound - ed - ing
express - ed - ing - ly - ive
 - ively - iveness
expression - al - ism - ist
expropriat/e - ed - ing - ion
expulsion; *but* expel
expun/ge - ged - ging - ction
expurgat/e - ed - ing - ion - or
 - ory - orial

EX*Q

exquisite - ly - ness

EX*TA-EX*TO

extant
extasy? *No,* ecstasy
extempor/e - ise - ised - ising
 - isation (z)
extemporaneous - ly - ness
extend - ed - ing - ible
extensib/le - ly - ility
extens-ion - ive - ively or extent
extenuat/e - ed - ing - ion
exterior - ly - ity - ise - ised
 - ising (z)
exterminat/e - ed - ing - ion - or
 - ory
external - ly - ity
externalis/e - ed - ing - ation (z)
extinct - ion
extinguish - ed - ing - ment - er
 - able

extirpat/e - ed - ing - ion - or
extol - led - ling
extort - ed - ing - ion - ionate
 - ive

EX*TR

extra
extract - ed - ing - ion - or - ive
 - able
extradit/e - ed - ing - ion - able
extramural
extraneous - ly - ness
extraordinar/y - ily - iness
extrapolat/e - ed - ing - ion
extravagan/t - tly - ce
extravert *or* extrovert
extrem/e - ely - ity - ities - ism
 - ist - eness
extricat/e - ed - ing - ion
extricab/le - ly
extrinsic - ally
extrover/t - ted - sion
extru/de - ded - ding - sion
 - sive

EX*U

exuberan/ce - t - tly
exud/e - ed - ing - ation
exult - ed - ing - ation - ant
 - antly
(EXHU)

EY

eyas (young hawk) - es
eye, eyed, eying, *or* eyeing
eyelet (small hole); *not* islet
(small island)
eyot *or* ait (islet)
eyre (court of law)
eyrie(brood of eagle, etc.)
 (AI AY EII)

F

FAB

fab, *for* fabulous
fabian
fabl/e - ed - er
fabric
fabricat/e - ed - ing - ion - or
fabul/ous - ously - ousness

---

* If the word you wish to spell is not in this list, omit the prefix
and look for the rest of the word.

-ist
FAC
façade
fac/e - ed - ing - er - ial - ially
facet
faceti/ae - ous - ously
 - ousness
facia *or* fascia
facile
facilit/y - ies - ate - ated - ating
 - ation
facsimile
fact - ual - ually
fact/ion - ious - iously
 - iousness
factitious (artificial) - ly - ness;
 not fictitious (fiction)
factitive
factor - ial - ially - age
factor/y - ies
factotum
facul/a - ar - ous
facult/y - ies - ative
 (FAS FAK PHA)
FAD
fad - dy - diness - dish
 - dishness
fad/e - ed - ing - eless - elessly
FAE
faec - al - es
faerie *or* fairy
faeton? *No*, phaeton
 (FAI FAY)
FAG
fag - ged - ging
faggot *or* fagot
 (PHAG)
FAH
fah (music)
Fahrenheit
 (FAR PHAR)
FAI
faience
fail - ed - ing - ure
faille (fabric)
fain (willing); *not* fane
 (temple)
faint - er - est - ed - ing - ly
 - ness; *not* feint (pretence)
fair - er - est - ly - ness; *not*

fare (go)
fairing
fair - y - ies
fait accompli (*F*)
faith - ful - fully - fulness - less
 - lessly - lessness
 (FAY FEI FEY)
FAK
fak/e - ed - ing - er
fakir
 (FAC)
FAL
falc/ate - ated - iform
falchion (sword)
falcon (bird) - er - ry
falconet
fallac/y - ies - ious
fall - ing - en; *but* fell
falli/ble - bly - bility
fallopian
fallow
fals/e - er - est - ely - ity - eness
falsehood
falsetto - s
falsies; *not* fallacies
 (delusions)
falsif/y - ies - ied - ying - ication
falter - ed - ing - ingly
 (FAUL FEL PHAL THAL)
FAM
fam/e - ed - ous - ously
familial (in a family)
familiar (well known) - ly - ity
 - ities
familiaris/e - ed - ing - ation (z)
famil/y - ies; family's,
 families'
famine
famish - ed - ing
famous - ly
 (FERM FOM)
FAN
fan - ned - ning
fan, *for* fanatic
fanatic - al - ally - ism
fanciful - ly - ness
fanc/y - ier - iest - ied - ying
fandango - es
fane (temple); *not* fain
 (willing)

90

fanfar/e -onade
fang -ed
fanmail
fan -tan
fantasia
fantastic -ally
fantas/y or phantas/y -ies
  (PHAN THAN)

FAR

far -ther -thest, or fur/ther
  -thest
farad -aic
farc/e -eur -ical -ically -icality
farcy
far/e (go) -ed -ing; not fair
farewell
farin/a -ose -aceous
fari (Sc)
farm -ed -ing -er
faro (card game); not
  Pharaoh
farouche (sullen); not
  ferocious
farrago -s (medley); not
  virago (fierce woman)
farrier -y
farrow -ed -ing
fart -ed -ing
farth/er -est or furth/er -est
farthing
farthingale
  (FAIR PHAR)

FAS

fasade? No, façade
fascia or facia
fascic/le -led -ule -ular -ulate
  -ulation
fascinat/-ed -ing -ion -ingly
  -or
fascine
fasc/ism -ist
fash -ed -ing (Sc)
fashion -ed -ing -able -ably
  -ableness
fasset? No, facet
fast -er -est -ed -ing -ness
fasten -ed -ing -er
fastidious -ly -ness
fastigiate
  (FAC PHAS)

FAT

fat -ter -test -ten -tened
  -tening -ty -tish -ling
fatal -ly -ity -ities -ism -ist
  -istically
fat/e -ed -ing -eful -efully;
  not fête (festival)
father -ed -ing -ly -liness
fathom -ed -ing
fatigu/e -ed -ing
fatu/ous -ously -ousness -ity

FAU

fauc/es -al (throat)
faucet (tap)
faugh!
fault -ed -ing -y -ily -iness
faultless -ly -ness
faun (rural god); not fawn
  (deer)
fauna (animals)
faux pas (F)
  (AL FAW FOR FOU PHOR)

FAV

favour -ed -ing -able -ably
  -ite -itism

FAW

fawn -ed -ing -ingly -er
  (FAL FAU FOR FOU PHOR)

FAY

fay (fairy); not fey (Sc, fated)
  (FAI)

FEA

fealty
fear -ed -ing -ful -fully
  -fulness
fearless -ly -ness
fearsome -ly -ness
feasib/le -ly -ility
feast -ed -ing -er; but
  festive
feat (deed); not feet (foot) or
  fête (festival)
feather -ed -ing -y -less
featur/e -ed -ing -eless
  (FEE FIA FIE PHEA)

FEB-FED

febrifug/e -al
febrile
February
feckless -ly -ness

fecul/ent -ence
fecund -ity -ate -ation
fed (did feed)
feder/al -ally -ate -ated -ating
 -ation
 (FA FI)

FEE

fee, feed or fee'd (paid a fee)
feeb/le -ly -leness
feed -ing -er; but fed
feedback
feel -ing -er; but felt
feet (foot); not feat (deed) or
 fête (festival)

FEI

feign -ed -ing
feint (pretence) -ed -ing; not
 faint
 (FAI FAY FIE PHY)

FEL

feldspa/r or felspa/r -thic
felicit/y -ies -ous -ously
felicitat/e -ed -ing -ion
felin/e -ity
fell (cut down) -ed -ing
fell (did fall)
fell (mountain; animal's skin)
fellah -een
felloe or felly (of wheel)
fellow
felo de se (L)
felon -y -ious -iously
felstone
felt (cloth) -ed -ing; not veldt
felt (did feel)
felteric
felucca
 (FALL FIL PHIL)

FEM

female
femin/ine -inely -inity -ality
 -ist -ism
fem/ur -oral
 (FAM)

FEN

fen -ny
fenc/e -ed -ing -er -eless

fend -ed -ing -er
fenestr/ate -ated -ating
 -ation
fenian
fennel
fenugreek
 (FAN PHEN)

FER

feral, ferine (wild)
ferial (non -festal)
ferment (leaven) -ed -ing
 -ation -able -ative; not
 foment (warm up)
fern -ery
feroc/ity -ious -iously
ferret -ed -ing
ferro-*, prefix meaning iron
ferr/ate -ic -ous -iferous
 -uginous
ferrul/e -ed
ferr/y -ies -ied -ying
fertil/e -ity
fertilis/e -ed -ing -er -ation
 -able (z)
ferv/ent -ently -our -id -idly
 (FAR FIR FOR FUR THUR
 VER)

FES

fescue
festal -ly; but feast
festiv/e -ely -eness -al -ity
 -ities
festoon -ed -ing -ery
 (FEAS FEZ PHEAS)

FET

fetch -ed -ing
fête (festival) -d -ing; not fate
 or feet
fetid or foetid -ly -ness
fetish -es -ism -ist -istic
fetlock
fetor (stink)
fetter (shackle)
fettle
fet/us or foet/us -ses -al
 -icide
 (FAT FEAT FEET)

* If the word you wish to spell is not in this list, omit the prefix
and look for the rest of the word.

FEU

feu (*Sc*, fee)
feud
feudal -ly -ism -istic
feudalis/e -ed -ing -ation (z)
feudatory
feul? *No*, fuel
feushia? *No*, fuchsia
(FEW FU PHEW)

FEV

fever -ed -ish -ishly -ous; *not*
feather (of bird)
feverfew

FEW

few -er -est
(FEU FU PHEW)

FEY

fey (*Sc*, fated); *not* fay (fairy)
(FAI FEI FAY)

FEZ

fez
(FEAS FES PHEAS)

FIA

fiancé, fiancée (*F*)
Fianna Fail
fiasco -s
fiat
(FEA PHIA)

FIB

fib -bed -bing -ber
fibr/e -ed -ous -ously
-ousness
fibril -ar -ary -ate -ose -ation
fibr/in
fibro/in -id -sitis
fibula

FIC

ficelle
fichu
fickle
fictile
ficti/on -onal -tious -tiously
-ve

FID

fid
fiddl/e -ed -ing -er
fidelity
fidget -ed -ing -y -iness
fido
fiduci/al -ary

FIE

fie!
fief *or* feoff -ment -or -ee
field -ed -ing -er
fieldfare
fiend -ish -ishly -ishness
fierce -r -est -ly -ness
fier/y (flaming) -ier -iest -ily
-iness; *but* fire
fiesta
(FEA FEE PHE PHI)

FIF

fife -r
fife -rail
fifteen (15) -th
fifth (5th) -ly; *but* five
fift/y (50) -ies -ieth yfold

FIG

fig -ged -ging -gy
fight -ing -er; *but* fought
figment
figurat/ion -ive -ively
-iveness
figur/e -ed -ing
figurine

FIL

filament -ary -ed
filari/a -al -asis
filature
filbert
filch -ed -ing -er
fil/e (tool) -ed -ing; *not* phial
(bottle)
filet (net); *not* fillet
filia/l -tion
filibeg (*Sc*, kilt)
filibuster -ed -ing -er
filigree -d
Filipino -s
fill -ed -ing -er
fillet (ribbon, meat, etc.) -ed
-ing; *not* filet
fillip (flip)
fillister
fill/y -ies
film -ed -ing -y -iness
filter -ed -ing; *not* philtre
filth -y -ier -iest -ily -iness
filtrate
(FIEL PHIL PHYL)

FIM
 fimbriat/e -ed
FIN
 fin -ned -ny
 final -ly -ity
 finale (*It*)
 financ/e -ed -ing -ier -ial -ially
 finch
 find -ing -er -able; *but* found
 fin de siècle (*F*)
 fin/e -er -est -ed -ing -eness
 finery
 finesse
 finger -ed -ing
 finial
 finic/al -king -ky
 finis (*L*)
 finish -ed -ing -er; *not*
  Finnish
 finite -ness
 Fin/land -nish -n
 finnan (haddock)
FIO
 fiord *or* fjord
  (VIO)
FIR
 fir (tree); *not* fur (coat)
 fir/e -ed -ing -er; *also* afire
  (on fire); *but* fiery
 firkin
 firm -er -est -ly -ness
 firmament -al
 first (1st) -ly -ling -hand
 firth
  (FER FUR THIR);
FIS
 fiscal
 fish -ed -ing -er -y -iness
 fisher/y -ies -man -men
 fishmonger
 fissil/e -ity
 fission -able
 fissur/e -ed
 fist -ed -ic -icuffs
 fistul/a -ar -ous
  (FIZZ PHYS)

FIT
 fit -t -ed -ting -ter -ness -test
 fitch
 fite? *No*, fight
 fitful -ly -ness
 fitment
  (PHYT)
FIVE
 five (5); *but* fifth, fifteen, fifty
 five/fold -some -sided
 fiver
 fives
FIX
 fix -ed -ing -er -ity -edly
  -edness
 fixat/ion -ive
 fixture
FIZ
 fizz -y -le -led -ling
  (FIS PHYS)
FLAB
 flabbergasted
 flabb/y -ier -iest -ily -iness
 flabell/ate -iform
FLAC-FLAM
 flaccid -ly -ity
 flag -ged -ging -gy
 flagell/ate -ated -ating -ation
  -ator -atory -ant
 flageolet
 flagitious -ly -ness
 flagon
 flagran/t (glaring) -tly -cy; *not*
  fragrant (sweet -smelling)
 flail -ed -ing
 flair (instinct); *not* flara
  (flame)
 flak
 flak/e -ed -ing -y
 flambeau
 flamboyan/t -tly -ce
 flam/e -ed -ing -eless; *also*
  aflame (in flames)
 flaming -es
 flammab/le †-ility
FLAN-FLAT
 flan

† For practical reasons 'flammable' is a safer word to use than
'inflammable', since the prefix 'in'-can sometimes mean 'not'.

flang -d
flank -ed -ing -er
flannel -led -ling -ly
flannelette
flap -ped -ping -per
flapdoodle
flapjack
flar/e (flame, etc.) -ed -ing;
 not flair (instinct)
flash -ed -ing -er -y -ier -iest
flask
flasket
flat -ter -test -ly -ness -tish
flatilla? *No,* flotilla
flatter -ed -ing -y -er
flatulen/ce -t -tly

FLAU

flaunt -ed -ing -ingly -er
flautist; *but* flute
 (FLAW FLO)

FLAV

Flavian
flav/in -escent
flavour -ed -ing -less

FLAW

flaw -ed -ing -less -lessly
 -lessness
 (FLAU FLO)

FLAX

flax -en
flaxid? *No,* flaccid

FLAY

flay -ed -ing
 (FLAI)

FLE

flea (insect); *not* flee (run
 away)
fleck -ed -ing
fled (did flee)
fledg/e -ed -ing -ling *or* -eling
flee -ing; *but* fled
fleec/e -ed -ing -y -ier -iest
 -iness
fleer -ed -ing
fleet -er -est -ing -ingly
 -ness
Flem/ing -ish
flens/e -ed -ing -er
flesh -ed -ing -er -y -ier -iest
 -iness -less

fleshl/y -iness
fleur -de -lis (*F*)
flew (did fly); *not* flue
(chimney), flu (influenza)
flews (of bloodhound)
flex -ed -ing -ure -ion -ional
flexib/le -ly -ility
flexil/e -ity
 (PHLE)

FLI

flibbertigibbet
flick -ed -ing
flicker -ed -ing -ingly
flier *or* flyer
flight -y -ier -iest -ily -iness
flims/y -ier -iest -ily -iness
flinch -es -ed -ing
flinders
fling -ing -er; *but* flung
flint -y -iness
flip -ped -ping -per
flip -flop
flippan/t -tly -cy -cies
flirt -ed -ing -ation -atious
flit -ted -ting -ter
flitch -es
flittermouse
flivver

FLOA-FLOP

float -ed -ing -er -able -age;
 also afloat; *but* flotation
floccul/e -ent -ence -ous -ate
 -ated -ating -ation
flock -ed -ing; *not* phlox
(plant)
floe (ice); *not* flow
flog -ged -ging -ger
flong
flood -ed -ing
floor -ed -ing -er
flop -ped -ping -py -pier
 -piest
 (PHLO)

FLOR

flora -l
flor/et -escence -iate -iferous
 -ist
floricultur/e -al -ist
florid -ly -ity -ness
florin

95

(FLAU FLAW PHLOR)

FLOS-FLOT

floscul/ar-ous
floss-y
flotation; *but* float
flotilla
flotsam
(PHLO)

FLOU

flounc/e-ed-ing
flounder-ed-ing
flour (meal)-y-ier-iest; *not*
 flower (bloom)
flourish-ed-ing
flout-ed-ing
(FLOW)

FLOW

flow-ed-ing-ingly
flower (bloom)-ed-ing-y;
 not flour (meal)
flown (fly); *not* flowed (flow)
(FLOA FLOE FLOU)

FLU

flu, *for* influenza; *not* flew,
 flue
fluctuat/e-ed-ing-ion
flue (chimney); *not* flew, flu
fluen/t-cy-tly
fluff-y-ier-iest-ed-ing
 -iness
fluid-ity-ify-ified-ifying
fluk/e-y-ier-iest-iness-ily
flummery
flump-ed-ing
flung (did fling)
flunkey-s
fluor-ine-ide-spar-esce
 -escent-escence
flurr/y-ies-ied-ying
flurt? No, flirt
flush-ed-ing-er
fluster-ed-ing
flut/e-ed-ing-y-ist *or*
 flautist
flutter-ed-ing
fluvi/al-atile
flux-ion-ional-ionary
(FLA FLOO FLOU)

FLY

fly, flies, flier *or* flyer

FOA-FOE

foal-ed-ing
foam-y-ier-iest-ed-ing
fod-bed-bing
foc's'le, *for* forecastle
foc/us-i *or*-uses
focus-ed *or*-sed-ing *or*
 -sing
focal
fodder
foe-man-men
foet/us *or* fet/us-uses-al
(PHO)

FOG-FOM

fog-gy-gier-giest-gily
 -giness
fogey-s-ish
föhn
foible
foil-ed-ing
foist-ed-ing
fold-ed-ing-er
foli/age-ar-ate-ated-ation
folio-s
folk-lore-lorist-sy
follow-ed-ing-er
foll/y-ies
foment (warm up)-ed-ing
 -er-ation; *not* ferment
 (leaven)

FON

fond-er-est-ly-ness
fondant
fondl/e-ed-ing
font
fontanel-le
(PHON)

FOO

food
fool-ery-ish-ishly-ishness
foolhard/y-ier-iest-ily
 -iness
foot-ed-ing-er; *also* afoot
football-ing-er
footl/e-ed-ing-er
foozl/e-ed-ing
(FOU)

FOP

fop-pish-pishly-pery
fopa? No, faux pas (F)

FOR-FORD

for (in place of); *not* fore *or* 4
forag/e - ed - ing - er
foram/en - inate - inifera
forasmuch as
foray - s
forbear (refrain) - ing - ingly;
  but forbore/e - ne
forbear *or* forebear (ancestor)
forbid - den - ding - dingly; *but*
  forbade
forbor/e - ne *but* forbear
forbye (*Sc*)
forc/e - ed - ing - ible - ibly
forceful - ly - ness
forceps ford - ed - ing - able
  (FAU FAW FORE FOUR)

FORE*

fore - *, *preflx meating* front
(position), before (time)
forebear *or* forbear (ancestor)
forecast - ing - er (*not* - ed)
foregather *or* forgather - ed
  - ing
fore/go *or* for/go - went - gone
foreign - er
foremost
forenoon
forensic - ally
foresee - n - ing - able
forest - ed - er - ry; *also*
afforest
  (FAU FAW FOR FOUR)

FORF

forfeit - ed - ing - able - ure
forfend - ed - ing
  (FORTH)

FORG

forgather *or* foregather - ed
  - ing
forgave (did forgive)
forg/e - ed - ing - er - ery - eable
forget - ting - table - ful - fully
  - fulness; *but* forgot - ten
forgiv/e - ing - en - er - eness
  - able - ably - ingly - ingness

forgo *or* forego - ing - ne; *but*
  forwent *or* forewent
forgot - ten
  (FORE)

FORK

fork - ed - ing
  (FORE)

FORL

forlorn
  (FALL FORE)

FORM

form - ed - ing - er - less
  - lessness
formal - ly - ity - ities - ist - istic
formalis/e - ed - ing - isation (z)
format
format/ion - ive - ively
  - iveness
forme (printing)
former - ly
form/ic - ate - ine - yl - ica
formidab/le - ly - leness
formul/a - ae *or* - as - ate - ated
  - ating - ary
  (FORE PHOR)

FORN

fornicat/e - ed - ing - ion
  (FAUN FAWN FORE THOR)

FORR

forrard (more forward) - er
  (FORA FORE)

FORS

forsak/e - ing - en
forsook
forsooth
forswear - ing
forswor/e - n
forsythia
  (FAUC FORC FORE)

FORT

fort - ress - alice
forte (*lt*, strong)
forth (forward); *not* fourth
  (4th)
forthcoming
forthright - ness
forthwith

---

* If the word you wish to spell is not in this list, omit the prefix
and look for the rest of the word.

fortif/y -ied -ying -iable
-ication
fortissimo (*It*, very strong)
fortitude
fortnight -ly
fortuit/y -ous -ously
-ousness -ism -ist
fortun/e -ate -ately
fort/y (40) -ieth -yfold
(FORE FOUGH THOUGHT)
FORU-FORW
forum
forward -ed -ing -ness
forwent *or* forewent
(FORE)
FOS
fosse
fossick -ed -ing -er
fossil -iferous -ise -ised
-ising -isation (z)
foster -ed -ing -age -ling
(PHOS)
FOT
(PHOT)
FOU
fought (did fight); *not* fort
foul (offensive) -er -est -ed
-ing -ness -ly; *not* fowl
(bird)
foulard
found -ed -ing -er -ress
-ation
founder -ed -ing
foundling
foundr/y -ies
fount
fountain -ed
four (4) -th -thly -fold -sided
-some; *not* for, forth
fourteen (14) -th -thly -fold
fourty? *No*, forty (40)
(FAU FOO FOW PHOR)
FOW
fowl (bird) -ing -er; *not* foul
(offensive)
(FOU)
FOX
fox -ed -ing -y -iness
FOY
foyer (*F*)

(FOI)
FRAC-FRAG
fracas
fraction -al -ise -ised -ising
-isation (z)
fractious -ly -ness
fractur/e -ed -ing
fraenum *or* frenum
fragil/e -ity
fragment -ed -ing -ation -ary
-ariness
fragran/t -tly -ce
FRAI
frail -er -est -ty
fraise (tool); *not* phrase
(words)
(FRAY FREI PHRA)
FRAM FRAN
framboesia
fram/e -ed -ing -er
franc (money); *not* frank
France
franchise (*not* z)
Francis -can
Franco- phil -phobe -phobia
francolin
frangible -ly
frangipani
frank -ly -ness; *not* franc
Frankenstein
frankfurter
frankincense
franklin
frantic -ally
FRAP-FRAT
frap -ped -ping
frass
frater
fratern/ity -ities -al -ally
fraternis/e -ed -ing -isation
(z)
fratricid/e -al -ally
(PHRA THRA)
FRAU
Frau (*Ger*, Mrs.)
fraud -ulent -ulence -ulently
fraught
Fräulein (*Ger*, Miss)
(FROW)

FRAY
fray - ed - ing
(FRAI FREI PHRA)
FRAZ
frazzle
(PHRA)
FREA-FREE
freak - ed - ing - ish - ishly
 - ishness
freckl/e - ed - y
fre/e - er - est - ely - ed - eing
 - edom; *not* three (3)
freebooter
freemason - ry
freesia
freez/e - ing - er; *but* froze - n;
not frieze
(FREI FRIE FREQ THRE)
FREI
freight (cargo) - er - age; *not*
fright (fear)
(FRAI FRAY PHRA)
FREN
French - ify - ifiied
frend? *No,* friend
frenetic *or* phrenetic
frenz/y - ied
(FRIE PHRE THRE)
FREQ
frequent - ed - ing - er - ation
frequen/cy - cies - tly - tative
(FREAK)
FRES-FREU
fresco - s *or* - es
fresh - er - est - ly - ness; *also*
afresh (again)
freshen - ed - ing - er
freshet
fret - ted - ting - ful - fulness
Freud - ian
(THRE)
FRIA
friab/le (crumbling) - ility; *not*
fryable
friar - y - ies
(FRY)
FRIC
fricandeau - x
fricassee
fricative

friction - al
FRID
Friday
fridge, *for* refrigerator
(THRI)
FRIE
fried (did fry).
friend - ly - lier - liest - liness
 - ship
Friesian
frieze (wool, decoration)
(FREA FREE)
FRIG-FRIZ
frigate
fright - en - ened - ening - ful
 - fully - fulness
frigid - ly - ity - ness
frill - ed - ing - y - ies; *not* thrill
fring/e - ed - ing
frippery
frisk - ed - ing - er - y - ily - iness
frit (calcine, etc.) - ted - ting
frit - fly
fritillary
fritter - ed - ing
Fritz (*Ger*)
frivol/ity - ities - ous - ously
 - ousness
frizz/y - le - led - ling - ly
(THRI)
FRO
fro (from); *not* throw
frock - ed
Froebel - ian
Froid? *No,* Freud - ian
frog - ged - gy
frolic - ked - king - some
from
frond - age - ose
front - ed - ing - al - age
frontier
frontispiece
frontier
frost - ed - ing - y - ier - iest - ily
froth - y - ier - iest - ily - iness
frown - ed - ing - ingly
frowst - y - ier - iest - iness
frowz/y - ier - iest - iness
froze - n
(THRO)

99

FRU

fructif/y - ied - ying - ication
  - iferous
fructose
fructous
frugal - ly - ity
frugivorous
fruit - ed - ing - er - arian - erer
fruition
fruitless - ly - ness
frumen
a - ish - y
frunt? *No*,front
frustrat/e - ed - ing - ion
frustum
frut/ex - escent - icose
  (THRO THRU)

FRY

fry, fried, frying, frier *or* fryer;
  not friar (relig.)
  (FRI)

FUC-FUG

fuchsia
fuchsine
fuc/us - oid
fuddl/e - ed - ing
fuddy - dudd/y - ies
fudg/e - ed - ing
fuehrer *or* führer (*Ger*)
fuel - led - ling
fug - gy - gier - giest
fugac/ity - ious
fugitive
fugleman
fugue
  (FEU FUT THU)

FUL

fulcr/um - a
fulfil - led - ling - ment
fuliginous
full - er - est - y - ness *or*
  fulness
fulmar
fulmin/ic - ate - ant - ation
fulsome - ly - ness
fulv/ous - escent

FUM

fumarole
fumbl/e - ed - ing - er
fum/e - ed - ing

fumigat/e - ed - ing - ion - or
fumitory
  (THUM)

FUN

fun - ny - nier - niest - nily
function - ed - ing - al - ally - ary
  - aries
fund - ed - ing
fundament - al - ally - ality
  - alism - alist
funer/al - ary - eal - eally
fung/us - i *or* - uses - al - iform
  - icide
funicular
funk - ed - ing
funnel - led - ling
  (THUN)

FUR

fur (coat) - ry - rier - riest - red
  - ring; 20fir (tre)
furbelow
furbish - ed - ing - er
fucat/e - ion
furious - ly
furl - ed - ing
furlong
furlough
furnace
furnish - ed - ing - er
furniture
furore
furrow - ed - ing
further - more - most - ance
furthest *or* farthest
furtiv/e - ly - ness
furunc/le - ular - ulous
fur/y - ies - ious - iously; *not*
  furry (fur)
furze (gorse); *not* furs *or* firs
  (fer fir for thir thur)

FUS

fuscous
fus/e - ed - ing - ion - ible
fusee
fusel (oil)
fuselage
fusha? *No*, fuchsia
fusilier
fusillade
fusion

fuss- ed - ing - y - ier - iest - ily
  - iness
fustian
fust/y - ier - iest
  (FUZ)

FUT
futil/e - ly - ity - ities
futur/e - ity - ism - ist

FUZ
fuzz - y - ily - iness
  (FUS)

G

GAB
gab
gabardine *or* gaberdine
gabbl/e (talk) - ed - ing - er
gabbro
gabl/e (building) - ed - ing
gab/y - ies

GAD
gad - ded - ding
gad - fly
gadget - ry
gadwall

GAE
Gael - ic
  (GAI GAY)

GAF
gaff - ed - ing
gaffe (blunder)
gaffer

GAG
gag - ged - ging
gage (pledge); *not* gauge
gage (fruit)
gaggl/e - ed - ing

GAI
gai/ety - ly *but* gay
gain - ed - ing - er - ful - fully
gain/say - said - saying
gait (walk); *not* gate (entry)
gaiter
  (GAE GAY)

GAL
gala (fair)
galah (*Aus*, cockatoo)
galactic
galantine
galatea

gala/xy - xies - ctic
gale
gale/a - ate - ated
galeeny (guinea fowl)
galen/a - ic (lead ore)
Galileo
Galile/e - an
galingale
  (GALL)

GALL
gall - ed - ing
gallant - ly - ry - ries
gallon
galler/y - ies - ied
galley - s
gallic - ism - ise - ised - ising (z)
gallimaufry
gallinaceous
galliot
gallipot
gallium
gallivant - ed - ing
gallon (measure)
galloon (braid)
gallop - ed - ing - er; *not* galop
  (dance)
Galloway
gallows
Gallup poll
  (GEL)

GALO-GALV
galop (dance); *not* gallop
galore
galosh - es
galumph - ed - ing
galvanis/e - ed - ing - ation - er
  (z)
galvan/ism - ic - ometer

GAM
gamba
bambit
gambl/e (chance) - ed - ing - j;
  not gambol (caper)
gamboge
gambol (caper) - led - ling
*gam/e - ing - est - ely - eness
  - esome - ester*
gam/y - ier - iest - ily
gamete
gamin - e (F)

101

gamma (*Gr*)
gammon-ed-ing
gammy
gamp
gamut

GAN

Gana? *No*, Ghana-ian
gander
gang-ed-ing-er; *not* gangue
gang (*Sc*, go)
gange (in fishing)
Gange/s-tic
gang-gang (*Aus*)
Ganging
gangling
gangli/on-a-ated-onic-form
gangren/e-ed-ous
gangster-ism-dom
gangue (ore matrix); *not*
  gang
gangway
ganister
gannet
ganoid
gantr/y-ies
Ganymede

GAO

gaol *or* jail-ed-ing-er-bird;
  not goal

GAP

gap-py-pier-piest
gap/e-ed-ing-er

GARA-GARG

garag/e-ed-ing
garantee? *No*, guarantee
garb-ed-ing
garbage
garbl/e-ed-ing
garboard
garçon (*F*)
garden-ed-ing-er
gardenia
gargantuan
garget
gargl/e (wash throat)-ed-ing
gargoyle (carved spout)
  GUAR

GARI-GART

Garibaldi
garish-ly-ness
garland-ed-ing
garlic-ky
garment
garner-ed-ing
garnet
garnish-ed-ing
garniture
garret
garrison-ed-ing
garron
garrott/e-ed-ing; *or* garo-
garrul/ous-ously-ousness
  -ity
garter-ed-ing
garth

GAS

gas-es-eous-ify-ified
  -ifying-ification
gass/ed-ing-y-ier-iest-ily
  -iness
gascon-ade
gash-ed-ing
gasket
gasoline *or* gasolene
gasometer
gasp-ed-ing-er
gasteropod *or* gastropod
gastly? *No*, ghastly
gastr/ic-itis
gastro-*, *prefix meaning*
  stomach
gastrolog/y-ist-er
gastronom/e-y-ic-ical
  -ically
  (GAZ GHAS)

GAT

gat/e-ed-ing-eway; *not* gait
(manner of walking)
gateau (*F*)-x *or*-s
gather-ed-ing-er
gatling
  (GHAT)

* If the word you wish to spell is not in this list, omit the prefix
and look for the rest of the word.

GAU

gauche (*F*)
gaucho (*Sp*)
gaud/y -ier -iest -ily -iness
gauffer *or* gofer *or* gopher
 -ed -ing
gaug/e (measure) -ed -ing
 -eable; *not* gage, gorge
gault
gaunt -ness
gauntlet
gauss (magnetic unit) -age;
 not gorse
gauz/e (thin fabric) -y -iness
 (GAW GOR)

GAV

gave (did give)
gavel
gavelkin
gavotte

GAW

gawk -y -ier -iest -ily -iness
 (GAU GOR)

GAY

gay -er -est; *but* gaiety,
 gaily; *not* gey (*Sc*)

GAZ

gaz/e -ed -ing -er
gazebo
gazelle
gazett/e -ed -ing
gazetteer
 (GAS)

GEA-GEI

gear -ed -ing
gecko
gee!
geebung (*Aus*)
gee-gee
geese (goose)
geezer
geiger counter
geisha (*Jap*)
geissler tube
 (GHE JE)

GEL

gel -led -ling; *not* jelly

gelatin/e -eous
gel/id (cold) -ation; *not* jellied
geld -ed -ing -er
gelignite
 (GUEL JEAL JEL)

GEM

gem -med -ming
gemm/a -ae -ule -ate -ative
 -ation
gemm/ology -ologist -iferous
gemsbock
 (CHEM JEM)

GEN-GENE

gen, *for* general information
genappe
gendarme (*F*) -rie
gender
gene
genealog/y -ical -ically -ist
genera (more than one
 genus)
generaly -ly
generalis/e -ed -ing -ation -er
 (z)
generalissimo -s
generalit/y -ies
generat/e -ed -ing -ion -ive
 -or
generic -ally
gener/osity -ous -ously
 -ousness
genesis
genet (fur); *not* jenet (horse)
genetic -ally
geneva *or* gin
 (JEN)

GENI-GENO

genial -ly -ity
geniculat/e -ed
genie *or* djinn
genista
genital -ia
genitiv/e -al
genito-*, *prefix meaning*
 genital
genius -es
genocid/e -al

* If the word you wish to spell is not in this list, omit the prefix
and look for the rest of the word.

(JEN)
GENT
gent, *for* gentleman
genteel -ly
gentian
gentile
gentility
gentl/e -e -er -est -y -eness
gentleman -ly -liness -like
gentlewoman -ly -liness -like
gentry
GENU
genu/al -flect -flexion
genuine -ly -ness
gen/us -era -eric
GEO
geo-*, *prefix meaning* earth
geocentric -ally -ity
geod/e -ic
geode/sy -sic -tic -tically
geograph/y -ic -ical -ically -er
geolog/y -ic -ical -ically -ist
geologis/e -ed -ing (z)
geomet/ry -ric -rical -rically
 -rician
geomorpholog/y -ical -ically
 -ist
geophysic/s -al -ist
georgette
(JO)
GER
geranium
gerfalcon
geriatric -ian
gerkin? *No*, jerkin, *or* gherkin
germ -icide -icidal
German -icophil -ophobe
germander
germane
germanium
germin/al -ally
germinat/e -ed -ing -on -ive
geronto/logy -cracy
gerrymander -ed -ing
gerund -ive
(GAR GHER GIR GUER GOR
 JER JOUR JUR)

GES
gesso
gestalt (*Ger*)
gestapo (*Ger*)
gestation
gesticulat/e -ed -ing -ion -ive
 -ory
(GUES JES)
GET
get -ting -ter -table; *but* got
 -ten; *also* beget
getatable (accessible)
getaway
(GHET JET)
GEU GEW
geum
gew -gaw
(JEU JEW JOU JUI)
GEY
gey (*Sç*, very); *not* gay
geyser
(GHEE JEA)
GHA
Ghana -ian
ghastl/y -ier -iest -iness
ghat
(GA)
GHE
ghee
gherkin
ghetto -s
(GE JE)
GHO
ghost -ed -ing -ly -liness
ghoul -ish -ishly
(GO GOO)
GHY
ghyll *or* gill (ravine)
(GI GUI GUY)
GIA GIB
giant; *but* gigantic
gib (wedge); *not* jib
gibber -ed -ing -ish
gibbet -ed -ing
gibbon
gibb/ous -ously -osity
giblets

* If the word you wish to spell is not in this list, omit the prefix
and look for the rest of the word.

(GYB JIB)

GID GIF

gidd/y -ier -iest -ily -iness
gidgee (*Aus*)
gift -s -ed
giftie (*Sc*)
(JI)

GIG

gig
gigantic -ally; *but* giant
giggl/e -ed -ing -er
gigolo -s
gigot
(JIG)

GIL

Gilbert -ian
gild (gold) -ed -ing -er; *but*
 guild (society)
gilgai (*Aus*)
gill *or* ghyll (ravine)
gill -s (of fish)
gillaroo
gillie (*Sc*)
gillyflower
gilt (gilding); *not* guilt (guilty)
(JIL)

GIM

gimbal
gimcrack
gimlet
gimmer
gimmick -y
gimp
(GYM JIM)

GIN

gin *or* geneva (drink)
gin -and -it *for* gin and Italian
 vermouth
gin (machine, snare) -ned
 -ning
ginger -ly -y -ish
gingerade
gingham
ginglymus
ginkgo *or* gingko (tree) -es
ginseng
(GYN JIN)

GIP

gips/y *or* gyps/y -ies -yish
(GYP)

GIR

giraffe
gird -ing, girded *or* girt
girder -ed
gird/le -ed -ing
girl -ish -ishly -ishness -ie -y
girt *or* girded
girth
(GER GUR GYR JER)

GIS-GIZ

gist
gitar? *No,* guitar
gittern (ancient guitar)
gitters? *No,* jitters
giv/e -en -ing -er; *but* gave
gizzard
(GY JI)

GLA

glabrous
glacé (*F*)
glaci/er -al -ate -ated -ating
 -ation
glaciolog/y -ist
glacis
glad -der -dest -ly -ness
 -some
gladden -ed -ing
glade
gladiator -ial
gladiol/us -i *or* -uses
glamo/ur -rous -rously
 -rousness
glanc/e -ed -ing -ingly
gland -ular
glar/e -ed -ing -ingly
glass -y -ier -iest -ily -iness
 -ful
glaz/e -ed -ing -y -er -ier
 -iery

GLE

gleam -ed -ing
glean -ed -ing -er
glebe
glee -ful -fully -some
gleet -y
glen
glengarry
glenoid

GLI

glib -ber -best -ly -ness

glid/e - ed - ing - ingly - er
glim
glimmer - ed - ing
glimps/e - ed - ing
glint - ed - ing
glissad/e - ed - ing
glissando
glissé (F)
glisten - ed - ing
glitter - ed - ing
(GLY)

GLO
gloaming
gloat - ed - ing - ingly
glob/e - al - ose - osity - oid
globul/e - ar - arity - arly - in
glockenspiel
gloom - y - ier - iest - ed - ing
 - ily - iness
glorif/y - ies - ied - ying - ication
glor/y - ies - ied - ying - yingly
 - ious - iously
gloss - ed - ing - al - ary - aries
 - arial
gloss/y - ier - iest - ily - iness
gloss/itis - ology - ographer
glott/is - al - ic
glov/e - ed - ing - er - eless
glow - ed - ing - ingly - worm
glower - ed - ing - ingly
gloxinia
gloz/e - ed - ing - ingly
(GLU)

GLU
glucinum
glucose
glu/e - ed - ing - ey
glum - mer - mest - ly - ness
glum/e (bot.) - aceous - ose;
 not gloom
glut - ted - ting
glut/en - inous - inously
 - inosity
glutton - y - ous - ously
(GLO)

GLY
glycer/ine - ol - yl - ate - ide
 - inate
glyco/l - lic - gen - genic
 - genesis

glycosur/ia - ic
glyphograph - y - ic - er
glypt/ic - ography
glyptodon
(GLI)

GN
gnarl - ed - y
gnash - ed - ing
gnat
gnath/ic - ous
gnaw - ed - ing
gneiss - ic
gnocchi (It)
gnome
gnomic
gnomon - ic
gnos/is - tic - ticism
gnu
(KN N)

GO GOA
go, goes, gone, going, goer;
 but went
goad - ed - ing
goal - post - keeper - ie
goanna or iguana
goat - ish - ishness - y
goatee (beard)
(GAU GHO)

GOB-GOG
gob - bed - bing - ber
gobbet
gobbl/e - ed - ing - er
gobbledegook
gobelin (tapestry)
goblet
goblin (imp)
goby
God
god - dess - head - like - ly
 - liness - less
godet (F)
godetia
godwit
Goeth/e - ian
gofer or gopher or gauffer - ed
 - ing
go - getter
goggl/e - ed - ing - er

GOI
goitr/e - ed - ous

(GOY)

GOK
go-kart -ing -er

GOL
gold -en
golf -ed -ing -er
golliwog
golly!
(GAL GUL)

GON
gonad
gondol/a -ier
gone (did go); *also* begone
gonfalon
gong -ed -ing
gonorrhoe/a -al

GOO
good -ness -ly -ish -y -ies
good-bye
good-o!
goodwill
goof -y
googl/y -ies
goon
goondie (*Aus*)
goorie (*Aus*)
goosander
goose -y -flesh -step
goose/berry -gog
(GHOU GOU GU)

GOPH
gopher *or* gofer *or* gauffer;
not golfer

GOR
Gorblimey! *for* God blind me!
gorcock
gordian
gor/e -ed -ing -y -ier -iest
-iness
gor/e -ed -ing
gorgeours -ly -ness
gorget
gorgon -ian -ise -ised -ising
(z)
gorgonia
gorgonzola
gorilla (ape); *not* guerilla *or*
guerilla (irregular war)
gormandis/e -ed -ing -er (z)
gormless

gorse
gorsedd (*W*)
(GAU GAW)

GOS
gosh!
goshawk
gosling
gospel -ler
gossamer
gossip -ed -ing -er
gossoon (*Ir*)
(GHOS)

GOT
got (did get) -ten; *also* begot
-ten
Goth -ic

GOU
gouache (*F*)
goug/e -ed -ing
goulash
gourd
gourmand (*F*, glutton)
gourmet (*F*, connoisseur of
food and wine)
gout -y -ily -iness
(GHOU GOO GOW)

GOV
govern -ed -ing -ment
-mental -mentally
govern/ance -or -orship -ess
(GAV)

GOW
gowan (*Sc*)
gowk
gown -ed -ing
(GHOU GOU)

GOY
goy (*Heb*, gentile); *not* guy
(GOI)

GRAA-GRAB
graafian
grab -bed -bing -ber
grabbl/e -ed -ing

GRAC
grac/e -ed -ing -eful -efully
-efulness
graceless -ly
gracil/e -ity
gracious -ly -ness
grackle

(GRAS)

GRAD

gradation - al - ally
grad/e - ed - ing
gradely
gradient
gradual - ly - ness
graduat/e - ed - ing - ion - or

GRAF

graffit/o - i
graft - ed - ing - er
(GRAPH)

GRAI

grail
grain - ed - ing - er - y - iness;
  but graniferous
graip (*Sc*); *not* grape (vine)
(GRAY GREA GREY)

GRAM

gram (fodder)
gram *or* gramme (weight)
gramin/aceous - ivorous
grammalogue
gramma/r - rian - tical - tically
gramophone
grampus
(GRAN)

GRAN

granar/y - ies
grand - er - est - ness - ly - eur
  - ee
grand - father - mother - pa
  - ma - (d)ad
grandiloqu/ence - ent - ently
grandios/e - ely - ity
grange
grani/form - iferous - ivorous
granit/e - ic - oid
grann/y - ies
granolithic
grant - ed - ing - able - or - ee
granul/e - ar - arity - ous - ate
  - ated - ating - ation

GRAP

grape
graph - ed - ing - ic - ical - ically
graphit/e - ic - oid
graphiti? *No*, graffiti

grapholog/y - ist
graphotype
grapnel
grappl/e - ed - ing
(GRAF)

GRAS

grasp - ed - ing - ingly
  - ingness - able - er
grass - ed - ing - y - ier - iest
(GRAC GRAZ)

GRAT

grat/e - ed - ing - er; *not* great
(big)
grateful - ly - ness
graticule
gratif/y - ies - ied - ying - yingly
  - ication
gratin (*F*)
gratis
gratitude
gratuit/y - ies - ous - ously
(GREAT)

GRAV

gravamen
grav/e - en - ing
grav/e - er - est - ely
gravel - led - ling - ly
graves (*F*, wine)
gravid
gravit/y - ies
gravitat/e - ed - ing - ion - ional
  - ive
gravure
grav/y - ies

GRAY

gray
grayling
(GRAI GREA GREY)

GRAZ

graz/e - ed - ing - ier

GREA

greas/e - ed - ing - er - y - iness
great - er - est - ly - ness
greaves
(GRAI GREE GRIE)

GREB-GREE

grebe
grecian

Gree/ce - k; *but* Graeco -* as
  prefix
greed - y - ier - iest - ily - iness
green - er - est - ness - ery - ish
greengage
Greenwich
greet - ed - ing
  (GREA GRIE)

GREG-GREN
gregarious - ly - ness
gregorian
gremlin
grenad/e - ier
grenadine

GREW
grew (did grow)
  (GROO GRU)

GREY
grey - er - est - ed - ing - ness
  - ly - ish; gray (*Am*)
greyhound
greylag
  (GRAI GRAY GREA)

GRID
grid - ded - ding - iron
griddl/e - ed - ing
grid/e - ed - ing

GRIE
grief - s
grievance
griev/e - ed - ing - ous - ously
  (GREA GREE)

GRIF-GRIP
griffin *or* griffon *or* gryphon
  (fabulous animal)
griffon (breed of dog)
grig
grill (cookery) - ed - ing
grillage
grille (grating)
grilse
grim - mer - mest - ly - ness
grimac/e - ed - ing - er - ier
grimalkin
grim/e - y - ier - iest - ed - ing
  - iness
grin - ned - ning - ner

grind - ing - er - ery; *but*
  ground
gringo - s (*Sp*)
grip - ed - ing - per
grip/e - es - ed - ing
grippe (*F*, influenza)
  (GRE)

GRIS
grisaille (*F*)
grisette (*F*)
griskin
grisly (horrible); *not* gristly,
grizzly
grist
gristl/e (cartilage) - y
  (GRIZ)

GRIT
grit - ty - tier - tiest - tiness

GRIZ
grizzl/e (whimper) - ed - ing
grizzled (grey haired)
grizzly (bear); *not* grisly,
gristly
  (GRIS)

GROA-GROM
groan - ed - ing - ingly - er
groat
grocer - y - ies
grog - gy - gier - giest - ily
  - iness
grogram
groin (anat., archi.) - ed - ing;
  but groyne (beach defence)
grommet *or* grummet
gromwell
  (GROW)

GROO
groom - ed - ing
groov/e - ed - ing - y - ier - iest
  - iness
  (GRU GREW)

GROP-GROT
grop/e - ed - ing - ingly - er
grosgrain
gross (bloated) - er - est - ly
  - ness; *not* grocer
grotesque - ly - ness

* If the word you wish to spell is not in this list, omit the prefix
and look for the rest of the word.

grotto - s *or* - es
grott/y - ier - iest
GROU
grouch - ed - ing - er - y
ground - ed - ing - less - lessly
ground (did grind)
groundage
groundling
groundsel
group - ed - ing - er
grous/e - ed - ing - er
grout - ed - ing - er
(GROO GROW)
GROV
grove
grovel - led - ling - ler
GROW
grow - n - ing - ingly - able - er;
 but grew
growl - ed - ing - er
grown (did grow); *not* groan
 (low sound)
growth
(GROA GROU)
GROY
groyne (beach defence); *not*
 groin (anat., archi.)
GRUB-GRUE
grub - bed - bing - by - bier
 - biest - ber
grudg/e - ed - ing - ingly; *also*
 begrudge
gruel - ling
gruesome - ly - ness
(GREW GROO GROU)
GRUF-GRUY
gruff - er - est - ly - ness
grumbl/e - ed - ing - ingly - er
grum/e - ous
grummet *or* grommet
grump/y - ier - iest - ily - iness
grunt - ed - ing - er
gruyère (*F*)
GUA
guage? *No*, gauge
guanaco - s
guano - s
guarant/ee - eed - eeing - or - y
guard - ed - ing - edly - edness
guardian - ship

guava
 (GA GHA)
GUB-GUD
gubernatorial - ly
gudgeon
GUE
guelder rose
guerdon
Guernsey
guerilla *or* guerrilla (irregular
 war); *not* gorilla (ape)
guess - ed - ing - er
guest (visitor); *not* guessed
 (GE)
GUF
guffaw - ed - ing
GUI
guichet (*F*)
guid/e - ed - ing - er - ance
 - able
guidon
guilder (Dutch coin); *not*
 gilder
guile - ful - fully - less - lessly
 - lessness; *also* beguile
guillemot
guillotin/e - ed - ing
guilt - y - ier - iest - ily - less
 - lessly - lessness
guinea - fowl - pig
guise (appearance); *not* guys
guitar - ist
 (GHY GI GUY)
GUL-GUN
gulch
gules
gulf
gull - ed - ing - ible - ibility
gullet
gull/y - ies
gulp - ed - ing - ingly - er
gum - med - ming - my - mier
 - miest - miness
gumption
gun - ned - ning - ner - nery
gunge
gunny
gunter
gunwale *or* gunnel
gunya (*Aus*)

gunyang (*Aus*)

GUR
gurgitation
gurgl/e -ed -ing
Gurkha
gurnard *or* gurnet
guru -s
 (GER GHER GIR GUER)

GUS
gush -ed -ing -er -ingly
gusset -ed
gust -ed -ing -y -ier -iest -ily
gustati/ion -ive -ory
gusto
 (GUZ)

GUT
gut -ted -ting
gutta-percha
gutter -ed -ing
guttural -ly

GUY
guy -ed -ing
 (GHY GI GUI)

GUZ
guzzl/e -ed -ing -er
 (GUS)

GYB-GYM
gyb/e *or* jib/e -ed -ing
gym, *for* gymnasium
gymkhana
gymnas/ium -ia *or* -iums -tic
 -tically
gymnosperm -ous
gymnotus
 (JI)

GYN
gynaecolog/y -ist
gynobase
gynocracy
gynophore
 (GIN JIN)

GYP
gyp -ed -ing
gypsophila
gyps/um -eous -iferous
gyps/y *or* gips/y -ies
 (GIP)

GYR-GYV
gyrat/e -ed -ing -ion -ory
gyroscop/e -ic

gyver (*Aus*)
gyves (shackles)
 (GI JI)

H

HAB
habeas corpus (*L*)
haberdasher -y -ies
habiliment
habit -ed -ing -able
habitu/al -ally -ate -ated
 -ating -ation
habitat -ion
 (AB)

HAC
hachur/e -ed -ing
hack -ed -ing -er
hackle
hackney -s
 (AC AQU HEC)

HAD
had -n't
haddock
Hades
 (AD AID)

HAE
haem/al *or* hem/al -atic -atin
 -atology
haematite *or* hematite
haemo/rrhage *or*
 hemo/rrhage -rrhoids -philia
 -globin
haeremai (*NZ*)
 (HE)

HAF
hafnium
haft -ed
 (AF APH HAPH)

HAG
hag -gish
haggard -ly -ness
haggis
haggle/e -ed -ing -er
hagiarchy
hagio/graphy -rapher -logy
 -scope
 (AG)

HAH
ha ha!
ha -ha (sunken garden wall)

111

HAI
hail (greet) - ed - ing - er; *not*
  hale (robust)
hail (frozen rain) - ed - ing
hailo? *No,* halo
hainous? No, heinous
hair - y - ier - iest - ed - iness;
  not hare, heir
  (AI HEI HAY)
HAK
haka (*NZ*)
hake
  (AC HAC)
HALA-HALI
halation
halberd - ier
halcyon
hale (robust) - ness; *not* hail
hal/f - ve - ves - ved - ving
halibut
halidom
halitosis
  (AL EL HALL)
HALL
hall (room); *not* haul (pull)
hallelujah *or* alleluia
hallo! *or* hello! *or* hullo!
halloo! (in hunting)
hallow (make holy) - ed - ing
Hallowe'en
hallucinat/e - ed - ing - ion
hallucinogen
  (AL EL HAL)
HALM-HALY
halm *or* haulm
halma
halo - es
halo/gen - id
halt - ed - ing - ingly
halter
halv/e - es - ed - ing
halyard
  (AL HALL HAR HAUL)
HAM
ham - my
hamburger
hames
Hamit/e - ic
hamlet
hammer - ed - ing

hammock
hamper - ed - ing
hamster
hamstr/ing - ung - inging
  (AM HEM)
HAN
hand - ed - ing - er
hand/ful - cuff - cuffed
handicap - ped - ping - per
handi/craft - work
handkerchief - s
handl/e - ed - ing - er
handsom/e - ly - ness; *not*
hansom (cab)
handwrit/ing - ten
hand/y - ier - iest - ily - iness
hang - ed - ing - er; *but* hung
hangar (aircraft shed)
hangi (*NZ*)
hank
hanker - ed - ing
hank/y - ies, *for*
handkerchief(s)
hanky-panky
hansom (cab); *not* handsome
  (AN)
HAP
ha'pen/ny - ce
haphazard - ly - ness
hapless
ha'p'orth, *for* halfpennyworth
happen - ed - ing
happ/y - ier - iest - ily - iness
  (AP)
HARA
hara - kiri (*Jap*)
harangu/e - ed - ing
harass - ed - ing - ment
  (ARA ARRA HARR)
HARB-HARL
harbinger
harbour - ed - ing - age
hard - er - est - en - ened
  - ening - ly - ness
hard/y - er - iest - ily - iness
hare (animal); *not* hair, heir
harem *or* hareem
haricot
hark! *but* hearken
harlequin - ade

harlot - ry
(AR HOR)

HARM-HARP
harm - ed - ing
harmful - ly - ness
harmless - ly - ness
harmattan
harmonica
harmonis/e - ed - ing - ation
  - er - t (z)
harmonium
harmon/y - ies - ic - ically - ious
  - iously
harness - ed - ing
harp - ed - ing - er - ist
harpoon - ed - ing - er - ist
harpsichord
harp/y - ies
(AR)

HARR
harridan
harrier
Harro/w - vian
harrow - ed - ing
harr/y - ied - ying - ier
(ARR)

HARS-HARV
harsh - er - est - ly - ness
hart (deer); *not* heart
hartebeest
hartshorn
harum (lily)? *No*, arum
harum - scarum
harvest - ed - ing - er
(AR HEAR)

HAS
has - n't
has - been
hash - ed - ing
hashish
hasp (fastening); *not* asp
hassle
hassock
hast (thou hast, *old form of*
  you have)
hastate
hast/e - en - ened - ening

hast/y - ier - iest - ily - iness
(AS HAZ)

HAT
hat - ted - ting - ter - less
hatch - ed - ing - er - ery
hatchet
hatchment
hat/e - ed - ing - er - eful - efully
hath, *old form of* has
hatred
(AT)

HAU
hauberk
haugh (*Sc*)
haught/y - ier - iest - ily - iness
haul - ed - ing - ier - age
haulm *or* halm
haunch
haunt - ed - ing - er
haute école (*F*)
hauteur (*F*)
(AU AW HAW HOR WHO)

HAV
Havana
hav/e - ing - en't
haves (and have - nots)
haven
haver - ed - ing
haversack
havoc - ked - king
(AV)

HAW
haw - thorn
hawk - ed - ing - er
haws/e - er
(AU AW HAU HOR WHO)

HAY
hay - cock - rick - stack
(HAE HAI)

HAZ
hazard - ed - ing - ous - ously
  - ousness
haz/e - y - ier - iest - ily - iness
hazel
(AZ HAS)

HE
he; he-* *as prefix meaning*

* If the word you wish to spell is not in this list, omit the prefix
and look for the rest of the word.

male
he'd, *for* he had *or* he would; *not* heed
he'll, *for* he will; not heel, hell
he's, *for* he is *or* he has

HEAD
head -ed -ing -er; *also* ahead (in front)
head/long -most -strong
head/y -ier -iest -ily -iness
  (HED HEED)

HEAL
heal (cure) -ed -ing -er; *not* heel (foot)
health -y -ier -iest -ily -iness
healthful -ly -ness
  (HEEL HEL)

HEAP
heap -ed -ing
  (HEP)

HEAR
hear -ing -er; *not* here (in this place)
heard (did hear); *not* herd (of animals)
hear, hear! (agreement); *not* here
hearken -ed -ing
hearsay
hearse
heart -ed -en -ened -ening
hearth
heart/y -ier -iest -ily -iness
  (EAR HAR HERE)

HEAT
heat -ed -ing -er -edly
heath -y
heathen -ish -ishness
heather -y
  (EAT HET)

HEAV
heav/e -ing -er
heaved *or* hove
heaven -ly -liness -ward
heaviside layer
heav/y -ier -iest -ily -iness
  (EAV EV)

HEB
hebdomadal
hebetude
Hebr/ew -aic -aism -aist

HEC
hecatomb
heck
heckl/e -ed -ing -er
hectare
hectic -ally
hecto-*, *prefix meaning* hundred
hector -ed -ing
  (EC HAC)

HED
he'd, *for* he had *or* he would; *not* heed
heddle -s
hedg/e -ed -ing -er -ehog
hedon/ic -ism -ist -istic
  (HEAD HEED)

HEE
heed -ed -ing -ful -fully -fulness
heedless -ly -ness
hee-haw!
heel (foot) -ed -ing; *not* heal
heelamon (*Aus*)
  (HEA HE HIE)

HEF
heft/y -ier -iest
  (EF EPH HEI)

HEG
hegemon/y -ies -ic
hegira
  (EG)

HEI
heifer
heigh-ho!
height -en -ened -ening; *but* high
heinous -ly -ness
heir (inheritor) -ess -less -loom; *not* air, ere, hair, hare
hei-tiki (*NZ*)
  (HI HAI)

* If the word you wish to spell is not in this list, omit the prefix and look for the rest of the word.

HELD-HELI
held (did hold)
hel/e (set in soil) - ed - ing
heliacal (sun)
helianthus
helic/al (spiral) - ally - oid
 - oidal; *but* helix
helicopter
helio-*, *prefix meaning* sun
heliocentric - ity - ally
helio/gram - graph - graphic
heliotrop/e - ic - ism
heliosis
helium
helix - es
 (ELE)

HELL
hell - ish - ishly - ishness
he'll, *for* he will
hellebore
Hellen/e - ic - ism - ise - ised
 - ising (z)
hello! *or* hallo! *or* hullo!
 (EL HEL-)

HELM-HELV
helm (tiller); *not* elm (tree)
helmet
helminth - ic - iasis
helmsman
helot - ry - ism
help - ed - ing - er - ful - fully
 - fulness
helpless - ly - ness
helpmate
helter- skelter
helve
 (EL HELL)

HEM
hem - med - ming
hem-, *prefix, see* haem-
hemi-*, *prefix meaning* half
hemisphere
hemlock
hemp
hem - stitch
 (EM HAM)

HEN
hen
hence
hench/man - men
henna - 'd
henpecked
 (EN)

HEP
hepat/ic - itis - ise - ised
 - isation (z)
hepatica
hepta-*, *prefix meaning*
 seven
heptagon - al
heptarchy
 (EP HEAP)

HER-HERD
her, hers (*not* her's)
herald - ry - ic
herb - age - al - alist - arium
herbaceous
Hercule/s - an
herd - ed - ing - er
 (ERR HAR HIR HUR UR)

HERE
here (in this place); *not* hear
here/after - by - in - inafter - of
 - to - tofore - under - upon
 - with
heredit/y - ary - arily - able
 - ament
heres/y - ies - iarch - iologist
heretic - al - ally
 (ERE ERI ERY HEAR HERI)

HERI
heriot
herit/or - age - able - ably
 (ERI ERY HARI HERE)

HERM
hermaphrodit/e - ic - ism
hermeneutic - al
hermetic - ally
hermit - age
 (ERM)

HERN
hern - shaw
hernia

---

* If the word you wish to spell is not in this list, omit the prefix
and look for the rest of the word.

(EARN ERN URN)

HERO

hero - es - ic - ically - ism
heroin (drug)
heroine (female hero)
heron - ry
(ERO ERRO HERA)

HERP-HERT

herpe/s - tic
Herr (*Ger*)
herring
hers (not her's)
herself
herzian
(ER HUR)

HES

he's, *for* he is
hesitat/e - ed - ing - ion - ingly
  - ive
hesit/ant - ance - ancy
hessian
(ES HAS)

HET

het, *for* heated *or* heterodyne
hetero*, *prefix meaning*
  different
heterocyclic
heterodox - y
heterodyne
heterogam/y - ous
heterogene/sis - tic - ous
  - ously - ity
heterography (incorrect
  spelling!)
heterozygote
hetman
(ET HAT HEAT)

HEV

(EAV EV HEAV)

HEW

hew (chop) - ed - ing - n - er;
  not hue (colour)
(EU EW HU YOU)

HEX

hexa-*, *prefix meaning* six;
  see also sex-
hexad

hexagon - al
hexagram
hexahedr/on - al
hexapod - y
hexameter
hexateuch
(EX)

HEY

hey!
heyday
(EY HAI HAY)

HI-HID

hi!
hiatus - es
hibernat/e - ed - ing - ion - or
Hibernia - n
hibiscus
hiccup - ped - ping
hickory
hid (did hide) - den
hid/e - ing - er
hideous - ly - ness
hide - out
(HIGH HY)

HIE

hie (go), hied, hying
hierarch - y - ies - ical - ism
hieratic
hieroglyph - ic
hierophant - ic
(HIGH HIR HYE)

HIF

hi - fi, *for* high fidelity
(HYPH)

HIG

higgl/e - ed - ing - er
higgledy - piggledy
high - er - est - ly - ness; *but*
  height
highfalutin(g)
high - handed
(HYG IG)

HIJ

hijack - ed - ing - er
(HYG)

HIK

hik/e - ed - ing - er

* If the word you wish to spell is not in this list, omit the prefix
and look for the rest of the word.

(HIC IK)

HIL
hilar/ity -ious -iously
hill -y -ier -iest -iness -ock
hilt -ed
(IL)

HIM
him -self; *not* hymn (song)
(HYM IM)

HIN
hinau (*NZ*)
hind -er
hinder -ed -ing
hindrance
Hindu -ism -stan -stani
hing/e -ed -ing
hinn/y -ies
hint -ed -ing -er
hinterland
(IN)

HIP
hip -ped
hippo-, *for* hippopotamus
hippocampus
hippodrome
hippogryph
hippopotam/us -i *or* -uses
hipp/y -ies
(HYP IP)

HIR
hircine
hir/e -ed -ing -able -er -eling
hire -purchase
hirsute -ness
(HER HIER HUR IR)

HIS
his
hiss -ed -ing -es
hist!
histogen/y -esis -etic
histolog/y -ist -ical
histor/y -ies -ic -ical -icity
-ian
historiograph/y -er -ical
histrionic -ally
(HYS IS)

HIT
hit -ting -ter
hitch -ed -ing
hither -to

(IT)

HIV
hiv/e -ed -ing
(IV)

HOA
hoar/y -ier -iest -iness
hoarfrost
hoard -ed -ing -er; *not* horde
(gang)
hoars/e (husky) -er -est -ely
-eness; *not* horse
hoax -es -ed -ing -er
(AUR HAU HAW HOR OA
OR WHO)

HOB
hob
hobbl/e -ed -ing
hobbledehoy
hobb/y -ies
hobgoblin
hobnail -ed
hobnob
hobo -s (*Am*)
(OB)

HOC
hock (wine); *but* hough (of
animal's leg)
hockey
hocus -sed -sing
hocus -pocus
(HOK OC)

HOD
hod
hodden (*Sc*)
hodge -podge *or*
hotch -potch
hodiernal
hodometer *or* odometer
(OD)

HOE
hoe -d -ing
(EAU HOA OWE)

HOG
hog -ged -ging -gish -gishly
-gishness
hogget
hoggin
hogmanay (*Sc*)
hogshead
(OG)

117

HOI

hoik or hoick - ed - ing
hoi polloi (Gr)
hoist - ed - ing
hoity - toity
(HI HOY OI OY)

HOK

hokey - pokey
hokum (bunkum); not oakum
(HOC OC)

HOL

hold - ing - er; but held
hol/e - ed - ing; not whole
(complete)
holiday
holism
Holland - s - er
hollo (shout) - ed - ing; or
hollow or holler
hollow - er - est - ed - ing - ly
- ness
holl/y - ies
hollyhock
holm
holocaust
holograph
holster
holt
holus - bolus
hol/y - ier - iest - ily - iness
holystone
(OL WHOL)

HOM

homage
hombre (Sp)
homburg
home - ly - lier - liest - liness
- ward - y
hom/e - ed - ing - er
homeopath - y - ic or homaeo
Homer - ic
homicid/e - al
homil/y - ies - etic
hominy
homo sapiens (L, man as a
species)
homo-*, prefix meaning

same
homoeopath - y - ic or homeo
homogen/y - eous - eously
- eity - etic
homogenis/e - ed - ing - ation
(z)
homolog/y - ue - ous - ical
homologis/e - ed - ing (z)
homonym - ic - ous
homun/cule or /cle
(OM)

HON

hon., for honorary or
honourable
hon/e - ed - ing
honest - y - ly
honey - s - ed
honeycomb
honeymoon - er
hongi (NZ)
honk - ed - ing
honor/ary (unpaid)
honorarium
honorific
honour - ed - ing - able - ably
(ON)

HOO

hoo? No, who
hooch (Am)
hood - ed
hoodie
hoodlum
hoodoo
hoodwing - ed - ing
hooey
hoof - ed - ing; hooves
hook - ed - ing - er
hookah (Arab)
hookey
hooligan - ism
hoom? No, whom
hoop - ed ; not whoop (yell)
hooping - cough? No, whoop -
hoop - la
hoopoe
hoose? No, whose
hoosh - magundy

* If the word you wish to spell is not in this list, omit the prefix
and look for the rest of the word.

hoot -ed -ing -er
hoover -ed -ing
hooves (more than one hoof)
(HU OO OU WHO)

HOP
hop -ped -ping -per
hop/e -ed -ing -eful -efully
-efulness
hopeless -ly -ness
hopscotch
(OP)

HORD-HORN
horde (gang); *not* hoard
hore? *No,* whore
horehound
horizon -tal -tally -tality; *not*
orison (prayer)
hormone
horn -ed -ing -er -y -iness
horn/blende -beam -pipe
hornet
(AUR HAU HAW OR)

HORO
horlog/y -e -er -ist -ical
horopito (*NZ*)
horpter
horoscop/e -y -ic
(HORR ORO)

HORR
horribl/e -y -eness
horrid -er -est -ly -ness
horrif/y -ied -ying -ic -ically
horror
(ORR)

HORS HORT
hors de combat (*F*)
hors d'oeuvres (*F*)
hors/e -y -iness; *not* hoarse
(husky)
horse/man -woman -shoe
hortat/ive -ory
horticultur/e -al -ally -ist
(AU HAU HAW OR)

HOS
hosanna!
hos/e -ed -ing -ier -iery
hospice
hospital -ler -ise -ised
-isation (z)
hospit/ality -able -ably

HOST
host -s -ess -esses
hostage
hostel -ler
hostil/e -ity -ities -ely
(OS OZ)

HOT
hot -ter -test -ly -ness
hot/bed - head -house
hotch-potch *or*
hodge-podge
hotel -ier
Hottentot
(OT)

HOU
hough (of animal's leg)
houhere (*NZ*)
hound -ed -ing
hour -ly
houri
hous/e -ed -ing
household -er
housewife -ry -ly
(HOW OU)

HOV
hove (did heave)
hovel
hover -ed -ing -er -craft -port
(OVE)

HOW
how -ever -soever
howdah
howitzer
howl -ed -ing -er
(HOU OW)

HOY
hoy (small ship)
hoy! *or* ahoy!
hoyden
(HOI OI OY)

HUB
hub
hubb/y -ies
hubbub
hubris -tic
(HAB UB)

HUC
huckaback
huckle
huckleberry
huckster -ed -ing -y

(EUC HAC UK)

HUD
huddl/e -ed -ing
(EUD UD)

HUE
hue (cry, colour) -d; *not* hew
(chop)
(EU YEW YOU YU)

HUF
huff -ed -ing -y -ily -iness
-ish -ishly
(EUPH)

HUG
hug -ged -ging
huge -ly -ness
hugger -mugger
Huguenot (*F*)
(EUG UG)

HUI
hui (*NZ*)

HUL
hula -hula
hulk -ing
hull -ed -ing
hullabaloo
hullo! *or* hallo! *or* hello!
(EUL UL)

HUM
hum -med -ming
human -ly -ity -ism -ist
-itarian
humane -ly -ness
humanis/e -ed -ing -ation (z)
humanities
humbl/e -ed -ing -y -eness
humble -bee *or* bumble -bee
humbug -ged -ging
humdinger
humdrum
humer/us (bone) -al; *not*
humorous (funny)
humid -ity -ify -ified -ifying
-ifier
humiliat/e -ed -ing -ion
humility
hummock -y
humor/ous -ously -ist -istic
humour -ed -ing -less
hump -ed -ing -y

humus
(UM)

HUN
Hun -nish
hunch -es
hundred -th -fold
hung (did hang)
Hungar/y -ian
hunger -ed -ing
hungr/y -ier -iest -ily -iness
hunk -y
hunkers
hunt -ed -ing -er -ress
(EUN UN)

HUR
hurdl/e -ed -ing -er
hurdy -gurdy
hurl -ed -ing -er
hurley
hurly -burly
hurrah! *or* hurray!
hurricane
hurr/y -ied -ying -iedly
hurst
hurt -ing -ful -fully -fulness
hurtl/e -ed -ing
(HEAR HER HIR UR)

HUS
husband -ed -ing -man -ry
hush -ed -ing
husk -ed -ing -y -ier -iest
hussar
huss/y *or* huzz/y -ies
hustings
hustl/e -ed -ing -er
(US)

HUT
hut -ted -ting -ment
hutch
(UT)

HYA HYB
hyacinth
hyaena *or* hyena
hyal/ine -ite -oid
hybrid -ise -ised -ising
-isation -isable (z)
hybridism
(HI IA IB YA)

120

HYDR

hydr-*, *prefix meaning* water
hydr/a -oid
hydrangea
hydrant
hydrat/e -ed -ing -ion
hydraulic -ally
hydric
hydro, *for* hydropathic
hydrocarbon
hydrocephal/y -ic -ous -us
hydrochloric
hydrofoil
hydrogen -ous -ate -ated
  -ation
hydrograph/y -er -ical
hydrolog/y -ist -ical
hydroly/sis -tic
hydropath/y -ic
hydrophob/ia -ic
hydrophon/e -ic
hydrophyt/e -ic
hydroponics
hydrostatic -al -ally
hydrous
hydroxide
hydrozo/on -a

HYE HYG

hyena *or* hyaena
hygien/e (science of health)
  -ic -ically -ist
hygromet/er -ry -ric
hygroscop/e -ic
  (HIE HIJ)

HYM

hymen
hymenopter/a -al -ous
hymn -al -ody -ology
  (HIM IM)

HYO

hyoid
hyosc/ine -amine
  (IO)

HYP

hyper-*, *prefix meaning*
excessive; *not* hypo-
  (under)

hyperaesthe/sia -tic
hyperbol/a (geometry) -ic
hyperbol/e (exaggeration)
  -ical -ically -ism
hypermetrop/ia -ic
hypertension (high
  blood-pressure); *not* hypo-
  (low blood-pressure)
hypertroph/y -ic
hyphen -ate -ated
hypno/sis -tic -tism -logy
  (HIP)

HYPO

hypo-*, *prefix meaning*
under; *not* hyper-
  (excessive)
hypocaust
hypochondri/a -ac -asis
hypocri/sy -te -tical -tically
hypogen/e -ous
hypogynous
hypophosphite
hyposta/sis -tic -tically
hypostasis/e -ed -ing (z)
hypotension (low blood
  pressure); *not* hyper- (high)
hypotenuse
hypothe/sis -tical -tically
hypothesis/e -ed -ing (z)
  (HYPER HIPPO)

HYR

hyrax
  (HIR IR)

HYS

hyssop
hyster/ia -ic -ical -ically
  -ogenic -ectomy
  (HIS)

I

I-IB

I, I'd (I had, would), I'll (I will),
  I'm (I am), I've (I have)
iamb -ic -us
Iberia -n
ibex -es
ibid *or* ib, *for* ibidem (*L*)

---

* If the word you wish to spell is not in this list, omit the prefix
and look for the rest of the word.

ibis -es
(EY HI HY)

ICE
ic/e -ed -ing -y -icle
iceberg
Iceland -ic -er
(EIS IS)

ICH
ichneumon
ichor
ichthyo-*, *prefix meaning*
fish
ichthyograph/y -er
ichthyoid
ichthyolite
ichthyolog/y -ical -ist
ichthyophag/y -ous -ist
ichthyornis
ichthyosaurus
ichthyo/sis -tic
(ECH HITCH IK ITCH)

ICO
icon *or* ikon -ic -ography
-ology -olatry
iconocl/asm -ast -astic
iconometer
icosahedr/on -al
(HIC ICH)

ID
id
I'd, *for* I had *or* I would

IDE
idea
ideal -ly -ist -istic -ism -ity
idealis/e -ed -ing -ation (z)
ideat/e -ion -ional
idée fixe (*F*)
identic -al -ally
identif/y -ies -ied -ying -iable
-ication
identikit
identit/y -ies
ideogra/m -ph -phy
idelog/y -ies -ical -ically
id est *or* i.e. (*L,* that is)
(EID EYED HID)

IDI-IDY
idio/cy -t -tic -tically
idiom -atic -atically
idioplasm
idiosyncra/sy -tic -tically
idl/e (lazy) -ed -ing -y -eness
-er
idol (image) -ise -ised
-isation -ising (z)
idolat/ry -ries -rous -rously
-er
idyll -ic -ically
(HID)

IF
if
(EFF)

IG
igloo
igneous
ignit/e -ed -ing -ion
ignob/le -ly
ignomin/y -ious -iously
ignoramus -es
ignor/e -ed -ing
ignor/ant -antly -ance
iguan/a -odon
(HIG HYG YGG)

IK
ikon *or* icon -ic -ography
-ology -olatry
(ICH HIC)

ILA-ILK
iland? *No,* island
ile? *No,* isle *or* aisle *or* oil
ilex
ili/ac -um
Iliad
ilk
(EL ILL HIL)

ILL ILLA
ill -ness
I'll, *for* I will *or* I shall
illat/ion -ive -ively
(EL HIL IL)

ILLE
illegal -ly -ity -ities
illegib/le (unreadable) -ly

---

* If the word you wish to spell is not in this list, omit the prefix
and look for the rest of the word.

-ility; *not* eligible (suitable)
illegitima/te -tely -tion -cy
(ALLE ELE)

ILLI

illiberal -ly -ity
illicit (illegal) -ly; *not* elicit
(draw out)
illimitab/le -ly -ility
illiter/ate -acy -ateness
(ELI ILI)

ILLO

illogical -ly -ity
(ALO ELO)

ILLU

illumin/e -ed
illuminat/e -ed -ing -ion -ive
-or
illus/ion (deception) -ive
-ively -iveness; *not* allusion
(reference), elusion
(avoidance)
illusor/y -ily -iness
illustrat/e -ed -ing -ion -ive
-ively -or
illustrious -ly -ness
(ALLU ALU ELU HALLU)

IM IMA

I'm, *for* I am
imag/e -ed -ing -ery -ist
imagin/e -ed -ing -ary
imaginat/ion -ive -ively
-iveness
imag/o -os *or* -iness
imam
(AMA EMA IMMA)

IM*B

im -*, *prefix used before* b,
instead of in -
imbecil/e -ity -ities
imbib/e -ed -ing -ition
imbricat/e -ed -ing -ion -ive
Imbroglio (*It*)
imbru/e (stain) -ed -ing
imbu/e (inspire) -ed -ing
(EMB)

IMI

imitat/e -ed -ing -ion -ive

-ively -or
(EMI IMMI)

IM*M

im -*, *prefix used before* m,
instead of in -
immaculate -ly -ness
immanen/t (in -dwelling) -ce
-cy; *not* imminent
(impending) *or* eminent
(outstanding)
immedia/te -tely -teness -cy
immens/e -ely -ity
immers/e -ed -ing -ion
immigrant (arrival); *not*
emigrant (leaver)
immigrat/e -ed -ing -ion
imminen/t -ce -tly
(impending); *not* immanent,
eminent
immiscib/le -ly -ility
immitate? *No,* imitate
immitigab/le -ly
immolat/e -ed -ing -ion -or
immortal -ly -ity
immortalis/e -ed -ing
-ation (z)
immun/e -ity -ise -ised -ising
-isation (z)
immur/e -ed -ing -ement
immutab/le -ly -ility
(AM EM IM-)

IM*PA

im -*, *prefix used before* p,
instead of in -
imp -ish -ishly -ishness
impact -ed -ing -ion
impair -ed -ing -ment
impala
impal/e -ed -ing
impalpab/le -ly -ility
impanel *or* empanel -led -ling
impassab/le (uncrossable) -ly
-ility; *not* impossible
impasse (*F*)
impassion -ed
impasto
(EMPA)

---

* If the word you wish to spell is not in this list, omit the prefix
and look for the rest of the word.

IM*PE

impeach -ed -ing -ment
-able -ably
impecc/able -ably -ability
-ant
impecuni/ous -ously -osity
impedance
imped/e -ed -ing -iment
-imenta
impel -led -ling -lent
impend -ed -ing -ence -ency
-ent
imperativ/e -ely -eness
imperial -ly -ism -ist -istic
imperil -led -ling
imperious -ly -ness
impertinen/t -tly -ce
imperturbab/le -ly -ility
impetig/o -inous
impet/us -uses -uous
-uously -uousness -uosity

IM*PI

impi/ety -eties -ous -ously
imping/e -ed -ing -ement
(EMPI IMPE)

IM*PL

implacab/le -ly -ility
implement -ed -ing -ation
implicat/e -ed -ing -ion
implicit -ly -ness
implo/de -ded -ding -sion
implor/e -ed -ing -ingly
impl/y -ies -ied -ying -ication
(EMPL)

IM*PO

impolitic
import -ed -ing -ation -able
-ability -er
importan/t -tly -ce
importun/e -ed -ing -ity -ate
impos/e -ed -ing -ingly -ition
impost/or -ure
impoten/t -tly -ce -cy
impound -ed -ing
impoverish -ed -ing -ment
(EMPO)

IM*PR IM*PU

imprecat/e -ed -ing -ion
impregnab/le -ly -ility
impregnat/e -ed -ing -ion
impresario -s
impress -ed -ing -ment -ible
impression -able -ably
-ability -ism -ist -istic
impressive -ly -ness
imprest
imprimatur (L)
impromptu
improv/e -ed -ing -ement -er
improvis/e -ed -ing -ation -er
(not z)
impuden/t -ce -tly
impugn -ed -ing
impuls/e -ive -ively -iveness
impunity
imput/e -ed -ing -ation

IN*

in-*, prefix meaning either
not, negative, or else
inward; in the former sense
it is often interchangeable
with un-
in -ner -most -nermost
-ward -wardly
(INN)

IN*A

inadverten/t -tly -ce -cy
inan/e -ly -ity
inapt (unskilful) -ly -ness
-itude; not inept (absurd)
inasmuch
inaugur/ate -ated -ating
-ation -al
(ENA INNA UN)

IN*CA

Inca
incandesc/e -ent -ence
incantation
incapacit/y -ate -ated -ating
-ation
incarcerat/e -ed -ing -ion -or
incarnadin/e -ed
incarnat/e -ion

---

* If the word you wish to spell is not in this list, omit the prefix
and look for the rest of the word.

(ENCA UN)

IN*CE

incendiar/y -ist -ism
incens/e -ed -ing -ory; *not*
 insensate (mad)
incentive
incept/ion -ive
incessant -ly
incest -uous -uously
 (ENCE ENSE INSE UN)

INCH

inch -es -ed -ing
inchoat/e -ion
 (EN UN)

IN*CI

incidence
incident -al -ally
incinerat/e -ed -ing -ion
incipien/t -tly -ce -cy
incis/e -ed -ing -ion (*not* z)
incisor
incisive -ly -ness
incit/e -ed -ing -ment
 (ENCI ENCY ENSI INSI UN)

IN*CL

inclin/e -ed -ing -ation
includ/e -ed -ing
inclus/ion -ive -ively -iveness
 (EN UN)

IN*CO

incognit/o -a -i
incoheren/t -ce -tly
income
incommod/e -ed -ing
incommunicado (*Sp*)
incongru/ous -ously -ity -ities
inconsolab/le -ly
 (EN UN)

IN*CR

increas/e -ed -ing -ingly
increment -al
incriminat/e -ed -ing -ion -ory
incrust -ed -ing -ation -ation

IN*CU

incubat/e -ed -ing -ion -or
 -ory
incubus

inculcat/e -ed -ing -ion -or
 -ory
inculpat/e -ed -ing -ion -or
 -ory
incumben/t -cy
incunabula (*L*)
incur -red -ring
incurs/ion -ive
 (EN UN)

IN*DE

indebted -ness
indeed
indefatigab/le -y -ility
indelib/le -ly -ility
indemni/fy -fied -fying
 -fication
indemnit/y -ies
indent -ed -ing -ation
indentur/e -ed -ing
independ/ent -ently -ence
index -es (of books)
ind/ex -ices (algebra)
 (EN INDI UN)

IN*DI

India -n
indicat/e -ed -ing -ion -ive
 -ively -or
indict (accuse) -ed -ing -able
 -ment; *not* indite (compose)
indigen/e -ous -ously
indigen/t -ce
indign/ant -antly -ation
indignit/y -ies
indigo -s
indit/e (compose) -ed -ing
individual -ly -ity -ist -istic
 -ism
individualis/e -ed -ing -ation
 (z)
individuat/e -ed -ing -ion
 (EN INDE UN)

IN*DO

Indo-, *prefix meaning* Indian
indoctrinat/e -ed -ing -ion
indolen/t -tly -ce
indomitab/le -ly
indoor -s

---

* If the word you wish to spell is not in this list, omit the prefix
and look for the rest of the word.

(EN UN)

IN*DU

indubitab/le -ly
induc/e (persuade) -ed -ing
  -ement -ible
induct (introduce) -ed -ing
  -ion -or
induct/ance -ile -ive -ively
  -iveness
indulg/e -ed -ing -ence -ent
  -ently
indurat/e -ed -ing -ion -ive
industr/y -ies -ial -ialism
  -ialist
industrialis/e -ed -ing
  -ation (z)
industrious -ly
(EN UN)

IN*E

inebri/ate -ated -ating -ety
ineffab/le -ly
ineffaceab/le -ly
ineluctab/le -ly
inept (absurd) -ly -itude
  -ness; not inapt (unskilful)
inerrab/le -ly -ility
inert -ia -ly -ness
inevitab/le -ly -ility
inexorab/le -ly
(UNE)

IN*FA

infam/y -ies -ous -ously
infan/t -cy
infanta (Sp)
infant/ile -ilism -ine -icide
  -icidal
infantry
infatuat/e -ed -ing -ion -edly
(EMPH ENFA UN)

IN*FE

infect -ed -ing -ion -ious
  -iously -ive -ivity
infer -red -ring -ence -ential
  -rble
inferior -ity
infernal -ly
inferno -s

infest -ed -ing -ation
(EN INFI UN)

IN*FI

infidel -ity -ities
infiltrat/e -ed -ing -ion -or
infinit/y -e -ely -ude -ive
infinitesimal -ly
infirm -ly -ity -ities -ary -aries
(EMPH EN INFE UN)

IN*FL

inflam/e -ed -ing -mation
  -matory
inflammab/le -ility; but see
  note on flammable
inflat/e -ed -ing -ion -or
inflect (bend) -ed -ing -ion or
  inflexion
inflict -ed -ing -ion -able
inflorescen/t -ce
influen/ce -tial -tially
influenza
(UN)

IN*FO

inform -ed -ing -ant -er
informat/ion -ional -ive -ively
(EN UN)

IN*FR

infra dig, for infra dignitatem
  (L)
infra -red
infring/e -ed -ing -ement
(EN UN)

INFU

infuriat/e -ed -ing -ion
infus/e -ed -ing -ion -ible -ory
infusori/a -an -al

IN*G

ingeminat/e -ed -ing -ion
ingen/ious (clever) -iously
  -uity
ingenuous (innocent) -ly
  -ness
ingest -ed -ing -ion -ive
ingle -nook
ingot
ingratiat/e -ed -ing -ion -ingly
ingratitude; but ungrateful

---

* If the word you wish to spell is not in this list, omit the prefix
and look for the rest of the word.

ingredient
ingress
inguinal
ingurgitat/e - ed - ing - ion
  (EN HING INJ UN)

IN*H
inhabit - ed - ing - ation - ant
  - able - ancy
inhal/e - ed - ing - ation - ant
  - er
inher/e - ed - ing - end - ently
inherit - ed - ing - ance - or
  - ress *or* - rix
inheritab/le - ly - ility
inhibit - ed - ing - ion - ory
inhum/e - ed - ing - ation
  (EN)

IN*I
inimical (harmful) - y
inimitab/le (defies imitation)
  - ly
iniquit/y - ies - ous - ously
initial - ed - ing - ly
initiat/e - ed - ing - ion - or - rix
  - ive - ory
  (EN INNI UN)

IN*J
inject - ed - ing - ion
injunction
injur/e - ed - ng - y - ies - ious
  - iously
injustice; *but* unjust
  (ENGE ENJ HING INGE)

INK
ink - ed - ing - er - y - iness
inkling
  (ENC INC)

INL
inlaid
inland
in - law
inlay - ing
inlet
inlier (geology)
inlying
  (EN UN)

INM
inmate
inmost
  (ENM UNM)

IN*N
inn
innards (insides)
innate - ness
inner - most
innings
innocen/t - tly - ce
innocuous - ly - ness; *but*
  inoculate
innominate
innovat/e - ed - ing - ion - or
  - ory
innuendo - es
innumerable
  (HIN IN- UNN)

IN*O
inoculat/e - ed - ing - ion; *but*
  innocuous
inordinate - ly
inosculat/e - ed - ing - ion
  (EN INNO UN)

INQ
inquest
inquietude
inquir/e *or* enquir/e - ed - ing
  - er - y - ies
inquisit/ion - or - orial
inquisitive - ly - ness
  (EN UN)

IN*SA
insalivat/e - ed - ing - ion
  (UN)

INSC
inscrib/e - ed - ing
inscript/ion - ive
inscrutab/le - ly - ility - leness
  (EN UN)

IN*SE
insect - ology - arium - icide
  - ivore - ivora - ivorous
insecur/e - ity - ely
inseminat/e - ed - ing - ion - or
insensate - ly

* If the word you wish to spell is not in this list, omit the prefix
and look for the rest of the word.

insert -ed -ing -ion
inset -ting
(INCE UNS)

INSH
inshore (near land); *not*
insure, ensure
(EN UN)

IN*SI
inside -s -r
insidious -ly -ness
insight -ful -fully
insignia
insinuat/e -ed -ing -ion -or
-ingly -ive
insipid -ly -ness -ity
insist -ed -ing -ence -ency
-ent -ently
(ENCI ENCY ENSI INCI UN)

IN*SO
insofar
insolation (from sun); *not*
insulation
insolen/t -tly -ce
insomnia
insoucian/t -ce
(UN)

IN*SP
inspan -ned -ning
inspect -ed -ing -ion -orate
-oral -orial
inspir/e -ed -ing -ation
-ational -er
inspissat/e -ion
(UN)

INST
instability; *but* unstable
install -ed -ing -ation; *but*
instalment
instanc/e -ed -ing
instant -ly -aneous -aneously
instead
instep
instigat/e -ed -ing -ion -or
instil -led -ling -lation -ment;
or instill
instinct -ive -ively
institut/e -ed -ing -ion -ional

-ionally
instruct -ed -ing -ion -or
-ress
instructive -ly -ness
instrument -ed -ing -ation
instrumental -ly -lity
(UN)

IN*SU
insufferab/le -ly
insufflat/e -ed -ing -ion
insular -y -ism -ity
insulat/e (isolate) -ed -ing
-ion -or; *not* insolation
insulin
insult -ed -ing -ingly
insuperab/le -ly -ility
insupportab/le -ly
insur/e -ed -ing -ance -er
insurgen/t -cy
insurrection -al -ary -ist
(EN UN)

IN*TA
intact
intagli/o -os -ated
intake
(EN INTER UN)

IN*TE
integ/er -ral -rally -rity -rant
integrat/e -ed -ing -ion -or
-ive
integument
intellect -ion -ive -ual -ually
-ualism
intellectualis/e -ed -ing (z)
intelligen/t -tly -tsia -ce -cer
intelligib/le -ly -ility
intend -ed -ing; *but* intention
intendant (manager); *but*
superintendent
intens/e -ely -eness -ity -ive
-ively
intensif/y -ies -ied -ying
-ication
intent -ly -ion -ional -ionally
-ness
(EN HINT UN)

* If the word you wish to spell is not in this list, omit the prefix
and look for the rest of the word.

INTER*

inter-*, *prefix meaning*
  between, among
inter, *or* intermediate
  examination
inter (bury) - red - ring - ment;
  not intern (confine)
intercal/ary - ate - ated - ating
  - ation; *not* - calorie
interce/de - ded - ding - ssion
  - ssor - ssory
intercept - ed - ing - ion
intercom, *for* - munication
interdict - ion - ory
interest - ed - ing - ingly - edly
interfer/e - ed - ing - ence
interferometer
interim
interior - ly
interject - ed - ing - ion - ory
interland? *No,* hint -
interlocut/or - ress - rix - ory
interloper
interlude
intermediary
intermediat/e - ion - or - ory
intermezzo (*It*) - s
interminab/le - ly - leness
intermission (pause); *not*
  intromission (insertion)
intermit - tent - tently - tence;
  not intromit
intern (confine) - ed - ing
  - ment - ee; *not* inter (bury)
internal - ly - ity
internecine
interpolat/e - ed - ing - ion
interpos/e - ed - ing - ition
interpret - ed - ing - ation - er
  - able - ative
interregnum
interrogat/e - ed - ing - ion - or
  - ry - ories - ive - ively
interrupt - ed - ing - ion - er
intersect - ed - ing - ion - or
interspers/e - ed - ing - ion
intersti/ce - tial

interval
interven/e (interfere) - ed - ing
  - tion; *not* intravenous
interview - ed - ing - er
  (EN)

INTES

intesta/te - cy - cies
intestin/e - al

INTI

intimat/e - ed - ing - ion - ely
intimac/y - ies
intimidat/e - ed - ing - ion - or
  - ory
  (EN UN)

IN*TO

into
inton/e - ed - ing - ation
intoxicat/e - ed - ing - ion
intoxicant
  (EN UN)

IN*TR

intra-*, *prefix meaning* on
  the inside
intractab/le - ly - ility
intrados
intransigen/t - tly - ce
intravenous - ly
intrepid - ly - ity
intrica/te - tely - cy
intrigu/e - ed - ing - er
intrinsic - ally
intro-*, *prefix meaning* to the
  inside
introduc/e - ed - ing - tion - tory
introit
intromit (insert) - ted - ting
  - tent; *not* intermit (break)
intromission; *not*
  intermission
introspect - ion - ve - ively
  - iveness
introver/t - ted - sion - sible
  - sive *or* - tive
intru/de - ded - ding - der - sion
  - sive - sively - siveness
  (EN UN)

---

* If the word you wish to spell is not in this list, omit the prefix
and look for the rest of the word.

IN*TU

intubate
intuit -ed -ing -ion -ional -ive
  -ively -iveness
intussusception
  (INTO INTER)

IN*U

inundat/e -ed -ing -ion
inur/e -ed -ing
  (EN INNU UN)

IN*VA

inva/de -ded -ding -sion -sive
  -der
invaginat/e -ed -ing -ion
invalid -ly -ity -ate -ated
  -ating -ation
  (ENVE UN)

IN*VE

invective
inveigh -ed -ing
inveigl/e -ed -ing -ement
invent -ed -ing -ion -ive
  -ively -veness -or
inventor/y -ies
invers/e -ely -ion
invert -ed -ing
invest -ed -ing -ment -or
investigat/e -ed -ing -ion -or
investiture
inveterate
  (EN UN)

IN*VI

invidious -ly -ness
invigilat/e -ed -ing -ion -or
invigorat/e -ed -ing -ion -ive
  -or
invincib/le -ly -ility
inviolab/le -ly -ility
inviola/te -teness -cy
invit/e -ed -ing -ingly -ation
  (EN UN)

IN*VO

invoic/e -ed -ing
invo/ke -ked -king -cation
  -catory
involut/e -ed -ion
involv/e -ed -ing -ement

(EN UN)
INW

inward -ly -ness
inwrought
  (UNW)

IO

iod/ine -ide -oform -ic
iodis/e -ed -ing -ation (z)
iolit/e -ic
ion -ium -osphere
ionis/e -ed -ing -ation (z)
Ion/ia -ian -ic
iota
I O U, for I owe you
  (AEO EO YO)

IP

ipecacuanha
ipso facto (L)
  (EP HIP)

IRA-IRO

Iran -ian
Iraq -i
irascib/le -ly -ility
irate
ire -ful -fully
irenic (aimed at peace) -al
irgent? No, urgent
iridescen/t -tly -ce
iridium
iri/s -ses -sitis
Irish
irksome -ly -ness
iron -ed -ing -monger
  -mongery
iron/y -ies -ic -ical -ically -ist
  (ER EYR HIR IRR)

IRR

ir-* replaces in before r
irradiat/e -ed -ing -ion -ive
irreparab/le -ly -leness
irrigable
irrigat/e -ed -ing -ion -or
irritab/le -ly -ility
irritat/e -ed -ing -ion -ive
irritan/t -cy
irrupt (invade) -ed -ing -ion;
  not erupt

* If the word you wish to spell is not in this list, omit the prefix
and look for the rest of the word.

IS-ISL

is, isn't
ishue? *No,* issue
isinglass
Islam -ic -ism -ite -itic
island -er; *not* highland
isl/e -et (small island); *not a*
  aisle (of church)
  (ESC HIS)

ISO*

iso-*, *prefix meaning* equal,
  same
isobar -ic
isoclin/e -ic -al
isogon -ic -al
isohaline
isohel
isohyet -al
isolat/e -ed -ing -ion -ionism
  -ionist
isomer -ic -al
isomorph -ic -ism
isoneph
isopleth -ic
isopod
isosceles
isotop/e -ic -y
  (ASSO ESO)

ISR-IST

Israel -i -ite -itish
issu/e -ed -ing -able -ance
isthm/us -uses -ian
  (ES HIS)

IT

it, its (belonging to it), it's (*for*
  it is), itself
it, *for* Italian vermouth
italic -ise -ised -sing (z)
Ital/y -ian
itch -ed -ing -y -iness
item -ise -ised -ising -isation
  (z)
iterat/e -ed -ing -ion -ive
ither? *No,* either
itinerar/y -ies
itiner/ate -ation -ant -ancy

IV

I've, *for* I have
ivor/y -ies
iv/y -ies -ied
  (HIV)

J

JAB

jab -bed -bing
jabber -ed -ing
jabot (*F*)

JAC

jacaranda
jacinth
jack -ed -ing
jackal
jackaroo (*Aus*)
jackass
jackdaw
jacket -ed -ing
jack -knif/e -ed -ing
jackshay (*Aus*)
Jacob/ean -ite
jacobin (pigeon)
jaconet
jacquard
  (JOC)

JAD

jad/e -ed (weary)
jade -ite (mineral)

JAF

Jaffa -s
  (CHAF)

JAG-JAP

jag -ged -gedly -gedness
jaguar
jail, *see* gaol
Jain -ism -ist
jalap
jalopy *or* jaloppy
jalousie (*F*)
jam -med -ming -my -mier
  -miest
Jamaica -n
jamb (of doorway, etc.)
jamboree

* If the word you wish to spell is not in this list, omit the prefix
and look for the rest of the word.

jangl/e -ed -ing
janitor
jannock
January
Japan -ese
japan -ned -ning
jap/e -ed -ing
japonica
(CHA SHA)

JAR-JAZ
jar -red -ring -ringly; *also* ajar
jarful
jardinière (*F*)
jargon -ise -ised -ising
 -isation (z)
jarrah
jasmine *or* jessamine
jasper
jaundic/e -ed
jaunt -ed -ing -y -ily -iness
Java -n -nese
javelin
jaw -ed -ing
jay
jazz -ed -ing -y -ier -iest
(CHA SHA)

JEA-JEO
jealous -y -ies -ly -ness
jean -s
jeep
jeer -ed -ing
Jehovah *or* Jah *or* Yahweh
jell -ed -ing -y -ies; *but* gel,
 gelatine
jemm/y -ies
jennet
jenn/y -ies
jeopard/y -ise -ised -ising (z)
(GE)

JER
jerboa
jereboam
Jeremia/h -d
jerk -ed -ing -y -ily -iness
jerkin
jerr/y -ies -ican
jersey
Jerusalem
(CHER GER GIR JOU
SHER)

JES
jess -es
jessamine *or* jasmine
jest -ed -ing -ingly -er
jesuit -ry -ical -ically -ism
(GES CHES)

JET
jet -ted -ting
jetsam
jettison -ed -ing
jetton
jett/y -ies

JEU-JEW
jeu d'esprit (*F*)
Jew -ess -ry -ish
jewel -led -ling -ler -lery *or*
 -ry; *not* dual *or* duel
(DU JU)

JI
jib -bed -bing -ber
jibbah *or* djibbah
jib/e *or* gyb/e -ed -ing
jiffy
jig -ged -ging -ger -saw
jigger *or* chigoe
 (skin -burrowing flea)
jiggery-pokery
jiggl/e -ed -ing
jilt -ed -ing
jimp
jingl/e -ed -ing
jingo -istic -ism
jink -ed -ing -er
jinnee *or* genie
jinx
jitter -s -ed -ing -y
jiv/e -ed -ing
(CHI GE GI GY)

JOB-JOH
job -bed -bing -ber -bery
jockey -s -ed -ing
jocos/e -ely -ity -eness
jocular -ity -ly
jocund -ly -ity
jodhpurs
joey -s
jog -ged -ging
joggl/e -ed -ing
Joh/n -annine
johnn/y -ies

(GEO CHO SHO)

JOI

join - ed - ing - er - ery
joint - ed - ing - er - ly
jointur/e - ed - ing
joist - ed
(JOY CHOI)

JOK-JON

jok/e - ed - ing - er - y
joll-y - ier - iest - ity - ied - ying
 - ification
jolt - ed - ing - y
jonquil

JOR

Jordan - ian
jorum
(CHOR GEOR JAW)

JOS

josh - ed - ing
joss - stick
josser
jostl/e - ed - ing - er
(JUS)

JOT

jot - ted - ting - ter

JOU

joule (electricity); *not* jewel
 or jowl
journal - ism - ist - istic - ese
journalis/e - ed - ing - ation (z)
journey - s - ed - ing
joust - ed - ing - er
(DEU DU GER JER JEW
JOW JU)

JOV

jovial - ly - ity

JOW

jowl (jaw); *not* joule
(JOU)

JOY

joy - ful - fully - fulness - ous
 - ously - ousness
joyless - ly - ness
(JOI CHOI)

JUB-JUG

jubilat/e - ed - ing - ion
jubilan/t - tly - ce
jubilee
Juda/h - ism - ic - ist
judas - tree

judder - ed - ing
judg/e - ed - ing
judgment *or* judgement
judic/ial - ally - iary - ation
 - ature
judicious - ly - ness
judo
jug - ged - ging - ful
juggernaut
juggl/e - ed - ing - er - ery
Jugoslav - ia *or* Yugoslav - ia
jugular
(CHU TU)

JUI-JUM

juic/e (fluid) - y - ier - iest
 - iness; *not* deuce
ju - ju (fetish)
ju - jube (sweet)
juke - box - es
julep
Juli/us - an
julienne (soup)
July
jumbl/e - ed - ing
jumbo - s
jumbuck (*Aus*)
jump - ed - ing - er - able - y - er
 - iest - iness
(DEU DEW DU JEW)

JUN-JUP

junction
juncture
June
jungl/e - y
junior
juniper
junk
Junker (*Ger*)
junket - ed - ing
junta
jupe
Jupiter
(DU)

JUR

Jura - ssic
juridical
juris/consult - diction
 - prudence
jurist - ic - ically
jur/y - ies - or

JUS-JUX
just - er - est - ly - ness
justic/e - iar - iary - iable
justif/y - ies - ied - ying - iable
 - iably
justificat/ion - ive - ory
jut - ted - ting
jute
juven/ile - ility - ilia - escent
 - escence
juxtapos/e - ed - ing - ition
 (DEU)

K

KAD-KAN
kadi (*Arab*); *not* caddy *or*
 caddie
Kaffir
kahawai (*NZ*)
kahikatea (*NZ*)
kai (*NZ*)
kaiga (*NZ*)
kainit *or* kainite
kaiser
kaka - po - rike (*NZ*)
kakemono (*Jap*)
kale *or* kail - yard
kaleidoscop/e - ic
Kalmuck
kamahi (*NZ*)
kanaka
kangaroo
Kant - ian
 (CA CHA KHA)

KAO-KAY
kaolin
kaos? *No,* chaos
kapok
kappa (*Gr*)
kaput (*Ger*)
karaka (*NZ*)
karamu (*NZ*)
karate (*Jap*)
karma
karri (*Aus*)
kaross
karroo
kart (go - kart)
Kashmir (state) - i; *but*

cashmere (fabric)
katabatic - ally
katabolism *or* catabolism
kathode *or* cathode
kation *or* cation
katipo (*NZ*)
katydid
kauri (*NZ*)
kayak
 (CA CHA)

KEA-KEL
kea (*NZ*)
kearoscuro? *No,* chiaroscuro
kebab
kedg/e - ed - ing
kedgeree
keel - ed - ing
keelson *or* kelson
keen - ed - ing
keen - er - est - ly - ness
keep - ing - er; *but* kept
keepsake
keg
kelp
kelpie (*Sc*)
kelson *or* keelson
Kelt - ic *or* Celt - ic
kelt (fish)
 (CA KAL KIL)

KEM
kemp - y
 (CHEM)

KEN-KEP
ken
kennel - ed - ing - man
keno/sis - tic - ticism
Kent - ish
kentledge
kepi (*F*)
kept (did keep)
 (CA)

KER
kerat/in - ose
kerb (stone) - ed - ing; *not*
 curb (restrain)
kerchief - ed
kerf
kernel (of nuts, etc.); *not*
 colonel (army)
kerosene

Kerry
  (CHIR CUR)
KES-KEY
kestrel
ketch (boat); *not* catch
ketchup
ketone
kettle -ful
kevel
key (lock) -ed -ing; *not* quay
  (wharf)
  (CA)
KHA
khaki
khamsin (*Arab*)
khan (*Arab*)
  (CA KA)
KIA-KID
kia ora! (*NZ*)
kibbl/e -ed -ing
kibbutz (*Heb*) -im -nik
kibe
kibosh
kick -ed -ing -er
kickshaws
kid -ded -ding -dy -dies
Kidderminster
kiddle
kidnap -ped -ping -per
kidney -s
  (CHI)
KIE
kie -kie (*NZ*)
kier
kieselguhr
KIL
kilderkin
kill -ed -ing -ingly -er
killick
kiln
kilo -*, *prefix meaning*
  thousand
kilocycle
kilogram *or* kilogramme
kilolitre
kilomet/er -ric -re
kilowatt -age

kilt -ed -ing -ie *or* -y
kilter
KIM-KIP
kimera? *No,* chimera
kimono -s (*Jap*)
kin -ship; *also* akin (like)
kins/man -woman -folk
kincob
kind -er -est -ness -ly -liness
kindergarten
kindl/e -ed -ing
kindred
kine (cows)
kinema *or* cinema
kinemat/ic -ical -ograph
kinetic
king -ly -liness -ship -dom
kink -ed -ing -y -ier -iest
kinkajou
kino
kiosk
kip -ped -ping
kipper -ed -ing
KIR
Kirghiz
kirk (*Sc*)
kirsch -wasser (*Ger*)
kirtle
  (CHIR CUR KER KUR)
KIS-KIWI
kismet
kiss -ed -ing -er -able -ably
kit -ted -ting
kit -cat
kitchen -er -ette
kite
kith (and kin)
kitsch (*Ger*)
kitten -ed -ing -ish
kittiwake
kittle
kitt/y -ies
kiwi
KL
klaxon
kleptomania
klipspringer (*Af*)

* If the word you wish to spell is not in this list, omit the prefix
and look for the rest of the word.

kloof (*Af*)
(CHL CL)

KNA
knack
knacker - y - ies
knag
knap (chip) - ped - ping - er;
  not nap (sleep)
knapsack
knapweed
knar
knav/e (rogue) - ery - ish - ishly
  - ishess; *not* nave (of
  church)
  (GNA NA)

KNE
knead (massage, etc.) - ed
  - ing - able - er; *not* need
  (want)
knee - d - ing - bone
kneel - ing - er; *but* knelt
knell
knesset (*Heb*)
knew (did know); *not* new
  (fresh)
  (GNE NE)

KNI
knickerbocker
knickers
knick - knack
knif/e - ed - ing; *but* knives
knight (rank) - ed - ing - ly
  - hood - age; *not* night
knit - ted - ting - ter; *not* nit
knittle
  (GNEI NAI NI NY)

KNO
knob - bed - bing - by - bier
  - biest - biness
knobbl/e - y; *not* nobble
  (catch)
knobkerr/ie *or* - y
knock - ed - ing - er
knoll
knop
knot (tie) - ted - ting - ter - ty
  - tier - tiest; *not* not
know - n - ing - ingly - able; *but*
  knew
knowledge - able

(GNO NO)

KNU
knuckl/e - ed - ing
knurl
knurr
  (GNU NU)

KO
k.o., *for* knock out
koala
kobold
kodak
koel (*Aus*)
kohekohe (*NZ*)
kohl (powder); *not* coal
kohl - rabi
kola *or* cola (nut)
kolinsky
kookaburra (*Aus*)
kopje (*Af*)
koradji (*Aus*)
koran - ic
kosher
kowtow - ed - ing
  (CHO CO)

KR
kraal (*Af*)
krait (*Hind*)
kraken (*Nor*)
krans (*Af*)
kremlin (*Rus*)·
kriegspiel (*Ger*)
kris (*Malay*)
kromesk/y - ies
krone (coin); *not* crone
  (witch)
kroo - man; *not* crew - man
krypton
  (CHR CR)

KU
kudos
kudu
kukri (knife); *not* cookery
kulak (*Rus*)
kumara (*NZ*)
kümmel (*Ger*)
Kurd - ish - istan
kurrajong (*Aus*)
kursaal (*Ger*)
  (COO COU CU KER KIR)

KY

kylie (*Aus*)
kyrie eleison (*Gr*)
  (KI)

L

LA

la *or* lah (music)
laager (*Af,* camp); *not* lager
  (beer)

LAB

lab, *for* laboratory
label - led - ling
labia/l - ly - te - ise - ised - ising
  - isation (z)
labile
labi/um - a
laborator/y - ies - ial
laborious - ly - ness
labour - ed - ing - er - ite
Labrador
laburnum
labyrinth - ine - odon - odont

LAC

lac (resin); *not* lack *or* lakh
lac/e - ed - ing - y - ier - iest
lacerat/e - ed - ing - ion - or
lachrym/a - ation - atory - ose
  - osely - osity
lacinat/e - ed
lack - ed - ing; *not* lac *or* lakh
lackadaisical - ly
lackey - s
laconic - ally
lacquer - ed - ing
lacrosse
lact/action - ic - ate - eal
  - escent - escence
lactose
lacuna - e *or* - s
lacustrine
  (LAK LAS LAX)

LAD

lad - die *or* - dy
ladder
lad/e - en - ing
la-di-da
ladl/e - ed - ing - eful
lad/y - ies; lady's (of a
  lady); ladies' (of ladies)
lady/like - ship - hood

ladif/y - ied *or* ladyf/y - ied

LAG

lag - ged - ging - gard - gardly
lager (beer); *not* laager
  (camp)
lagoon

LAI

laid (did deposit, see
  footnote, p. 141)
lain (been lying, *see* p. 141)
lair (hiding place); *not* layer *or*
  liar
laird (*Sc*)
lair/y - ier - iest
laissez - faire (*F*)
lai/ty (non - clergy) - c - cally
  - cise (z)
  (LAY LEY)

LAK

lake
lakh (*Hind,* 100,000)
  (LAC)

LAM

lam (hit) - med - ming; *not*
  lamb
lama (monk) - ism - sery
  - series; *not* llama (animal)
lamb - ed - ing - kin
lambast/e - ed - ing
lambda (*Gr*)
lambent
lam/e - ed - ing - er - est - ly
  - eness
lamé (*F*)
lamell/a - ate - ated - ose
  - iform
lament - ed - ing - able - ably
  - ation
lamia
lamin/a - ae - ate - ated - ation
lammas - tide
lammergeyer
lamp
lampas
lampoon - ed - ing - er
lamp - post
lamprey - s

LAN

Lancast/er - rian
lanc/e - ed - ing - er

lancet
lancinating
land -ed -ing -lubber
landau -lette
landlord -ism
landscap/e -ed -ing -ist
lane (road); *not* lain (did lie)
lang (*Sc*)
language; *but* linguistic
languid -ly -ness
languish -ed -ing -ingly
languor -ous -ously
langur (monkey)
lani/ferous -gerous
lank -y -ier -iest -iness
lanner -et
lanolin
lantern
lanyard
  (LAU LAW)

LAO
Laodicea -n
Laos
  (LOU LOW)

LAP
lap -ped -ping -dog
lapar/ectomy -otomy
lapel
lapicide
lapid/ary -ate -ify -ified
  -ification
lapis lazuli
Lap/p -land -lander -ponian
lappet -ed
laps/e -ed -ing
lapsus linguae (*L*)
Laputa -n
lapwing

LAR
larcen/y -ous -ously -ist -er
larch
lard -ed -ing -aceous -y
larder
larg/e -er -est -ely -eness
largesse
largo
lariat
lark -ed -ing -y -ier -iest
larrikin
larva (grub) -e -l; *not* lava

laryn/x -geal -gitis -goscope
  (LAU LAW)

LAS
lasagne
Lascar
lascivious -ly -ness
laser
lash -ed -ing -er
lass -es -ie
lassitude
lasso *or* lasoo -ed -ing
last -ed -ing -ly
  (LAC LAZ)

LAT
latakia
latch -ed -ing -et
lat/e -er -est -ely -en -ened
  -ening; *not* latter
lateen
laten/t -tly -cy
lateral -ly
latex
lath (wood) -y
lathe (machine)
lather -ed -ing
Latin -ism -ist -ity
latitud/e -inal -inarian
latrine
latter -ly; *not* later
lattic/e -ed -ing

LAU
laud -ed -ing -able -ably
  -ation -atory
laudanum
laugh -ed -ing -ingly -able
  -ably -ter
launch -ed -ing -er
laund/er -ered -ering -ry -ries
  -erette -erer -ress
laureate -ship
laurel -led
  (LAW LOR)

LAV
lava (volcanic); *not* larva
  (grub)
lavator/y -ies -ial
lav/e -ed -ing -er
lavender
lavish -ed -ing -ly -ment
  (LEV)

138

LAW

law -ful -fully -fulness
lawless -ly -ness
lawyer
lawn
(LAU LOR)

LAX

lax -ity -ative
(LAC)

LAY

lay † (deposit), laid, laying,
  layer; *not* lie, lain
lay † (did lie)
lay (song)
lay (not of the clergy); *but*
  laity
lay figure (dummy)
layed? *No,* laid
layer -ed -ing
layette
(LAI LEY)

LAZ

laz/e -ed -ing
laz/y -ier -iest -ily -iness -yish
(LAS)

LEA

lea *or* ley
leach (percolate) -d -ing; *not*
  leech (worm)
lead -ing -er; *but* led (did
  lead)
lead (metal)‡ -en
leaf -y -ier -iest -iness; *but*
  leaves
leagu/e -ed -ing -er
leak -ed -ing -age -y -ier -iest
  -ily; *not* leek (plant)
lean (thin) -er -est -ness
lean (slope) -ed *or* -t -ing
leap -ed *or* -t -ing
leapyear
learn -ed *or* -t -ing -er
leas/e -ed -ing; *but* lessee,
  lessor
leash -ed -ing
least
leather -ed -ing -y -iness

leav/e -ing -er; *but* left (did
  leave)
leav/es -ed
leaven -ed -ing
(LEE LEI LI)

LEB

Leban/on -ese

LEC

lecher -y -ous
lectern
lectionary
lectur/e -ed -ing -er -ership
(ELEC LAC)

LED

led (did lead); *not* lead (metal)
ledge
ledger
ledger -line *or* leger -line
(LAD LEAD LEG)

LEE

lee -ward
leech (worm); *not* leach
leek (plant); *not* leak
leer -ed -ing -y -iest -ily
  -iness
less
leethal? *No,* lethal
(LEA LI)

LEF

left -ward -most -ism -ist
  -ish
left (did leave)
leftenant? *No,* lieutenant
(LEV)

LEG

leg -ged -ging -gy -gier
  -giest -giness
lega/cy -cies -tee
legal -ly -ity -ism -ist
legalis/e -ed -ing -ation (z)
legat/e -ion
legato
legend -ary
leger -line *or* ledger -line
leghorn
legib/le (readable) -ly -ility;

---

† See footnote on Lie and Lay, page 141.
‡ It has been suggested that the metal be spelt 'ledd'.

not illegible, eligible
legion -ary -naire
legislat/e -ed -ing -ion -ive
 -ure
legitim/ate -ately -acy -ism
 -ist
legitimis/e -ed -ing -ation (z)
legum/e -inous
 (LEDG LAG)

LEI
leisur/e -ed -ely
 (LEA LEE)

LEM
lem? *No,* eleven
lemming
lemon -y -ade
lemur
 (LIM)

LEN
lend -ing -er; *but* lent
length -y -ier -iest -ways
 -wise
lengthen -ed -ing
lenien/t -tly -ce -cy
lenit/y -ive
Lenin -ism -ist
lens-es
lent (did lend); *not* leant (did
 lean)
Lent -en
lenth? *No,* length
lenticular
lentil
lentisk
 (LIN)

LEO
Leo -nid
leonine; *but* lion
leopard -ess
leotard
 (LIO)

LEP
lep/er -rosy -rous
lepidopter/a -ous
leporine
leprechaun

LER
lern? *No,* learn
 (LIR LUR)

LES
lesbian -ism
lèse majesté (*F*)
lesion
less -en -ened -ening -er;
 not lesson (teach)
less/or -ee (of lease); *not*
 lesser
lesson (teach)
lest
lesure? *No,* leisure

LET
let -ting
lethal -ly -ness
letharg/y -ic -ical -ically
Lett -ish
letter -ed -ing
lettuce
 (LEC)

LEU
leuco/cyte -tomy
leukaemia
 (LEW LIEU LOO LU)

LEV
levant -ed -ing
Levant -ine -er
levee
level -led -ling -ler -ly
lever -ed -ing -age
leveret
leviathan
levitat/e -ed -ing -ion
Levit/e -icus -ical
levit/y -ies
lev/y -ies
 (LIV)

LEW
lewd -ly -ness
Lewis -ian
 (LEU LIEU LOO LU)

LEX
lexic/on -al -ography
 -ographer

LEY
ley *or* lea
leyden -jar
 (LAI LAY)

LIA
liab/le -ility
liaison

liais/e - ed - ing
liana
liar; *but* lie
lias - sic
  (LIO)

LIB
libation
libel - led - ling - lous
liberal - ly - ity - ism
liberalis/e - ed - ing - ation (z)
liberat/e - ed - ing - ion - or
libertin/e - ism - age
libert/y - ies
libid/o - os - inous
Libra - n
librar/y - ies - ian
librett/o - i - ist
Libya - n

LIC
lice; *but* louse
licence (a permit)
licens/e (to permit) - ed - ing
  - er - ee
licentiate
licentious - ly - ness
lichen
lichgate *or* lychgate
lick - ed - ing
licorice *or* liquorice
  (LIK LIQ LYC)

LID
lid
lido - s
  (LYD)

LIE
lie† (tell lies), lied, lying, liar
lie† (get into a flat position),
  lying, lay, lain
lief - er - est
liege

lien
lieu (place)
lieutenan/t - cy
  (LIGH LY)

LIF
life - like - less
lift - ed - ing - er

LIG
liga/ment - ture
light - er - est - ed - ing - some;
  also alight; *but* lit (did light)
lighten - ed - ing (make
  lighter)
lightning (electric storm)
lighter - age
lign/ite - eous
lignum vitae (*L*)
  (LEG)

LIK
lik/e - ed - ing - able; alike
likel/y - ier - iest - iness - ihood
likewise
liken - ed - ing - ess
  (LIC LYC)

LIL
lilac
Lilliput - ian
lilt - ed - ing
lil/y - ies - ied

LIM
limb (of body) - ed; *not* limn
  (draw)
limber - ed - ing
limbo - s
lim/e - ed - ing
lim/en - inal
Limerick
limey (*Am*)
limit/ed - ing - ation - ative
limn (draw) - ed - ing - er

† *Lie and Lay examples:*
1 Lie in bed. Last night I lay in bed. I was lying in bed. I have lain in bed.
2 He lies when accused. He lied when accused. He was lying to the police.
3 I now lay down my burden. I am laying it down. I have laid it down.
4 The hen lays egg. It laid an egg. It is laying eggs.

limousine
limp - ed - ing
limpet
limpid - ly - ity
  (LEM LYM)

LIN

linchpin
linden
lin/e - ed - ing - ear - eal - eage
  - eament; *but* align (line up)
linen
liner
ling (fish, heather)
linger - ed - ing
lingerie
lingo - es
lingu/ist - istic - al - istically
liniment
link - ed - ing - age
links (golf, cuff); *not* lynx
  (animal)
Linnae/us - an
linnet
lino, *for* linoleum
linotype
linseed
linsey - woolsey
lint
lintel
  (LEN LYN)

LIO

lion - ess; *but* leonine
lionis/e - ed - ing (z)
  (LEO LIA)

LIP

lip - ped

LIQ

lique/fy - fied - fying - fiable
  - faction - factive
liquescent
liquid - ate - ated - ating - ation
  - ator - ity
liquidis/e - ed - ing - ation (z)
liqueur
liquor
liquorice *or* licorice
  (LIC)

LIR

lir/a - e (*It*)
  (LYR)

LIS

lisle
lisp - ed - ing - ingly - er
lissom
list - ed - ing
listen - ed - ing - er
listless - ly - ness
  (LIZ)

LIT

lit (did light)
lit. hum., *for* literae
  humaniores (*L*)
litan/y - ies
litera/cy - te - tely
literal - ly - ism - ist (by the
  letter); *not* littoral
literar/y - ily - iness
literature
lithargic? *No,* lethargic
lithe - ly - ness
lithium
litho - graph - graphy - graphic
lithotomy
litig/ate - ation - ant - ious
litmus
litotes
litre
litter - ed - ing
litterateur (*F*)
little; *also* belittle
littoral (by the shore); *not*
  literal
liturg/y - ies - ical - ically

LIV

liv/e - ed - ing - er - able; *also*
  alive
live/ly - lier - liest - liness
livelihood
livelong
liven - ed - ing
liver - ish
Liver/pool - politan - pudlian
liver/y - ies - ied
livid
  (LEV LITH)

LIX

lixiviat/e - ion
  (LIC)

LIZ

lizard

LL
llama (animal); *not* lama
(monk)
Lloyd's

LO
lo! (behold!)
(LOW)

LOA
loach
load-ed-ing-er; *not* lode
(vein of ore)
loaf-ed-ing-er
loa/f-ves
loam-y-ier-iest
loan (lend)-ed-ing; *not* lone
(solitary)
loath *or* loth
loath/e-ed-ing-some
(LOW)

LOB
lob-bed-bing-ber
lobate
lobb/y-ies-ied-ying-yist
lob/e-ed-ate-ule-ular
-otomy
lobelia
lobster
(LOP)

LOC
local-ly-ity-ism
localis/e-es-ng-ation (z)
locale
locat/e-ed-ing-ion-or-ive
loch (*Sc*)
lock-ed-ing-er
locket
locomot/ion-ive
locum, *for* locum tenens (*L*)
loc/us-i
locust
locution

LOD LOE
lode (vein of ore); *not* load
lodestone
lodg/e-ed-ing-er-ment *or*
-ement
loess

LOF
loft-y-ier-iest-ed-ing-ily

-iness; *also* aloft
(LOA LOTH)

LOG
log-ged-ging
log, *for* logarithm
logan-stone
logarithm-ic-al
loggerheads
loggia
logic-al-ally-ality-ian
logistic-s-al-ally
logos

LOI
loin
loiter-ed-ing-er
(LOY)

LOL
loll-ed-ing
loll/y-ies, *for* lollipop-s
(LUL)

LON
London-er
lone-ly-lier-liest-liness-r
-some; *also* alone
long-er-est-ways-wise
longeron
longevity
longitud/e-inal-inally
long-sleever
(LOAN LUN)

LOO
loo; *not* lieu (in place of)
looard? *No*, leeward
loofah
look-ed-ing-er
loom-ed-ing
loon
loop-ed-ing-er-y
loop-hole
loos/e (slack)-er-est-ely-ed
-ing; *not* lose, lost
loosen-ed-ing-er
loot-ed-ing-er
(LEU LEW LIEU LOU LU)

LOP
lop-ped-ping-sided
lop/e (run)-ed-ing
(LOB)

LOQ
loquac/ity-ious-iously

143

loquat

LOR
lorcha
lord - ed - ing - ly - ship - ling
lordosis
lore (knowledge); *not* law
lorgnette (*F*)
lorn (forlorn); *not* lawn
lorr/y - ies
lor/y - ies (bird)
(LAU LAW)

LOS
los/e - t - ing - er - able; *not*
  loose (slack)
loss - es
(LOZ)

LOT
lot; *also* allot
loth *or* loath
lotion
lotter/y - ies
lotto
lotus - es

LOU
loud - er - est - ly - ness; *also*
  aloud
lough (*Ir*)
loung/e - ed - ing - er
lour *or* lower (frown) - ed - ing
lous/e - y - ier - iest
lout - ish
louver *or* louvre
(LAO LOO LOW)

LOV
lov/e - ed - ing - er - able - ably
  - eless - elessly
lovel/y - ier - iest - iness

LOW
low - er - est - ermost
low (moo) - ed - ing
lowl/y - ier - iest
lowan (*Aus*)
lower *or* lour (frown) - ed - ing
(LOA LOU)

LOY
loyal - ty - ties - ly - ism - ist
(LOI)

LOZ
lozeng/e - y

LUB
lubber - ly - liness
lubra (*Aus*)
lubricat/e - ed - ing - ion - nt - er
lubricity

LUC
lucerne
lucid - ly - ity
lucifer
luck - y - ier - iest - ily - less
lucr/e - ative
lucubration
(LOOK LUS)

LUD-LUG
ludicrous - ly
ludo
luff - ed - ing
lug - ged - ging
lug/e - ed - eing
luggage
lugger
lugsail
lugsury? *No,* luxury
lugubrious - ly - ness

LUK
lukewarm - ly - ness
(LEU LUC LOOK)

LUL
lull - ed - ing - ingly
lullab/y - ies
(LOL)

LUM
lumbago
lumbar (of the loin)
lumber (timber, etc.) - ed - ing
  - er
lumbrical
lumin/ous - osity - ously
  - iferous - escence
luminar - y - ies
lump - ed - ing - y - ier - iest - ily
  - iness
lumpish - ness
(LOM LOOM)

LUN
luna/cy - cies - tic
luna/r - te - tion
lunch - eon - ed - ing - er
lune
lunette

144

lung - ed
lung/e - ed - ing
  (LON)
LUP
lupin (plant)
lupine (wolf - like)
lupus
  (LOOP)
LUR
lurch - ed - ing - er
lur/e - ed - ing
lurid - ly - ness
lurk - ed - ing
  (LEAR LYR)
LUS
luscious - ly - ness
lush - ed - ing
lust - ed - ing - ful - fully
  - fulness
lustr/ate - al - ation
lustr/e - ous - ously
lustrine
lustr/um - a or ums
lust/y - ier - iest - ily - iness
LUT
lute (music); not loot
lutanist
Luther - an - ism
LUX
luxat/e - ed - ing - ion
luxur/y - ies - ious - iously
  - iousness
luxuri/ant - antly - ance
luxuri/ate - ated - ating
LY
lycanthropy
lychgate or lichgate
lyddite
lye (alkalised water)
lying, see footnote, p. 141
lyle? No, lisle
lymph - atic
lynch - ed - ing
lynx - es
lyr/e - ist - ate
lyric - al - ally - ism - ist
  (LI)

M
MA
ma, for mamma
ma'am, for madam
  (MAH MAR)
MACA
macabre
macadam - ise - ised - ising
  - isation (z)
macaron/i - is - ic
macaroon
macassar
macaw
  (MACK MEC)
MACE
mace
macedoin (F)
macerat/e - ed - ing - ion
  (MAS)
MACH
mach (speed of sound); not
  match
machete or matchet
Machiavelli - an
machicolat/e - ed - ing - ion
machinat/e - ed - ing - ion - or
machin/e - ed - ing - ery - ist;
  but mechanical
  (MASH MATCH)
MACK-MACU
mackerel
mac(k)intosh - es
macle
macramé
macro - *, prefix meaning
  great; not micro -
macrocosm
macul/a - ae
  (MACA MAK)
MAD
mad - der - dest - ly - ness
madam
madame, mesdames, or
  Mme., Mmes. (F)
madden - ed - ing - ingly
madder (plant, dye)
made (did make); not maid

---

* If the word you wish to spell is not in this list, omit the prefix
and look for the rest of the word.

Madeira
mademoiselle,
  mesdemoiselles *or* Mlle.
  Mlles. (*F*)
mado (*Aus*)
madonna
madrigal
MAE
maelstrom
maenad
maestoso (*It*)
maestro (*It*)
mae-west
  (MAI MAY)
MAF
maffick -ing
mafia (*It*)
MAG-MAGM
mag, *for* magazine, magneto
magazine
Magdalen -e
magenta
maggot -y
magi (magus)
magic -al -ally -ian
magist/rate -rature -erial
  -erially
magma
  (MAJ)
MAGN-MAGY
magnanim-ity -ous -ously
  -ousness
magnate (big boss); *not*
  magnet
magnesi/a -um -an
magnet -ic -ically -ism -ite
magnetis/e -ed -ing -ation (z)
magneto -s
magnificat
magnificen/ce -t -tly
magnif/y -ies -ied -ying
  -ication -ier
magniloquen/ce -t -tly
magnitude
magnolia
magnum -s
magpie

mag/us -i
Magyar
MAH
mahara/jah -nee *or* -ni
mahatma
mah -jongg
mahlstick
mahoe
mahogany
Mahometan, *see*
  Mohammedan
mahout (*Hind*)
  (MA MAR)
MAI
maid -en -enly -ish -enish;
  not made (did make)
mail -ed -ing (post); *not* male
  (masculine)
maim -ed -ing
maimai (*NZ*)
main -ly
maintain -ed -ing -able
maintenance
maire (*NZ*)
maisonette
maître d'hôtel (*F*)
maize
  (MAE MAY)
MAJ
majest/y -ies -ic -ically
majolica
major -ed -ing -ity
majuscul/e -ar
  (MAGE MAJI)
MAK
mak/e -ing -er; *but* made
make-up
mako -mako (*NZ*)
  (MAC)
MAL MALA
mal-*, *prefix meaning* bad
Malacca
malachite
malacolog/y -ist
maladroit -ly -ness
malad/y -ies
Malagasy

---

* If the word you wish to spell is not in this list, omit the prefix
and look for the rest of the word.

malaise
malanders
malapert
malaprop/os -ism
malar
malari/a -al -ous -an
Malay -a -an
(MALL MARL)
MALC MALD
malcontent
mal de mer (*F*)
MALE
maledict/ion -ory
malefact/or -ion
malefic -ent -ence
malest? *No,* molest
malevolen/t -tly -ce
(MALI MALLE)
MALF
malfeasan/t -ce
MALI
malic (acid)
malic/e -ious -iously
malign -ed -ing -ly
malig/nant -nantly -nancy
-nity
malinger -ed -ing -er
(MALE MALL)
MALL
mallard
malleab/le -ly -ility
mallet
mallow
(MAHL MAL MAUL)
MALM MALN
malm
malmaison
malmsey
malnutrition
(MAM MARM)
MALO
malodorous -ly -ness
(MALL MELL MELO)
MALT
malt -ed -ing -ster -ose
Malt/a -ese
malthusian
maltreat
(MOLT MOULT)

MALV
malvaceous
malversation
malvoisie
(MARV)
MAM
mamba
mamelon
mameluke
mamill/a -ary -ate -ated
-iform
mama, mamma, mamm/y
-ies (mother)
mamm/a (milk gland) -ae -ary
-iferous -iform
mammal -ia -ian -ogy -ogist
-iferous
mammon
mammoth
(MEM MUM)
MAN MANA
man -ned -ning
man -ful -fully -ly -liness
-hood
mann/ish -ishness
mana
manacl/e -ed -ing
manag/e -ed -ing -ement -er
-erial
manageab/le -ly -ility
manaia (*NZ*)
manatee
(MANN MENA)
MANC
Man/chester -cunian
manciple
(MANK MANS)
MAND
mandamus
mandarin -e
mandat/e -ed -ing -ory *or*
-ary
mandib/le -ular -ulate
mandolin(e)
mandrake
mandragora
mandrel *or* mandril (tool)
mandrill (baboon)
manducat/e -ed -ing -ion,
-ory

(MEND)
MANE
mane (hair); *not* main (chief)
manège (*F*, riding school);
not ménage
(MAIN MANN)
MANG MANH
mangan/ese - esian - ic
mang/e - y - iness
mangeao (*NZ*)
mangel *or* mangold - wurzel
manger
mangl/e - ed - ing
mango - es
mangosteen
mangrove
Manhattan
manhood
MANI
man/ia - iac - iacal - iacally
manic
manicur/e - ed - ing - ist
manifest - ed - ing - ly - ation
manifesto - s
manifold - ed - ing - er
manikin
manilla
manioc
manipulat/e - ed - ing - ion - or
- ory - ive
(MANN MEN)
MANK-MANO
mankind
manna
mannequin (dress model)
manner - ed - ly - ism - ist
manoeuvr/e - ed - ing - er
manomet/er - ric
ma non troppo (*It*)
manor - ial
(MONO)
MANQ
manqué (*F*)
MANS
mansard
manse
mansion
manslaughter
(MANC)

MANT-MANY
mantel - piece
mantic
mantilla (*Sp*)
mantis (insect)
mantissa (math.)
mantl/e - ed - ing
manual - ly
manufactor/y - ies
manufactur/e - ed - ing - er
manuka (*NZ*)
manum/it - itted - itting - ission
manur/e - ed - ing - ial
manuscript
manuver? *No,* manoeuvre
Manx
many
MAO
Mao - ism - ist
maomao (*NZ*)
Maori - s - tanga (*NZ*)
(MOU)
MAP
map - ped - ping - per
mapau (*NZ*)
maple
MAR MARA
mar - red - ring
marabou
maraschino - s
marathon
maraud - ing - er
(MAH MARR MORA)
MARB
marbl/e - ed - ing - y
MARC
Marcan (of St. Mark)
marcasite
marcel - led - ling
march - ed - ing - er
marchioness
marconi - gram
(MARK MARQ MARS)
MARE
mare (she - horse); *not* mayor
mare (*L*, lunar 'sea')
MARG
margarine *or* marge
margin - ed - al - ally - alia
marguerite

(MARJ)

MARI
marigold
marijuana
marimba
marina
marina/te - ted - ting - tion - de
marine, mariner
marionette
Mari/st - olatry
marital (of marriage) - ly
maritime
(MARR)

MARJ
marjoram
(MARG)

MARK
mark - ed - edly - ing - er
market - ed - ing
(MARC MARQ)

MARL
marl
marline - spike

MARM
marmalade
marmite
marmo/lite - real
marmoset
marmot
(MAAM MALM)

MARO
marocain
maroon - ed - ing
(MARR MORO)

MARQ
marquee
marquetry
marqu/is or - ess, - ise; but
marchioness
(MARC MARK)

MARR
marram
marriage - able
marron glacé (F)
marrow
marr/y - ied - ying
(MAR-)

MARS
Mar/s - tian
marsala

Marseill/es - aise
marsh - y - ier - iest - iness
marshal - led - ling; not
martial (warlike)
marsupial
(MARC MARZ)

MART-MARZ
mart
martello tower
marten (weasel)
martial (warlike) - ly; not
marshal, marital
Martian
martin (bird)
martinet
martingale
martini
martlet
martyr - ed - ing - dom - ology
marvel - led - ling - lous - lously
Marx - ism - ist - ian
marzipan

MASC-MASQ
mascara
mascot
masculin/e - ity
mash - ed - ing - er
mashie
mask - ed - ing - er
masoch/ism - ist - istic
- istically
mason - ic - ry
masque (entertainment)
masquerad/e - ed - ing - er

MASS
mass - es - ed - ing - y - iness
massacr/e - ed - ing
massag/e - ed - ing
mass/eur - euse
massif (highland)
massive - ly - ness
(MACE MAS- MAZ)

MAST
mast - ed - er
mastaba
master - ed - ing - y - ly - liness
- ship
masterful - ly - ness
mastic
masticat/e - ed - ing - ion - or

149

-ory
mastiff
mastitis
mastodon -tic
mastoid
masturbat/e -ed -ing -ion
MAT MATA
mat -ted -ting
matador
matagouri (*NZ*)
matai (*NZ*)
(MATT)
MATCH
match -ed -ing -less -lessly
matches
matchet *or* machete
(MACH)
MATE
mat/e -ed -ing -ey
maté (*Sp*)
matelot (*F*) *or* matlow
material -ly -ism -ist -istic
materialis/e -ed -ing -ation (z)
matern/al -ally -ity -nalism
(MAIT MATT)
MATCH-MATR
mathematic/s -al -ally -ian
matilda
matin -s *or* mattins
matinée
matlow *or* matelot (*F*)
matrass (glass vessel); *not*
  mattress
matriarch -y -ies -al
matricid/e -al
matriculat/e -ed -ing -ion
  -ory
matrimon/y -ial -ially
matri/x -ces *or* -xes
matron -ly
(MATT)
MATT
matt (dull -surfaced)
matter -ed -ing -y
matting
mattins *or* matin -s
mattock
mattoid
mattress -es
(MAT-)

MATU
maturat/e -ed -ion -ive
matur/e -ed -ing -ely -ity
matutinal
MAU
maudlin
maul -ed -ing -er
maunder -ed -ing
maundy
mausoleum
mauve
(MAW MOR)
MAV
maverick
mavis
mavourneen (*Ir*)
MAW
maw (gullet); *not* more
mawkish -ly -ness
mawseed
(MAU MOR)
MAX
maxill/a -ae -ary -iform
maxim
maximis/e -ed -ing -ation (z)
maxim/um -a -al
MAY
may
May Day
mayday (signal: m'aider, *F*)
mayhem
mayonnaise
mayor -ess -al -alty
(MAE MAI)
MAZ
mazard *or* mazzard
mazarine
maz/e -ed -y -ily -iness
mazer
mazurka
(MAS)
ME MEA
me; *but* my, mine
me/seems -thinks -thought,
  etc.
mead (drink, meadow)
meadow
meagre -ly -ness
meal -y -iness
mealies (maize)

mean - t - ing - ingly - ingful;
  not mien (bearing)
mean - ly - ness; *not* mesne
  (intermediate)
meander - ed - ing
measl/es - y
measur/e - ed - ing - ement
  - able - ably
meat - y - less - ier - iest
meatus - es
  (MEE MIS MIE)

MEC
Mecca
meccano
mechanic - al - ally - ian; *but*
  machine
mechanis/e - ed - ing - ation (z)
mechan/ism - ist - istic
  (MAC)

MEDA MEDD
medal - led - list (decoration)
medallion
meddl/e (interfere) - ed - ing
  - er - esome - esomeness
  (MAD MEAD MID)

MEDI
media (mediums)
medi(a)eval - ism - ist
medial - ly
median
mediant (music)
mediat/e - d - ing - ion - or - rix
  - ory - orial
medic/al - ally - able - ament
medicin/e - al - ally
medico - s
mediocr/e - ity
meditat/e - ed - ing - ion - or
  - ive - ively - iveness
Mediterranean
medi/um - a - umistic

MEDL-MEDU
medlar (fruit); *not* meddler
medley - s
medoc
medulla - ry

MEE
meed (reward); *not* mead
meek - er - est - ly - ness
meerschaum (*Ger*)
meet (get together), met,
  meeting; *not* meat *or* mete
meet (suitable) - ly - ness
  (MEA MIE)

MEF
  (MEPH)

MEG
mega-*, megalo-*, *prefixes
  meaning* great
megalith - ic
megaloman/ia - ic - iac
megalosaur/us - ian
megaphone
megatheri/um - a
megaton
megawatt
megasse
megilp
megrim
  (MAG)

MEI
meiosis
Meistersinger (*Ger*)
  (MAI MAY MY)

MEL
melamine
melanchol/y - ia - ic
Melanesia - n
mélange (*F*)
melan/ism - osis - otic
melasses? *No,* molasses
meld - ed - ing
melée (*F*)
melinite
melior/ate - ation - ism - ist
melliferous (honey - yielding)
mellifluous (sweet voiced) - ly
mellow - er - est - ly - ness
melod/eon *or* - ion *or* - ium
melod/ic - ist - ious - iously
  - iousness
melod/y - ies
melodis/e - ed - ing - er (z)

* If the word you wish to spell is not in this list, omit the prefix
and look for the rest of the word.

melodrama -tic -tically
melon
melt -ed -ing -ingly; *but*
  molten
melton
(MAL)

MEM

member -ed -less -ship
membran/e -ous -eous
  -aceous
memento -s *or* -es
memoir
memor/able -ably -ability
memorand/um -a *or* -ums
memor/y -ies -ial -ialise
  -ialised (z)
memoris/e -ed -ing -ation (z)
memsahib (*Hind*)
(MAM)

MEN

men
menac/e -ed -ing -ingly
ménage (*F*)
menagerie
mend -ed -ing -able; *also*
  amend (improve), emend
  (correct)
mendac/ity (lying) -ities -ious
  -iously; *not* mendicity
Mendel -ism -ian
mendic/ity (begging) -ant
  -ancy; *not* mendacity
menhir
menial -ly
menin/x -ges -geal -gitis
meniscus
menopause
menses
menstruat/e -ed -ing -ion
menstru/um -al -ous
mensur/al (of measuring)
  -able -ation
mental -ly -ity
menthol
mention -ed -ing -able
mentor
menu -s
menure? *No,* manure
meny? *No,* many

MEPH

Mephistophel/es -ean *or* -ian
mephitic
(METH)

MERC

mercantil/e -ism -ist
Mercator
mercenar/y -ies
mercer -y -ise -ised -ising (z)
merchandise (*not* z)
merchant -able
mercur/y -ial -ic -ous
merc/y -ies -iful -ifully -iless
  -ilessly -ilessness
(MURK)

MERE

mere -ly
meretricious -ly -ness
(MEER MERI)

MERG

merganser
merg/e -ed -ing -er -ence

MERI

meridi/an -onal
meringue
merino -s
merit -ed -ing -orious
  -oriously
(MERE)

MERL-MERR

merlin (falcon)
merlon (architecture)
mer/maid -man
merr/y -ier -iest -ily -iness
  -iment
(MUR MYR)

MES

mesa
mesdames (*F,* Mmes.)
mesdemoiselles (*F,* Mlles.)
meself? *No,* myself
mesembrianthemum
mesenter/y -ic -itis
mesh (net) -es -ed -ing; *not*
  mash
mesmer/ism -ist -ic
mesmeris/e -ed -ing (z)
mesne (intermediate); *not*
  mean

meso-*, *prefix meaning*
  middle
meso/lithic - phyll - zoic
meson
mess - y - ier - iest - ily - iness
message
messenger
Messia/h - nic
messieurs (*F*, MM.)
Messrs (*plural of* Mr)
messuage
mestizo - s (*Sp*)
  (MEZZ)

MET META

met (did meet)
met., *for* meteorological
meta-*, *prefix meaning with*,
  after, change
metabol/ism - ic - ise - ised (z)
metacarpus
metage
metal - lic - loid - lography; *not*
  mettle (courage)
metallis/e - ed - ing - ation (z)
metallurg/y - ic - ical - ist
metamer/e - ic - ism
metamorph/ic - ism - osis
  - ose - osed
metaphor - ical - ically
metaphysic/s - al - ian
metaplasm
metasta/sis - tic
metatars/us - al
metathesis
  (METO)

METE

met/e (measure) - ed - ing;
  not meat *or* meet
metempsychosis
meteor - ic - oid - ite - olite
meteorolog/y (weather) - ic
  - ical - ically - ist; *not*
  metrology
meter (measuring
  instrument); (*also Am* 1,000
  mm)
  (MEAT MEET)

METH

methane
metheglin
me/thinks - thought
method - ical - ically - ology
methodis/e - ed - ing (z)
Method/ism - ist - istic
methyl - ic - ate - ated
  (MEPH MYTH)

METI

meticulous - ly - ness
métier (*F*)
  (MATI)

METO

metonic
metonym/y - ic - ical - ically
metope (architecture)
  (META)

METR

metr/e (1,000 mm) - ic
metric/al - ally - ation
metrolog/y (measuring); *not*
  meteorology (weather)
metronom/e - ic
metropoli/s - tan
  (MATR MATT)

METS

  (MEZZ)

METT

mettle (courage) - some; *not*
  metal

MEW

mew - ed - ing
mews
  (MU)

MEZZ

mezzanine (architecture)
mezzoforte (*It*, mf)
mezzorelievo (*It*)
mezzotint (*It*)
  (MES)

MIA

mia - mia (*Aus*)
miaow - ed - ing
miasm/a - al - atic
  (MEA)

---

* If the word you wish to spell is not in this list, omit the prefix
and look for the rest of the word.

MIC

mica - ceous
mice (mouse)
micker/y or - ie (Aus)
mickle (Sc)
micky
micro-*, prefix meaning
  small (see also mu)
microb/e - ial
microcosm - ic
micron
microphone
microphyte
microscop/e - ic - ically - y
microtome
microzyme
micturition
  (MIK MYC)

MID

mid or amid - st
midday
midden
middl/e - ing
midd/y - ies (Aus)
midge
midget
midland - er
midnight
midriff
midship - s - man - men
midsummer
midwife - ry
  (MED)

MIE

mien (bearing); not mean
  (MEA MEE MEI MY)

MIG

might (may); not mite (tiny
  insect)
might - y - ier - iest - ily - iness
mignonette
migraine
migrant
migrat/e - ed - ing - ion - ory

MIK

mikado - s

mike, for microphone
  (MIC MYC)

MIL

milage or mileage
Milan - ese
milch
mild - er - est - ly - ness
mildew - ed - ing
mile
miler (athlete); not miller
milieu (F)
militan/t - tly - cy
militar/y - ily - ism - ist - istic
militat/e - ed - ing
militia
milium
milk - ed - ing - er - y - ier - iest
  - iness
mill - ed - ing - er
mille-*, mill-*, prefixes
  meaning thousand
millenni/um - a - al
millenar/y - ian; not millinery
millet
milliard
millinery (women's hats)
million - th - fold - aire
millipede
milt - ed - ing - er
Mil/ton - ic
  (MEL)

MIM

mim/e - ed - ing
mimeograph - ed - ing
mime/sis - tic - tically
mimic - ked - king - ry
mimosa
mimulus
  (MEM)

MINA-MING

mina or mynah (bird)
minaret
minatory
minc/e - ed - ing - er - ingly
mind - ed - ing - er - ful - fully
  - fulness
mine (belonging to me)

* If the word you wish to spell is not in this list, omit the prefix
and look for the rest of the word.

min/e -ed -ing -er
mineral -ogy -ogist -ogical
mineralis/e -ed -ing -ation (z)
mingl/e -ed -ing
ming/y -ier -iest
  (MEN)

MINI*

mini-*, *prefix meaning* small
miniat/e -ed -ing
miniatur/e -ist -ise -isation (z)
minif/y -ies -ied -ying
minikin
minim
minim/um -a -al -alist -ally
minimis/e -ed -ing -ation (z)
minion
minister -ed -ing -ial -ially
ministr/y -ies -ation -ative
  -ant
minit? *No,* minute
miniver *or* minever
  (MANI MENI)

MINK-MINT

mink -s (furs); *not* minx
minnit? *No,* minute
minnow
minor -ity -ities
Minocra *or* Menorca
minster
minstrel -sy
mint -ed -ing -age

MINU

minuet
minus
minuscul/e -ar
minut/e -ed -ing -ely
minutia -e

MINX

minx (hussy); *not* mink -s
  (furs)

MIO

miocene
  (MYO)

MIR

mirac/le -ulous -ulously
  -ulousness
mirage

mir/e -ed -y
miro (*NZ*)
mirror -ed -ing
mirth -ful -fully -fulness -less
  -lessly
  (MER MUR MYR)

MIS*-MIS*P

mis-*, *prefix that gives an
  unfavourable sense to the
  word it precedes*
misanthrop/e -y -ic -ist
miscegenation
miscellane/a -ous -ously
  -ousness
mischief
mischievous -ly -ness; *not*
  -vious
miscib/le -ly -ility
miscreant
mis -cu/e -ed -ing
miser -ly -liness
misericord
miser/y -ies -able -ably
mishap
mis -hit -ting
mishmash
misled (did mislead)
misnomer
misogynist
misprision
  (MISS MIZ)

MIS*S

miss -ed -ing; *for* unmarried
  woman, *use* Miss *or* Ms.
missal (mass -book); *not*
  missile *or* mizzle
missel -thrush
mis -shapen
missile (thrown weapon)
mission -er -ary -aries
missis? missus? *Use* Mrs *or*
  Ms.
missive
mis -spel/l -t *or* -led -ling
  (MIS-MYS)

MIS*T

mist -ed -ing -y -ier -iest -ily

* If the word you wish to spell is not in this list, omit the prefix
and look for the rest of the word.

-iness
mistak/e -en -ing -enly -able
mister, *use* Mr.
mistletoe
mistral
mistress -es
(MYST)

MIT
mite (tiny insect); *not* might
mitigat/e -ed -ing -ion
mitosis
mitr/e -ed -ing -al (*Am* miter)
mitten *or* mitt

MIX
mix -ed -ing -er -ture
(MYX)

MIZ
mizpah -ring
mizzen
mizzl/e -ed -ing -y
(MIS)

MNE
mnemonic -ally

MO-MOB
mo, *for* moment; *not* mot (*F*)
moa (extinct bird)
moan -ed -ing -er -ful; *also*
bemoan
moat (ditch); *not* mote
mob -bed -bing
mobil/e -ity -ise -ised -ising
-isation (z)

MOC
moccasin
mocha
mock -ed -ing -er -ingly -ery
(MAC MEC MOK MOQ)

MOD
mod/e -al -ality
model -led -ling -ler
modena
moderat/e -ed -ing -ion -or
-ely -eness
modern -ise -ised -ising
-isation (z)
modern/ness -ism -ist -ity
modest (humble) -y -ly; *not*
modiste
modicum
modif/y -ied -ying -ication

-iable
modillion, *not* medallion
modish -ly -ness
modiste (milliner); *not*
modest
modulat/e -ed -ing -ion -or
modul/e -us -ar

MOG-MOI
mogo (*Aus*)
mogul
mohair
Mohammed -an -anism
Mohawk
moiet/y -ies
moir/e -é
moist -er -est -en -ened
-ening -ure -urise -uriser (z)

MOK
moke
moki (*NZ*)
moko (*NZ*)
(MOC MOQ)

MOL
molar
molatto? No, mulatto
molasses
mole
molecul/e -ar -arity -arly
molest -ed -ing -ation
moll
mollif/y -ied -ying -ication
mollusc
molly -coddl/e -ed -ing -er
Molotov cocktail
molten
molto (*It*)
molybdenum
(MAL MOUL)

MOM
moment -um -ly
momento? No, memento
momentar/y -ily -iness
momentous -ly -ness
(MUM)

MONA-MONK
monad -ic -ology; *not* nomad
(wanderer)
monandr/y -ous
monarch -y -ic -ical -ically
-ism -ist

monast/ery - ic - ically - icism
mondaine (F)
Monday - ish
monet/ary - ise - ised - ising
  - isation (z)
money - s - ed - 's worth
monger
Mongol - ian - oid - ism
mongoose - s
mongrel - ism - ise - ised
  - ising - isation (z)
mon/ism - ist - istic
monition
monitor - ed - ing - y - ial - ship
monitress
monk - ish
monkey - s - ed - ing - ish; *not*
  manqué
  (MOAN MUN)

MONO*

mono - *, *prefix meaning*
alone, single
monocle - d
monocoque
monod/y - ic
monogam/y - ous - ist
mono/gram - graph
monolith - ic
monologue
monomer
monomial
monopol/y - ies - ist
monopolis/e - ed - ing
  - ation (z)
monoton/y - ous - ously - e

MONS-MONU

monsieur, messieurs (F, M,
  MM.)
monsignor - i (*It*)
monsoon - al
monster
monstrosit/y - ies
monstrous - ly - ness
monstrance
montage
montane
montbretia

Montessori - an
month - ly
monument - al - ally
  (MUN)

MOO

moo - ed - ing; *not* moue
  (pout)
mooch *or* mouch - ed - ing
mood - y - ier - iest - ily - iness
moon - ed - ing - y - light
moor - ed - ing
moose (deer); *not* mousse
moot - ed - ing
moove? *No,* move
  (MOU)

MOP

mop - ped - ping
mop/e - ed - ing - er - ish - ishly
moped, *for* motor - pedal
mopoke *or* morepork (*Aus*)

MOQ

moquette
  (MOC MOK)

MORA-MORE

morain/e - ic
moral - ly - ism - ist - ity - ities;
  but amoral (not moral)
moralis/e - ed - ing - ation - er
  (z)
morale
morass - es
moratori/um - a
morbid - ly - ity - ness
morbific
mordan/t (caustic) - tly - cy
mordent (music)
more - over
moreen
morel (a plant)
morello
morepork *or* mopoke (*Aus*)
mores (*L*)
  (MAU MAW)

MORG-MORP

morgage? *No,* mortgage
morganatic - ally
morgue

* If the word you wish to spell is not in this list, omit the prefix
and look for the rest of the word.

moribund
Mormon -ism
morn -ing (before noon); *not*
. mourn
Morocc/o -an
moron -ic
morose -ly -ness
morpheme
Morpheus
morph/ia -ine -inism
morpholog/y -ical -ically -ist
(MARI MAU MAW MERI)

MORR-MORW

morris
morrow
morse
morsel
mort
mortal -ly -ity
mortar
mortgag/e -ed -ing -ee -or
mortician (*Am*, undertaker)
mortif/y -ies -ied -ying
-ication
mortis/e *or* mortic/e -ed -ing
mortmain
mortuar/y -ies
morwong (*Aus*)
(MAU MAW)

MOS

mosaic
moschatel
Moscow; *but* Muscovite
moselle
Moslem *or* Muslim
mosque
mosquito -es
moss -y -ier -iest
most -ly

MOT

mot (*F*)
mote (dust particle); *not*
moat
motel
motet
moth -y -eaten
mother -ed -ing -ly -hood
motif
motil/e -ity
motion -al -less

motiv/e -ate -ated -ating
-ation -ity
motley
motocross
motor -ed -ing -ise -ised
-ising -isation (z)
motorcade
mottl/e -ed -ing
motto -es
(MAT MET)

MOU

moue (pout); *not* moo (cow)
moufflon
moujik
mould -ed -ing -y -ier -iest
-iness
moulder -ed -ing
moult -ed -ing
mound
mount -ed -ing
mountain -ous -y -eer
-eering
mountebank
mount/y -ies, *for* Royal
Canadian Mounted Police
mourn -ed -ing -er -ful -fully
-fulness
mous/e -y -er
mousse (froth); *not* moose
(deer)
moustache
mouth -ed -ing -y -ful
(MAO MOO)

MOV

movab/le -ility -leness -ly
mov/e (shift) -ed -ing -er
-ement -ingly; *not* mauve
(colour)
movies

MOW

mow -ed -ing -er
(MAU MOU)

MU-MUG

mu, *Greek letter, used as*
sign for micro-
much -ness
mucilage
muck -ed -ing -y -ier -iest
muckle (*Sc*)
muc/us -ous -osity

mud -dy -dier -diest -dily
 -diness
muddl/e -ed -ing -er
muezzin
muff -ed -ing -ish
muffin
muffl/e -ed -ing -er
mufti
mug -ged -ging -ger -gy
 -giness
muggins
mugwump

MULA-MULI

mulatto -s
mulberr/y -ies
mulch -ed -ing
mulct -ed -ing
mul/e -ish -ishly -ishness
muleteer
mulga (*Aus*)
muliebrity
 (MAL MOL MULL)

MULL

mull -ed -ing
mullah
mullein
muller
mullet
mulligatawny
mullion -ed
mullock (*Aus*)
mulloway
 (MAL MOL MUL-)

MULT

multangular
multi -*, *prefix meaning*
 many
multifarious -ly -ness
multifid
multifoil
multinomial
multiparous
multiple -x
multiplic/ation -ative -and
multipl/y -ies -ied -ying -ier
 -iable -icity
multitud/e -inous -inously

-inousness
 (MAL MOUL)

MUM

mum
mumbl/e -ed -ing -er
mumbo -jumbo
mummer -y
mumm/y -ies -ify -ified
 -ifying -ification
mumps
 (MOM)

MUN

munch -ed -ing
mundane -ly -ness
munga (*Aus*)
mungo
municipal -ly -ity -ities
municipalis/e -ed -ing -ation
 (z)
munificen/t -tly -ce
munition
 (MON)

MUR

mural
murder -ed -ing -er -ess -ous
 -ously
murex
muriat/e -ic
murk -y -ier -iest -ily -iness
murmur -ed -ing -ous
murph/y -ies
murrain
 (MER MIR MYR)

MUS

musca/dine -tel
muscl/e (flesh) -ed -ing
 -eless
Muscov/y -ite; *but* Moscow
muscul/ar -arity -ature
mus/e -ed -ing; *also* bemuse
museum
mush -y -ier -iest -iness
mushroom -ed -ing
music -al -ally -ality -ology
 -ologist
musician
musk -y

* If the word you wish to spell is not in this list, omit the prefix
and look for the rest of the word.

musket - ry - eer
Muslim or moslem or
  Mussulman
muslin
musquash
mussel (shellfish); not
  muscle
must
mustache? No, moustache
mustang
mustard
muster - ed - ing
must/y - ier - iest - iness
  (MAS MUZ)

MUT
muta/tion (change) - ble
  - bility; not nutation
mutatis mutandis (L)
mut/e - ed - ing - ism
mutilat/e - ed - ing - ion - or
mutin/y - ies - ied - ying - ous
  - ously - eer
mutt
mutter - ed - ing - er
mutton - y
mutual - ly - ity

MUZ
muzz/y - ily - iness
muzzl/e - ed - ing
  (MUS)

MY-MYO
my (belonging to me, mine)
myalgia
myall (Aus)
myceli/um - al
mycetoma
myco/sis - logy
mynah or mina (bird)
myocard-ium -itis
myology
myop/e - ia -ic
myo/sis -tic
  (MI)

MYR
myriad
myriapod
myrmidon
myrobalan
myrrh
myrt/le -aceous

(MER MIR MUR)
MYS
myself
mystagog/ue - ic
myster/y - ies - ious - iously
mystic - al - ally - ism
mystif/y - ies - ied - ying
  - ication
mystique
  (MIS)
MYTH
myth - ical - ically
mytholog/y - ies - ical - ically
  (METH)
MYX
myxodema
myxoma - tosis
  (MIX)

N
NAB-NAK
nab - bed - bing
nacelle
nacre - ous
nadir
nag - ged - ging - ger
naiad
naïf (see naïve)
nail - ed - ing - er - ery
nainsook
naïve - ly - ty (or - té F)
naked - ly - ness
  (KNA NEI)
NAM-NAP
namby - pamby
nam/e - ed - ing - ely - eless
  - able
namma (Aus)
nanc/y - ies
nankeen
nann/y - ies
nannygai (Aus)
nap - ped - ping (sleep,
  game); not knap (chip)
napalm
nape
napery
naphtha - lene or - line
napoo (from F, il n'y en a
  plus)

160

napp/y -ies, *for* napkin -s
  (KNA)
NAR
narciss/ism -istic
narciss/us -i
narcolepsy
narco/sis -tic -tically -tism
  -tist
nard
nardoo (*Aus*)
nark -ed -ing
narks *for* nitrogen narcosis
narrat/e -ed -ing -ion -ive -or
narrow -er -est -ed -ing -ly
  -ness -ish
narthex
narwhal
nary (never)
  (GNAR KNAR)
NAS
nasal -ly -ity -ise -ised -ising
  -isation (z)
nascen/t -cy
nassella (*NZ*)
nasturtium
nast/y -ier -iest -ily -iness
  (GNAS NAZ)
NAT
natal -ity
natat/ion (swimming) -ory
  -orial; *not* notation, nutation
nation -hood
national -ly -ity -ism -ist
nationalis/e -ed -ing -ation (z)
native
nativit/y -ies
natron
natter -ed -ing -er
natterjack
natt/y -ier -iest -ily -iness
natur/e -ed
natural -ly -ism -ist -istic
  -istically
naturalis/e -ed -ing -ation (z)
  (GNAT)
NAU
naught (nothing); *not*
  nought (0)
naught/y -ier -iest -ily -iness
nausea -te -ted -ting -tingly

nauseous -ly
nautch -girl
nautical -ly
  (GNAW NOR)
NAV
naval (of a navy); *not* navel
nave (of church); *not* knave
navel (umbilicus); *not* naval
navigat/e -ed -ing -ion -or
navigab/le -ly -ility
navv/y (labourer) -ies -ied
  -ying
nav/y -ies
  (KNAV)
NAW
  (GNAW NAU NOR)
NAY
nay (no); *not* neigh
  (NAI NEI)
NAZ
Nazar/eth -ene -ite
naze
nazi -(i)sm -fy -fied -fying
  -fication
  (NAS)
NEA
Neandertal (*or* -thal) -er
neap
Neapolitan (of Naples)
near -er -est -ed -ing -ly
  -ness
neat -er -est -ly -ness
  (KNE NEE NEI NIE)
NEB
neb (*Sc*)
nebul/a -ae -ar -ous -ously
  -osity
NEC
necessar/y -ies -ily
necessit/y -ies -ous -ously
  -ousness
necessitat/e -ed -ing -ion
neck -ed -ing
neckerchief
neck/lace -let
necroman/cy -cer -tic
necrophag/y -ous
necropolis
necrop/sy -tic
necro/sis -tic

161

nectar -y -ous -ine
(NEK NES)

NEE

née (*F*, born, maiden name)
need -ed -ing -y -ier -iest
 -iness -ily
need/ful -fully -fulness -less
 -lessly -lessness
needl/e -ed -ing
ne'er, *for* never
(KNE NEA NEI NIE)

NEF

nefarious -ly -ness
(NEPH)

NEG

negat/e -ed -ing -ion -ory
negativ/e -ed -ing -ely
 -eness -ity
neglect -ed -ing -ful -fully
 -fulness
negligé (*F*) -e
neglig/ent -ence -ently -ible
negotiat/e -ed -ing -ion -or
negotiab/le -ly -ility
negr/o -oes -ess -esses
negr/ito -itos -illo -illos -oid
negus
(NIG)

NEI

neice? *No,* niece
neigh (horse sound); *not* nay
neighbour -ly -liness -hood
neinei (*NZ*)
neither
(GNEI KNI NAI NAY NIE)

NEK

nekton
(NEC)

NEL

nell/y -ies
nelson
(KNEL)

NEM

nemato/de -id
nem. con., *for* nemine
 contradicente (*L*)
nemesis

nemonic? *No,* mnemonic

NEO

neo-*, *prefix meaning* new
neolithic
neolog/y -ism -ist -ise (z)
neon
neontolog/y -ist
neophron
neophyte
neoteric
neozoic
(NEU PNEU)

NEP

nepenthe
nephew
nephrit/is -ic
nephr/ology -otomy (ectomy)
nepot/ism -ist
Neptun/e -ian
neptunium
(NEF)

NER

nereid
Nero -nian
nervat/e -ion
nerv/e -y -ier -iest -ous
 -ously -ousness
nerv/ed -ing -iness -less
 -lessly -lessness
(KNUR NAR NIR NUR)

NES

ness
nest -ed -ing -ling
nestl/e -ed -ing
(NAS NEC)

NET

net (mesh) -ted -ting -ter
net *or* nett (after deductions)
nether -most
Netherland/s -er -ish
netsuke (*Jap*)
nettl/e -ed -ing

NEU

neur(o)-*, *prefix meaning*
 nerve
neural
neuralg/ia -ic

* If the word you wish to spell is not in this list, omit the prefix and look for the rest of the word.

neurasthen/ia -ic
neurectomy
neur/ine -itis -ology -ologist
 -ological
neuroma -ta
neuropath -y -ic -ology
 -ologist
neuropter/a -ous
neuro/sis -tic -tically
neurotomy
neusance? *No,* nuisance
neuter -ed -ing
neutral -ly -ity
neutralis/e -ed -ing -ation (z)
neutron
 (GNU KNEW NEW NU
 PNEU)

NEV
névé (*F*)
never
 (NEPH NETH)

NEW
new -er -est -ly -ness
newel
newfangled
Newfoundland -er
Newmarket
news -y -ier -iest -less
 -paper
newsance? *No,* nuisance
news -sheet
newt
Newton -ian
New Zealand -er
 (GNU KNEW NEU NU
 PNEU)

NEX
next
nexus

NGA
ngaio (*NZ*)

NIA-NID
Niagara
nialism? *No,* nihilism
nib -bed
nibbl/e -ed -ing -er
niblick
nic/e -er -est -ely -eness
nicet/y -ies
niche

nick -ed -ing
nickel
nickname
nicot/ine -inism -ian
nictat/e *or* nictitat/e -ed -ing
 -ion
nidif/y -ied -ying -ication
nidus
 (KNI NY)

NIE
niece
Nietzsche -an
 (GEI KNE KNI NEA NEI NY)

NIF
niff -y
nifty
 (KNIF)

NIG
niggard (stingy) -ly -liness
nigger (dark brown)
niggl/e -ed -ing
nigh -er -est
night (not day) -ly; *also*
 benighted; *not* knight
nightingale
nightjar
nightmare
night/y -ies
nigr/itude -escent -escence
 (KNI NEG)

NIH
nihil/ism -ist -istic

NIK
nikau palm (*NZ*)
 (NIC KNI)

NIL
nil
Nil/e -otic -ometer
 (NYL)

NIM
nimbl/e -y -er -est -eness
nimbus
niminy -piminy
 (NYM)

NIN
nincompoop
nin/e (9) -th -efold -esided
nineteen (19) -th -fold
ninet/y (90) -ies -ieth -yfold
ninn/y -ies

ninon

NIP

nip -ped -ping -py -pier
 -piest
nipple
Nippon -ian

NIR

nirvana
 (KNUR NER NUR)

NIS

nisi (*L*)
 (NAS NICE)

NIT

nit (louse egg); *not* knit
nitr/e -ate -ation -ic -ite -ous
nitrif/y -ied -ying -cation
nitro-*, *prefix meaning*
 combined with nitre
nitro/gen -genous
nitroxyl
nitty -gritty
nitwit
 (KNIT NIGHT)

NIX

nix

NO-NOD

no (negative); *not* know (ken,
 be aware of)
nob -by
nobbl/e (catch) -ed -ing -er
nobl/e -y -eness; *also*
 ennoble
nobility
noctiflorous
noctule
nocturnal
nocturne
nod -ded -ding -der -dle
nod/e -al -ose -osity -ical
nodul/e -ar -ate -ous -ose
 -ation
nod/us -i
 (KNO)

NOE NOI

noel
noetic
nog

noggin
no -hoper (*Aus*)
noil
nois/e -y -ier -iest -ily -eless
 -lessly
noisette
noisome -ness

NOL

 (KNO)

NOM

nomad -ic -ically -ism
nom de plume (*F*)
nomenclature
nominal -ly -ism -ist -istic
nominat/e -ed -ing -ion -ive
nominee
 (GNOM)

NON*

non -*, *prefix meaning* not
nonage
nonagenarian
nonary
nonce
nonchalan/ce -t -tly
nondescript
none (not any); *not* nun
nonentit/y -ies
nones
nonpareil
nonplus -sed
nonsens/e -ical -ically
 (NUN)

NOO

noodle
nook
noon -day -tide
noose
 (GNU NOU)

NOR

nor (neither); *not* gnaw
nor', *for* north
nordic
Norfolk
norm -ative
normal -ity -ly -ise -ised
 -ising -isation (z)
normalcy? (*Am for* normality)

* If the word you wish to spell is not in this list, omit the prefix
and look for the rest of the word.

Norman
Norse
north -ward -ing -ern -erner
 -erly
north -east -ern -erly
north -west -ern -erly
Nor/way -wegian
 (GNAW NAU)

NOS

nos/e -ed -ing -y -ier -iest -er
nostalg/ia -ic -ically
nostril
nostrum
 (GNOS NAS NOZ)

NOT

not (negative); *not* knot
 (intertwine)
notab/le -ly -ility
notar/y -ial -ially
notation (note); *not* natation
notch -es -ed -ing
not/e -ed -ing
nothing -ness
notic/e -ed -ing -eable -eably
notif/y -ies -ied -ying -ication
notion -al -ally
notochord
notori/ous -ously -ety
notornis
notwithstanding
 (KNOT)

NOU

nougat
nought (0); *not* naught
noumen/on -a -al -ally
noun
nourish -ed -ing -ment
nous (*Gr,* gumption)
nouveau riche (*F*)
 (GNU NOO NOW)

NOV

novel -ette -ist
novelt/y -ies
November
novena
novi/ce -ciate *or* -tiate
novacaine

NOW

now
nowadays

nowhere
 (KNO NOU)

NOX

noxious -ly -ness

NOZ

nozzl/e -ed
 (NOS)

NUA-NUL

nuance
nub
nubbl/e -y
nubil/e -ity
nuci/form -ferous -vorous
nuclear
nucle/us -i -al -ary -ate -ated
 -ating -ation
nucleol/e -ar -ate
nud/e -ity -ism -ist
nudg/e -ed -ing
nugatory
nugget -y
nuisance
null -ity -ify -ified -ifying
 -ification
nulla -nulla (*Aus*)
 (KNU NEU NEW)

NUM

numb -ed -ing -ness
number -ed -ing -less
numbles
numera/cy -te
numer/al -ation -able -ator
numeric -al -ally
numerous -ly -ness
numinous
numismat/ic -ism -ist -ology
numm/ary -ulary -ulite
numskull
 (NOM PNEUM)

NUN

nun -nery -neries -nish; *not*
 none
nunatak
nun -buoy
nunci/o -ature
nuncupat/e -ed -ing -ion
 (NON)

NUP

nuphar
nuptial -ly

NUR

nurs/e - ed - ing - ery - eling
nurtur/e - ed - ing
(KNUR NER NIR)

NUS

nusance? *No,* nuisance
(NAS NOS)

NUT

nut - ted - ting - ter - ty - tier
- tiest
nutat/e (of earth's axis; nod)
- ed - ing - ion; *not* mutation
nutmeg
nutria
nutri/ent - ative - ment
nutrit/ion - ious - iously
- iousness
(NEUT NEWT)

NUX

nux vomica (*L*)

NUZ

nuzzl/e - ed - ing

NY

nyctalopia
nyctitropic
nylghau
nylon
nymph - s - et
nympholep/sy - tic - t
nymphoman/ia - iac
nystagmus
(KNI NI)

O

O OA

O (*as in* 'O Lord, help me!')
not eau, owe, oh
o', *for* of
oaf - s (*or* oaves) - ish
oak - en
oakum
Oamaru stone (*NZ*)
oar (rowing); *not* or, o'er
oas/is - es
oast - house
oat - en - meal
oath - s
(HOA OW)

OBB-OBF

obbligato - s

obdura/te (stubborn) - tely - cy
obedien/t - tly - ce
obeisance
obelisk
obes/e - ity
obey - ed - ing
obfuscat/e - ed - ing - ion
(AB HOB)

OBI

obi (*Jap*)
obiit (*L*)
obituar/y - ies
(ABI ABY HOB)

OBJ

object - ed - ing - ion - ionable
- or; *not* abject (degraded)
objectif/y - ies - ied - ying
- ication
objectiv/e - ely - eness - ity
- ism - ist
objurgat/e - ed - ing - ion - ory
(ABJ)

OBL

oblate
oblat/ion - ory - ional
obligat/e - ed - ing - ion - ory
obligato? *No,* obbli
oblig/e - ed - ing - or - ee
obliqu/e - ely - ity
obliterat/e - ed - ing - ion
oblivi/on - ous - ously
- ousness
oblong
obloquy
(ABL)

OBN

obnoxious - ly - ness
(ABN HOBN)

OBO

obo/e - ist
(ABO HOB)

OBS

obscen/e - ity - ities - ely
obscurant - ism - ist
obscur/e - ed - ing - ity - ation
obsequi/es - al
obsequious - ly - ness
observ/ance - ant - antly
observ/e - ed - ing - er - ation
- ationally

observator/y -ies
obsess -ed -ing -ion
obsidian
obsolescen/t -ce
obsolete -ness
obstacle
obstetric -al -ally -ian
obstin/ate -ately -acy
obstreperous -ly -ness
obstruct -ed -ing -ion -ive
-ively -iveness
(ABS OPS)

OBT

obtain -ed -ing -able
obtrud/e -ed -ing
obtrus/ion -ive -ively
-iveness
obturat/e (stop up) -ed -ing
-ion -or
obtuse -ly -ness
(OPT)

OBV

obverse -ly
obver/t -sion
obviat/e -ed -ing -or
obvious -ly -ness

OCA

ocarina
(ACA OCC OKA)

OCC

occasion -ed -ing -al -ally
occident (west) -al -ally
-alism -alist
occidentalis/e -ed -ing -ation
(z)
occip/ut -ital
occlu/de -ded -ding -sion
-sive -sor
occult (cut off) -ed -ing -ation
occult (mysterious) -ly -ness
-ism -ist
occup/ation -ant -ancy
occup/y -ies -ied -ying -ier
occur -red -ring -rence
(ACC ACK HOC OX)

OCE-OCL

ocean -ic -ography

-ographical
ocell/us -i -ate
ocelot
ochr/e -ous
o'clock
(OSCI OSS)

OCT

oct * (octa-, octo-), *prefix
meaning* eight
octachord
octagon -al -ally
octahedr/on -al
octane
octant
octave
octavo (8vo) -s
octet *or* octette
October
octogenarian
octopus -es
octupl/e -ed -ing

OCU

ocular -ly -ist
oculist -ic
ocul(o) -*, *prefix meaning* eye
(ACCU ACU HOCU OCCU)

OD

odd -er -est -ly -ness -ity
-ment
odds
ode
Odeon
odious -ly -ness
odium
odonto -*, *prefix meaning*
tooth
odont/ology -oid
odontoglossum
odo/ur -rous
odoriferous -ly
odyssey -s
(AD HOD)

OE

(*The modern tendency,
especially in America, is to
reduce* oe *to* e; *so,* oe/*or* e/
-cology, -dema, *etc.*)

---

* If the word you wish to spell is not in this list, omit the prefix
and look for the rest of the word.

o'er, *short for* over; *not* oar
Oersted (Danish physicist;
  unit of magnetism)
oesophag/us - eal
oestrogen *or* estrogen

OF OFF
of (belonging to)
off (not on)
offal
offend - ed - ing - er
offence - less
offensive - ly - ness
offer - ed - ing
offertor/y - ies
offic/e - er
offici/al - ally - alism - ous
  - ously - ousness - alese
officialis/e - ed - ing - ation (z)
officiat/e - ed - ing - ion
offing
offish - ness
offset - ting
offspring
oft - en
  (AF OPH)

OG
ogee
ogiv/e - al
ogl/e - ed - ing - er
ogr/e - ess
  (HOG)

OH
oh! oho!
ohm - age - meter
  (OA)

OI
oil - ed - ing - y - ier - iest - er
ointment
Oireachtas (*Ir*)
  (HOI HOY OY)

OK
o.k.
okapi
  (HOC HOK OC)

OL
old - er - est - en - ster
oleaginous

oleander
oleograph - y - ic
olfact/ion - ory
oligarch - y - ic - ically
oligocene
oliv/e - ine - ary - aceous
olympiad
Olymp/us - ic - ian
  (AL HOL WHOL)

OM
ombudsman
omega (*Gr*)
omelet *or* omelette
omen
omicron (*Gr*)
ominous - ly - ness
omission (leaving out); *not*
  emission (giving off)
omit - ted - ting
omni *, *prefix meaning* all
omnibus
omnipoten/t - ce
omniscien/t - ce
omnium gatherum
omnivorous - ly - ness
omphalos
  (AM HOM)

ON
on - going - ward
onager
once - r
oncore? *No*, encore
one (1) - ness - r - self - sided;
  not won (did win)
onerous - ly - ness
onion
onlooker
only
onomatopoe/ia - ic - ically
onset
onslaught
onto *or* on to
ontolog/y - ical - ist
onus
onward - s
onyx
  (AN EN HON UN)

* If the word you wish to spell is not in this list, omit the prefix
and look for the rest of the word.

OO

oodles
oogene/sis - tic (*pronounced* o-o-)
oolit/e - ic (*pronounced* o-o-)
oolong
oom (*Dutch* uncle)
ooz/e - ed - ing - y - ier - iest - ily
  - iness
  (HOO OU WHO)

OP-OPE

op, *for* operation *or* opus
opacity; *but* opaque
opair? *No*, au pair (*F*)
opal - escent - escence
  - esque
opaqu/e - er - est - ely - eness;
  but opacity
open - ed - ing - er - ness - ly
  - able
opera - tic - tically
operat/e - ed - ing - ion - ive
  - ively
opercul/um - a - ar - ate - ated
operetta
  (AP HOP OPI)

OPH

ophicleide
ophidian
ophiolat/ry - er
ophit/e - ic
ophthalm/ia - ic - itis - ology
  - ologist - oscope
  (APH OFF)

OPI

opiate
opin/e - ed - ing
opinion - ated - ative
opium
  (OPE OPP)

OPO

opoponax
opossum
  (APO OPP)

OPP

oppidan
oppilat/e - ed - ing - ion
opponent
opportun/e - ity - ities - ism
  - ist - ely - eness

oppos/e - ed - ing - ition - er
opposite - ly - ness; *not*
  apposite (appropriate)
oppress - ed - ing - ion - or
oppressiv/e - ely - eness
opprobri/um - ous - ously
oppugn - ed - ing - er - ant
  - ance
  (OP HOP)

OPS

ops, *for* operations
opsimath - y - ic
opsonic
  (OBS)

OPT

opt - ed - ing - ant - ative
opthalmia? *No*, ophthalmia
optic - al - ally
optician
optim/ism - ist - istic - istically
optimis/e - ed - ing (z)
optim/um - a
option - al - ally
optomet/er - ry - ric - rist
  (OBT)

OPU

opulen/t - tly - ce
opus, opera
opuscul/e - um - a - ar
  (OPPU)

OR ORA

or
orac/le - ular
oracy
oral - ly
orange - ry - ade
orang - outang
orat/e - ed - ing - ion - or
oratorio
orator/y - ies - ian - ical - rically
  (AUR HOR ORR)

ORB

orb - ed
orbicul/ar - arity - ate
orbit - ed - ing - al
  (AUB)

ORC

Orcadian (of Orkney)
orchard
orchestr/a - al - ate - ated

-ating -ation
orch/id or orch/is -idaceous
orchil
orchitis
orchin
 (AUC AWK HAWK)

ORD
ordain -ed -ing; but
 ordination
ordeal
order -ed -ing -ly -liness
ordinal
ordinance (decree); not
 ordnance
ordinand
ordinar/y -ies -ily -iness
ordinate
ordin/ation -and -ee
ordnance (guns, survey); not
 ordinance
ordure
 (AUD HORD HOAR)

ORE
ore
oreide
 (AUR HOR OAR WHOR)

ORF
 (AWF OFF ORPH)

ORG
organ -ic -ically
organ/die -za
organism
organis/e -ed -ing -ation -er (z)
organist
organ/on -um
orgas/m -tic
org/y -ies -iastic
 (AUG)

ORI
oriel
orient -ed -ing -ate -ated
 -ating -ation
orienteer -ing
orient/al -ly -ism -ist
orientalis/e -ed -ing -ation (z)
orifice
oriflamme

origan -um
origin -al -ally -ality
originat/e -ed -ing -ion -or
oriole (bird)
Orion -id
orison (prayer); not horizon
 (AURI HORRI ORRI)

ORL
Orleans
orlon (fabric)
orlop (deck)
 (ALL AUL AWL HAU
 HAW)

ORM
ormolu
 (AUM HORM)

ORN
ornament -al -ally -ed -ing
 -ation
ornate -ly -ness
ornitholog/y -ical -ically -ist
ornithorhyncus
 (AWN HORN)

ORO
orogen/y -esis -etic -etically
orograph/y -ic -ically
oroide
orotund
 (AURO ERO HORO ORR)

ORP
orphan -ed -age -hood
Orph/eus -ean -ic
orpiment
orpine
Orpington

ORR
orrer/y -ies
orris -root
 (OR)

ORS
 (AUS HORS)

ORTH
orth(o) -*, prefix meaning
 right, straight
orthoclas/e -tic
orthodontic
orthodox -y

* If the word you wish to spell is not in this list, omit the prefix
and look for the rest of the word.

170

orthogonal
orthograph/y -ic -ical -ically
orthopaed/y -ic
orthopter/a -ous
orthoptic
orther? *No*, author
orthorhombic
(AUTH)

ORTO
ortolan
(AUTO)

OSC
oscar
oscillat/e (swing) -ed -ing
 -ion -or -ory
osculat/e (kiss) -ion -ory
(OCE OSS)

OSI-OSP
osier
osmium
osmo/sis -tic -tically
osmund
osprey -s
(HOS OZ)

OSS
oss/eous -uary -uaries -icle
ossif/y -ies -ied -ying -ication
ossifrage
(HOS OCE)

OST
ostensib/le -ly
ostentat/ion -ious -iously
osteo -*, *prefix meaning*
 bone
osteolog/y -ical
osteomyelitis
osteopath -y -ic
ostler
ostracis/e -ed -ing (z)
ostracism
ostrich
(AUST)

OT
other -ness -wise; *also*
 another
otic
otiose -ly -ness

otolog/y -ical
otter
ottoman
(AUT HOT)

OUB-OUS
oubliette
ouch!
ought (owe a duty); *not*
 aught
ouija
ounce
our (belonging to us); *not*
 hour
ours (*not* our's)
oursel/f -ves
ousel *or* ouzel
oust -ed -ing -er
(OO OW)

OUT*
out, *also used as prefix* *
 outer-
outage (time off)
outing
outlandish
outlaw -ed -ing -ry
outlay
outl/ier -ying
outrag/e -ed -ing -er
outrageous -ly -ness
outré (*F*)
outsid/e -er
outspan -ned -ning
outstanding -ly
outstrip -ed -ping
out-thrust
out-turn
outward
outwith (*Sc*)
(AUT)

OVA OVEN
ov/a -um -ary -arian -aritis
ov/al -ate
ovation
oven

OVER*
over, *also used as prefix* *
overdraft

* If the word you wish to spell is not in this list, omit the prefix
and look for the rest of the word.

over-eat-ate-eaten
overjoyed
over/lay (something laid over)
  -laid; *see footnote , p141*
over/lie (lie on top of) -lain
  -lying; *see footnote, p.141*
overrat/e -ed -ing
overreach -ed -ing
over/ride -rode -ridden
overrul/e -ed -ing
over/run -ran -running
overseer
overt -ly
overture
over-us/e -ed -ing
overweening
overwhelm -ed -ing
overwr/ite -ote -itten
overwrought
  (AVER HOVE)

OVI-OVU
ovi -duct -parous -positor
  -form
ovine (of sheep)
ovoid (egg-shaped)
ovolog/y -ist
ov/um -a -ule -ular

OW
ow/e -ed -ing
owl -ish -ishly -et
own -ed -ing -er
  (EAU HOW OA)

OX-OXT
ox - en
oxal/ate -ic
Oxford -ian *or* Oxonian
oxid/e
oxidis/e -ed -ing -ation -able
  (z)
oxter (*Sc*)
  (AUX OCCI)

OXY
oxy -acetyline
oxygen -ous
oxygenat/e -ed -ing -ion
oxygenis/e -ed -ing (z)
oxymoron
  (AUX OCCI)

OY
oyez! *or* oyes!

oyster
  (HOI HOY OI)

OZ
ozocerite *or* ozokerit
ozone
  (HOS)

PA PAB
pa *or* papa
pa *or* pah (*NZ*)
pabulum

PAC
pac/e -ed -ing -er
pachyderm -atous
pacific -ation -atory
pacif/ism -ist
pacif/y -ied -ying
pack -ed -ing -er -et
packag/e -ed -ing
pact
  (PAK PAS PEC)

PAD
pad -ded -ding -der
paddl/e -ed -ing -er
paddock
padd/y -ies
padlock -ed -ing
padre (*Sp*)
  (PED)

PAE
paella (*Sp*)
paean
  (PEA PEE)

PAG
pagan
pag/e -ed -ing
pagin/al -ate -ated -ating
  -ation
pageant -ry
pagoda

PAI
paid (did pay)
pail (bucket); *not* pale (faint)
pain (hurt) -ed -ing; *not* pane
  (window)
painful -ly -ness
painless -ly -ness
paint -ed -ing -er -erly
pair (set of two) -ed -ing; *not*

172

pare, pear
(PAY)
PAJ
(PAG PYJ)
PAK
pakeha (*NZ*)
Pakistan - i - is
(PAC)
PAL PALA
pal (friend) - ly - led - ling; *not*
pall
pala/ce - tial - tially
palais - de - danse (*F*)
paladin
palaeo - *or* paleo -*, *prefix
meaning* ancient
palaeograph/y - ic - er
palaeolithic
palaeontolog/y - ical - ist
palaeozoic
palanquin
palat/e - able - al - alise (z)
palatin/e - ate
palaver
(PALL PAL PEL)
PALE PALF
pal/e (faint) - er - est - ed - ing
- ely - eness
paleo -, *see* palaeo -
palette *or* pallet
palfrey
PALI
palimpsest
palindrom/e - ic
paling
palingene/sis - tic
palinode
palisade
(PALAE PALL PEL POLI)
PALL)
pall (cloth); *not* pal *or* pawl
pall (cloy) - ed - ing
Palladian
palladium
pallet *or* palette
palliasse
palliat/e - ed - ing - ion - ive

pallid - ly - ness
pallium
pallor
(PAL - PARL PAUL PER
PUL)
PALM
palm - ed - ing - er - y
palm/ar - ary
palmat/e - ed
palmiped - al
palmist - ry
(PARM)
PALP-PALT
palp - us - al
palpab/le - ly - ility
palpat/e - ed - ing
palpebral
palpitat/e - ed - ing - ion
palstave
pals/y - ied
palter - ed - ing
paltry
(PAUL)
PAMP
pampa - s (*Sp*)
pamper - ed - ing
pampero (*Sp*)
pamphlet - eer
PAN PANA
pan - *prefix meaning* all; e.g.
pan - African
pan - ned - ning
panacea
panache
Panama - nian
(PANN PANO)
PANC PAND
panchromatic
pancre/as - atic - atin
panda
pandemic
pandemonium
pander - ed - ing
pandit *or* pundit
Pandora
PANE
pane (glass); *not* pain

* If the word you wish to spell is not in this list, omit the prefix
and look for the rest of the word.

panegyr/ic -ical -ist
panegyris/e -ed -ing (z)
panel -led -ling -list
 (PAIN)

PANG-PANJ

pang
panga
pangolin
panic -ked -king -ky
panicle
panjandrum
 (PANN PENI)

PANN

pannage
panne (F)
pannier
pannikin
 (PAN-)

PANO

panopl/y -ies -ied
panopticon
panoram/a -ic -ically
 (PANA)

PANS

pans/y -ies
 (PANZ)

PANT

pant -ed -ing
pantal/oon -ette
pantechnicon
panthe/on -ism -ist -istic
panther
panties
pantile
pantograph -ic
pantomim/e -ic
pantoscop/e -ic
pantr/y -ies
pants
 (PENT)

PANZ

panzer (Ger)
 (PANS)

PAP

pap
papa
pap/acy -al -alism -alist -ist

 -istical
papaver/ous -aceous
paper -ed -ing -y
papier maché (F)
papoose
paprika
papyr/us -aceous
 (PEP PUP)

PAR

par (equal)
par, for paragraph

PARA*

para-*, prefix meaning either
 beyond or shelter
para, for paratrooper
parable
parabol/a -ic -ically
parachut/e -ed -ing -ist
paraclete
parad/e -ed -ing
paradigm -atic
paradis/e -al -iac -iacal
parados (mound behind
 trench)
paradox (seemingly absurd
 statement) -ical -ically
paraffin
paragon
paragraph -ic
parakeet or paroquet
parall/ax -active
parallel -ed -ing -ism -ogram
 -epiped
paraly/se -sed -sing -sis -tic
 -tically
parameter
paramount -cy -ly
paramour
paranoi/a -ac
parapet
paraphernalia
paraphras/e -ed -ing -tic
parapleg/ia -ic
paraquat
parasit/e -ic -ism -ology
 -icide
parasol

* If the word you wish to spell is not in this list, omit the prefix
and look for the rest of the word.

paravane
(PARR)

PARB

parboil - ed - ing
parbuckl/e - ed - ing

PARC

parcel - led - ling
parcen/er - ary
parch - ed - ing
parchment
(PARS PERC)

PARD

pardalote (*Aus*)
pardon - ed - ing - er - able
- ably
(PERD)

PARE

par/e (cut away) - ed - ing; *not*
pair *or* pear
paregoric
parent - al - ally - age - hood
parenthe/sis - ses - tic - tically
parenthesis/e - ed - ing (z)
parera (*NZ*)
paresis
par excellence (*F*)
(PER)

PARG

parget - ed - ing

PARI

pariah
parietal
Paris - ian
parish - es - ioner; *but*
parochial
parit/y - ies
(PARR PERI)

PARK-PARN

park - ed - ing - er
parka (*Eskimo,* garment)
parkin
parky; *not* parquet
parlance
parley - ed - ing
parliament - ary - arian
parlour
parlous
Parm/a - esan
Parnass/us - ian
(PER)

PARO

parochial - ly - ism
parod/y - ies - ied - ying - ist
parol/e - ed
paronomasia
paroquet *or* parakeet
parot/id - itis
paroxysm - al
(PARA PARR PERO)

PARQ

parquet (floor)
(PARK)

PARR

parr (young salmon) *not* par
parricide
parrot - ed - ing - ry
parr/y - ies - ied - ying
(PAR-)

PARS

pars/e - ed - ing
parsec
Parsee
parsimon/y - ious - iously
parsley
parsnip
parson - ic - age
(PAS PERC PERS)

PART

part - ed - ing - ible - ly; *also*
apart
partak/e - en - ing - er
partan (*Sc*)
parterre (*F*)
parthenogene/sis - tic
partial - ly - ity
participat/e - ed - ing - ion - or
particip/le - ial - ially
particle
particoloured
particular - ly - ity - ism
particularis/e - ed - ing - ation
(z)
partisan *or* partizan - ship
partition (division) - ed - ing;
not petition
partitive - ly
partner - ed - ing - ship
partridge
parturi/tion - ent
part/y - ies

(PERT)

PARV
parvenu
(PERV)

PAS-PASQ
pas (*F*)
paschal
pasha
pashence? *No*, patience
paspalum
pasque-flower
pasquinade
(PAC PARS PES)

PASS
pass - es - ed - ing - er - able
- ably
passag/e - ed - ing
passant (heraldry)
passé - e (*F*)
passenger
passe-partout (*F*)
passerine
passion - al - ate - ately
- ateness
passiv/e - ely - eness - ity
pass/over - port - word
passtime? *No*, pastime
(PARS)

PAST
past
pasta (*It*)
past/e - ed - ing
pastel
pastern
pasteuris/e - ed - ing - ation (z)
pastiche
pastille
pastime
pastor - al - ally - ate
pastr/y - ies
pastur/e - age
past/y - ies
(PARS)

PAT-PATE
pat - ted - ting
pataka (*NZ*)
patch - ed - ing - y - ily - iness
patchouli
pate (head) - ed
pâté (*F*)

patell/a - ar - ate
paten (plate); *not* patten
(overshoe)
patent - ed - ing - ly - ee
pater - nal - nally - nity
pater/familias - noster (*L*)
(PATT PET)

PATH
path - s
pathetic - ally; *not* apathetic
(unfeeling)
pathogen/y - ic - ous - esis
- etic
patholog/y - ical - ically - ist
pathos

PATI
patien/t - tly - ce
patina
patio (*Sp*)
(PATT)

PATR
patriarch - y - al - ally - ate
patrici/an - ate
patricid/e - al
patrimon/y - ial
patriot - ic - ically - ism
patristic
patrol - led - ling
patron - ess - age - al
patronis/e - ed - ing - ingly (z)
patronymic
(PETR)

PATT
patten (overshoe); *not* paten
(plate)
patter - ed - ing
pattern - ed - ing
patt/y - ies
(PAT-)

PAU
paua (*NZ*)
paucity
Paul - ine
paunch - y - iness
pauper - dom - ise - ised - ising
- isation (z)
paus/e - ed - ing
(PAW POR)

PAV
pavane (*F*)

176

pav/e -ed -ing -er -iour
pavement
pavilion

PAW

paw -ed -ing
pawk/y -ily -iness
pawl (lever with catch); *not*
  pall
pawn -ed -ing -ee -shop
pawpaw
  (PAU POO POR)

PAX

pax (*L*)
  (PAC PAK)

PAY

pay -ing -able -ment -er -ee;
  but paid
  (PAI)

PEA

pea -s *or* -se
peace -ful -fully -able -ably;
  not piece (portion)
peach -ed -ing -y -iness
pea/cock -hen -fowl
pea-jacket
peak -ed -ing -y; *not* peke
  (dog)
peal (of bells) -ed -ing; *not*
  peel
peanut
peaple? *No,* people
pear (fruit); *not* pair *or* pare
pearl (gem) -y -iness -ing
  -ies; *not* purl
pearmain
peasant -ry
peascod
pease-pudding
peat -y -iness
  (PEE PEI PIA)

PEB

pebbl/e -y iness
  (PAB)

PEC

pecan
peccab/le -ly -ility
peccadillo -es
peccan/t -cy
peccar/y -ies
peccavi! (*L*)

pêche Melba (*F*)
peck -ed -ing -er -ish
pect/en (zoology) -ines -inate
  -inated
pectin (chemistry) -ic
pectoral
pectose
peculat/e -ed -ing -ion -or
peculiar -ly -ity -ities
pecuniar/y -ily
  (PIC PERC)

PED

pedagog/ue -y -ical -ically
pedal (by foot) -led -ling -ler;
  not peddle
pedant -ic -ically -ry
pedate
peddl/e (retail) -ed -ing; *but*
  pedlar
pederast -y
pedestal -led
pedestrian
pedic/el -le -ellate -ulate
pedicul/ar -ous
pedicure
pedigree -d
pediment -ed -al
pedlar (small trader) -y; *not*
  pedaller
pedolog/y -ist
pedometer
  (PAD PERD)

PEE

pee (urinate) -d -ing ; *not* pea
peel (skin) -ed -ing; *not* peal
  (bells)
peen
peep -ed -ing -er
peeple? *No,* people
peer (look) -ed -ing; *not* pier
  (landing-stage)
peer (lord, equal) -age -less
  -lessly
peev/ish -ishly -ed
peewit
  (PEA PIE)

PEG-PEK

peg -ged -ging
pejorative -ly
pekan

177

peke, *for* pekinese; *not* peak
  (point)
pekoe
  (PAG)

PEL

pelargonium
pelerine
pelf
pelican
pelisse; *not* police
pellagra
pellet - ed
pellic/le - ular
pellitory
pell - mell
pellucid - ly - ity
pelmet
pelorus
pelota
pelt - ed - ing
pelv/is - ic
  (PAL)

PEM

pemmican
  (PAM PIM)

PEN-PENA

pen - ned - ning - manship;
  also pent (penned)
penal - ly
penalis/e - ed - ing - ation (z)
penalt/y - ies
penance
penannular
  (PAN PENN)

PENC

pence (pennies)
pencil - led - ling - ler
  (PENS)

PEND

pend - ed - ing
pendant (ornament)
pendent (hanging)
pendul/um - ous - ate - ine

PENE

penepla/in - nation
penetrat/e - ed - ing - ion
  - ingly - ive

penetrab/le - ility
  (PENN PENI)

PENG

penguin

PENI

penicill/in - ate
peninsula
peninsular (belonging to a
  peninsula) - ity
pen/is - es - ial
peniten/t - ce - tial - tly - tiary
  (PENE PENN PERN)

PENK-PENN

penkni/fe - ves
pennant (flag)
penni/form - ferous
pennon (flag)
penn'orth
penn/y - ies (*or* pence) - iless
pennyroyal
  (PEN-)

PENO

penolog/y - ist - ical
  (PENN)

PENS

pensile (hanging down)
pension - able - ary - er
pensive - ly - ness
penstock
  (PENC)

PENT

pent *or* penned
pent -*, *prefix meaning* five
penta/cle - gram
pentad
pentadactyl - ic
pentagon - al
pentahedr/on - al
pentameron
pentameter
pentane
pentateuch - al
pentathlon
pentatonic
pentecost - al
penthouse *or* pentice
pentode

* If the word you wish to spell is not in this list, omit the prefix
and look for the rest of the word.

pentstemon
(PANT)

PENU

penultimate
penumbra
penur/y -ious -iously
(PENA PNEU)

PEO

peon (*Sp*); *not* paean (song)
peon/y -ies
peopl/e -ed -ing

PEP

pep -ped -ping -py
pepper -ed -ing -y
pep/sin -tic -tone
(PAP PIP)

PER PERA

per (*L*, by)
per-*, *prefix used in
chemistry, e.g.,* perchloride
peradventure
perambulat/e -ed -ing -ion
-or -ory
(PARA PUR)

PERC

perceiv/e -ed -ing
percent -age -ile
percept -ion -ional -ible
-ibility
perceptiv/e -ely -eness -ity
perch -ed -ing -er
perchance
percheron
percipien/ce -t -tly
percolat/e -ed -ing -ion -or
percuss -ed -ing -ion -ive
percutaneous
(PEC PERK PURS)

PERD

perdition
perdue (*F*)
perdurab/le -ly -ility
(PARD PED PURD)

PERE

père (*F*)
peregrinat/e -ed -ing -ion -or
peregrine

peremptor/y -ily -iness
perennial -ly -ity
(PARE PERR)

PERF

perfect -ed -ing -ly -ible
-ibility
perfection -ist -ism
perfervid
perfid/y -ious -iously
perforat/e -ed -ing -ion -or
perforce
perform - ed -ing -er
perfum/e -ed -ing -er -ery
perfunctor/y -ily -iness

PERG

pergola
(PERJ PURG)

PERH

perhaps

PERI*

per-*, *prefix meaning* around
peri (fairy)
perianth
pericard/ium -iac -ial -itis
pericarp
periclin/e -al
perigee
perihelion
peril -ous -ously
perimeter
perineum
period -ic -ical -ically -icity
peripatetic -ally
peripher/y -al -ally
perphras/is -tic -tically
periscop/e -ic
perish -ed -ing -ingly -able
-ableness
peristal/sis -tic -tically
peristyle
periton/eum (*or* /aeum) -itis
-eal
periwig
periwinkle
(PARI PERE)

PERJ

perjur/e -ed -ing -y -ious

---

* If the word you wish to spell is not in this list, omit the prefix
and look for the rest of the word.

-iously
(PURG)

PERK

perk - ed - ing - y - ier - iest - ily
-iness
perks, *for* perquisites
(PEC PERC PERQ)

PERL

perlite (geol.); *not* polite
(PEAR PEL POL PURL)

PERM

perm, *for* permutation *or*
'permanent' wave
permafrost
permalloy
permanen/t - tly - ce - cy
permangan/ate - ic
permeat/e - ed - ing - ion
perme/able - ability - ance
-ant
Permian
permiss/ion - ive - ively
-iveness - ible - ibly
permit - ted - ting
permut/e - ed - ing - ation

PERN

pernicious - ly - ness
pernickety
pernoctation
(PEN)

PERO

perorat/e - ed - ing - ion
peroxide
(PARO)

PERP

perpend
perpendicular - ly - ity
perpetrat/e - ed - ing - ion - or
perpetu/al - ally - ity
perpetuat/e - ed - ing - ion - or
perplex - ed - ing - ity - ingly
-edly
(PURP)

PERQ

perquisite
(PECU)

PERR

perry
(PER PUR)

PERS

persecut/e - ed - ing - ion - or
Perse/us - id
persever/e - ed - ing - ance
-ingly
Persia - n
persiflage
persimmon
persist - ed - ing - ent - ently
-ence - ency
person - al - ally - ality - able
-age
persona grata (*L*)
personalis/e - ed - ing - ation
(z)
personalty (personal estate)
personat/e - ed - ing - ion - or
personif/y - ies - ied - ying
-ication
personnel
perspective - ly
perspex
perspicac/ious (discerning)
-iously - ity
perspicu/ous (clear in
meaning) - ously - ity
perspir/e - ed - ing - ation
-atory
persuad/e - ed - ing - able - er
persuas/ion - ive - ively
-iveness
(PERC PURS)

PERT

pert - ly - ness
pertain - ed - ing
pertinac/ity - ious - iously
pertinen/t - tly - ce - cy
perturb - ed - ing - ation
(PART PET POT PRET)

PERU

Peru - vian
peruke
perus/e - ed - ing - al
(PRU)

PERV

pervad/e - ed - ing
pervas/ion - ive - ively
-iveness
pervers/e - ely - eness - ity
-ion - ive

pervert - ed - ing - ible
pervious - ly - ness
  (PAV PURV)

PES

peseta, peso
pessar/y - ies
pessim/ism - ist - istic
  - istically
pest - ology - ologist - icide
  - iferous
pester - ed - ing
pestilen/ce - t - tly - tial
pestle
  (PIS)

PET-PETI

pet - ted - ting
petal - led
petard
peter (out) - ed - ing
petersham
pethetic? *No,* pathetic
pethology? *No,* pathology
petiol/e - ar - ate
petit(s) four(s) (*F*)
petit mal (*F*)
petite (*F*)
petition (ask) - ed - ing - er; *not*
  partition
  (PAT PERT PET PIT POT)

PETR

petrel (bird); *not* petrol
petrif/y - ies - ied - ying - action
petrograph/y - ic - er
petrol - eum; *not* patrol
  (march)
petrolog/y - ist
petrous
  (PATR)

PETT

petticoat
pettifogging
pettish - ly - ness
pettitoes (pigs' feet); *not*
  potatoes
pett/y - ier - iest - ily - iness
  (PATT)

PETU

petulan/ce - t - tly
petunia
  (PERT)

PEW

pew
pewter
  (PU)

PHA

phagocyte
phalange - al
phalanger
phalan/x - xes *or* - ges
phalarope
phall/us - ic - icism
phanerogam - ic - ous
phantasm - al - ally - ic
phantasmagor/ia - ic
phantas/y - ies, *or* fantasy
phantom
pharaoh
pharis/ee - aic - aically - aism
pharmac/y - ies - eutical
  - eutically
pharmacolog/y - ist
pharmacopoeia
pharos
pharyn/x - gal - geal - gitis
  - gotomy
phas/e - ed - ing
  (FA PHE PHI)

PHE

pheasant
phenacetin
phen/ol - olic - yl
phenolog/y - ical
phenomen/on - a - al - ally
  - alism - alistic
phew!
  (FE PHA PHI PHOE PHY)

PHI

phi (*Gr*)
phial (small bottle); *not* file
phil - *, *prefix meaning* lover
  of
philander - ed - ing - er
philanthrop/ist - ic - ical - ically

---

* If the word you wish to spell is not in this list, omit the prefix
and look for the rest of the word.

philanthrop/y -ise -ised -ising
   (z)
philatel/y -ic -ist
philharmonic
philippic
philistin/e -ism
phillumenist
philolog/y -ical -ically -ist
philoprogenitive -ness
philosoph/y -ies -ic -ical
   -ically -er
philosophis/e -ed -ing (z)
philtre (love potion); *not* filter
   (FI PHA PHE PHY)

PHL
phlebitis
phlebotom/y -ise -ised -ising
   (z)
phlegm -atic -atically
phlegmon -ic -ous
phloem
phlogiston
phlorizin
phlox (plant)
   (FL)

PHOB-PHOE
phobia
Phoenicia -n
phoenix -es
   (FO)

PHON
phon-*, phono-*, *prefix
   meaning* sound
phon
phon/ate -ation -atory
phone, *for* telephone
phonem/e -ic
phonetic -ally -ian -ist
phoney *or* phony
phonic
phonogram
phonograph -y -ic -ically
phonolite
phonolog/y -ical -ically -ist
phonotype
   (FON)

PHOR
phormium
   (FAL FAU FAW FOR
   FOUR)

PHOS
phosgene
phosph/ine -ate -atic -ide -ite
phosphor-bronze
phosphor/us -ic -ous
phosphoro/genic -graphic
   -scopy
phossy-jaw
   (FOS)

PHOTO
photo-*, *prefix meaning* light
photogenic
photograph -y -ic -ically -er
photogravure
photon
photophobia
photosphere
photostat
photosynthesis

PHR
phras/e -ed -ing
phraseo/logy -gram -graph
phrenetic -ally
phrenolog/y -ical -ically -ist
   (FR)

PHT
phthis/is -ical

PHU
phut
   (FU)

PHYL
phylacter/y -ies
phylloxera
phyl/um -a -etic
   (FIL PHIL)

PHYS
physic -al -ally
physician
physicist
physiognom/y -ic -ically
physiograph/y -ic -er
physiolog/y -ic -ical -ically
   -ist

* If the word you wish to spell is not in this list, omit the prefix
and look for the rest of the word.

physiotherap/y -eutic -ist
physique
  (FIS FIZZ)
PHYT
phyto -*, *prefix meaning*
  plant
phytogen/y -esis
phytography
phytomer
phytozoon
  (FIGHT)
PI PIA
pi (*Gr*, 3.14159)
pi, *for* pious
pian/o -oforte -ist
piano (*p*), pianissimo (*pp*) (*It*)
pianola
piastre
piazza (*It*)
  (PIE PIO PY)
PIB
pibroch (*Sc*)
PIC
pica
picador
picar/oon (rogue) -esque
picayune (insignificant)
piccalilli (pickle)
piccaninn/y (child) -ies
piccolo
pick -ed -ing -er
pick -a -back
pickerel
picket -ed -ing
pickl/e -ed --ng
Pickwick -ian
picnic -ked -king
pico -*, *prefix meaning*
  a million -millionth of
picot
picric
Pict -ish
pictorial -ly
pictur/e -ed -ing -ise -ised (z)
picturesque -ly -ness
  (PIQU PYK)

PID
piddl/e -ed -ing
piddock
pidgin (business); *not* pigeon
pi -dog *or* pye -dog
PIE
pie
piebald
piec/e (portion) -ed -ing -er;
  also apiece; *not* peace
piecemeal
pied
pier (landing stage); *not* peer
  (lord, stare)
pierc/e -ed -ing -ingly
pierr/ot -ette
pieta (*It*)
piet/y -ism -ist -istic; *but*
  pious
  (PIA PIO)
PIF
piffl/e -ing
PIG
pig -gy -gies -let -ling -gery
  -geries
piggish -ly -ness
pigeon (bird) -ry; *not* pidgin
  (business)
pigment
pigm/y *or* pygm/y -ies
pigtail -ed
  (PYG)
PIK
pike
pikelet
piker
  (PIC PIQU PYK)
PIL
pilaster
pilaff *or* pilau
pilch
pilchard
pil/e -ed -ing
pilfer -ed -ed -ing -er
pilgrim -age
pili/form -ferous
pill

* If the word you wish to spell is not in this list, omit the prefix
and look for the rest of the word.

pillag/e -ed -ing -er
pillar
pillion
pillory
pillow -ed -ing -y
pilos/e -ity
pilot -age
pilul/e -ar -ous
(PYL)

PIM
pimento
pimp -ed -ing
pimpernel
pimpl/e -ed -ing -y
(PEM)

PIN
pin -ned -ning
pinafor/e -ed
pince -nez (F)
pincers
pinch -ed -ing -er
pinchbeck
pin/e -ed -ing -ery -y
pineal
pinfold
ping -ed -ing -pong
pinion -ed -ing
pink -er -est -ness -y -ish
pink -ed -ing
pinnace
pinnacl/e -ed
pinnate -ly
pinnule
pinny, for pinafore
pint
pintle
(PEN)

PIO
pioneer -ed -ing
piopio (NZ)
pious -ly -ness; but piety
(PIA PIE PYO)

PIP
pip -ped -ping -py -less
pip/e -ed -ing -er
pipette
pipistrelle
pipit
pipkin
pippin

pip -squeak
(PEP)

PIQ
piquan/t -tly -cy
piqu/e -ed -ing
piqué (fabric)
piquet (card game)
(PIC PIK)

PIR
pira/te -tical -tically -cy
pirouett/e -ed -ing
(PER PUR PYR)

PIS
pis aller (F)
piscator/y -ial
piscicultur/e -al -ist
piscina
piscin/e -ivorous
pisé
pish!
piss -ed -ing -er
pistachio -s
pistil (of flower) -late -lary
 -line
pistol (gun)
piston
(PES PIZ)

PIT
pit -ted -ting -tite
pit -a -pat
pitch -ed -ing -y
pitcher (jug); not picture
pitchfork
pitchi (Aus)
piteous -ly -ness ; see pity
pith -y -ily -iness
pithecanthrop/e -us -oid
pithecoid
pithon? No, python
piti/ful -fully -able -ably; see
 pity
pitiless -ly -ness; see pity
piton
pittance
pitter -patter
pittosporum
pituit/ary -ous -rin
pituri (Aus)
pit/y -ies -ied -ying; but
 piteous

PIU

piupiu (*NZ*)
(PEW PIO PU)

PIV-PIZ

pivot -ed -ing -al
pixy *or* pixie, pixies
pizza (*It*)
pizzicato (*It*)
pizzle
(PY)

PLAC

placab/le -ility
placard
placat/e -ed -ing -ory
plac/e (position) -ed -ing -er;
   not plaice (fish)
placebo
placent/a -ae -al
placid -ly -ity
plack? *No,* plaque
placket
(PLAS PLAQ)

PLAG

plage (*F*)
plagiar/y -ism -ist
plagiaris/e -ed -ing (z)
plagu/e -ed -ing -ily -y -ier
   -iest

PLAI

plaice (fish)
plaid (*Sc*)
plain -er -est -ly -ness; *not*
   plane (flat)
plaint -iff
plaintive -ly -ness
plait (entwine) -ed -ing; *not*
   plat
(PLAY)

PLAN

plan -ned -ning -ner
planchette
plan/et (flat) -ed -ing -ation;
   not plain
planet -ary -oid -esimal
planetar/ium -ia
plangen/t -tly -cy
planimet/er -ric -rical -ry

planish -ed -ing -er
planispher/e -ic
plank -ed -ing
plankton
plant -ed -ing -er -ation
plantain
plant/ar -igrade
(BLAN)

PLAQ

plaqu/e -ette
(PLAC)

PLAS

plash -ed -ing -y
plasm -a -ic -atic -odium
   -odia
plasmolys/e -ed -ing -is
plaster -ed -ing -er
plastic -ally -ity
plasticis/e -ed -ing -er (z)
plasticine (modelling clay);
   not pleistocene
plastisol
plastron
(PLAC)

PLAT

plat (plot of ground); *not* plait
   (entwine)
plat/e -ed -ing -er -eful
plateau -x *or* -s
platen
platform -ed
platin/um -oid -ic -iferous
platinotype
platitud/e -inous -inously
platonic (of Plato, asexual
   love) -ally; *not* plutonic (of
   Pluto, rocks)
platoon
platter
platypus -es
platyrrhine
(BLAT)

PLAU

plaudits
plausib/le -ly -lity

PLAY

play -ed -ing -er -ful -fully

---

* If the word you wish to spell is not in this list, omit the prefix
and look for the rest of the word.

-fulness
playwright
  (PLAI)

PLEA

plea
pleach - ed - ing
plead - ed (pled, *Sc*) - ing
  - ingly - er
pleasant - ly - ness - ry
pleas/e - ed - ing - ingly
pleasur/e - ed - ing - able - ably
pleat - ed - ing
  (PLE-)

PLEB-PLEI

pleb - s - eian
plebiscite
plectrum
pledg/e - ed - ing - able - er - ee
Pleistocene (geology)
  (PLI PLY)

PLEN-PLEX

plenar/y - ily
plenipotentiary
plenitude
plenteous - ly - ness
plent/y - iful - ifully - ifulness
plenum
pleonas/m - tic - tically
plesiosaurus
plethor/a - ic - ically
pleur/a - isy - itic
plex/or - imeter
plex/us - iform
  (PLEA PLI)

PLI

pliab/le - ly - ility; *but* ply
plian/t - tly - cy
plicat/e - ed - ing - ion
pliers
plight - ed - ing
plimsoll
plinth
Pliocene
plissé (fabric)
  (PLEI PLY)

PLO

plod - ded - ding - dingly - der

plonk
plop - ped - ping
plosive - ly
plot - ted - ting - ter
plough - ed - ing
ploughshare
plover
ploy

PLU

pluck - ed - ing
pluck/y - ier - iest - ily - iness
plug - ged - ging
plum (fruit) - my - mier - miest
plumage
plumb (measure depth) - ed
  - ing
plumbag/o - aginous
plumb/er - ery
plumb/ic - iferous - ism
plum/e - ed - ing - ose - y
plummer - block
plummet - ed - ing
plump - er - est - ed - ing
plumul/e - er - aceous
plunder - ed - ing - age
plung/e - ed - ing - er
pluperfect
plural - ly - ity - ism - ist - istic
pluralis/e - ed - ing - ation (z)
plus
plush - y - ier - iest
Pluto - nic; *not* platonic
plutocra/t - tic - cy
plutonium
pluvi/al - ous - ometer
  (PLEU)

PLY

pl/y - ied - ying; *but* pliable
  (PLEI PLI)

PNEU

pneuma - *, pneumo - *, *prefix
  meaning* air
pneumatic - ally
pneumocyst
pneumogastric
pneumolog/y - ical
pneumon/ia - ic

* If the word you wish to spell is not in this list, omit the prefix
and look for the rest of the word.

PO-POD

po, *for* pot, po-faced
poach -ed -ing -er
poaka (*NZ*)
pochard
pock -s *or* pox
pocket -ed -ing
pod -ded -ding -dy
podagr/a -al -ic -ous
podg/e -y -ier -iest
podi/um -a

POE

poe/m -t -try -sy
poetic -al -ally
poeticis/e -ed -ing (z)
(POI)

POI

poi (*NZ*)
poignan/t -tly -cy
poinsettia
point -ed -ing -er -less
 -lessly -lessness
pointill/ism -ist
pois/e -ed -ing
poison -ed -ing -er -ous
 -ously
(POE)

POK

pok/e -ed -ing -er
pok/y -ier -iest
(POC POLK)

POLA-POLE

Po/land -le -lish
polar -ity
polari/meter -metric -scope
 -scopic
polaris/e -ed -ing -ation (z)
polder -ed -ing
pol/e -ed -ing -er -eward; *not*
 poll (voting)
pole -axe
polecat
polemic -al -ally
polenta (*It*)
(POLL)

POLI

polic/e -ed -ing -eman

polic/y -ies
polio, *for* poliomyelitis
polish -ed -ing -er
Polish (of Poland)
polit/e -er -est -ely -eness
politic -al -ally -ian
polit/y -ies
(POLL POLY)

POLK

polka
(POK)

POLL

poll -ed -ing -able -ater
pollack *or* pollock
pollard -ed -ing
pollen
pollinat/e -ed -ing -ion
pollut/e -ed -ing -ion
(POL-)

POLO

polo
polonaise
polonium
polon/y -ies
(PELO)

POLT

poltergeist
poltroon -ery
(PALT POUL)

POLY*

poly-*, *prefix meaning* many
polyacetal
polyamide
polyandr/y -ous -ously -ist
polyanthus
polycarpous
polyester
polyethylene
polygam/y -ous -ously -ist
polyglot -tal -tic -tism
polygon (shape) -al -ally
polygonum (plant)
polyhedr/on -al -ic
polymath
polymer -ous -ic -ism
polymeris/e -ed -ing -ation (z)
polymorph -ous -ic -ism

---

* If the word you wish to spell is not in this list, omit the prefix
and look for the rest of the word.

polynomial
polyp -ary -oid
polyphon/y -ic -ous
polypod
polypropylene
polyvinyl chloride (PVC)
polytechnic -al
polythene
polyurethane
polyzo/a -ic
  (POLI POLL)

POM

pom, *for* Pomeranian dog
pom -mie *or* -my (*Aus*)
pomace (crushed apples);
  not pumice
poma/de -tum -ded -ding
pomander
pom/e -iculture -iferous
pomegranate
pomelo -s
Pomerania -n
pomfret
pommel (of saddle, etc.); *not*
  pummel (hit)
pomolog/y -ical -ist
pomp -ous -ously -osity
Pompadour
Pompey
pompier
pom-pom
  (PUM)

PON

ponce
poncho -s
pond -ed -ing -age
ponder -ed -ing -ingly -able
  -ability
ponder/ous -ously -ousness
  -osity
pongee
pong/o -oid
poniard
pons asinorum (*L*)
pontifex (*L*)
pontif/f -ical -ically -icate
pontoon
pon/y -ies
  (PUN)

POO

poodle
poodle -fak/er -ing
pooh -pooh!
pool -ed -ing
poop -ed -ing
poor (needy) -er -est -ly
  -ness; *not* pore, pour
  (POU PU)

POP

pop, *for* popular
pop -ped -ping
pop/e -ish; *but* papal
popery; *not* pot -pourri (*F*)
pop -eyed
popinjay
poplar (tree); *not* popular
poplin
poppet
poppl/e -ed -ing -y
popp/y -ies
poppycock
popul/ace -ous -ousness
popular -ly -ity
popularis/e -ed -ing -ation (z)
populat/e -ed -ing -ion
popul/ism -ist
  (PUP)

PORC-PORR

porcelain
porcellan/eous -ic -ous
porch -ed
porcine
porcupine
por/e (small opening) -ous
  -ousness -osity
por/e (read intently) -ed -ing;
  not poor *or* pour
pork -er -ling -y -ier -iest
pornograph/y -ic
poroporo (*NZ*)
porphyry
porpoise
porridge
porrig/o -inous
porringer
  (PAU PAW POOR POUR)

PORT

port -ed -ing -er -able -ability
portag/e -ed -ing

portal
portamento (*It*)
portcullis
portend (foreshadow) - ed
 - ing; *not* pretend
portent (omen) - ous - ously;
 not pretentious
portfolio - s
porthole
portico - s
portion - ed - ing
Portland
portly
portmanteau - s *or* - x
portrait - ure - ist
portray - ed - ing - al
Portu/gal - guese

POSE-POSS

pos/e - ed - ing - er
poseur (*F*)
posh
posies (posy)
posit - ed - ing
position - ed - ing - al
positive - ly - ness
positiv/ity - ism - ist - istic
positron
posse
possess - es - ed - ing - ion - or
possessive - ly - ness
posset
possib/le - ly - ility - ilities
possum, *for* opossum

POST*

post - ed - ing - age - al - man
 - haste
post - *, *prefix meaning* after
poster
poste restante (*F*)
posterior - ity
posterity
postern
posthumous
postillion
post meridiem (*L*, p.m.)
post mortem (*L*)
postpon/e - ed - ing - ement

postscript (p.s.)
postula/te - ted - ting - tion
 - tor - nt
postur/e - ed - ing - er - al

POSY

pos/y - ies
 (POSI)

POT

pot - ted - ting - ful - ter - tery
pot, *for* potential
potable
potage (*F*)
potash *or* potass
potass/ium - ic
potat/ion - ory
potato - es
poteen *or* potheen
poten/t - tly - cy - tate
potential - ly - ity
potentiometer
pother (fuss) - ed - ing; *not*
 bother
pothol/e - ed - ing - er
potion
potoroo (*Aus*)
pot - pourri (*F*)
potsherd
pottage
potter - ed - ing - er
potter/y - ies
potto
potty

POU POV

pouch - ed - ing - y
pouffe (*F*)
poult (fabric)
poulterer
poultic/e - ed - ing
poultry
pounc/e - ed - ing
pound - ed - ing - er
poundage
pour (make flow) - ed - ing
 - er; *not* poor, pore
pout - ed - ing - ingly - er
poverty
 (POO POW)

---

* If the word you wish to spell is not in this list, omit the prefix
and look for the rest of the word.

POW

powder - ed - ing - y - iness
power - ful - fully - less - lessly
powwow

POX

pox
(POC POK)

PRA

practicab/le - ly - ility
practical - ly - ity - ness
practice (*e.g.*, his practice)
practis/e (*e.g.*, we practise)
 - ed - ing
practitioner
pragmat/ic - ically - ism - ist
prairie
prais/e - ed - ing - eful - efully
 - efulness
praiseworth/y - ily - iness
praline
pram, *for* perambulator
prang - ed - ing
prank - ish - ishness
prank - ed - ing
prat/e - ed - ing - er
prattl/e - ed - ing - er
prawn - ing
pray (ask) - ed - ing - er
prayer - ful - fully - fulness

PRE*-PREB

pre-*, *prefix meaning* before
preach - ed - ing - er - y - iness
preamble
prebend - al - ary - aries
(PROB)

PRE*C

precarious - ly - ness
precaution - ary
preced/e (go before) - ed
 - ing; *not* proceed (go)
preced/ent - ented - ence
precentor
precept - ive - or - orial
precession (astron.) - al; *not*
 procession
precinct
preci/ous - ously - ousness

 - osity
precipice
precipitat/e - ed - ing - ion
precipit/ous - ously - ousness
précis (*F*)
precis/e - ly - eness - ion - ian
preclu/de - ded - ding - sive
precoci/ty - ous - ousness
precurs/or - ory - ive
(PRES PRIS PROC)

PRE*D

preda/tor - tory - cious - city
predecessor
predial
predic/able (affirmable) - ably
 - ability; *not* predictable
predicament
predicant
predicat/e (affirm) - ed - ing
 - ion - ive - ory
predict (foretell) - ed - ing - ion
 - or
predictab/le - ly - ility
predilection
(PREJ PROD)

PRE*E

pre - eminen/t - tly - ce
pre - empt - ed - ing - ion - ive
preen - ed - ing
(PREA PRIE)

PRE*F

prefab, *for* prefabricated
 house
prefa/ce - ced - cing - tory
 - torial
prefect - orial
prefectur/e - al
prefer - red - ring - ence - able
 - ably - ment
preferential - ly
prefix - ed - ing
(PROF)

PRE*G-PRE*M

pregnable
pregnan/t - tly - cy
prehensil/e - ity
prehension

* If the word you wish to spell is not in this list, omit the prefix
and look for the rest of the word.

prejudic/e - ed - ing - ial - ially
prela/te - ture - tic - cy
prelim, for preliminary
preliminar/y - ies - ily
prelu/de - sive
premier
première (F)
premis/e - ed - ing (not z)
premises (houses, etc.)
premiss (in logic) - es
premium
  (PRA PRO)

PRE*N

prenatal
prentice, for apprentice
  (PRON)

PRE*P PRE*R

prep, for prepara/tion - tory
prepar/e - ed - ing - edness
preparat/ion - ive - ively
preparator/y - ies - ily
prepense
preponder/ate - ated - ating
  - ant - antly - ance
preposition - al - ally
preposterous - ly - ness
prepu/ce - tial
prerogative
  (PROP)

PRE*S

presag/e - ed - ing - eful
presbyop/ia - ic
presbyter - ian - ianism - y - ial
prescien/t - tly - ce
prescrib/e (order) - ed - ing;
  not proscribe (condemn)
prescript - ion - ive - ively
presence
present - ed - ing - er - ee
  - ment
presentab/le - ly - ility
presentat/ion - ional - ive
presenti/ent - ment - ve
presently
preserv/e - ed - ing - ation
  - ative - er
preservab/le - ly - ility

presid/e - ed - ing - iary
presiden/t - tial - tially - cy
presidium
press - ed - ing - ingly - er
pressur/e - ise - ised - ising
  - isation (z)
prestidigitat/ion - or - ory
prestig/e - ious
prest/o - issimo (It)
prestress - ed
presum/e - ed - ing - able - ably
  - ingly - edly
presumpt/ion - ive - ively
  - uous - uously - uousness
  (PREC PROS)

PRE*T

pretence
pretend - ed - ing - edly - er
preten/sion - tious - tiously
  - tiousness
preterit/e - ion
pretermit - ted - ting
preternatural - ly
pretext
prett/y - ier - iest - iness - ily
  - yish
prettif/y - ied - ying
  (PROT)

PRE*V

prevail - ed - ing - ingly
prevalen/t - tly - ce
prevaricat/e - ed - ing - ion - or
prevenient
prevent - ed - ing - ion - er
  - able or - ible
preventive - ly
previous - ly - ness
  (PROV)

PREY

prey (hunt) - ed - ing; not pray
  (ask)

PRIC-PRIG

pric/e - ed - ing - eless - ey
prick - ed - ing - er
pricket
prick/le - ed - ing - y - iness
prid/e - ed - ing - eful - efully;

---

* If the word you wish to spell is not in this list, omit the prefix
and look for the rest of the word.

but proud
priest -ly -liness -hood
prig -gish -gishly -gishness

PRIM

prim -mer -mest -ly -ness
prima donna (*It*)
prima facie (*L*)
primal
primar/y -ies -ily
prima/te -cy
prim/e -ed -ing -er
primeval -ly
primitive -ly -ness
primo
primogenit/or -ure
primordial -ly
prim/rose -ula
primus

PRIN-PRIT

prince -ss -let -ling -dom -ly
  -liness
principal (chief) -ly -ity
principl/e (law) -ed
prink -ed -ing
print -ed -ing -er -able
prior -ess -y -ies -ate
priorit/y -ies
pris/e (force) -ed -ing; *not*
  price *or* prize
prism -al -oid -oidal -atic
  -atically
prison -ed -ing -er
pristine
prithee, *for* I pray thee
pritty? *No,* pretty
  (PRET)

PRIV

priv/acy -ate -ately
privateer -ing
privat/ion -ive
privet (bush)
privileg/e -ed -ing
privit/y -ies
priv/y -ies -ily
  (PREV)

PRIZ

priz/e (reward) -ed -ing; *not*

price *or* prise

PRO*-PRO*B

pro, *for* professional
pro-*, *prefix meaning* for, in
  front of, before
probab/le -ly -ility -ilities
probat/e -ive
probation -ary -er
prob/e -ed -ing
probity
problem -atic -atically
probosc/is -idian *or* -idean

PRO*C

procedur/e -al
proceed -ed -ing
procellarian
process -ed -ing -er *or* -or
procession -al -ary -ist
proclaim -ed -ing
proclamat/ion -ory
proclitic
proclivit/y -ies
proconsul -ar -ate
procrastinat/e -ed -ing -ion
  -ive -or
procreat/e -ed -ing -ion -ive
procrustean
proctor -ial
procumbent
procur/e -ed -ing -er -ess
  -ement
procurat/or -ion -ory -orial
  -orship
  (PREC PROS)

PRO*D

prod -ded -ding
prodigal -ly -ity
prodigious -ly -ness
prodig/y -ies
produc/e -ed -ing -er -ible
  -ibility
product -ive -ively -ivity
  -iveness -ion
  (PRED)

PRO*F

prof, *for* professor
profan/e -ed -ing -ely -ity

---

* If the word you wish to spell is not in this list, omit the prefix
and look for the rest of the word.

-ation
profess -ed -ing -ion
professional -ly -ism
professionalis/e -ed -ing
  -ation (z)
professor -ial -ially -iate -ship
proffer -ed -ing
proficien/t -tly -cy
profile
profit (gain) -ed -ing -able
  -ably; *not* prophet
profiteer -ed -ing
proflig/ate -ately -acy
prof/ound -oundly -undity
profus/e -ely -eness -ion
  (PREF PROPH)

PRO*G-PRO*J
prog -ged -ging
progenit/or -ress -orial -ure
  -ive -ively -iveness
progen/y -ies
prognath/ous -ic -ism
prognos/is -tic -ticable
prognosticat/e -ed -ing -ion
  -ive -ory
program -me -med -ming
  -mer
progress -ed -ing -ion -ional
progressive -ly -ness
prohibit -ed -ing -ion -ory
prohibitive -ly -ness
project -ed -ing -ion -ive -ively
  -iveness
project/or -ile

PRO*L
prolaps/e -ed -ing
prolate -ly
prolegomena
prolep/sis -tic -tically
proletari/at -an -anism
proliferat/e -ed -ing -ion -ive
prolif/ic -erous
prolix -ly -ity
prologue
prolong -ed -ing -ation

PRO*M
prom, *for* promenade

promenad/e -ed -ing -er
prominen/t -tly -ce -cy
promiscu/ous -ously -ity
promis/e -ed -ing -er -ee
  -sory
promontor/y -ies
promot/e -ed -ing -ion -ive
  -er
prompt -ed -ing -er -ly -itude
  -ness
promulgat/e -ed -ing -ion -or
  (PREM)

PRO*N
prone -ness
prong -ed
pronominal -ly
pronoun
pronounc/e -ed -ing -edly;
  but pronunciation
pronto (*Sp*)
prontosil
pronunciation

PROO
proof (against water, etc.)
  -ed -ing
proof (evidence, etc.) -s; *but*
  prove
  (PRU)

PRO*P
prop, *for* propeller *or* stage
  property
prop -ped -ping
propaedeutic -al
propagand/a -ism -ist -istic
propagat/e -ed -ing -ion -or
  -ive
propel -led -ling -lant -lent
  -ler; *but* propulsion
propensit/y -ies
proper -ly
propert/y -ies
  (PREP)

PRO*PH
prophec/y -ies
prophes/y -ied -ying
prophet -ic -ically; *not* profit
  (gain)

* If the word you wish to spell is not in this list, omit the prefix
and look for the rest of the word.

prophyla/xis -ctic
(PREF PROF)

PRO*PI-PRO*PU

propinquity
propitiat/e -ed -ing -ion -ory
propitious -ly
proponent
proportion -ed -ing -al -ally
  -ate -ately -able -ably
propos/e -ed -ing -al -er
proposition -al
propound -ed -ing -er
propriet/or -ress -ary -orial
  -orially -orship
propriet/y -ies
propuls/ion -ive; *but* propel
  (PREP)

PRO*S

prosaic -ally
proscenium
proscri/be (reject, etc.) -bed
  -bing -ption -ptive; *not*
  prescribe (order)
pros/e -y -ier -iest -ily -iness
prosecut/e -ed -ing -ion -or
  -rix
proselyt/e -ism
proselytis/e -ed -ing -er (z)
prosod/y -ic -ical
prospect -ed -ing -or -ive
  -ively
prospectus -es
prosper -ed -ing -ous -ously
  -ity
prostat/e -ic
prosthe/sis -tic
prostitut/e -ed -ing -ion
prostrat/e -ed -ing -ion
  (PRES PROC)

PRO*T

protagonist
prota/sis -ses -tic
protean
protect -ed -ing -ion -ive
protector -ate
protégé, protégée (*F*)
protein -ic -ous

protest -ed -ing -ingly -ation
  -er -or
protestant -ism
protium
proto-*, *prefix meaning*
  chief, original
protocol
proton
protophyt/e -a
protoplas/m -mic -t -tic
prototyp/e -al -ic
protozo/on -a -ic -al -ology
protract -ed -ing -ion -ile -or
protrud/e -ed -ing -ent
protrus -ion -ive -ively -ile
  -ible
protuberan/t -ce
  (PRET)

PROU

proud -er -est -ly; *but* pride
  (PROO PROW)

PRO*V

prov/e -ed -ing -en -able
  -ably; *but* proof
provenance
Proven/ce -çal
provender
proverb -ial -ially -iality
provid/e -ed -ing -er
providen/ce -tial -tially
provident -ly
provinc/e -ial -ially -ialism
provincialis/e -ed -ing
  -isation (z)
provision -ed -ing -ment
provisional -ly -ity -ness
proviso -s
provisor/y -ily
provocat/ion -ive -ively
  -iveness
provok/e -ed -ing -ingly -er
provost
  (PREV)

PROW

prow -ed
prowess
prowl -ed -ing -er

* If the word you wish to spell is not in this list, omit the prefix
and look for the rest of the word.

(PROU)

PROX

prox, *for* proximo (next
  month)
proximal - ly
proxim - ity - ate - ately
prox/y - ies

PRU

prud/e - ery - ish - ishly
  - ishness
pruden/t - tly - ce
prudential - ly - ism - ist
prun/e - ed - ing - er - ello
prunella
prurien/t - tly - ce - cy
Prussia - n
prussic
(PERU PROO)

PRY

pr/y - ied - ying
(PRI)

PSA-PSO

psalm - ist - ody - odic - odist
psalter
psaltery
psepholog/y - ist
pseudo -*, *prefix meaning*
  false
pseudomorph - ic - ous - ism
  - osis
pseudonym - ous - ity
psi (*Gr*)
psilosis
psittac/ine - osis
psoriasis

PSYCH*

psych(o) -*, *prefix meaning* of
  the mind
psyche
psychedelic
psychiatr/y - ic - ical - ist
psychic - al - ally
psycho - analy/sis - tic
psycholog/y - ical - ically - ist
psychologis/e - ed - ing (z)
psychometr/y - ic - ical
psychoneuro/sis - tic

psychopath - y - ic - ology
psycho/sis - tic; *not* sycosis
  (barber's itch)
psychosomatic
psychotherap/y - eutic
psychrometer
(SCI SI)

PT

ptarmigan
pterodactyl
pteropod
pterosaur
pteropus
pterygoid
ptomaine
ptosis

PUB

pub, *for* public house
pub/erty - ic - escent
  - escence
public - ly
publication
public/ity - ist
publicis/e - ed - ing (z)
publish - ed - ing - er - able
  - ability

PUC

puce
puck - ish
puckeroo (*NZ*)
pucker - ed - ing
(PUK)

PUD

pud (hand)
pudding - y
puddl/e - ed - ing - er - y
pudency
pudend/um (*L*) - a - al - ic
pudg/e - y
(PAD POD)

PUE

pueblo (*Sp*)
pueril/e - ely - ity - ities
puerperal
(PEW)

PUF

puff - ed - ing - er - y - iness

---

* If the word you wish to spell is not in this list, omit the prefix
and look for the rest of the word.

-ery
puffin
PUG
pug -gish -gy -ging
puggaree (*Hind*)
pugil/ist -istic -ism
pugnac/ity -ious -iously
PUI
puisne (judge); *not* puny
puissan/t -tly -ce
PUK
pukatea (*NZ*)
puk/e -ed -ing
pukka (*Hind*)
puku (*NZ*)
(PUC)
PUL
pulchritude
pul/e -ed -ing
pull -ed -ing -er
pullet
pulley -s
pullulat/e -ed -ing -ion
pulmon/ary -ate -ic
pulp -ed -ing -y -iness
pulpit -eer
pulsat/e -ed -ing -ion -or -ory
 -ile
pulsatilla
puls/e -ed -ing
pulsimeter
pulveris/e -ed -ing -ation -er
 (z)
pulverulent
pulvinat/e -ed
(PAL)
PUM
puma
pumice (stone) -ous
pummel (hit) -led -ling; *not*
 pommel
pump -ed -ing -er
pumpernickel (*Ger*)
pumpkin
(PAM POM)
PUN
pun -ned -ning -ster
punch -ed -ing -er
puncheon
punctat/e -ed

punctili/o -ous -ously
 -ousness
punctual -ly -ity
punctuat/e -ed -ing -ion
punctur/e -ed -ing
pundit *or* pandit
pungen/t -tly -cy
punish -ed -ing -ment -er
 -able -ably
punit/ive -ory
punk
punkah (*Hind*)
punnet
punt -ed -ing
punty
pun/y -ier -iest -iness
(PAN)
PUP
pup -ped -ping -py -pies
pupa -e -te -ted -ting -tion
pupil -lary -lage
puppet -ry
(POP)
PURB-PURP
purblind -ness
purchas/e -ed -ing -er -able
purdah (*Hind*)
pur/e -er -est -ely -ity -ist
purée (*F*)
purgat/ion -ive
purgator/y -ial
purg/e -ed -ing
purif/y -ies -ied -ying -ier
purific/ation -ator -atory
purilent? *No,* purulent
puriri (*NZ*)
puritan -ical -ically -ism
purl -ed -ing -er; *not* pearl
 (gem)
purlieu -s
purlin
purloin -ed -ing -er
purpl/e -ed -ing -y -ish
purport -ed -ing -edly
purpos/e -ed -ing -ive
 (intend); *not* propose
 (suggest)
purpose -ly -ful -fully
 -fulness
purposeless -ly -ness

purpur/a - in - ic
(PER PEAR PYR)

PURR-PURV
purr - ed - ing
purs/e - ed - ing - er - y - iness
pursu/e - ed - ing - it - er - ant
  - ance
pursuivant
purulen/t - tly - ce
purvey - ed - ing - ance - or
purview
  (PER)

PUS
pus
push - ed - ing - er
pusillanim/ity - ous
puss - y - ies - yfoot
pustul/e - ar - ous - ate
  (PUZ)

PUT
put - ting
putative - ly
putref/y - ied - ying - action
  - active
putresc/ent - ence
putrid - ly - ness - ity
putsch (Ger)
putt (golf) - ed - ing - er
puttee
putt/y - ied - ying

PUZ
puzzl/e - ed - ing - ingly
  - ement - er
  (PUS)

PY-PYO
pyaem/ia - ic
pyalla (NZ)
pygm/y or pigm/y - ies
pyjamas (Am, pajamas)
pyknic (thickly built person);
  not picnic
pylon
pylor/us - ic
pyorrhoea
  (PI)

PYR*
pyr - *, prefix meaning fire

pyracanth
pyramid - al - ally
pyre
pyrethrum
pyre/xia - tic
pyrheliometer
pyridine
pyrit/es - ic - iferous - ise - ised
  (z)
pyrogallic
pyrogen/ic - etic - ous
pyrolat/ry - rous
pyromani/a - ac
pyrosis
pyrotechn/y - ic - ical - ically
pyroxene
pyroxylin
  (PER PIR PUR)

PYTH
Pythagor/as - ean
python
  (PITH)

PYX
pyx - ed - ing
pyxi/s - dium
  (PIX)

Q

QUAC
quack - ed - ing - ery; not
  quake (shudder)

QUAD
quad, for quadr/angle, - uplet,
  etc.; not quod
quadr(i) - *, prefix meaning
  four
quadrable
quadragesima - l
quadrang/le - ular
quadrant - al
quadrat
quadrat/e - ed - ing - ic - ure
quadrennial - ly
quadrifid
quadrilateral
quadrille
quadrillion

* If the word you wish to spell is not in this list, omit the prefix
and look for the rest of the word.

quadrinomial
quadrivalent
quadruped - al
quadrupl/e - ed - ing - ly - et
 - icate
(QUOD)

QUAF-QUAL
quaff - ed - ing
quag - gy - mire
quail - ed - ing
quaint - er - est - ly - ness
quak/e - ed - ing - ingly; *not*
 quack (duck, etc.)
quaker - ess - ism - ish
qualif/y - ies - ied - ying
 - ication - icatory
qualit/y - ies - ative - atively
qualm

QUAN
quandar/y - ies
quandong (*Aus*)
quango - s
quantif/y - ied - ying - iable
 - ication
quantit/y - ies - ative - atively
quantivalence
quant/um - a
(QUON)

QUAQ
quaquaversal - ly

QUAR
quarantin/e - ed - ing
quarenden (apple)
quarrel - led - ling - ler - some
quarr/y - ies - ied - ying - ier
(QUOR)

QUART
quart - s (liquid measure); *not*
 quartz
quartan
quarter - ed - ing - ly - age
quarter centenary? *No,*
 quater -
quarern
quartet *or* quartette
quartile
quarto

quarz (rock)
(QUAT)

QUAS
quasar
quash - ed - ing
quasi -*, *prefix meaning*
 almost
quassia

QUAT
quatercentenary (400th); *not*
 quar -
quatern/ary - ion - ity
quatrain
quatrefoil
quattrocento (*It*)
(QUART)

QUAV
quaver - ed - ing - ingly
(GUAV)

QUAY
quay (wharf) - age; *not* key

QUE
queas/y - ier - iest - iness
quebracho (*Sp*)
queen - ed - ing - ly - like
queer - er - est - ed - ing - ly
 - ness
quell - ed - ing - er
quench - ed - ing - able - less
 - er
quern
querulous - ly - ness
quer/y - ies - ied - ying - ist
quest - ed - ing; *also* bequest
question - ed - ing - er - able
 - ably
questionnaire
quetzal
queue (line up) - d - ing; *not*
 cue (billiards, entry)

QUIB-QUIL
quibbl/e - ed - ing - er
quick - er - est - ly - ness
quicken - ed - ing - er
quickie
quid
quiddit/y - ies

* If the word you wish to spell is not in this list, omit the prefix
and look for the rest of the word.

quid pro quo (*L*)
quiescen/t - tly - ce
quiet - er - est - ly - ness - ude
quiet/ism - ist - istic
quietus
quiff
quill - ed
quilt - ed - ing - er

QUIN*

quin -*, quinqu -*, *prefix*
  meaning five
quin/ary - ate
quince
quin/centenary *or* gentenary
quincun/x - cial - cially
quin/ine - quina
quinquagesima
quinquennium - al - ally - ad
quinquereme
quinquivalent
quins, *for* quintuplets
quins/y - ied
quint
quintain
quintal
quintan (fever)
quintessen/ce - tial
quintet *or* quintette
quintup/le - ly - licate - let

QUIP-QUIZ

quip - ped - ping
quire (paper); *not* choir
quirk - y
quisling
quit - ted - ting - ter
quitch
quite; *not* quiet (silent)
quit/s - tance
quiver - ed - ing - ingly
quivive (*F*)
Quixot/e - ic - ism - ically - ry
quiz - zed - zing - zer - zical
  - zically
  (CUI)

QUO

quod (prison); *not* quad
quod erat demonstrandum

(*L*, Q.E.D.)
quoin (corner - stone, etc.);
  not coin, coign
quoit
quondam
quorum
quota
quot/e - ed - ing - ation - able
quoth
quotidian
quotient
  (QUA)

R

RAB

rabbet (joinery) - ed - ing; *not*
  rabbit
rabbi - s - nical - nate
rabbit (animal) - ing - y; *not*
  rabbet
rabble - ment
Rabelais - ian
rabid - ly - ness - ity
rabies
  (RHAB)

RAC

rac/e - ed - ing - er - ism - ist
rac/y - ier - iest - ily - iness
raceme
rach/is - ides
rachitis *or* rickets
racial - ism - ist
rack - ed - ing; *not* wrack
  (seaweed, etc.)
racket *or* racquet (bat)
racket (din, etc.) - ed - ing - y
  - eer
raconteur
racoon *or* raccoon
  (RAK WRAC)

RAD-RADIC

radar
raddl/e - ed - ing
radial - ly
radian
radian/t - tly - ce
radiat/e - ed - ing - ion - or

* If the word you wish to spell is not in this list, omit the prefix
and look for the rest of the word.

radical -ly -ism
radic/le (part of plant) -ular
RADIO
radio -s -ed -ing
radio -*, *prefix meaning* of
  rays, of radius, of radio
radioactiv -e -ely -ity
radio -carbon
radio -carpal
radiogenic
radiogram
radiograph/y -ic -er
radiolog/y -ical -ist
radiosonde
radiotherap/y -eutic -ist
RADIS-RADO
radish -es
radium
radi/us -i
radi/x -ces
radome
radon
RAF
R.A.F., *for* Royal Air Force
raffia
raffish (dissipated) -ly
  -ness; *not* ravish
raffl/e -ed -ing
raft -ed -ing
rafter
RAG
rag -ged -ging -ger -gedly
  -gedness
ragamuffin
rag/e -ed -ing -ingly
raglan
ragout (*F*)
ragwort
RAI
raid -ed -ing -er
raidio? *No,* radio
rail -ed -ing -ingly
raillery
railway
raiment
rain -ed -ing -y -iness; *not*
  reign, rein

rainbow
rais/e (lift) -ed -ing; *not* rays,
  raze, rise
raisin
raison d'être (*F*)
  (RAR RAY REI WRAI)
RAJ
raj
rajah
  (RAGE)
RAK
rak/e -ed -ing -ish
  (RAC)
RAL
rallentando (*It*)
rall/y -ies -ied -ying
  (REL)
RAM
ram -med -ming -mer -mish
Ramadan
rambl/e -ed -ing -ingly -er
ramie
ramif/y -ies -ied -ying
  -ication
ramose
ramp -ed -ing
rampag/e -ed -ing -eous
rampan/t -tly -cy
rampart
rampion
ramshackle
ramson
RAN
ran (did run)
ranch -ed -ing -er
rancid -ly -ness -ity
ranco/ur -rous -rously
rand
randan
random -ly -ness
rand/y -ier -iest -iness
ranee *or* rani (*Hind*)
rang (did ring)
rangatira (*NZ*)
rang/e -ed -ing -er
rangle? *No,* wrangle
rank -ed -ing -er

* If the word you wish to spell is not in this list, omit the prefix
and look for the rest of the word.

rankl/e - ed - ing
ransack - ed - ing
ransom - ed - ing
rant - ed - ing - er
ranuncul/us - i or - uses

RAP

rap (tap) - ped - ping; *not* wrap
(enfold)
rapaci/ty - ous - ously
rap/e - ed - ing - er - ist
rapid - ly - ity
rapier
rapine
rapport
rapprochement (*F*)
rapt (in a rapture); *not*
wrapped
raptor
raptur/e - ed - ous - ously
(RHAP WRAP)

RAR

rar/e - er - est - ely - eness - ity
- ities
rarebit (Welsh delicacy); *not*
rabbit
raref/y - ied - ying - action
- active - ication

RAS

rascal - ly - ity
rash - er - est - ly - ness
rasher (of bacon)
rasp - ed - ing - er - atory
raspberr/y - ies
(RAIS RAZ WRAS)

RAT-RATH

rat - ted - ting - ter - ty - tier
- tiest
rata (*NZ*)
ratab/le *or* rateab/le - ly - ility
rataplan
ratchet
rat/e - ed - ing - er
rather
(RATT WRAT)

RATI

ratif/y - ies - ied - ying - ication
ratio - s

ratiocinat/e - ed - ing - ion - ive
ration - ed - ing
rational - ly - ity - ism - ist - istic
rationale
rationalis/e - ed - ing - ation (z)
(RACI RASH)

RATT

rattan
rattl/e - ed - ing - er
(RAT-)

RAU

raucous - ly - ness
raughty *or* rorty
rauriki (*NZ*)
(RAW WRA WRO)

RAV

ravag/e (plunder) - ed - ing
- er; *not* ravish
rav/e - ed - ing
ravel - led - ling
ravelin
raven (bird)
raven (devour) - ed - ing - ous
- ously
ravin/e (valley) - ed
ravioli (*It*)
ravish (rape, charm) - ed - ing
- ingly - ment - er; *not* ravage

RAW

raw - er - est - ness - ish; *not*
roar
(RAU WRA WRO)

RAY

ray - ed - ing - less
rayon
(RAI WRAI)

RAZ

raz/e (destroy) - ed - ing; *not*
raise *or* rays
razor
razzle - dazzle
razzmatazz
(RAS)

RE*

re (*L*, in the matter of)
re - *, *prefix meaning again,
etc., which can be used*

---

* If the word you wish to spell is not in this list, omit the prefix
and look for the rest of the word.

with a very large number of words

RE*A

reach -ed -ing -able
react -ed -ing -ion; *but*
  reagent
read -ing -er -able -ability
read (did read); *not* red
readdress -ed -ing
read/y -ier -iest -ily -iness;
  also already
reagen/t -cy
real -ly -ity -ities -ism -ist
  -istic -istically
realis/e -ed -ing -ation -able
  (z)
realm
realt/y (*Am,* real estate) -or
ream -ed -ing -er
reap -ed -ing -er
rear -ed -ing -er
reason -ed -ing -er -able
  -ably
  (REE REI RERE RIE WREA)

RE*B

rebarbative
rebate
rebel -led -ling -lion -lious
rebuff -ed -ing
rebuk/e -ed -ing -ingly
rebus
rebut -ted -ting -tal -ter
  -ment

RE*C-RECC

recalcitran/t -ce
recant -ed -ing -ation
recap, *for* recapitulat/e -ed
  -ing -ion
recce, *for* reconnaissance
reccomend? *No,* recommend
  (WREC)

RE*CE

reced/e (go away) -ed -ing;
  not re -seed
receipt -ed -ing; *not* reseat
receiv/e -ed -ing -er -able
recension

recen/t -tly -cy
receptacle
recept/ion -ionist -ive -ively
  -ivity -iveness
recess -ed -ing -ive -ively
  -iveness
recession -al
  (RECI RESC RESI WRES)

RE*CH

réchauffé (*F*)
recherché (*F*)
  (RESH RETCH WRET)

RE*CI

recidiv/ism -ist
recipe *or* receipt
recipient
reciproc/ity -al -ally
reciprocat/e -ed -ing -ion
recit/e -ed -ing -al -ation -er
  (RECE RESC RESI)

RECK

reck (care) -ed -ing; *not*
  wreck
reckless -ly -ness
reckon -ed -ing -er
  (WREC)

RE*CL

reclaim -ed -ing
reclamation
reclin/e -ed -ing
recluse

RE*CO

recognis/e -ed -ing (z)
recognit/ion -ory
recogniz/ance -ant
recoil -ed -ing
recollect -ed -ing -ion
recommend -ed -ing -ation
  -atory -able
recompens/e -ed -ing
reconcil/e -ed -ing -iation
  -able -ability
recondite -ly -ness
reconnaissance
reconnoitr/e -ed -ing
record -ed -ing -er -able
recount (narrate) -ed -ing;

---

* If the word you wish to spell is not in this list, omit the prefix
and look for the rest of the word.

not re-count
recoup -ed -ing -ment
recourse
recover -ed -ing -y; *not*
re-cover

RE*CR

recrean/t -cy
recreat/e -ion -ive
recrement -itious
recriminat/e -ed -ing -ion -ive
-ory
recrudesc/e -ed -ing -ent
-ence
recruit -ed -ing -ment -er

RECT

rectang/le -ular -ularity
rectif/y -ies -ied -ying
-ication -ier -iable
rectilin/ear -eal -earity
rectitude
recto
rector -ial -ially -ate -ship
rector/y -ies
rectum

RE*CU

recumbent
recuperat/e -ed -ing -ion -ive
recur -red -ring -rence -rent
-rently
recusan/t -ce -cy
(REQU)

RE*D

red (colour) -der -dest -ness
-dish; *not* read
redact -ed -ing -ion -or
redden -ed -ing -er
redeem -ed -ing -able -er
redempt -ion -ive
redingote
redolen/t -ce
redoubt (fort)
redoubt/able (formidable)
-ably
redound -ed -ing
redress (remedy) -ed -ing;
not re-dress
reduc/e -ed -ing -tion -er

-ible
redundan/t -tly -cy -cies
(RID)

RE*E

re-echo -ed -ing
reed (plant) -y -iness; *not*
read
re-edit -ed -ing
reedling (bird)
reef -ed -ing -er
reek (stink, smoke) -ed -ing;
not wreak
reel (winder, spin) -ed -ing;
not real
re-enforc/e -ed -ing; *not*
reinforce (support)
re-enact -ed -ing
re-ent/er -ered -ering -rant
-ry
re-establish -ed -ing -ment
reev/e -ing; *but* rove (did
reeve)
re-examin/e -ed -ing -ation
re-exist -ed -ing -ent -ence
re-export -ed -ing -ation
(REA RHE RIE WREA)

RE*F

ref, *for* referee, reference
refect/ory -ion
refer -red -ring -ence -ential
-able
refer/ee -eed -eeing
referend/um -a
refin/e -ed -ing -ement -er
-ery -eries
reflat/e -ed -ing -ion
reflect -ed -ing -ion -ingly -or
reflective -ly -ness
reflex -ed -ible -ive -ively
refluen/t -ce
reform -ed -ing -er -able
reformat/ion -ive -ively -ory
-ories
refract -ed -ing -ion -ional
-ive -or
refrain -ed -ing
refrangib/le -ility

* If the word you wish to spell is not in this list, omit the prefix
and look for the rest of the word.

refresh -ed -ing -ingly -ment
-er
refrigerat/e -ed -ing -ion -or
-ory
refrigerant
refug/e -ee
refulgen/t -tly -ce
refund -ed -ing -ment
refus/e -ed -ing -al -able
refuse (rubbish); *not* re -fuse
re -fus/e -ed -ing -ion
refut/e -ed -ing -ation -able
RE*G
regal -ly -ity -ism -ia
regal/e -ed -ing -ement
regard -ed -ing -ful -fully
-fulness
regardless -ly -ness
regardant
regatta
regelat/e (re -freeze) -ed -ing
-ion; *not* relegate, regulate
regen/t -cy
reggae
regicid/e -al
regime
regimen
regiment -al -ally -ation
regin/a -al
region -al -ally -alism -alist
register -ed -ing
registr/y -ies -ar -ation -able
regn/al -ant
regress -ed -ing -ion -ive
-ively -iveness
regret -ted -ting -ful -fully
-fulness
regrettabl/e -ly
regular -ly -ity
regularis/e -ed -ing -ation (z)
regul/ate -ated -ating -ation
-ator -able
regurgitat/e -ed -ing -ion
(REJ)
RE*H
rehabilitat/e -ed -ing -ion
rehears/e -ed -ing -al

RE*I
reign (rule) -ed -ing; not rain,
rein
re -ignit/e -ed -ing
reimburs/e -ed -ing -ement
rein (harness) -ed -ing; *not*
rain, reign
reindeer
reinforc/e -ed -ing -ement;
not re -enforce (support)
reinstat/e -ed -ing -ement
reinter -red -ring -ment
reissu/e -ed -ing
(RAI REA REE RHI WRAI
WREA)
RE*J
reject -ed -ing -ion -or -able
rejoic/e -ed -ing -ingly
rejoin -ed -ing -der
rejuvenat/e -ed -ing -ion
rejuvenesc/e -ed -ing -ent
-ence
(REG)
RE*L
relaps/e -ed -ing
relat/e -ed -ing -ion -ional
-ionship -edness
relativ/e -ely -eness -ism -ity
relax -ed -ing -ation
relay -ed -ing
releas/e -ed -ing -able
relegab/le -ility
relegat/e -ed -ing -ion
relent -ed -ing -ingly
relentless -ly -ness
relevan/t -tly -ce -cy
reliab/le -ly -ility; *but* rely
reli/es -ed -ance -ant
relic (remnant)
relict (widow, survival)
relie/f -ve -ved -ving -vable
religi/on -ous -ously -osity
-ousness
relinquish -ed -ing -ment
reliquar/y -ies
relish -ed -ing -able
reluctan/t -tly -ce

* If the word you wish to spell is not in this list, omit the prefix
and look for the rest of the word.

rel/y - ies - ied - ying

RE*M

remain - ed - ing

remainder - ed - ing

remand - ed - ing

remark - ed - ing - able - ably

remed/y - ies - ied - ying - ial
- ially - iable

rememb/er - ered - ering
- rance - rancer

remind - ed - ing - er

reminisc/e - ed - ing - ent
- ence - ently

remiss - ly - ness - ion - ible

remit - ted - ting - tance - ter
- tee - tal

remnant

remonetis/e - ed - ing
- ation (z)

remonstrat/e - ed - ing - ion - or
- ive - ingly

remonstran/t - ce

remorse - ful - fully - fulness
- less - lessly

remote - ly - ness

remov/e - ed - ing - al - able
- ability

remunerat/e - ed - ing - ion - ive
- ively - iveness

RE*N

renaissance *or* renascen/ce
- t

ren/al - iform

rend - ing; *but* rent

render - ed - ing

rendezvous (*F*) - ed - ing

rendition

renega/de - tion

reneg(u)/e - ed - ing

renew - ed - ing - al - able

rennet

renounc/e - ed - ing; *but*
renunciation

renovat/e - ed - ing - ion - or

renown - ed

rent - ed - ing - al - er - able

renumerate? *No,* remunerate

renunciat/ion - ive - ory
(RHEN WREN)

RE*O

reorganis/e - ed - ing - ation (z)
(RHEO)

RE*P-RE*PL

rep, *for* representative,
repertory, repetition

rep *or* repp (fabric)

repair - ed - ing - able

repar/ation - able - ative

repartee

repast

repatriat/e - ed - ing - ion

repeal - ed - ing - able - er

repeat - ed - ing - edly; *but*
repetition

repel - led - ling - lent - lently

repent - ed - ing - ance - ant
- antly

repertoire

repertor/y - ies

repetend

repetit/ion - ive - ively - ious
- ional

repin/e - ed - ing

replac/e - ed - ing - ement
- eable

replenish - ed - ing - ment

replet/e - ion

replic/a - ate - ated - ating
- ation

repl/y - ies - ied - ying

RE*PO-RE*PU

report - ed - ing - able - age - er

repos/e - ed - ing - eful - efully
- efulness

repositor/y - ies

repoussé (*F*)

repp (fabric)

reprehen/d - ded - ding - sible
- sibly - sion

represent - ed - ing - ation
- ative - able - ational

repress - ed - ing - ion - ive
- ively - iveness

repriev/e - ed - ing

* If the word you wish to spell is not in this list, omit the prefix
and look for the rest of the word.

reprimand -ed -ing
reprisal
reproach -ed -ing -ingly
reproachful -ly -ness
reprobat/e -ed -ing -ion
reproof (blame)
re -proof (proof again)
reprov/e -ed -ing -ingly
reptant
reptil/e -ian -iform -iferous
republic -an -anism
repudiat/e -ed -ing -ion -or
repugnan/t -tly -ce
repuls/e -ed -ing -ion
repulsive -ly -ness
reputab/le -ly
reput/e -ed -edly -ation

RE*QU
request -ed -ing
requiem (L)
requiescat (L)
requir/e -ed -ing -ement
requisite -ness
requisition -ed -ing
requit/e -ed -ing -al
(REC WREC)

RE*RE
re -read -ing
reredos
(REAR)

RE*SC-RE*SI
resc/ind -inded -inding
-ission
rescript
rescu/e -ed -ing -er
reseat -ed -ing; not receipt
(acknowledgement)
resect -ed -ing -ion
reseda
resembl/e -ed -ing -ance
resent -ed -ing -ment -ful
-fully
reserv/e -ed -ing -ation -ist
-edly
reservoir
resid/e -ed -ing -ence -ency
resident -ial -iary

residu/e -um -al -ally -ary
resign -ed -ing -ation -edly
resilien/t -tly -ce
resin -ous
resist -ed -ing -ance -ant -er
resistib/le -ly -ility
(RECE RECI)

RE*SO
resoluble
resolut/e -ely -ion
resolv/e -ed -ing -ent -able
resonan/t -tly -ce
resonator
resorb -ed -ing -ent -ence
resorption
resort -ed -ing; not re -sort
resotto? No, ris-
resound -ed -ing -ingly
resource -ful -fully -fulness
-less

RE*SP
respect -ed -ing -ful -fully
respectab/le -ly -ility
respective -ly
respir/e -ed -ing -ation -atory
-ator
respite
resplenden/t -tly -ce
respond -ed -ing -ent
respons/e -ive -ively
-iveness
responsib/le -ly -ility

RE*ST
rest -ed -ing -ful -fully
-fulness
restless -ly -ness
restaurant
restitution
restive -ly -ness
restor/e -ed -ing -ation -ative
restrain -ed -ing -t -able
-edly
restrict -ed -ing -ion -ive
-ively
(WRES)

RE*SU
result -ed -ing -ant -ful -less

* If the word you wish to spell is not in this list, omit the prefix
and look for the rest of the word.

resum/e -ed -ing -ption
 -ptive
résumé (F)
resurgen/t -tly -ce
resurrect -ed -ing -ion -ionist
resuscitat/e -ed -ing -ion -or
 -ive
 (RHES)

RE*T RE*TA
ret -ted -ting -ter -tery
retail -ed -ing -er
retain -ed -ing -er -able; but
 retention
retaliat/e -ed -ing -ion -ive
 -ory
retard -ed -ing -ation -atory;
 but ritardando (It)

RETC
retch (strain to vomit) -ed
 -ing; not wretch
 (RECH)

RE*TE-RE*TO
retent/ion -ive -ively
 -iveness; but retain
reticen/t -tly -ce
reticle (observation line in
 telescope)
reticule (handbag)
reticulat/e -ed -ing -ion -ive
 -ely
reticul/um -a -ar -ose
retin/a -as or -ae -al
retinue
retir/e -ed -ing -ingly -ement
retort -ed -ing
 (RHET WRET)

RE*TR
retrac/e -ed -ing
retract -ed -ing -ion -or -able
 -ile -ive
retread (on foot), retrod,
 retrodden
retread (tyre) -ed -ing
retreat -ed -ing
retrench -ed -ing -ment
retribut/ion -ive -ively
retriev/e -ed -ing -al -able

retro-*, prefix meaning
 backwards, behind
retroce/de -ded -ding -dent
 -ssion -ssive
retrograd/e -ely -ation
retrogress -ed -ing -ion -ive
 -ively
retrospect -ion -ive -ively
retroussé (F)
retrover/t -ted -ting -sion
 -sive

RE*TU
return -ed -ing -able

RE*U
re -us/e -ed -ing
 (REW RHEU RU)

RE*V-RE* VE
rev, for revolution -ved -ving
reveal -ed -ing -able; but
 revelation
reveille (awakening signal)
revel (make merry) -led -ling
 -ry -ler
revelation -ist; but reveal
reveng/e -ed -ing -ful -fully
 -fulness
revenue
reverberat/e -ed -ing -ion -or
 -ory -ive
rever/e -ed -ing -ent -ently
reveren/ce -ced -cing -tial
 -tially
reverend (title)
reverie
revers (turned-back edge of
 garment)
revers/e (turn around) -ed
 -ing -al -ible -ibility
rever/t -ted -ting -tible -sion
revet -ment

RE*VI
review (survey) -ed -ing -able
 -er; not revue
revil/e -ed -ing -ingly -er
revis/e -ed -ing -ion -ional -er
reviv/e -ed -ing -al -able -er
 -lism -alist

* If the word you wish to spell is not in this list, omit the prefix
 and look for the rest of the word

RE*VO

revo/ke - ked - king - cation
- cable - catory
revolt - ed - ing - ingly
revolution - ary - ism - ist
revolutionis/e - ed - ing - er (z)
revolv/e - ed - ing - er

RE*VU

revue (entertainment); *not*
review
revuls/ion - ive

RE*W

rewa-rewa (*NZ*)
reward - ed - ing
rewrit/e - ing - ten
rewrote
(RU)

REX

rex (*L*)
(REC WREC)

REY

reynard
(RAI RAY REI)

RHA

rhabdomancy
Rhaet/ian - ic
rhapsod/y - ies - ic - ical - ically
rhapsodis/e - ed - ing (z)
(RA REI WRA)

RHE

Rhenish (of the Rhine)
rheo/stat - meter - logy
rhesus
rhetoric - al - ally - ian
rheum - y
rheumat/ism - ic - ically - oid
- icky
(RE WRE)

RHI

rhin/al - oscope - oscopy
rhinoceros - es
rhizome
(REI RHY RI RY WRI)

RHO

rhodium
rhododendron
rhomb - ic - oid - oidal - us

- ohedron
(RO WRO)

RHU

rhubarb
rhumb - line; *not* rum
(ROO RU)

RHY

rhym/e - ed - ing - er
rhythm - ic - ical - ically
(RY WRY)

RIB

rib - bed - bing
ribald
riband *or* ribbon - ed
ribes
riboflavine

RIC

rice
rich - es - er - est - ly - ness
rick - ed - ing
ricket/s - y - iness; *but* rachitis
rickshaw
ricochet - ed - ing
rictus

RID

rid - ding - dance; *not* ride
riddl/e - ed - ing
rid/e - ing - den - er - erless;
but rode
ridg/e - ed - ing
ridicul/e - ed - ing - ous - ously

RIE

riesling(*Ger*)
(REA REE RHE RHI WRI)

RIF

rife - ness
riffl/e - ed - ing
riff - raff
rifl/e - ed - ing - eman
rift - ed - ing

RIG

rig - ged - ging - ger
rigadoon
(WRIG)

RIGH

right - ed - ing - ly - ness
righteous - ly - ness

---

* If the word you wish to spell is not in this list, omit the prefix
and look for the rest of the word.

rightful -ly -ness
(RITE WRI)

RIGI-RIGO
rigid -ly -ity -ness
rigmarole
rigor (medical)
rigo/ur -rous -rously
(WRIG)

RIL
ril/e -ed -ing
rill (steam)
rille (canyon on moon)

RIM
rim -med -ming
rim/e (hoar-frost) -y; *not*
rhyme
rimu (*NZ*)
(RHY)

RIN
rind -ed
rinderpest
ring -ed -ing -er -let; *but*
rang, rung; *not* wring (twist)
rink -er
rins/e -ed -ing -er
(RHIN WRIN)

RIO
riot -ed -ing -er -ous -ously
-ousness; *not* ryot
(RHEO)

RIP
rip -ped -ping -per
riparian
rip/e -er -est -ely -eness
ripen -ed -ing -er
ripost/e -ed -ing
rippl/e -ed -ing -y

RIS
ris/e -ing -en -er; *also* arise;
but rose; *not* raise (lift)
risib/le -ility
risk -ed -ing -y -ier -iest -ily
-iness
risotto (*It*)
risqué (*F*)
rissole
(WRIS RHIZ)

RIT
ritardando (*It*)
rite (ceremony); *not* right,

write
ritual -ism -istic
ritualis/e -ed -ing -ation (z)
(WRIT)

RIV
rival -led -ling -ry -ries
riv/e -ed -ing
river -ine -ain
rivet -ed -ing -er
rivulet
(REV)

ROA
roach
road -way -ster; *not* rode
(did ride)
roam -ed -ing -er
roan
roar (noise) -ed -ing -er
roast -ed -ing -er; *not* roster
(list)
(RHO RO-WRO)

ROB
rob -bed -bing -ber -bery
rob/e -ed -ing
robin
robot
robust -ly -ness

ROC
rochet
rock -ed -ing -er -y -ier -iest
-ily -iness
rocker/y -ies
rocket -ed -ing -ry
rococo

ROD
rod -ded
rode (did ride); *not* road,
rowed
rodent -ial
rodeo
rodomontade
(RHOD ROAD ROE ROW)

ROE
roe (deer); *not* row
roe (fish's) -d
(RHO ROA)

ROG
rogation
rogu/e -ery -ish -ishly
-ishness

209

ROI
  roi (F)
  roister -ed -ing -er
  (ROY)
ROL
  role (function)
  roll -ed -ing -er -able
  rollick -ed -ing
  roly- pol/y -ies
  (ROW)
ROM
  roman/ce -ced -cing -cer -tic
   -tically
  Rom/or Rum/ania -anian
   -anish
  Romanis/e -ed -ing -ation
  Roman -ism -ist -istic -esque
  Roman/y -ies
  Rome
  romp -ed -ing -er
  (RHOM)
RON
  rondeau or rondel
  rondure
  roneo
  Röntgen
  (WRON)
ROO
  roo, for kangaroo
  rood (crucifix); not rude
  roof -s -ed -ing -er -age -less
  rook -ed -ing -er -ling
  rookie (recruit)
  room -ed -ing -y -ier -iest -ily
   -iness
  roost -ed -ing -er
  root -ed -ing -er -y -less
   -lessness; not route (road)
  rootl/e -ed -ing
  (RHEU ROU RUE)
ROP
  rop/e -ed -ing -y -iness
ROR
  rorqual
  rorty or raughty
  (RAU RAW ROA WROU)
ROS
  rosaceous
  rosar/y -ies
  ros/e (flower) -ery -ette -eate

  -y -ier -iest -iness
  rose (did rise); also arose;
   not roes, rows
  rosella (Aus)
  roseola (German measles)
  rosicrucian
  rosin -ed -ing
  roster (list); not roaster
  rostr/um -al -ated -iform
ROT
  rot -ted -ing -ten -tenly
   -tenness -ter
  rota -ry -rian
  rotat/e -ed -ing -ion -ive -ory
  rote (learning by repetition);
   not wrote
  rotifer
  rotor
  rotund -ity -ities
  rotunda
  (WRO)
ROU
  rouble
  roué (F)
  rouge
  rough -er -est -ed -ing -ly
   -ness -ish
  roughage
  roughen -ed -ing -er
  roulade
  rouleau
  roulette
  Roumania, see Romania
  round -er -est -ed -ing -ness
   -ly -ish; also around
  roundel
  roundelay
  rounders
  roup -y
  rous/e -ed -ing -ingly -er
  roustabout
  rout (defeat, etc.) -ed -ing
  rout/e (way) -ed -ing; not
   root
  routine
  (RHEU RHU ROO ROW RUI
  WROU)
ROV
  rov/e -ed -ing -er
  rove (did reeve)

210

ROW

row (noise) -ed -ing
row (propel boat) -ed -ing -er
rowan
rowd/y -ier -iest -ily -iness
-yism
rowel -led -ling
rowlock
(RHO ROA ROE ROU)

ROY

royal -ly -ty -ties -ism -ist
(ROI)

RUB

rub -bed -bing -ber
rubato (*It*)
rubbish -y
rubbl/e -y
rubicund
rubidium
rubric -ate -ation -ator
rub/y -ies
(RHU)

RUC

ruche (*F*)
ruck -le -led -ling
rucksack
ructions

RUD

rudd
rudder -less
ruddle
ruddock
rudd/y -ier -iest -ily -iness
rud/e -er -est -ely -eness
rudiment -al -ary
(ROOD)

RUE

rue (plant)
ru/e (repent) -ed -ing -eful
-efully
(RHEU RHU ROO)

RUF

ruff -ed -ing; *not* rough (opp.
to smooth)
ruffian -ly
ruffl/e -ed -ing
rufous
(ROOF ROUGH)

RUG-RUL

rug

rugby *or* rugger
rugged -ly -ness
rug/ose -osely -osity -ate
-ous
ruin -ed -ing -ous -ously
-ation
rul/e -ed -ing -er
(ROU)

RUM

rum -my -ness -mily -miness
rumba
rum -baba
rumbl/e -ed -ing
rumbustious -ly -ness
rum/en -inant
ruminat/e -ed -ing -ion -or
-ive -ively
rummag/e -ed -ing
rumour -ed -ing
rump -y
rumpl/e -ed -ing
rumpus -es
(RHEU RHUM)

RUN

run -ning -ner -ny; *but* ran
runagate
runcible
runcinate
run/e -ic
rung (of ladder, did ring); *not*
wrung
runlet
runnel
runt
runway

RUP RUR

rupee
ruptur/e -ed -ing
rural -ly -ity
ruralis/e -ed -ing -ation (z)
ruridecanal

RUS RUT

ruse
rush -ed -ing -er
rush -es -y -ier -iest
rusk
Russ/ia -ian -ify -ified -ophile
-ophobe
Russianis/e -ed -ing -ation (z)
russet

211

rust - ed - ing - y - ier - iest - ily
 - iness - less
rustic - ity - ally - ate - ated
 - ating - ation
rustl/e - ed - ing - er
rut - ted - ting - ty - tish
ruth - less - lessly - lessness
ruthenium

RY
rye
ryot (*Hind*, peasant); *not* riot
 (RHI RHY RI WRI WRY)

S

SAB
Sabbatarian - ism
Sabbat/h - ical - ically
sabl/e - ed - y
sabot/age - aged - aging - eur
sabr/e - ed - ing - eur
sabretache
 (SEB SUB)

SAC
sac (medical) - cule
sacchar/in - ine - ide - ic - ose
 - oid
sacerdotal - ly - ism - ist
sacerdotalis/e - ed - ing - ation
 (z)
sachem
sachet
sack - ed - ing - ful - less
sackbut
sacrament - al - ally - alism
 - alist
sacred - ly - ness
sacrific/e - ed - ing - ial - ially
sacrileg/e - ious - iously
sacring
sacrist - y - ies - an
sacrosanct - ity
sacr/um - al
 (SAK SAS SAX SEC)

SAD
sad - der - dest - den - dening
 - dened
saddl/e - ed - ing - er
sadducee
sadhu
sad/ism - ist - istic

 (CED SED)

SAF
safari
saf/e - er - est - ely - ety
saffron

SAG
sag - ged - ging - gy
saga
sagac/ity - ious - iously
sag/e - er - est - ely - eness
saggar
Sagittari/us - an
sago

SAH
Sahara - n
sahib (*Hind*)
 (SAR)

SAI
said (did say)
sail - ed - ing
sailer (ship)
sailor (seaman) - ing
sainfoin
saint - ly - liness - like
saith (doth say)
 (SAY SEI)

SAK
sake
saker
 (SAC SAX)

SALA-SALL
salaam - ed - ing
salac/ity - ious - iously
 - iousness
salad
salamand/er - rian - rine
salam/e *or* -i (*It*)
sal - ammoniac
salar/y - ies - ied
sale - able - ability (*or* salab/le
 - ility)
salem
salic
salic/in - ylic - ylate - ylous
salien/t - tly - ce - cy
saliferous
salin/e - ity - ometer
saliv/a - ary - ate - ated - ating
 - ation
sallee (*Aus*)

212

sallow -ness -y -ish
sall/y -ies -ied -ying
  (CEL SAIL SEL SOL SUL)

SALM-SALT

salmi, for salmagundi
salmon (fish)
salmonella (illness)
salon (F)
saloon
Salop (Shropshire) -ian
salsify
salt -er -est -ed -ing -ness
  -ern
salt/y -ier -iest -iness -cellar
saltat/ion -ory -orial
saltire -wise
saltpetre
  (PSAL)

SALU

salubri/ty -ous -ously
saluki
salutar/y -ily -iness
salut/e -ed -ing -ation -atory
  -er
  (SOLU)

SALV

salv/age (rescue) -aged
  -aging; not selvage
salvation -ism -ist
salv/e -ed -ing -able
salver
salvia
salvo -s or -es
sal volatile (L)

SAM

Samar/ia -itan
samba
sambur
same -ness
sammon? No, salmon
Sam/os -ian
samite (fabric); not semite
samlet (young salmon)
Samoa -n
samovar (Russ)
Samoyed -ic
sampan (Chinese)
samphire
sampl/e -ed -ing -er
samurai (Jap)

  (CEM SEM)

SAN

sanat/orium -ory -ive; not
  sanitary
sanctif/y -ies -ied -ying
  -ication
sanctimon/y -ious -iously
  -iousness
sanctit/y -ies
sanctuar/y -ies
sanctum
sand -ed -ing -y -ier -iest
  -iness
sandal -ed
sanderling
sandwich -es -ed -ing
san/e -er -est -ely -ity
sang (did sing)
sang -froid (F)
sanguin/e -ed -eous
sanguinar/y -ily -ness
sanhedrin
sanitar/y -ily -iness -ian
sanitat/e -ed -ing -ion
sank (did sink)
sanserif
Sanskrit
Santa Claus
  (SAUN ZAN)

SAP

sap -ped -ping -py -piness
  -per
sapid -ity
sapien/t -tly -tial -ce
sapling
saponaceous
saponif/y -ied -ying -iable
  -ication
sapper
Sapph/o -ic -ism -ist
sapphir/e -ine
sapraem/ia -ic
sapro/genic -phile -phyte
  -phytic
  (SOP SUP)

SAR

saraband
Saracen -ic
sarcas/m -tic -tically
sarco/ma -us -plasm -logy

sarcophag/us -i
sard
sardine
sardonic - ally
sardonyx
sargasso
sargeant? *No*, sergeant *or*
  serjeant
sar (*Hind*)
sark (*Sc*)
sarong (*Malay*)
sarsaparilla
sarsen
sarsenet
sartorial - ly
  (SER SUR TSAR)

SAS
sash - ed
sassafras
sassenach (*Sc*)
sastrugi
  (SUS)

SAT
sat (did sit)
Satan - ic - ism - ist
satchel - led
sat/e (satiate) - ed - ing - iety
sateen
satellite
satia/te - ted - ting - tion - ble
satin - y
satir/e (ridicule) - ic - ical - ically
  - ist; *not* satyr
satiris/e - ed - ing (z)
satisfact/ion - ory - orily
  - oriness
satisf/y - ies - ied - ying - yingly
  - iable
satrap - y - ies
saturat/e - ed - ing - ion
Saturday - ish
Saturn - ian - alia - alian
saturnine - ly
satyr (woodland god) - ic
  - iasis; *not* satire
  (SET)

SAU
sauc/e - ed - ing - y - ier - iest
  - ily - iness
saucer

sauerkraut (*Ger*)
sauna
saunter - ed - ing - er
saurian
sausage
sauté - ed
Sauterne(s)
  (SAW SOR)

SAV
savag/e - ed - ing - ely - eness
  - ery
savan/a *or* - na *or* - nah
savant
sav/e - ed - ing - ingly - able - er
saveloy
saviour
savoir faire (*F*)
savory (herb)
savour (taste) - ed - ing - y - ily
  - iness
Savoy - ard
  (SEV)

SAW
saw (did see)
saw - ed - ing - yer
  (SAU SOR)

SAX
sax, *for* saxophone
saxe (blue)
saxhorn
saxifrage
Saxon - y
  (SAC SAK SEX SUCC)

SAY
say, says, said, saying
  (SAI SEI)

SCAB-SCAF
scab - bed - bing - by - biness
scabbard
scabi/es (itch) - ous
scabious (herb)
scabrous - ness
scad
scaffold - ed - ing - er

SCAL
scald - ed - ing
scal/e - ed - ing - y - iness
scalene
scallion (onion); *not* scullion
scallop *or* scollop - ed - ing

scallywag *or* scalawag
scalp - ed - ing - er
scalpel
(ESCAL)

SCAM SCAN
scamp - ed - ing
scamper - ed - ing
scampi (*It*)
scan - ned - ning - ner
scandal - ous - ously - ousness
scandalis/e - ed - ing (z)
Scandinavia - n
scansion
scant - y - ier - iest - ily - iness
scantling

SCAP SCAR
scapegoat
scapegrace
scapement *or* escapement
scapula - r
scar - red - ring
scarab
scaramouch
scarc/e - er - est - ely - eness
 - ity
scarcement
scar/e - ed - ing
scarf - ed - ing, scarfs *or*
 scarves
scarif/y - ied - ying - ier - ication
scarlatina
scarlet
scarp - ed
scarper - ed - ing
(ESCA)

SCAT
scath/e - ed - ing - ingly - eless
scatolog/y - ical
scatter - ed - ing - er
scatt/y - ily - iness
(SKAT)

SCAV
scaveng/e - ed - ing - er

SCE
scenario - s
scen/e - ery - ic; *not* seen
 (see)
scent (smell) - ed - ing; *not*
 sent, cent
sceptic - al - ally - ism (*Am,*

skep -)
sceptr/e - ed
(ASCE SE SKE)

SCH
schedul/e - ed - ing
schema - ta - tic - tically
schem/e - ed - ing - er
scherz/o - ando (*It*)
schism - atic - atical - atically
schist - ose
schizanthus
schizo/id - phrenia - phrenic
schmaltz (*from Ger,* schmalz)
schnapps
schnorkel *or* snorkel
scholar - ly - liness - ship
scholastic - ally - ism
school - ed - ing
schooner
schottische
(ESCH SH SK)

SCI
scil *or* sc, *for* scilicet (*L,* to
 wit)
sciatic - a - ally
scien/ce - tific - tifically
Scill/y - ies - onian
scimitar
scintilla
scintillat/e - ed - ing - ion - ant
scion
scissor/s - ed - ing
(CI CY SCHI SI SCY SKI)

SCL
scler/a - iasis - itis - otomy
sclero/ma - sis - sed - tic
(SL)

SCOF-SCOP
scoff - ed - ing - er - ingly
scold - ed - ing
scollop *or* scallop
sconc/e - ed - ing
scone
scoop - ed - ing - er
scoot - ed - ing - er
scope
(ESCO SCHO)

SCOR
scorbutic - ally
scorch - ed - ing - ingly - er

scor/e - ed - ing - er
scoria - ceous
scorif/y - ied - ying - ier
 - ication
scorn - ed - ing - er - ful - fully
scorp/ion - ioid
(ASCO)

SCOT
Scot - land - tish - ch - ticism
scotch - ed - ing
scot-free

SCOU SCOW
scoundrel - ly - ism
scour - ed - ing - er
scourg/e - ed - ing
scout - ed - ing - er
scow
scowl
(SCHO SCOO)

SCRA
scrabbl/e - ed - ing
scrag - ged - ging - gy - gier
 - giest - gily - giness
scram!
scrambl/e - ed - ing - ingly - er
scran
scrap - ped - ping - ping - py
 - pier - piest - pily - piness
scrap/e - ed - ing - er
scratch - ed - ing - er - y - ier
 - iest - ily - iness
scrawl - ed - ing
scrawn/y or scrann/y - ier
 - iest

SCRE
scream - ed - ing - er
scree
screech - ed - ing
screed
screen - ed - ing
screev/e - ed - ing - er
screw - ed - ing - y - eye - eyed

SCRI
scribbl/e - ed - ing - er
scribbly gum (*Aus*)
scrib/e - er; *also* ascribe
scrim
scrimmage *or* scrum
scrimp - y
scrimshank

scrip (certificate, etc.)
script (writing) - ed
scriptur/e - al
scrivener
(ASCR)

SCRO
scroful/a - ous - ousness
scroll - ed - ing
scrot/um - a - al - itis - ocele
scroung/e - ed - ing - er

SCRU
scrub - bed - bing - ber - by
 - biness
scruff - y - ier - iest - ily - iness
scrum *or* scrimmage
scrump - ed - ing
scrumptious - ly - ness
scrunch - ed - ing
scrupl/e - ed - ing
scrupul/ous - ously - osity
scrutator
scrutin/y - ies - eer
scrutinis/e - ed - ing - ingly (z)
(SCREW)

SCU-SCUP
scuba
scud - ded - ding
scuff - ed - ing
scuffl/e - ed - ing
scull (oar) - ed - ing - er; *not*
 skull
scull/ery - ion
sculptor
sculptur/e - ed - ing - al - ally
scum - med - ming - my - mier
 - miest
scumbl/e - ed - ing
scunner
scupper - ed - ing
(SKU)

SCUR
scurf - y - ier - iest - iness
scurril/ity - ous - ously
 - ousness
scurr/y - ied - ying
scurv/y - ied
(SKIR)

SCUT
scut
scutage

scutch -ed -ing -er
scutcheon *or* escutcheon
scutter -ed -ing
scuttl/e -ed -ing
scut/um -a
SCY
scyth/e -ed -ing
(CI CY SCI SY)
SEA
sea -board -borne -girt -side
-ward
seafar/ing -er
seakale
seal -ed -ing -er
sealyham
seam (in cloth) -ed -ing -less
-y; *not* seem
seamstress *or* sempstress
seaman -ship -like
séance (*F*)
sear -ed -ing -ingly (scorch);
not sere (withered), seer
(prophet)
search -ed -ing -ingly -er
seascape
season -ed -ing -al -ally
seasonab/le -ly -leness
seat -ed -ing -er
seaworth/y -ier -iest -ily
-iness
(CE SCE SEE SEI)
SEB
sebaceous
(SIB SUB)
SEC
sec, *for* second
secant
secateurs
sece/de (withdraw) -ded
-ding -der -ssion; *not*
succeed
seclu/de -ded -ding -sion
second -ed -ing -er
second/ly -ary -arily
secre/t -tly -cy
secretaire
secretar/y -es -ial -iat
secret/e -d -ing -ion
secretive -ly -ness
sect -arian -arianism

sectile
section -al -ally
sector
secular -ism -ist -istic -ity
secularis/e -ed -ing -ation (z)
secur/e -ed -ing -ity -ely
-able
(SEQ SES)
SED
sedan
sedate -ly -ness
sedat/ion -ive
sedentar/y -ily -iness
sedg/e -y
sedilia (stone seats for
priests); *not* cedilla
sediment -ary -ation
sediti/on -ous -ously
-ousness
seduc/e -ed -ing -tion -tive
-ively -tiveness -ible
sedul/ous -ously -ness
(CED)
SEE
see (vision), seen; *but* saw
see (diocese)
seed (of plant) -ed -ing; *not*
cede (give up)
seed/y -ier -iest -ily -iness
seek -ing -er; *but* sought
seem (appear to be) -ed -ing
-ingly; *not* seam
seeml/y -ier -iest -iness
seen (viewed); *not* scene
seep -ed -ing -age
seer (prophet); *not* sear
(scorch), sere (withered)
seersucker
seesaw -ed -ing
seeth/e -ed -ing
(CE SEA SEI)
SEF
(CEPH PSEPH SAF SUF)
SEG
segment -al -ally -ary
segment -ed -ing -ation
segregat/e -ed -ing -ion
(SAG SUG)
SEI
seiche (*F*)

seidlitz powder
seigneur or seignior -y -age -ial
sein/e -ing -er
seism/ic -ograph -ometer -ology
seiz/e -ed -ing -able -ure
(CEI SAI SAY SEA SEE SIE)

SEL

selacanth? No, coelacanth
seldom
select -ed -ing -ion -or
selectiv/e -ely -eness -ity
selen/ium -ite -ic -ate -ious
selen(o)-*, prefix meaning moon
seleno/graphy -logy -logist -tropic
self-*, can be used as a prefix to many words
self/ish -ishly -ishness -hood -less
sell -ing -er; but sold; not cell (room)
seltz/er -ogene
selvage or selvedge -ed; not salvage (saving)
selvagee
(CEL SAL SOL)

SEM

semantic -ally
semaphor/e -ed -ing
semblance
sem/en -inal -inally -ation
semi-*, prefix meaning half
seminar -y -ies -ist
Semit/e -ic -ism -ist
semitis/e -ed -ing -ation (z)
semolina
sempiternal
sempre (It)
sempstress or seamstress
(CEM)

SENA-SENO

senat/e -or -orial -orially
sence? No, sense
send -ing -er; but sent

senescen/t -ce
senhor -a -ita (Port)
senil/e -ity
senior -ity
senna
sennet
señor -a -ita (Sp)
(CEN SCEN)

SENS

sensation -al -ally -alism -alist
sensationalis/e -ation (z)
sense -less -lessly -lessness
sensib/le -ly -ility
sensitiv/e -ity -ely -eness
sensitis/e -ed -ing -ation -er (z)
sensor/y -ial -ium -ia
sensual -ly -ity -ism -ist
sensuous -ly -ness
(CENS)

SENT

sent (did send)
sentenc/e -ed -ing
sententious -ly -ness
sentien/t -tly -ce
sentiment -al -ally -ality -alism
sentimentalis/e -ed -ing (z)
sentinel
sentr/y -ies
(CENT SCENT)

SEP

sepal
separat/e -ed -ing -ion -ism -ist -or -ive
separ/able -ably -ability
sephalic? No, cephalic
sephology? No, psephology
sepia
sepoy
sepsis
sept-*, prefix meaning seven
September
septen/nium -nial -nate -ary
septet or septette
septic (putrefying) -ally -ity;

* If the word you wish to spell is not in this list, omit the prefix and look for the rest of the word.

but aseptic (preventing
  putrefaction); *not* sceptic
septicaemia
septuagenar/y - ian
septuagesima - l
septuagint
sept/um - a - al - ate - ation
septupl/e - ed - ing
sepulchr/e - ed - ing - al - ally
sepulture
  (SCEP SOP SUP)

SEQU
sequaci/ty - ous - ously
sequel
sequelae (*L*)
sequen/ce - t - tial - tially
sequester - ed - ing - able
sequestrat/e - ed - ing - ion - or
sequin
sequoia
  (SECU)

SERA-SERE
serac
seraglio
serape (*Sp*)
seraph - im *or* - s - ic - ically;
  not serif (type - face)
Serb - ia - ian
sercus? *No*, circus
sere (withered); *not* sear
  (scorch), seer (prophet)
serenad/e - ed - ing - er
serenata (*It*)
serendipity
seren/e - ly - ity
  (CERA CERE SERR)

SERF-SERJ
serf (slave) - dom; *not*
  surf(waves)
serge (textile) - tte; *not* surge
  (move)
sergeant (army)
serjeant (law)
  (SUR)

SERI
serial (in series) - ly - ity; *not*
  cereal

serialis/e - ed - ing - ation (z)
seriat/e - ed - ing - ion - im
sericin
sericultur/e - al - ist
series
serif (type - face); *not* seraph
  (angel)
serigraph - y - ic
serioso (*It*)
serious - ly - ness; *not* serous
  (of serum)
  (CERE CERI SERRI)

SERM-SERU
sermon - ette - ise - ising
  - iser (z)
serong? *No*, sarong
serotine
serous (of serum); *not*
  serious
serpent - ine
serpigenous
serpul/a - ae
serr/a - ae - ate - ated - ation
serried
serrulat/e - ed - ion
serum
  (CER CIR SOR SUR)

SERV
servant
serv/e - ed - ing - er - ery
servic/e - ed - ing - eable
  - eably - eableness
serviette
servil/e - ely - ity
servit/or - ude
servo -*, *prefix meaning*
  machine control of machine
  (CERV SERV)

SES
sesam/e - oid
seseli
sesqui -*, *prefix meaning*
  one- and - a - half
sesquipedalian
sessile
session - al
sestet *or* sextet

---

* If the word you wish to spell is not in this list, omit the prefix
and look for the rest of the word.

(CAES CES SUS)
SET
set - ting - ter
setaleen? *No*, acetylene
setaceous - ly
settee
settl/e - ed - ing - ment - er
settlor (law)
setts (stone paving)
(CET SAT)
SEU
(PSEU SUE)
SEV
seven (7) - th - thly - fold
 - sided
seventeen (17) - th - fold
sevent/y (70) - ies - yfold
sever - ed - ing - ance - able
several - ly - ty
sever/e - er - est - ely - ity
Seville (orange)
Sèvres (porcelain)
(SAV)
SEW
sew (stitch) - ed - n - ing - er;
 not sow (seed), so (thus)
sew/age - er - erage
(PSEU SUE)
SEX
sex - ed - ing - less
sex -*, *prefix meaning* six
sexagenar/y - ian
sexagesima - l
sext *or* sexte
sextant (navigating
 instrument)
sextet *or* sestet (music)
sexton (church official)
sextupl/e - ed - ing
sexual - ly - ity - ism - ist; *but*
 asexual (*not* sexual)
sexualis/e - ed - ing - ation (z)
sex/y - ier - iest - ily - iness
(SEC SAX SIX)

SF
sforzando (*It*)
(SPH)
SHAB-SHAK
shabb/y - ier - iest - ily - iness
 - yish
shabrack
shack
shackl/e - ed - ing
shad
shaddock
shad/e - ed - ing - eless
shad/y - ier - iest - ily - iness
shadoof *or* shaduf
shadow - ed - ing - y - er
shaft - ed - ing
shag - ged - gy - gier - giest - ily
 - iness
shagreen *or* chagrin
shah
shak/e - en - ing - able - er; *but*
 shook; *not* sheik
shak/y - ier - iest - ily - iness
Shakespear /e† - ian
shako
(CHA)
SHAL
shal/e - y - iness
shall, shalt, shan't
shalloon
shallot
shallow - er - est - ed - ing - ly
 - ness
(CHAL)
SHAM
sham - med - ming - mer
shaman - ism
shambl/e - ed - ing
shambles
sham/e - ed - ing - ful - fully
 - fulness
shameless - ly - ness
shammy *or* chamois - leather
shampoo - ed - ing
shamrock

* If the word you wish to spell is not in this list, omit the prefix
and look for the rest of the word.
† His six known signatures include the spellings: Shakspeare,
Shakspere, Shaksper, *but not* Shakespeare!

(CHAM SHEM)

SHAN
shand/y - ies - ygaff
shanghai - ed - ing
shank - ed
shan't (shall not)
shantung
shant/y - ies
(CHAN)

SHAP
shap/e - ed - ing - able - ely
 - eliness
shapeless - ly - ness
(CHAP)

SHAR
shard or sherd
shar/e - ed - ing - er
shark - ed - ing
sharp - er - est - ly - ness
sharpen - ed - ing - er
(CHAR)

SHAT SHAV
shatter (smash) - ed - ing
shatto? No, chateau (F)
shav/e - ed - ing - er

SHAW
shaw (copse)
Sha/w - vian
shawl - ed
shawm
(CHAU SHOR SURE)

SHE-SHED
she, she'd (she would), she'll
 (she will or shall), she's (she
 is or has); also she- as
 prefix

shea/f (of corn, etc.) - ves
shear (clip) - ed - ing - ling; not
 sheer
shear-legs or sheer-legs
sheath (a cover) - s
sheath/e - ed - ing
sheave (a pulley-wheel)
shebang
shebeen (Ir)
shed - ding - der
(SCH)

SHEE-SHEK
sheek? No, chic (F)

sheen - y
sheep - ish - ishly - ishness
sheer (simple); not shear
sheer-legs or shear-legs
sheet - ed - ing
shef? No, chef (F)
shei/k or - kh
sheila (Aus)
shekel
(CHEA CHIE SHE SHEA)

SHEL
shel/drake - duck
shel/f - ves - ved - ving
shell - ed - ing - y - less
shellac
shelter - ed - ing
shelt/y or - ie - ies
(SHAL SHIL)

SHEM
shemozzle
(CHEM SHAM)

SHEP
shepherd - ed - ing

SHER
Sheraton
sherbet
sherd or shard
sheriff - s; but shrieval - ty
sherpa
sherr/y - ies
(CHER CHIR SCHER SHIR)

SHEW
shew (old form of show) - ed
 - ing
(SHOE)

SHI
shibboleth
shicer (Aus)
shield - ed - ing - less
shieling (Sc)
shift - ed - ing - less - lessly
 - lessness
shift/y - ier - iest - ily - iness
shillelagh
shilling
shilly - shall/y - ied - ying
shimmer - ed - ing
shin - ned - ning
shind/y - ies
shin/e - ing - y - ier - iest - er;

but shone
shingl/e -y
shintiyan
Shinto -ism -ist
shinty
ship -ped -ping -per -wright
shippon *or* shippen
shiralee (*Aus*)
shire
shirk -ed -ing -er
shir(r) -ring
shirt -ed -ing -y -less
shit -ting -ter
shiver -ed -ing -y -ish
shivoo (*Aus*)
  (CHI SCHI SHER SHY)

SHOA-SHOP
shoal -ed -ing -y -iness
shock -ed -ing -er -ingly
shod (did shoe)
shodd/y -ier -iest -ily -iness
shoe -ing; *but* shod
shook (did shake)
shone (did shine)
shoo (drive away) -ed -ing
shoot -ing -er -able; *but* shot
shop -ped -ping -per -py
  (CHAU SCHO)

SHOR
shore -less -ward; *also*
  ashore; *not* sure (certain)
shor/e -ed -ing
shorn (clipped)
short -er -est -ness -age -ly
short -* *can be prefixed to
  many words, either with a
  hyphen* (short -circuit) *or
  without* (shorthand)
shorten -ed -ing
  (SHAW)

SHOT-SHOW
shot
should -n't
shoulder -ed -ing
shout -ed -ing
shov/e -ed -ing
shovel -led -ling -ful -ler

show -ed -ing -n -y -ier -iest
  -ily -iness
shower -ed -ing -y -iness
  (CHAU CHO SCHO)

SHR
shrank (did shrink)
shrapnel
shred -ded -ding -der
shrew -sh -ishly -ishness
shrewd -er -est -ly -ness
shriek -ed -ing -er
shrieval -ty; *but* sheriff
shrift (short shrift)
shrike
shrill -er -est -ed -ing -y
  -ness
shrimp -ed -ing -er
shrine (*also* enshrine)
shrink -ing -age -able; *but*
  shrank, shrunk
shriv/e -ing -en; *but* shrove
shrivel -led -ling
shroud -ed -ing
Shrove Tuesday
shrub -by -bery -beries
shrug -ged -ging
shrunk -en; *but* shrink

SHU
shuck -ed -ing
shudder -ed -ing -ingly -y
shuffl/e -ed -ing -ingly -er
shugar? *No,* sugar
shun -ned -ning
shunt -ed -ing -er
shut -ting -ter
shuttl/e -ed -ing
  (CHU)

SHY
shy -er -est -ly -ness
sh/y -ied -ying
shyster
  (CHI SHI)

SIA
Siam -ese
  (SCI)

SIB
sib -ling -ship

---

* If the word you wish to spell is not in this list, omit the prefix
and look for the rest of the word.

Siberia -n
sibilan/t -tly -ce -cy
sibilat/e -ed -ing -ion
sibyl -line
(CEB CIB SEB)

SIC
sic (L, so)
siccative
sice (6 on dice)
sice or syce (Hind, groom)
Sicil/y -ian
sick -er -est -ness -ly -lier
-liest -liness
sicken -ed -ing -ingly -er
sickle
(CIC CYC PSYC SEC SIK
SYC)

SID
side-* can be used as a
prefix to many words
sid/e -ed -ing -edly -edness;
also aside
sidelong
sidereal
side/ward -ways
sidl/e -ed -ing
(CID CYD SED)

SIE
siege, also besiege
sienna (It)
sierra (Sp)
siesta (Sp)
siev/e -ed -ing
(CEI SCI SEA SEE SEI)

SIF
siffleu/r -se (F)
sift -ed -ing -er
(CIPH SIPH SYPH)

SIG
sigh -ed -ing
sight -ed -ing -edly -edness
-less
sightl/y -ier -iest -iness
sigillate
sigma (Gr) -te -tic
sigmoid
sign -ed -ng; not sine (trig.)

signal -led -ling -ler -ly
signalis/e -ed -ing -ation (z)
signator/y -ies
signature
signet (seal); not cygnet
(young swan)
significan/t -tly -ce
signif/y -ies -ied -ying
-ication
signor -a -ina (It)
(CIG CYG SAG)

SIK
Sikh
(CYC PSYC SIC)

SIL
silage, from silo
silenc/e -ed -ing -er
silent -ly
Silesia -n
silhouett/e -ed -ing
silic/a -on -one -ic -ate -ated
silic/ious or -eous
silicif/y -ied -ying -ication
silico/sis -tic
silk -en -y -ier -iest -ily -iness
sillabub
sill/y -ier -iest -ily -iness
silo -s
silt -ed -ing
silurian
silv/an or sylv/an -iculture
silver -ed -ing
(CIL CYL PSIL SAL SCIL
SEL SYL)

SIM
simian
similar -ly -ity
simile
similitude
simmer -ed -ing
simnel
simon/y -ies -iac -iacal
simoom
simper -ed -ing -ingly -er
simpl/e -er -est -y -ism -istic
-icity
simpleton

---

* If the word you wish to spell is not in this list, omit the prefix
and look for the rest of the word.

simplif/y -ied -ying -ication
simulacr/um -a
simulant
simulat/e -ed -ing -ion -or
simultane/ous -ously
  -ousness -ity
  (CIM CYM SEM SYM)

SIN
sin -ned -ning -ner
sinful -ly -ness
sinless -ly -ness
Sinai -tic
since
sincer/e -er -est -ely -ity
sine (trig.); *not* sign
sine die (*L*)
sine qua non (*L*)
sinecur/e (without duties)
  -ism -ist; *not* cynosure
sinew -ed -y
sinfonia (*It*, symphony)
sing -ing -er -able; *but* sang,
  sung
sing/e -ed -eing
singl/e -ed -ing -y -eness
singlet
singleton
singsong
singular -ly -ity
Sinhalese (of Ceylon)
sinist/er -erly -ral -rally
sink -ing -able -er; *but* sank,
  sunk
Sinn Fein (*Ir*)
Sino-*, *prefix meaning*
  Chinese
Sinolog/y -ist
sinter
sinu/ous -ously -osity -ate
  -ately
sinus -es
  (CIN CYN SCIN SEN SYN)

SIP
sip -ped -ping
siphon -ed -ing -ic -age
siph/onet -uncle
sippet

(CIP CYP SUP SYP)

SIR
sir
sir/e -ed -ing
siren
sirloin
sirname? *No*, surname
sirocco
  (CER CIR CYR SUR SYR)

SIS
sisal
siskin
sissors? *No*, scissors
sister -ly -liness -hood -less
sistern? *No*, cistern
  (CIS CYS SIZ SYS)

SIT
sit -ting -ter; *but* sat
situat/e -ed -ing -ion
sit/e (for building) -ed -ing;
  not sight
sitz -bath
  (CIT CYT PSIT SET)

SIV
  (CIV SEV SIEV)

SIX
six (6) -th -thly -er -fold
  -sided
sixteen (16) -th -fold
sixt/y (60) -ies -ieth -yfold

SIZ
siz/e -ed -ing -er -able -y
sizar -ship
sizzl/e -ed -ing
  (SCIS SIS SYS)

SKA
skat
skat/e -ed -ing -er
  (SCA)

SKE
skeddaddl/e -ed -ing
skee? *No*, ski
skein
skelet/on -onic -al
skeletonis/e -ed -ing -ation
  (z)
skelp -ed -ing (*Sc*)

* If the word you wish to spell is not in this list, omit the prefix
  and look for the rest of the word

skep *or* skip (basket,
  bee-hive)
skeptic? *No*, sceptic; *but*
  Am, sk-
skerrick (*Aus*)
skerr/y -ies
sketch -ed -ing -er
sketch/y -ier -iest -ily -iness
skew; *also* askew
skewbald
skewer -ed -ing; *not* skua
  (bird)
  (SCE SCHE)

SKI-SKIP

ski, ski'd, skiing, skier
skid -ded -ding
skiff
skiffle
skil/l -led -ful -fully -fulness
skillion (*Aus*)
skilly
skim -med -ming -mer
skimp -ed -ing -y -ier -iest
skin -ned -ning -ner -ny -nier
  -niest
skink
skip -ped -ping -pingly -per
  (SCH)

SKIR

skirl -ed -ing
skirmish -es -ed -ing -er
skirret
skirt -ed -ing
  (SCUR SKER)

SKIT SKIV

skit
skit/e -ing -er (*Aus*)
skitsophrenia? *No*,
  schizophrenia
skitter -ed -ing
skittish -ly -ness
skittl/e -es -ed -ing -er
skiv/e -ed -ing -er
skivv/y -ies -ied -ying

SKU

skua (bird); *not* skewer
skulduggery
skulk -ed -ing -ingly -er
skull (head) -ed; *not* scull
  (oar)

skunk
  (SCU)

SKW

  (SQU)

SKY

sk/y -ies -ied -ying -yer
  -yward
Skye
  (SKI)

SLA

slab -bed -bing -ber
slack -ed -ing -ly -er -ness
slacken -ed -ing
slag -ged -ging -gy
slain (slay)
slak/e -ed -ing
slalom -ed -ing
slam -med -ming -mer
slander -ed -ing -er -ous
  -ously -ousness
slang -ed -ing -y -ier -iest -ily
  -iness
slant -ed -ing -ingly -wise;
  also aslant
slap -ped -ping -per
slapdash
slaphappy
slapstick
slash -ed -ing -er
slat -ted -ting
slat/e -ed -ing -er -y -ier -iest
  -iness
slather (*Aus*)
slattern -ly -liness
slaughter -ed -ing -er
Slav -ic -onic -onian
slav/e -ed -ing -er -ery -ish
slaver (dribble) -ed -ing
slaw
slay, slew, slain

SLE

sleaz/y -ier -iest -ily -iness
sled
sledg/e -ed -ing
sleek -er -est -ly -ness
sleep -ing -er -y -ier -iest;
  also asleep; *but* slept
sleepless -ly -ness
sleet -ing -y -iness
sleev/e -ed -eless

sleigh (sledge); *not* slay
sleight (dexterity); *not* slight
slender - er - est - ly - ness
slept (did sleep)
sleuth
slew (did slay)
slew (turn) - ed - ing
  (SCLE SEL)

SLI

slic/e - ed - ing - er
slick - er - est - ly - ness
slid/e - ing - er; slid (did slide)
slight - er - est - ly - ness
slight - ed - ing - ingly
slim - mer - mest - med - ming
  - ness
slim/e - y - ier - iest - iness
sling - ing - er; *but* slung
slink - ing - y; *but* slunk
slip - ped - ping - py
slipper - ed - ing
slipper/y - ier - iest - iness
slit - ting
slither - ed - ing
sliver (splinter); *not* saliva
  (SLEI SLY)

SLO

slobber - ed - ing - er
sloe (fruit); *not* slow
slog - ged - ging - ger
slogan
sloop
slop - ped - ping - py - pier
  - piest - pily - piness
slop/ed - ing
slosh - ed - ing
slot - ted - ting
sloth - ful - fully - fulness
slouch - ed - ing - ingly - er
slough - ed - ing - y
Slovak - ia - ian
sloven - ly - liness
Sloven/e - ia - ian
slow - er - est - ed - ing - ness;
  not sloe (fruit)
slow - worm
  (SALO)

SLU

slub - bed - bing - ber
sludg/e - y

slug - gish - gishly - gishness
sluggard - ly - liness
sluic/e - ed - ing
slum - med - ming - my - mer
slumber - ed - ing - er - ous
  - ously
slummock - ed - ing
slump - ed - ing
slung (did sling)
slunk (did slink)
slur - red - ring
slurry
slush - y - ier - iest - ily - iness
slusher (*Aus*)
slut - tish - tishly - tishness
  - tery
  (SALU SCLE)

SLY

sly - er - est - ly - ness
slype
  (SLEI SLI)

SMA

smack - ed - ing - er
small - er - est - ness - ish
smallage
smalt
smart - ed - ing
smart - er - est - ly - ness
smarten - ed - ening
smash - ed - ing - er
smatter - ing - er

SME

smear - ed - ing - y - iness;
  also besmear
smeech *or* smitch
smell - ing - er - y - ier - iest
  - iness - ed *or* smelt
smelt - ed - ing - er
smew

SMI

smilax
smil/e - ed - ing - ingly - er
  - eless
smirch - ed - ing; *also*
  besmirch
smirk - ed - ing
smit/e - ing - ten - er; *but*
  smote
smith - y - ery
smithereens

SMO

smock - ed - ing
smog
smok/e - ed - ing - er - less
 - lessness - able
smok/y - ier - iest - ily - iness
smoko (*Aus, NZ*)
smolt
smoodg/e - er (*Aus*)
smooth - er - est - ly - ness - ed
 - ing
smorgasbord (*Sw*)
smote (did smite)
smother - ed - ing
smoulder - ed - ing

SMU

smudg/e - ed - ing - y - ier - iest
 - ily - iness
smug - ger - gest - ly - ness
smuggl/e - ed - ing - er
smut - ted - ting - ty - tier - tiest
 - tily - tiness
smutch *or* smudge

SMY

Smyrn/a - iot
(SMI)

SNA

snack
snaffl/e - ed - ing
snafu *for* situation normal,
 etc.
snag - ged - gy
snail
snak/e - ed - ing - y - iness
snap - ped - ping - per - py
 - pier - piest
snappish - ly - ness
snar/e - ed - ing - er
snarl - ed - ing - er
snarl - ed - ing - ingly - er --y
snatch - ed - ing - er - y - ily

SNE

sneak - ed - ing - ingly - ers
sneck (*Sc*)
sneer - ed - ing - ingly - er
sneez/e - ed - ing

SNI

snib - bed - bing (*Sc*)
snick - ed - ing

snicker - ed - ing
snickersnee
snide - ly - sman
sniff - ed - er - y - ier - iest
snigger - ed - ing
snip - ped - ping - per - pet
snip/e - ed - ing - er
snivel - led - ling - ler

SNO

snob - bish - bishly - bishness
 - bery
snoek *or* snook (fish)
snood
snook (gesture)
snooker - ed - ing
snoop - ed - ing - er
snoot/y - ier - iest - ily - iness
snooz/e - ed - ing
snor/e - ed - ing - er
snorkel
snort - ed - ing - er
snot - ty - ties - tier - tiest - tily
 - tiness
snout - ed
snow - ed - ing - y - ier - iest
 - iness

SNU

snub - bed - bing - ber
snuff - ed - ing - er
snuff/y - ier - iest - iness - ily
snuffl/e - ed - ing - ingly - er
snug - ger - gest - ly - ness
 - gery
snuggl/e - ed - ing

SO-SOA

so (thus), *not* sew, sow
soak - ed - ing - er - age
soap - ed - ing - er - less
soap/y - ier - iest - ily - iness
soapsuds
soar (fly) - ed - ing - ingly - er;
 not sore
(PSO SOW)

SOB

sob - bed - bing - ber - stuff
sober - er - est - ed - ing - ly
sobriety
sobriquet *or* soubriquet

SOC

soccer, *for* association

football
sociab/le -ly -ility
social -ly -ity -ite
social/ism -ist -istic -istically
socialis/e -ed -ing -ation (z)
societ/y -ies
sociolog/y -ical -ically -ist
sock -ed -ing
socket -ed -ing
sockeye
socle
Socrat/es -ic -ically

SOD
sod
soda
sodalit/y -ies
sodden (soaked) -ness; *not*
  sudden
sodium
sodom/y -ite

SOF
sofa
soffit
soft -er -est -ly -ness -ish
soften -ed -ing -er
  (SOPH SAF)

SOG
sogg/y -ier -iest -ily -iness
  (SOJ)

SOI
soi disant (*F*)
soigné -e (*F*)
soil -ed -ing -er -less
soirée (*F*)
  (SOYA SWA)

SOJ
sojourn -ed -ing -er
  (SOLD)

SOLA-SOLF
solac/e -ed -ing
solan -goose
solanum
solar -ium -ia (of the sun)
solati/um (solace) -a
sold (did sell); *not* soled,
  souled
solder -ed -ing
soldier -y -ed -ing -ly -like
sol/e (foot,fish) -ed -ing; *not*
  soul

solecism
solemn -ly -ity -ities
solemnis/e -ed -ing -ation (z)
solenoid
sol-fa
solferino
  (CELE SAL SELE)

SOLI SOLL
solicit -ed -ing -ation
solicitor
solicit/ude -ous -ously
solid -ly -ity -arity
solidif/y -ies -ied -ying -iable
  -ication
soliloqu/y -ies -ise -ised
  -ising (z)
solips/ism -ist
solitaire
solitar/y -ily -iness
solitude
sollicker (*Aus*)
  (CIL SAL SIL)

SOLO-SOLV
solo -s
solsti/ce -tial
solub/le -ly -ility
solution -ist
solv/e -ed -ing -er -able
  -ability
solven/t -cy
  (SAL)

SOM
somat/ic -ically -ogenic
  -ology
sombre -ly -ness
sombrero -s
some -thing -times -what
  -when -where
somersault
Somerset
somnambul/ism -ist -ant
  -istic
somniferous
somnolen/t -tly -ce -cy
  (SUM)

SON
son -ny -ship
son et lumière (*F*)
sonar
sonata

228

song -ster -stress
sonic
sonnet -eer
sono/buoy -meter
sonor/ous -ously -ific -escent
sonsy (*Sc*)
  (SUN)

SOO
sook -y *or* -ie (*Aus*)
soon -er -est
soot -ed -ing -y -ier -iest
  -iness
sooth (truth)
sooth/e -ed -ing -ingly
  (SOU)

SOP
sop -ped -ping -py -pier
  -piest
soph/ism -ist -istical
sophisticat/e -ed -ing -ion
sophomore
soporific -ally
sopran/o -os *or* -i
  (SOF SUP)

SOR
sorb -ic -ate
sorbet
sorcer/y -ies -er -ess
sordid -ly -ness
sord? *No*, sword
sordine (mute, damper); *not*
  sardine
sore (hurt) -st -ly -ness; *not*
  soar (fly)
sorghum
soriasis? *No*, psoriasis
soroptimist
sororit/y -ies
sorra (*Ir*)
sorrel
sorrow -ed -ing -ful -fully
  -fulness
sorr/y -ier -iest -ily -iness
sort -ed -ing -er -able
sortie
sorti/tion -lege
  (SAU SAW SOAR)

SOS
S O S (morse signal)
so -so

sostenuto (*It*)
  (SAUS SOCI)

SOT
sot -tish -tishly -tishness
sotto voce (*It*)

SOU
sou
soubrette
soufflé
sough -ed -ing
sought (did seek); *also*
  besought
soul -ed -ful -fully -fulness
soulless -ly -ness
sound -er -est -ly -ness
sound -ed -ing -er -less
soup -ed -ing -y -ier -iest
soupçon (*F*)
sour -er -est -ed -ing -ly
  -ness
source
sous/e -ed -ing
soutane
souter (*Sc*)
south -ern -erly -ing -ward
  -erner -ron
south-east -ern -erly -er
south-west -ern -erly -er
souvenir
  (SOO SOW)

SOV
sovereign -ty
soviet

SOW
sow (seed) -ed -ing -er; *not*
  sew (stitch)
sow (female pig)
  (SOA SOU)

SOY
soy, soya (bean)
  (SOI)

SOZ
sozzl/e -ed -ing -er
  (SAUC SAUS)

SPA-SPAN
spa (health resort); *not* spar
spac/e -ed -ing -er
spacious -ly -ness; *but*
  spatial
spade -ful

spaghetti
Spain; *but* Spanish
spake (did speak)
spam
span - ned - ning
spandrel
spang/e - ed - ing
spaniel
Span/ish - iard
spank - ed - ing - er
spanner

SPAR

spar - red - ring; *not* spa
(health resort)
spar/e - ed - ing - ingly - ely
- eness
sparger
spark - ed - ing - er
sparkl/e - ed - ing - ingly - er
sparrow
sparrow - grass (asparagus)
spars/e - er - est - ely - eness
Sparta - n

SPAS-SPAY

spasm - odic - odically
spastic
spat (did spit, gaiter, spawn)
spatchcock - ed - ing
spate
spath/e - ose - ous - ic - iform
spatial - ly - ity
spatter - ed - ing; *also*
bespatter
spatul/a - ate
spavin - ed
spawn - ed - ing
spay - ed - ing

SPEA

speak - ing - er; *but* spoke,
spoken
spear - ed - ing
(SPEE)

SPEC

spec, *for* speculation
special - ly - ty - ity - ism - ist
specialis/e - ed - ing - ation (z)
specie (coins)
speci/es - fic - ology
specif/y - ies - ied - ying - iable
- ication

specimen
speci/ous - ously - ousness
speck - ed - ing - less
speckl/e - ed - ing
specs, *for* spectacles
spectac/le - led - ular - ularly
spectat/or - ress
spectr/e - al - ally
spectro/gram - graph - meter
spectroscop/e - y - ic - ical - ist
spectr/um - a - al
speculat/e - ed - ing - ion - ive
- ively
specul/um - a - ar

SPED

sped (did speed)

SPEE

speech - ify - ified - ifying - less
speed - ing - er - ometer; *but*
sped
speed/y - ier - iest - ily - iness
(SPEA)

SPEL

spel/l - t *or* - led - ling - ler
spelt (wheat)
spelter

SPEN

spencer
spend - ing - er - able; *but*
spent

SPER

sperm - ary - atic
spermaceti
spermato - zoon - zoa - logy
- cele - rrhoea
(SPIR SPUR)

SPES SPET

(SPEC)

SPEW

spew - ed - ing; *or* spu/e - ed
- ing; *but* sputum

SPH

sphagn/um - a
sphenoid - al
spher/e - ical - ically - icity
- ometer
spheroid - al - ally
spherulite
sphincter - ic - ial
sphinx - es

230

sphorzando? *No*, sforzando
sphygmo/gram -graph
 -manometer
sphygmus

SPIC-SPIL

spic/e -ed -ing -y -ier -iest
 -ily -iness
spick and span
spicul/e -ar -ate
spider -y -ish
spied (did spy)
spiel -er
spiflicat/e -ed -ing -ion
spigot
spik/e -ed -ing -y -ier -iest
 -iness
spikelet
spikenard
spil/e (peg) -ed -ing; *not* spoil
spill -ikin
spil/l -t *or* -led -ling -ler
 (SPY)

SPIN

spin -ning -ner; *but* spun *or*
 span
spina bifida (*L*)
spinach
spinal
spindl/e -y
spindrift
spin/e -ed -y -ier -iest -iness
spineless -ly -ness
spinel
spinet
spinifex (*Aus*)
spinnaker
spinster -hood

SPIR

spirac/le -ular -ulate
spiraea
spiral -led -ling -ly -ity
spire
spirit -ed -ing -uous -less
spiritual -ly -ity -ism -ist
spirit *or* spurt -ed -ing
 (SPER SPUR)

SPIT SPIV

spit -ting -ter -tle -toon; *but*
 spat
spitted (put on a spit)

spit/e -ed -ing -eful -efully
 -efulness
spiv -vish -vishly -vishness

SPL

splash -ed -ing -er
splatter -ed -ing
splay -ed -ing
sple/en -nic
splend/id -idly -our -iferous
splenetic -ally
splic/e -ed -ing -er
spline
splint -er -ery -eriness
split -ting -ter
splotch -y
splurg/e -ed -ing
splutter -ed -ing -er

SPOI-SPON

spoil -ed -ing -er -age
spoke (bar)
spok/e (did speak) -en
spokesman
spoliation (plunder); *not*
 spoil-
spondee
spondyle
spong/e -ed -ing -er -y -ier
 -iest -ily -iness
sponson (of ship)
sponsor -ed -ing -ial -ship
spontane/ous -ously -ity

SPOO

spoof -ed -ing -er
spook -y -ier -iest -ish
spool
spoon -ed -ing -ful
Spooner -ism
spoor
 (SPU)

SPOR

sporadic -ally
spor/e -ule
sporran
sport -ed -ing -ingly
sport/y -ier -iest -ive -ively
 (SPAW)

SPOT

spot -ted -ting -ter -less
 -lessly -lessness
spott/y -ier -iest -ily -iness

SPOU

spouse (husband or wife);
 but espouse (marry, etc.)
spout - ed - ing - er

SPRA SPRE

sprag
sprain - ed - ing
spraints
sprang (did spring)
sprat - ting - ter
sprawl - ed - ing
spray - ed - ing - er
spread - ing - er
spree

SPRI

sprig - ged - ging - gy
sprightl/y - ier - iest - iness;
 but sprite
spring - ing - er - y - ier - iest;
 but sprang, sprung
springbok
springe
sprinkl/e - ed - ing - er
sprint - ed - ing - er
sprit - sail
sprite; *but* sprightly
 (SPRY)

SPRO SPRU

sprocket
sprout - ed - ing
spruc/e - ed - ing - ely - eness
sprue
spruik - er (*Aus*)
spruit
sprung (spring)

SPRY

spry - er - est - ly - ness
 (SPRI)

SPUD-SPUN

spud - ded - ding - dy
spuddl/e - ed - ing - er
spu/e - ed - ing *or* spew - ed
 - ing
spum/e - y - ily - iness
spun (did spin)
spunk - y - ier - iest

SPUR

spur - red - ring - rier
spurge
spurious - ly - ness

spurling - line
spurn - ed - ing
spurry
spurt - ed - ing
 (SPER SPIR)

SPUT

sputnik
sputter - ed - ing - ingly - er
sputum

SPY

spy - ing, spied, spier
 (SPI)

SQUA

squab - by
squabbl/e - ed - ing - er
squad - ron
squal/or - id - idly
squall - y - ier - iest
squam/ous - ose
squander - ed - ing - er
squar/e - er - est - ed - ing - ely
 - eness - ish
squash - ed - ing
squat - ted - ting - ter
squaw
squawk - ed - ing - er

SQUE

squeak - ed - ing - er - y - ier
 - iest - ily - iness
squeal - ed - ing - er
squeamish - ly - ness
squeegee - d - ing
squeez/e - ed - ing - able
 - ability - er
squelch - ed - ing

SQUI

squib
squid
squiff/y - ier - iest - ily - iness
squill
squinch
squint - ed - ing - er
squir/e - ed - ing - (e)archy
 - een
squirm - ed - ing
squirrel
squirt - ed - ing
squish
squit
squiz (*Aus*)

SQUO
(SQUA)
STAB-STAG
stab - bed - bing - ber
stability
stabilis/e - ed - ing - ation (z)
stabl/e - er - est - y
stabl/e - ed - ing
staccato (It)
stack - ed - ing
stadi/um - a or - ums
staff - ed - ing - s; but stave - s
(music)
staflex (fabric)
stafyl - ? No, staphylococcus
stag - gard; not staggered
stag/e - ed - ing - er - y - iness
stagger - ed - ing - ingly
stagnat/e - ed - ing - ion
stagnan/t - tly - cy
STAI
staid - ly - ness
stain - ed - ing - er - less - lessly
- lessness
stair - s - way; not stare (gaze)
staith or staithe
(STAY STEA)
STAK
stak/e - ed - ing; not steak
(meat)
(STAC)
STAL
stalact/ite - itic - iform
stalagm/ite - itic - iform
stal/e - er - est - ely - eness
stalemate
stalk - ed - ing - er - y - less
stall - ed - ing - age
stallion
stalwart - ly - ness
STAM
stam/en - inal - inate
stamina
stammer - ed - ing - ingly - er
stamp - ed - ing
stamped/e - ed - ing
STAN
stance
stanch or staunch - ed - ing
stanchion

stand - ing; but stood
standard
standardis/e - ed - ing - ation (z)
stank (did stink)
stann/ary - ic - ate - iferous
stanza
(STEN)
STAP
staphylococc/us - i
stapl/e - ed - ing - er
STAR
star - red - ring - ry - dom - let
star-gaz/er - y - pie
starboard
starch - ed - ing - y - ier - iest
- iness
star/e - ed - ing - ingly - er
stark - ly
starling
starn? No, stern
start - ed - ing
startl/e - ed - ing - ingly
starv/e - ed - ing - ation - eling
STAS
stasis; but static
STAT
stat/e - ed - ing - edly - ement
statel/y - ier - iest - iness
statesman - ly - like - ship
static - al - ally
station - ed - ing
stationary (still)
stationer - y (paper)
statist - ic - ical - ically - ician
stator
statu/e - ary - esque
statur/e - ed
status - ed
statut/e (law) - ory - orily
STAU
staunch (loyal) - er - est - ly
- ness
staunch or stanch (check
flow) - ed - ing
(STOR)
STAV
stave (staff)
stav/e (in) - ing - ed or stove (in)
STAY
stay - ed - ing - er; not staid

233

(steady
(STAI)

STEA

stead -fast -fastly -fastness
steading
stead/y -ier -iest -ily -iness
steak
steal -ing -er; *but* stole -n;
  not steel (metal)
stealth -y -ier -iest -ily -iness
steam -ed -ing -er
steam/y -ier -iest -ily -iness
stear/in -ic -ate
steatit/e -ic
steato/sis -tic -pygia -pygous
  (STEE)

STEE

steed
steel -ed -ing -y -iness; *not*
  steal (thieve)
steep (slope) -er -est -ly
  -ness
steep (soak) -ed -ing
steepen -ed -ing
steepl/e -ed -ejack
steeplechas/e -ed -ing -er
steer -ed -ing -able -ability
  -er
steerage -way
steev/e -ed -ing
  (STEA STE-)

STEI

stein
steinbock
  (STEA STEE STI STY)

STEL-STEP

stele (inscribed pillar)
stell/ar -ate -ately -ular
stem -med -ming -mer -less
stemple
sten -gun
stench
stencil -led -ling -ler
stenograph/y -ic -er
stenter -ed -ing
Stentor -ian
step -ped -ping -per
step -father -mother, etc.
stephanotis
steppe (*Russ*)

STER

stereo -s, *for* stereotype, etc.
stereo/gram -graph -phony
  -phonic -scope -scopic, etc.
steril/e -ity
sterilis/e -ed -ing -ation (z)
sterling
stern -ly -ness -er -est
stern (of ship); *also* astern;
  not starn
stern/um -al
sternutat/ion -ive -ory
stertorous -ly -ness
  (STIR STUR)

STET STEV

stet (*L*)
stethoscop/e -ic -ically
stetson
stevedore

STEW

stew -ed -ing -er
steward -ess -ship
  (STU)

STIC-STIL

stick -ing -er; *but* stuck
stick/y -ier -iest -ily -iness
stickit (*Sc*)
stickleback
stickler
stiff -er -est -ly -ness -ish
stiffen -ed -ing -er
stifle -ed -ing
stigma -s *or* -ta -tic -tose
stigmatis/e -ed -ing -ation (z)
stile (over fence, etc); *not*
  style
stiletto -s
still -ed -ing -er -est -ness
stillage
stilt -ed -ing -edly -edness
Stilton

STIM-STIP

stimul/us -i -ant
stimulat/e -ed -ing -ion -ive
sting -ing -er; *but* stung
stingo
sting/y -ier -iest -ily -iness
stink -ing -ingly -er -ard; *but*
  stank, stunk
stint -ed -ing -ingly

234

stipend -iary -iaries
stippl/e -ed -ing -er
stipulat/e -ed -ing -ion -or
stipul/e -ar -ary -ate -iform

STIR

stir -red -ring -ringly -rer;
also astir
stirk
stirp(s) -iculture
stirrup
(STER STUR)

STIT STIV

stitch -ed -ed -ing -er
stith/y -ies
stiver

STOA-STON

stoat
stock -ed -ing -er -ist -less
stockade
stockinet
stocking; *not* stoking
 (fuelling)
stock/y -ier -iest -ily -iness
stodg/e -y -ier -iest -ily
 -iness
stoep
stoic -al -ally -ism
stok/e -ed -ing -er; *not* stock
stol/e (did steal) -en
stole (scarf)
stolid -ly -ity
stolon -ate
stomach -ed -ing -er -ic
stomat/ology -itis
ston/e -ed -ing -y -ier -iest
 -ily -iness
stonker -ed (*Aus*)

STOO

stood (did stand)
stog/e -ed -ing
stook -ed -ing
stool
stoop (bend) -ed -ing -ingly
 -er; *not* stoup
 (STOU STU)

STOP

stop -ped -ping -per -page

STOR

stor/e -ed -ing -able -age -er
storey (floor) -s -ed; *or* stor/y

-ies -ied
stork
storm -ed -ing -y -ier -iest
 -ily -iness
stor/y (tale) -ies -ied
 (STAU)

STOU-STOW

stoup (flagon, etc.); *not*
 stoop
stoush -ed -ing (*Aus*)
stout -er -est -ly -ness -ish
stove (heater)
stove (did stave)
stow -ed -ing -age

STRAB-STRAG

strabism/us -al -ic
straddl/e -ed -ing
strad, *for* Stradivarius
straf/e -ed -ing
straggl/e -ed -ing -er

STRAI

straight -er -est -ness; *not*
 strait (narrow)
straighten -ed -ing -er
strain -ed -ing -er
strait (narrow) -ly -ness; *not*
 straight
straits (narrow waters)
 (STRAY)

STRAK-STRAW

strake
strand -ed -ing
strang/e -er -est -ely -eness
strangl/e -ed -ing -er
strangulat/e -ed -ing -ion
strangur/y -ious
strap -ped -ping -per
strass
stratagem
strateg/y -ies -ic -ically
strath (*Sc*)
stratif/y -ied -ying -ication
 -icatory
stratigraph/y -ic -ically
stratospher/e -ic
strat/um -a
stratus
strato/ -cumulus -cirrus
straw -y
strawberr/y -ies

235

STRAY
stray - ed - ing; *also* astray
(STRAI)
STRE
streak - ed - ing - er
streak/y - ier - iest - ily - iness
stream - ed - ing - er - let
street
strength - en - ened - ening
strenuous - ly - ness
streptococc/us - i
streptomycin
stress - ed - ing
stretch - ed - ing - er - y - iness
strew - ed - ing - n
STRI
stria - e - te - ted - ting - tion
stricken (strike)
strict - er - est - ly - ness
stricture
strid/e - ing - den; *also*
  astride; *but* strode
strident - ly
stridulant
stridulat/e - ed - ing - ion - or
strife
stigil
strik/e - ing - ingly ,- er; *but*
  struck, stricken
string - ing - ed; *but* strung
string/y - ier - iest - ily
stringen/t - tly - cy
strip - ped - ping - per
strip/e - ed - ing - y - iness
stripling
striv/e - ing - en; *but* strove
(STRY)
STRO
strob/e - ed - ing - oscope
strode (did stride)
strok/e - ed - ing - ingly
stroll - ed - ing - er
strong - er - est - ly - ish
stronti/um - a - an
strop - ped - ping - per
stroph/e - ic
strove (did strive)
STRU
struck (did strike)
structur/e - ed - ing - al - ally

strue? *No*, strew
struggl/e - ed - ing - ingly - er
strum - med - ming - mer
strumpet
strung (did string)
strut - ted - ting - ter
STRY
strychnine
(STRI)
STUB-STUD
stub - bed - bing - by
stubbl/e - y
stubborn - ly - ness - est
stucco - es - ed
stuck (did stick)
stud - ded - ding
student - ship
studio - s
studious
stud/y - les - ied - ying - iedly
STUF-STUP
stuff - ed - ing - er
stuff/y - ier - iest - ily - iness
stultif/y - ies - ied - ying
  - ication
stum - med - ming
stumbl/e - ed - ing - ingly
stumer
stump - ed - ing - er - y - iness
stun - ned - ning - ner
stung (did sting)
stunk (stink)
stuns'l, for studding sail
stunt - ed - ing
stupef/y - ies - ied - ying
  - action
stupendous - ly - ness
stupid - ly - ity
stupor - ous
STUR
sturd/y - ier - iest - ily - iness
sturgeon
stutter - ed - ing - ingly - er
(STER STIR)
STY
sty, sties (for pigs)
sty *or* stye, sties (on eyelid)
stygian (of the Styx)
styl/e (manner, etc.) - ed - ing;
  not stile

styl/ist -istic -ish -ishly
  -ishness
stylis/e -ed -ing -ation (z)
styl/us -oid -ograph
stymie -d
styptic
styrax
styrene
Sty/x -gian
  (STEI STI)

SUA

suas/ion -ive
suav/e -ely -ity
  (SWA)

SUB*-SUB*P

sub -*, *prefix meaning* under
subaltern
subdu/e -ed -ing -able -al
subfusc
subjacent
subject -ed -ing -ion
subjectiv/e -ity -ely -eness
  -ism -ist
subjugat/e -ed -ing -ion -or
subjunctiv/e -ity -ely -eness
  -ism -ist
sublimat/e -ed -ing -ion
sublim/e -er -est -ely -ity
subliminal -ly
submarin/e -er
submerg/e -ed -ing -ence
submers/ion -ible
submit -ted -ting
submiss/ion -ive -ively
  -iveness
suborn -ed -ing -er -ation
subpoena -ed *or* 'd

SUB*S-SUB*V

subscri/be -bed -bing -ption
subsequent -ly
subservien/t -tly -ce -cy
subsid/e -ed -ing -ence
subsidiar/y -ies -ily
subsid/y -ies
subsidis/e -ed -ing -ation (z)
subsist -ed -ing -ence
substan/ce -tial -tially -tiality

substantiat/e -ed -ing -ion
substantiv/e -ely -al -ally
substitut/e -ed -ing -ion -ive
subsum/e -ed -ing -ption
subten/d -ded -ding -se
subterfuge
subterranean
subtl/e -y -ety -eties
subtopia
subtract -ed -ing -ion -ive
subtrahend
suburb -an -ia
subvention
subver/t -ted -ting -sion -sive

SUCC

succeed -ed -ing
success -ful -fully
success/ion -ive -ively -or
succinct -ly -ness
succory *or* chicory
succour -ed -ing
succub/us -i -a -ae
succulent
succumb -ed -ing
  (SUCK)

SUCH-SUCT

such
suck -ed -ing -er; *not*
  succour (aid)
suckl/e -ed -ing
sucrose
suction

SUD

Sudan -ese
sudator/y -ium
sudd (Nile weed)
sudden -ly -ness
sudorif/ic -erous
suds (soap)
  (PSEUD)

SUE

su/e -ed -ing
suède
suet (fat) -y; *not* suit
  (PSEU SEW SHOE SUI)

SUFF

suffer -ed -ing -able -ance

* If the word you wish to spell is not in this list, omit the prefix
and look for the rest of the word.

suffic/e - ed - ing - ient - iently
 - iency
suffix - ed - ing
suffocat/e - ed - ing - ion - ingly
suffragan
suffrag/e - ist - ette
suffus/e - ed - ing - ion
 (SOUGH)

SUG

sugar - ed - ing - y - iness
suggest - ed - ing - ion - ive
 - ively - iveness
suggestib/le - ly - ility

SUI

suicid/e - al - ally
suit (match, etc.) - ed - ing
suitabl/le - ly - ility - leness
suite (set of furniture, etc.)
suitor
 (SUE SWE SWI)

SUL

sulk - ed - ing - er
sulk/y - ier - iest - ily - iness
sullage
sullen - er - est - ly - ness
sull/y - ied - ying
sulph/amate - ate - ide - ite
 - onamide
sulphur - ate - ated - ating
 - ator
sulphur/ic - ous - eous - etted
sulphuris/e - ed - ing - ation (z)
sultan - a - ess - ate
sultr/y - ier - iest - ily - iness
 (SAL SOL)

SUM

sum (total) - med - ming
 - mation; *not* some
sumach
summar/y - ies - ily
summaris/e - ed - ing
 - ation (z)
summer - y - ish
summersault *or* somer-
summit
summon - ed - ing - er
summons - es

sump
sumpter
sumptu/ary - ous - ously
 (SOM)

SUN

sun - ned - ning
sunn/y - ier - iest - ily - iness
sun/beam - light - rise - set
 - ward - wise, etc.
sunbath - e - ed - ing - er
sunburn - t - ed
sundae
Sunday
sunder - ed - ing; *also*
 asunder
sundowner (*Aus*)
sundr/y - ies
sung (sing)
sunk (sink) - en
 (SAN SON)

SUP

sup - ped - ping - per

SUPER*

super-*, *prefix meaning*
 over, beyond; *see also*
 supra-
superannuat/e - ed - ing - ion
supercede? *No,* supersede
superable
superb - ly
supercili/ous - ously - ousness
supererogat/ion - ory
superficial - ly - ity
superflu/ous - ously - ousness
 - ity
superhet, *for* - heterodyne
superintend - ed - ing - ent
superior - ity
superjacent
superlative - ly - ness
supernal
supernumerar/y - ies
superscription
superse/de - ded - ding - ssion
supersonic - ally
superstiti/on - ous - ously
 - ousness

* If the word you wish to spell is not in this list, omit the prefix
and look for the rest of the word.

superven/e - ed - ing - tion
supervis/e - ed - ing - ion - or
 - ory (*not* z)
 (SUPRA)

SUPI

supinat/e - ed - ing - ion - or
supine - ly - ness

SUPP

supper
supplant - ed - ing - er
suppl/e - er - est - y - eness
supplejack (*Aus*)
supplement - ed - ing - ation
 - al - ary - aries
suppliant - ly
supplicat/e - ed - ing - ion
 - ingly - ory
suppl/y - ied - ying - ier - iable
support - ed - ing - er - ive
suppos/e - ed - ing - edly - ition
 - itional
supposititious - ly - ness
suppositor/y - ies
suppress - ed - ing - ion - or
 - ible
suppurat/e - ed - ing - ion - ive
suprise? *No*, surprise

SUPR

supra-*, *prefix similar in
 meaning to* super, *used
 mainly in words relating to
 anatomy, botany, etc., e.g.,*
 supra-axillary, suprarenal
supra (*L*)
suprem/e - ly - acy
 (SURP)

SUR

surcharg/e - ed - ing
surcingl/e - ed - ing
surd
sur/e - er - est - ely - ety - eties
 - eness
surf (foam) - ed - ing - y
 - iness; *not* serf (slave)
surfac/e - ed - ing
surfeit - ed - ing
surg/e (move) - ed - ing

surg/eon - ery - eries - ical
 - ically
surl/y - ier - iest - ily - iness
surmis/e - ed - ing (*not* z)
surmount - ed - ing
surnam/e - ed - ing
surpass - ed - ing - ingly
surplic/e (vestment) - ed
surplus (left over) - es - age
surpris/e - ed - ing - ingly - edly
 (*not* z)
surreal - ism - ist
surrender - ed - ing
surreptitious - ly - ness
surrogate
surround - ed - ing
surtax - ed - ing - ation
surveillance
survey - ed - ing - or
surviv/e - ed - ing - al - or
 (CER CIR SER SIR)

SUS

susceptib/le - ly - ility - ilities
susceptive
suspect - ed - ing - able
suspend - ed - ing - er
suspens/e - ible - ibility - ion
 - ive - ively
suspic/ion - ious - iously
 - iousness
suspir/e - ed - ing - ation
sustain - ed - ing - ingly - able
susten/ance - tation
sussuration
 (SUZ)

SUT

sutch? *No*, such
sutler (camp - follower); *not*
 subtler
sutra (*Hind*)
suttee *or* sati (*Hind*)
sutur/e - ed - ing - ation - al
 - ally
 (SUBT SUIT)

SUZ

suzerain - ty
suzette

* If the word you wish to spell is not in this list, omit the prefix
and look for the rest of the word.

SVE
svelte

SWA
swab - bed - bing - ber
swaddl/e - ed - ing
swag
swag/e - ed - ing
swagger - ed - ing - ingly - er
Swahili
swain
swal/e - ed - ing
swallet
swallow - ed - ing - er - able
swam (did swim)
swami (*Hind*)
swamp - ed - ing - y - ier - iest
-ily - iness
swan - ned - ning - nery - like
swang *or* swung
swank - ed - ing - er
swap *or* swop - ped - ping - er
sward (grass); *not* sword
swarf
swarm - ed - ing
swarth/y - ier - iest - ily - iness
swash - ed - ing
swashbuckl/er - ing
swastika
swat (slap) - ted - ting - ter;
not swot
swath (cut hay, etc.) - s
swath/e (wrap) - ed - ing
sway - ed - ing
(SOI SWO)

SWE
sweat - ed - ing - y - ier - iest
-ily - iness
sweater
Swed/e - en - ish
sweep - ing - ingly - er; *but*
swept
sweet - er - est - ly - ness - ish
sweet/y - ie - ies - ing
sweeten - ed - ing - er
swell - - ed - ing - ing - er - est;
but swollen
swelter - ed - ing
swept (did sweep)
swerve - ed - ing - er

SWI
swift - er - est - ly - ness
swig - ged - ging
swill - ed - ing
swim - ming - mingly - mer;
but swam, swum
swindl/e - ed - ing - er
swin/e - ery - ish - ishly
-ishness
swing - ing - ingly - er; *but*
swang, swung
swinge - ing
swingl/e - ed - ing
swip/e - ed - ing - er
swipes
swirl - ed - ing
swish - ed - ing
Swiss
switch - ed - ing
Switzerland
swivel - led - ling
swizzle - stick

SWO
swob *or* swab - bed - bing
swollen (swell)
swoon - ed - ing - ingly
swoop - ed - ing
swop *or* swap - ped - ping - er
sword (blade) - ed - less; *not*
sward (grass)
swor/e (did swear) - n
swot (study) - ted - ting - ter;
not swat (slap)
(SWA)

SWU
swum (swim)
swung (swing)

SYB-SYL
sybarit/e - ic - ically - ism
sybil? *No*, sibyl
sycamore
sycophan/t - tic - cy
sycosis (barber's itch); *not*
psychosis
syenit/e - ic
syllab/le - led - ic - ically
syllab/us - uses *or* - i
syllepsis
syllog/ism - istic - istically

240

sylph - like
sylvan or silvan
 (CI CY PSY SI SCI)
SYM
symbio/sis - tic - tically
symbol - ic - ically - ism - ist;
 not cymbal (music)
symmetr/y - ies - ical - ically
sympath/y - ies - etic - etically
sympathis/e - ed - ing - er (z)
symphon/y - ies - ic
symposi/um - a - al - arch
symptom - atic - atically
 - atology
 (CYM SIM)

SYN
synagogue
syncarp - ous
synchromesh
synchron/ic - ous - ously
 - ousness - icity
synchronis/e - ed - ing
 - isation (z)
synclin/e - al
syncopat/e - ed - ing - ion - er
syncop/e - ic or - tic
syncret/ism - ic - ist - istic
syndactyl/ism - ous
syndic - ate - ated - ating - ation
syndicalism
syndrome
syne (Sc)
synecdoche
synod - ic - ical - ically
synonym - ous - ously - ity
synop/sis - tic - tical - tically
 - tist
synovitis
synt/ax - actic
synthe/sis - ses - tic - tically
 - tist - sist
synthesis/e - ed - ing - er (z)
 (CYN SIN)

SYPH
sypher (join) - ed - ing; not
 cipher, cypher
syphil/is - itic
 (CIPH SIF SHIPH)

SYR
Syri/a - an - ac
syringa
syring/e - ed - ing
syrinx
syrup - y
 (CIR CYR SIR)

SYS-SYZ
system - atic - atically
systematis/e - ed - ing - ation
 (z)
syst/ole - olic - altic
systyl/e - ous
syzygy
 (CIS CYS SIS SIZ)

T

TAB
tab - bed - bing
tabard
tabb/y - ies
tabernac/le - led - ling - ular
tab/es - etic - escence
tabinet
tabl/e - ed - ing - er - eful
tableau - x
table d'hôte (F)
tabl/et - oid
taboo or tabu or tapu - ed - ing
tabor
tabouret
tabul/ar - ate - ated - ating
 - ation
 (TOB)

TAC
tacho/graph - meter - metry
tachycardia
tachylyt/e - ic
tacit - ly - urn - urnity
tack - ed - ing - er
tack/y - ier - iest - ily - iness
tackl/e - ed - ing - er
tact - ful - fully - fulness
tactless - ly - ness
tactic - s - al - ally - ian
tact/ile - ility - ual - ually
 (TAK TAS TEC)

TAD-TAG
tadpole
taffeta

taffrail *or* tafferel
tag -ged -ging -ger
TAI
taiga (*Russ,* forest); *not* tiger
taikoa (*NZ*)
tail -ed -ing -less; *not* tale
  (story)
tailor -ed -ing
tain
taint -ed -ing
taipan (*Aus*)
taipo (*NZ*)
  (TEA TI TY)
TAK
tak/e -ing -en -er; *but* took;
  also betake
takin (animal)
  (TAC)
TAL
talc -um -ite
tale (story); *not* tail
talent -ed
talion -ic
talip/es -ed
talisman -ic
talk -ed -ing -er -ie
talkativ/e -ely -eness
tall -er -est -ness -ish
tallow -y -iness
tall/y -ies -ied -ying -ier
tally -ho!
Talmud -ic -ist -istic
talon -ed
tal/us -i *or* -uses
  (TAIL TEL)
TAM
tamarack (American tree)
tamarind (tropical fruit)
tamarisk (seaside shrub)
tambour -ine
tam/e -er -est -ed -ing -ely
  -eness
tam/able *or* tameable -ability
tamm/y -ies, *for* tam -o'-
  shanter
tamp -ed -ing -er
tamper -ed -ing -er
tampion *or* tompion (plug for
  gun, organ -pipe, etc.)
tampon (blood -stopper)

  (TOM)
TAN
tan, *for* tangent
tan -ned -ning -ner
tanager (bird)
tangra (statuette)
tandem
tang -ed -ing -y -ier -iest -ily
  -iness
tangen/t -tial -tially -cy
Tang/ier -erine
tangi (*NZ*)
tangib/le -ly -ility
tangl/e -ed -ing -y
tango -s -ed -ing
tangram
tank -er -age
tankard
tann/ic -ate -iferous
tannoy
tans/y -ies
tantalis/e -ed -ing -ingly (z)
tantalus
tantamount
tantara!
tantivy!
tantrum -s
  (TEN)
TAO
Taoiseach (*Ir*)
Tao -ism -ist
TAP
tap -ped -ping -per -ster
tap/e -ed -ing -eless
taper -ed -ing -ingly
tapestr/y -ies -ied
tapioca
tapir (mammal)
tapis (*F*)
tappet
tapu *or* tabu *or* taboo
TAR-TARA
tar -red -ring -ry -riness
taradiddle
tara -fern (*NZ*)
trakihi (*NZ*)
tarantass (*Russ*)
tarantella (dance)
tarantula (spider)
taraxacum

(TARR TERE TERR)

TARB-TARP

tarboosh
tard/o - amente (*It*)
tard/y - ier - iest - ily - iness
 - igrade
tare (weight, vetch); *not* tear
 (rip)
target
tariff
tarlatan
tarmac
tarn
tarnish - ed - ing - able
taro - s
tarot *or* - oc (card game)
tarpan (horse)
tarpaulin
tarpon (fish)
 (PTAR)

TARR-TARZ

tarragon
Tarragona
tarriff? *No*, tariff
tarrock
tarr/y - ied - ying
tarsier
tars/us - i
tart - ly - ness - let
tartan
tartar - ic - ous
Tartar *or* Tatar - y
tartare (sauce)
tartrate
tarwhine (*Aus*)
Tarzan
 (TER)

TAS

task - ed - ing
taslan (yarn)
Tasmania - n
Tassie *or* Tazzie (*Aus*)
tass - ie (*Sc*)
tassel - ed - ing
tast/e - ed - ing - er - able
tasteful - ly - ness
tast/y - ier - iest - ily - iness
 (TAC TES)

TAT

tat - ted - ting

tatter - ed - demalion
tattl/e - ed - ing - ingly - er
tattoo - ed - ing
tatt/y - ier - iest - ily - iness

TAU

taught (did teach); *not* taut *or*
 tort
taunt - ed - ing - ingly - er
taupata (*NZ*)
Taur/us - ine
taut - er - est - en - ened - ly
 - ness; *not* taught (did teach)
tautolog/y - ical - ically
 (TAW TOR)

TAV

tavern - er

TAW

taw
tawa, tawhai, tawhiri (*NZ*,
 trees)
tawdr/y - ier - iest - ily - iness
tawn/y - ier - iest - iness
tawse (*Sc*)
 (TAU TOR)

TAX

tax - ed - ing - ation - able
 - ability
taxi - s - ed - ing - meter
taxiderm/y - al - ic - ist
taxin
taxonom/y - ic - ically - ist
 (TEX TUX)

TEA

tea (drink); *not* tee (golf)
teach - ing - er - able - ability;
 but taught
teak
teal
team (group) - ed - ing - ster;
 not teem
tear - ful - fully - fulness
tear (rip) - ing; *but* tore, torn
teas/e - ed - ing - ingly - er
teasle *or* teazel
teat - ed
 (TAI TEE TIA)

TEC

technic - al - ally - ality - ian
technicolor - ed
technique

243

technocra/t -cy
technolog/y -ical -ically -ist
tectonic -ally
tectorial

TED

ted -ded -ding -der
tedd/y -ies
te deum (L)
tedi/um -ous -ously
 -ousness

TEE

tee (golf) -d -ing; *not* tea
tee (T-shaped) -square -joint
teem (overflow) -ed -ing -er
teen -s -age -ager
teeny (tiny)
teeter -ed -ing
teeth (tooth) -ed -ed -ing
teetotal -ism -er
teetotum
 (TEA TIE)

TEG

teg
tegul/ar -arly -ated
tegument -al -ary

TELE*

tele -*, *prefix meaning* far
telecast -er
telegenic
telegram
telegraph -ed -ing -y -er -ist
 -ic -ese
telekine /sis -tic
telemark
teleolog/y -ic -ical -ically
telepath/y -ic -ically
telephon/e -ed -ing -y -ist -ic
 -ically
telergy
telescop/e -ed -ing -y -ic -ist
televis/ion -e -ed -ing
televiewer
telex

TELL-TELP

tell -ing -ingly -er -able; *but*
 told
tellurion

telly, *for* television
telpher -age

TEME

tem/erity -arious
 (TEA TEE)

TEMP

temp, *for* temporary
temper -ed -ing -able -edly
tempera
temperament -al -ally -ality
temper/aɪ ce -ate -ately
 -ateness
temperature
tempest -uous -uously
 -uousness
templar
template *or* templet
temple
tempo (*It*)
temporal (of this world) -ly
 -ity -ities
temporar/y (for a time) -ily
 -iness
temporis/e -ed -ing
 -ation -er (z)
tempt -ed -ing -ingly -ble

TEN

ten (10) -th -thly -fold -ner
tenable
tenaci/ty -ous -ously
tenan/t -try -cy *or* tenure
tench
tend -ed -ing -ency -entious
tender -er -est -ly -ness
ten/don -dinous
tendril -led
tenement
tenet
tenner (£10 note); *not* tenor
tennis
tenon
tenor (voice); *not* tenner
tens/e -er -est -ely -eness
 -ity
tens/ion -or -ile -ility
tent -ed
tentac/le -ular -ulate

* If the word you wish to spell is not in this list, omit the prefix
and look for the rest of the word.

tentative -ly -ness
tenter -hooks
tenu/ous -ously -ity
tenure
tenuto (*It*)
TEP
tepee *or* teepee
tepid -ly -ness -ity
TERA
teraglin (*Aus*)
terai
teratolog/y -ical -ist
  (PTER TERR)
TERC
tercel *or* tiercel
tercenten/ary -nial
  (TERS TURK)
TERD
  (TURD)
TERE
terebinth -ine
teredo
terephthalate
  (TERR TERY TURE)
TERG
tergiversat/e -ed -ing -ion
  (TURG)
TERI
  (TERE TERR TERY)
TERK
  (TURK)
TERM
term -ed -ing -ly
termagant
terminab/le -ly -ility
terminal -ly
terminat/e -ed -ing -ion -or
terminolog/y -ical -ically -ist
termin/us -i *or*-uses
termit/e -ary -arium
  (TURM)
TERN
tern (bird); *not* turn
tern/ary -ate
terne (tin -plate)
  (TURN)
TERO
  (PT)
TERP
Terpsichor/e -ean

  (TURP)
TERR
terrac/e -ed -ing
terracotta
terrain
terramare
terrapin
terraqueous
terrene
terrestrial -ly
terret
terrib/le -ly
terrier
terrif/y -ied -ying -yingly -ic
terrigenous
terrine *or* tureen
territor/y -ies -ial -ially
terror -ism -ist
terroris/e -ed -ing -ation (z)
terry
  (PTER TER-)
TERS TERT
terse -ly -ness
tert/ian -iary -ius
tertium quid (*L*)
  (TUR)
TERY
terylene
  (TERE TERR)
TESS
tess/era -erae -ellated
  -ellation
TEST
test -ed -ing -er -able
testace/an -ous
testament -ary -arily
testamur
testat/e -or -rix
testic/le -ular -ulate
testif/y -ies -ied -ying
testimon/y -ies -ial
testudin/ate -arious -eous
testud/o -inal
test/y -ily -iness
TET
tetan/us -ic
tetch/y -ier -iest -ily -iness
tête-à-tête (*F*)
tether -ed -ing

tetra-*, *prefix meaning*
 four (4)
tetrachord - al
tetrad
tetradactyl - ous
tetragon - al
tetrahedr/on - al
tetrarch - y - ical

TEU
Teusday? *No*, Tuesday
teuton - ic - ism
teutonis/e - ed - ing - ation (z)
 (CHEW TU)

TEXT
text - ual - ually
textile
textur/e - ed - al - eless
 (TAX)

THA
thalam/us - i
thalidomide
thallium
than
thanatoid
thane *or* thegn
thank - ed - ing - ful - fully
 - fulness
thankless - ly - ness
thanksgiving
that, that's (*for* that is)
thatch - ed - ing - er

THAU THAW
thought? *No*, thought
thaumatrope
thaumaturg/e - y - ic - ical - ist
thaw - ed - ing
 (THOR)

THE-THEN
the; *not* thee (you)
theatr/e - ical - ically
thee (you); *not* the
theft
thegn *or* thane
theif? *No*, thief
their (belonging to them); *not*
 there (that place), they're
 (they are)

theirs (*not* their's)
the/ism - ist - istic
them - selves
them/e - atic - atically
then
thence - forth - forward
 (THA)

THEO
theo -*, *prefix meaning* god
theocra/t - tic - cy
theodicy
theodolite
theolog/y - ies - ical - ian
theologis/e - ed - ing (z)
theorbo
theorem
theoretic - al - ally
theor/y - ies
theoris/e - ed - ing (z)
theosoph/y - ist - ic - ical
 (THIO)

THER
therap/y - ies - ist
therapeut/ic - ically
there (at that place); *not* their
 (belonging to them), they're
 (they are)
there - about - abouts - after
 - at - by - from - in - inafter
 - into - of - on - out - through
 - to - unto - upon - with
 - withal
therefore
 (THIR THUR)

THERM
therm - al - ally - ic
therm(o) -*, *prefix meaning*
 heat
thermion - ic
thermite
thermograph
thermomet/er - ry - ric
thermonuclear
thermos - es
thermostat - ic - ically

THES-THEY
thesaurus

* If the word you wish to spell is not in this list, omit the prefix
and look for the rest of the word.

these
thes/is -es
thespian
theta (*Gr*)
thew -s -ed -y
they, their, theirs, they'd
   (they had *or* would), they're
   (they are), they've (they
   have)

THI-THIO

thiamine
thick -er -est -ly -ness -ish
thicken -ed -ing -er
thicket
thie/f -ves; *but* theft
thiev/e -ed -ing -ery -ish
   -ishly -ishness
thigh -ed
thimble -ful -rig -rigger
thin -ner -nest -ned -ning -ly
   -ness
thine (yours)
thing
think -ing -er -able; *but*
   thought; *also* bethink
thio -acid -sulphide, etc.
   (THEO THY)

THIR

third (3rd) -ly
thirst -ed -ing -y -ier -iest -ily
   -iness; *also* athirst
thirteen (13) -th
thirt/y (30) -ieth -yfold
   (THER THUR THYR)

THIS THITH

this, these
thisis? *No* phthisis
thistl/e -y
thither
   (THES)

THO

tho' *for* though
thol/e -ed -ing (*Sc*)
thole -pin
thong -ed -ing
thora/x -ces -cic
thorium
thorn -y -ier -iest -iness -less
thorough -ly -ness -bred
   -fare

thorp *or* thorpe
those
thou (you)
though; *also* although
thought -ful -fully -fulness
thoughtless -ly -ness
thousand -th
   (THAU THAW)

THRA-THRI

thral/l -dom
thrash (beat) -ed -ing -er
thread -ed -ing -er -y -iness
threat -en -ening -eningly
three (3) -fold -sided -some;
   not free
threnod/y -ies
thresh (grain) -ed -ing -er
threshold
threw (did throw); *not*
   through
thrice
thrift -y -ier -iest -ily -less
thrill -ed -ing -ingly -er
thrips
thriv/e -ing -ingly -en -ed *or*
   throve
   (FR)

THRO

thro', *for* through
throat -ed -y -ier -iest -ily
   -iness
throb -bed -bing -bingly
throe -s (anguish); *not* throw
   (fling)
thrombo/sis -tic
thron/e -ed -ing; *also*
   enthrone
throng -ed -ing
throstle
throttl/e -ed -ing
through (from end to end);
   not threw
throughout; *not* threw out
throve (did thrive)
throw (fling) -ing -n -er; *but*
   threw; *not* throe
throwster
   (FRO)

THRU

thrum -med -ming -my

247

thrush -es
thrust -ing -er
  (FRU)
THU
thud -ded -ding
thug -gery -gish -gee
thumb -ed -ing
thump -ed -ing -er
thunder -ed -ing -y -er
thuri/ble -fer -ferous -fication
Thursday
thus
THW
thwack -ed -ing
thwaite
thwart -ed -ing -ingly -ships;
  also athwart
THY
thy -self, thine; *not* thigh
  (upper leg)
thym/e (herb) -y; *not* time
thymol
thymus
thyr/oid -oxin(e)
thyrsus
  (THI)
TIA-TIDY
tiara -'d
tibi/a -ae -al
tic (facial twitching)
tick -ed -ing -er
ticket -ed -ing
tickl/e -ed -ing -er
  -ish -ishness
tiddler
tiddl/y -iness
tiddly -winks
tid/e -ed -ing -al -ally -eless
tidings
tid/y -ier -iest -ily -iness
  (TY)
TIE
tie -d, tying
tier (row); *not* tear (-drop)
tierce
  (TEA TEE TY)
TIF
tiff -ed -ing
tiffany
tiffin

(TYPH)
TIG
tiger -ish -ishness; tigress
tight -er -est -ly -ness
tighten -ed -ing -er
tigon
TIL
tilde
til/e -ed -ing -ery -er *or* tyler
till *or* until
till (plough, etc.) -ed -ing -er
  -age
tiller -ed -ing
tilt -ed -ing -er
tilth
  (TYL)
TIM
timber (wood) -ed -ing
timbre (quality of sound)
timbrel
tim/e -ed -ing -er -eless; *also*
  betimes; *see* thyme
timel/y -ier -iest -iness
timid -er -est -ly -ity
timorous -ly -ness
timothy
timpan/o (orchestral drum) -i
  -ist; *not* tym- (ear -drum,
  space over door, etc.)
  (TYM)
TIN
tin -ned -ning -ner
tinn/y -ier -iest -ily -iness
tinct/ure -ured -uring -orial
tindal
tinder -y -ish
tin/e -ed
ting/e -ed -ing
tingl/e -ed -ing
tinker -ed -ing
tinkl/e -ed -ing -er
tinnitus
tinsel -led -ling
tint -ed -ing -er -y
tintinabul/um -a -ate -ated
  -ation
tin/y -ier -iest -ily -iness
  (TEN)
TIP
tip -ped -ping -per -ster

248

tippet
tippl/e -ed -ing -er
tips/y -ier -iest -ily -iness
 (TYP)

TIR
tirade
tir/e -ed -ing -ingly -eless
 -elessly -elessness
tire or tyre (on wheel)
tire or attire
tiresome -ly -ness
tiro or tyro -s
 (TER TUR TYR)

TIS
'tis, for it is
tissue -s -d

TIT
tit -lark -bit -ing; not teat
 (nipple)
titan -ic -ically
titan/ium -ate
tith/e -ing -able
titillat/e (excite) -ed -ing -ion
titivat/e (smarten) -ed -ing
 -ion
titl/e -ed -ing; also entitle
titrat/e -ed -ing -ion
titter -ed -ing -er
tittle
tittle -tattl/e -ed -ing -er
tittup -ped -ping
titular -ly
 (TIGH)

TO TOA
to (towards); not too (very)
 or two (2)
toad -ish
toad/y -ies -ied -ying -yism
toast -ed -ing -er
 (TOE TOO)

TOB
tobacco -s -nist
toboggan -ed -ing -er -ist
tobralco
toby-jug

TOC
toccata (It)
Toc H
tocher (Sc)
tocsin (alarm-bell); not toxin
 (poison)
 (TOK TOQ TOX)

TOD
tod
today or to-day
toddl/e -ed -ing -er
toddy
to-do

TOE
toe (of foot) -d -ing -less; not
 tow (pull)
 (TO TOO)

TOF
toff -ish
toffee
toft
 (TOPH)

TOG
tog -s -ged -ging -gery
toga
together -ness; also
 altogether
toggle

TOH
toheroa (NZ)
tohunga (NZ)

TOI
toi-toi (NZ)
toil -ed -ing -er
toilsome -ly -ness
toilet -ry -ries
 (TOY)

TOK
tokay
token; also betoken
 (TOC TOQ)

TOL
told (did tell)
Toledo
tolerat/e -ed -ing -ion -or
toler/ant -antly -ance -able
 -ably -ability
toll -ed -ing -able
tolu/ol -ene

TOM
tomahawk
tomaine? No, ptomaine
tomalley
tomato -es
tomb -ed -ing; also entomb

249

tombola
tomboy - ish
tome
tomfool - ery
tomm/y - ies - ygun
tomorrow
tompion *or* tampion
tomtit
tom - tom
  (TUM)
TON
ton (1016.05 kg) - nage - ner;
  not tonne, tun (cask)
ton/e - ed - ing - al - ally - ality
tonga
tongs
tongu/e - ed - ing - eless
tonic - ally - ity
tonight
tonne (1000 kg); *not* ton
  (1016.5 kg), tun (cask)
tonneau
tonsil - lar - litis
tonsorial - ly
tonsure
  (TUN)
TOO
too (very, etc.); *not* two (2) *or*
  to (towards)
took (did take); *also* betook
tool - ed - ing - er
toot - ed - ing
tooth - ed - ing - some - less
  - lessly - lessness; *but* teeth
tootl/e - ed - ing
toots/y - ies
  (TOU TU)
TOP
top - ped - ping - pingly - most
topless - ly - ness
topaz - es
top/e - ed - ing - er
topi *or* topee (*Hind*)
topiar/y - ist
topic - al - ally - ality
topograph/y - ic - ical - ically
  - er
topolog/y - ical - ically
topper
toppl/e - ed - ing

topsyturv/y - ier - iest
TOQ
toque
TOR
tor (rocky hilltop); *not* tore
  (did tear)
torc *or* torque
torch
torchon
tore (did tear); *not* tor
toreador
torii (*Jap*)
torment - ed - ing - ingly - or
tormentil
torn
tornado - es
torpedo - es - ed - ing
torp/or - id - idly - idity
torque *or* torc
torrent - ial - ially
Torricelli - an
torrid - ity - ness
tors/ion - ive - ional - ionally
torso - s
tort (legal); *not* taught, taut
tortoise
tortu/ous - ously - ousness
tortur/e - ed - ing - ingly - er
tor/y - ies - yism
  (TAU TAW TERR TOUR)
TOS
tosh
tosis? *No,* ptosis
toss - ed - ing
  (TOAS TOES)
TOT
tot - ted - ting
total - led - ling - y - ity
totalitarian
totalis/e - ed - ing - ation - ator
  (z)
totara (*NZ*)
tot/e (carry) - ed - ing
tote, *for* totalis(z)ator
totem
t'other, *for* the other
totter - ed - ing - ingly - er
TOU
toucan
touch - ed - ing - er - ingly - able

-ability
touch/y -ier -iest -ily -ness
tough -er -est -ly -ness; *not*
  tuff (rock)
toughen -ed -ing -er
toupee *or* toupet (false hair)
tour (travel) -ed -ing -er -ism
  -ist
tourmaline
tournament
tournedos
tourney -s
tourniquet
tousl/e -ed -ing
tout -ed -ing
tout ensemble (*F*)
  (TOO TOW TU)

TOW
tow -ed -ing -age (pull); *not*
  toe
toward -s
towel -led -ling
tower -ed -ing; *not* tour
  (travel)
town -y -ier -iest -ship -sfolk
  (TOU)

TOX
tox/in (poison) -ic -ically
  -icology -aemia; *not* tocsin
toxophil/y -ite
  (TOC TUX)

TOY
toy -ed -ing
  (TOI)

TRAC
trac/e -ed -ing -er -eable
  -eability
tracer/y -ies -ied
trache/a -al -ate -itis -otomy
trachoma -tous
trachyt/e -ic
track -ed -ing -er -age -less
tract
tractab/le -ly -ility
tract/ion -or -ive -al

TRAD
trad, *for* traditional

trad/e -ed -ing -er -esman
tradition -al -ally -alism -alist
traduce -ed -ing -ement -er
  -ible
  (TRAG TRAJ TREAD)

TRAF
traffic -ked -king -ker -ator

TRAG
tragacanth
traged/y -ies -ian -ienne
tragic -al -ally -alness
tragicom/edy -ic -ically
  (TRAJ)

TRAI
trail -ed -ing -er
train -ed -ing -er -ee -able
traips/e -ed -ing
trait
trait/or -ress -orous -orously
  -orousness
  (TRAY)

TRAJ
trajector/y -ies
  (TRAG)

TRAM
tram -med -ming
trammel -led -ling
tramp -ed -ing
trampl/e -ed -ing -er
trampoline
  (TREM)

TRAN
trance; *also* entrance
tranquil -ly -lity
tranquillis/e -ed -ing -er (z)

TRANS
trans*, *prefix meaning*
  across, through, etc.
transact -ed -ing -ion -or
transceiver
transcend -ed -ing -ent
  -ently -ence
transcendental -ly
transcri/be -bed -bing -ber
  -ption
transect -ed -ing -ion
transept (of church) -al

* If the word you wish to spell is not in this list, omit the prefix
and look for the rest of the word.

transfer - red - ring - ence
 - ential
transfer - able - ably - ability
 - ee - or *or* er
transgress - ed - ing - ion - or
tranship - ped - ping - ment
transhumance
transi/ent - ently - ence
transistor
transistoris/e - ed - ing
 - ation (z)
transit - ed - ing - ion - ional
 - ionally
transitiv/e - ely - eness
transitor/y - ily - iness
translat/e - ed - ing - ion - ional
transluc/ent - ently - ence
transmit - ted - ting - ter - table
transmiss/ion - ible - ibly
 - ibility
transmogrif/y - ied - ying
 - ication
transmut/e - ed - ing - ation
 - able
transom - ed
transpar/ent - ently - ency
 - encies
transpir/e - ed - ing - ation
 - atory
transpontine
transport - ed - ing - ation - er
 - able - ability
transpos/e - ed - ing - ition
 - itive - al - er
transvers/e - al - ely
transvest/ism - ist - ite

TRAP-TRAT
trap - ped - ping - per
trapes *or* traips/e - ed - ing
trapez/e - ium - ia - oid - oidal
trappings
Trappist - ine
trash - y - ier - iest - ily - iness
trattoria (*It*)

TRAU
trauma - s *or* - ta - tic - tically
 - tism
 (TRAW TROU TROW)

TRAV
travail - ed - ing

travel - led - ling - ler - ogue
travers/e - ed - ing - er
travertine
travest/y - ies - ied - ying

TRAW
trawl - ed - ing - er
 (TRAU)

TRAY
tray - ful
 (TRAI)

TREA-TREE
treacher/y - ies - ous - ously
 - ousness
treacl/e - ed - ing - y
tread - ing; *but* trod, trodden
treadl/e - ed - ing - er
treason - ous - ously
treason/able - ably - ableness
treasur/e - ed - ing - y - ies - er
 - ership
treat - ed - ing - er - ment - able
 - ability
treatise (written exposition)
treat/y (written agreement)
 - ies
trebl/e - ed - ing - y
trebucket
treck? *No*, trek
tree - ed - less - lessness

TREF-TREY
trefine? *No*, trephine
trefoil - ed
trek - ked - king - ker
trellis - ed - ing
trembl/e - ed - ing - ingly - y - er
tremend/ous - ously
 - ousness
tremol/o - ando (*It*)
tremor
tremul/ous - ously - ousness
trench - es - ed - ing - er
trenchan/t - tly - cy
trend - ed - ing - y - ier - iest - ily
 - iness
trepang
trephin/e - ed - ing - ation
trepidation
trespass - es - ed - ing - er
tress - es - ed - y
trestl/e - ed

trew (*Sc*)
trey (3, in cards, etc.)
  (TRA)
TRI* TRI* A
tri-*, *prefix meaning* three
triabl/e - y - ility
triad - ic
trial
triang/le - ular - ularly - ularity
triangulat/e - ed - ing - ion
trias - sic
triatic
  (TRY)
TRI*B-TRI*D
trib/e - al - ally - alness
triblet *or* tribolet
tribometer
tribulation
tribunal
tribun/e - ate - itial - ician
tributar/y - ies - ily - iness
tric/e - ed - ing
tricel
trichin/a - ae - iasis
trick - ed - ing - ery - eries - ster
trick/y - ier - iest - ily - iness
trickl/e - ed - ing - y
tricoline
tricorne
tricot (*F*)
tricycl/e - ed - ing - ist
trident
TRIE
tried (did try)
trienni/um - al - ally
trier, tries
  (TRIA TRY)
TRI*F-TRI*N
trifid
trifl/e - ed - ing - er
trifori/um - a
trig, *for* trigonometry
trig - ged - ging
trigger - ed - ing
triglyph
trigon - al
trigonomet/ry - ric - rical

  - rically
trihedr/on - al
trilb/y - ies
trilemma
trilith - on - ic
trill - ed - ing - er
trillion - th
trilobite
trilog/y - ies
trim - med - ming - mer - mest
  - ly - ness
trimaran
trimensual - ly
trin/e - al - ary
trinitrotolu/ol - ene (TNT *or*
  trotyl)
trint/y - ies - arian - arianism
trinket - ry
trinomial
TRI*O
trio - s
triode
triolet
  (TRIU)
TRI*P
trip - ped - ping - per - pingly;
  also atrip
tripartit/e - ely - ion
tripe - ry
triphthong - al
tripl/e - ed - ing - ly
triplet
triplex
triplicat/e - ed - ion
tripod
tripos
triptych
  (TRY)
TRI*R
trireme
  (TRIE)
TRI*S
trisect - ed - ing - ion
trismus
  (TRIC TRY)
TRI*T
trite - ly - ness

* If the word you wish to spell is not in this list, omit the prefix
and look for the rest of the word.

tritium
triton
triturab/le -ly -ility
triturat/e -ed -ing -ion -or
TRI*U
triumph -ed -ing -al -ant
triumvir -ate
triun/e -ity
  (TRIO)
TRIV
trivalen/t -cy
trivet
trivi/a -al -ally -ality -alities
TROC-TROM
troch/ee -aic
trochle/a -ae -ar -ate
trochoid -al
trod (did tread) -den
troglodyt/e -ic -ism
troika (*Russ)*
Trojan
troll -ed -ing
trolley -s *or* troll/y -ies
trollop -ish -y
tromba (*It*)
trombon/e -ist
trommel
trompe l'oeil (*F*)
TROO
troop -ed -ing -er; *not* troupe
  (actors)
  (TROU TRU)
TROP-TROT
trope
trophic (nutrition)
troph/y -ies -ied
tropic -al -ally
tropo/sphere -pause
troppo (*It*)
trot -ted -ting -ter
troth, *also* betroth
trotyl
  (TNT)
TROU
troubadour
troubl/e -ed -ing -er -ous
 -esome

trough
trounc/e -ed -ing
troup/e (actors) -er
trouser/s -ed -ing
trousseau -s *or* -x
trout -let -ling
trouvaille (*F*)
  (TROO TROW TRU)
TROV-TROY
trov/e -er
trow
trowel -led -ling -ler
Tro/y -jan
troy
  (TROU)
TRU
truan/t -ted -ting -cy
truble? *No*, trouble
truc/e -ial
truck -ed -ing -er -age
truckl/e -ed -ing -er
truculen/t -tly -ce
trudg/e -ed -ing
trudgen (swimming stroke)
tru/e -er -est -ly -ism -eness;
 also truth
truffle
trug
trump -ed -ing
trumpery
trumpet -ed -ing -er
truncat/e -ed -ing -ion; *but*
 trunk
truncheon
trundl/e -ed -ing -er
trunk -ed -ing -less; *but*
 truncate
truss -ed -ing
trust -ed -ing -ful -fully
 -fulness
trust/y -ier -iest -ily -iness
trustworth/y -ier -iest -ily
 -iness
truth -ful -fully -fulness
  (TROO TROU)
TRY
try -ing -ingly; *but* tries, tried,

---

* If the word you wish to spell is not in this list, omit the prefix
and look for the rest of the word.

trier
trypanosome
trypsin
tryst -ed -ing
  (TRI)
TS
tsar *or* czar -dom -ist
tsetse
  (TZ)
TUA
tuart (*Aus*)
tuatara (*NZ*)
  (TWA)
TUB
tub -bed -bing -y -ier -iest
  -ful
tuba (music); *not* tuber
  (vegetable)
tub/e -ed -ing -al -ular -iform
tuber -ous -ously -ousness
  -iform
tubercl/e -ed
tubercul/osis -in -ate -ar -ous
  -ose
tuberose
tubul/e -ar
TUC-TUG
tuck -ed -ing -er
Tudor
Tuesday
tufa (deposited calcite)
  -ceous
tuff (volcanic ash rock); *not*
  tough
tuft -ed -ing -y
tug -ged -ging
TUI
tuition -al -ary; *but* tutor
  (TWI)
TUL
tulip
tulle
  (TAL TOL)
TUM
tumbl/e -ed -ing -er
tumbler -ful
tumbril *or* tumbrel
tumef/y -ied -ying -action
  -acient
tumesc/ent -ently -ence

tumid -ly -ity
tumm/y -ies, *for* stomach
tumour
tumult -uous -uously
  -uousness -uary
tumul/us -i
  (TOM)
TUN
tun (cask) -nage; *not* ton,
  tonne (weights)
tuna *or* tunny
tundra
tun/e -ed -ing -er -able
tuneful -ly -ness
tuneless -ly -ness
tungsten
tunic -le -ate
tunnel -led -ling -ler
tunny *or* tuna
  (TON)
TUP
tup -ped -ping
tuppence, *for* twopence (2p
  or 2d)
  (TOP)
TUR
turban (headdress); *not*
  turbine
turbary
turbid -ly -ity -ness
turbin/ate -al -oid
turbine (engine)
turbo/jet -prop, etc.
turbot
turbulen/t -tly -ce
turd
turd/ine -iform -oid
tureen
turf -ed -ing -y -iness
turgid -ly -ity
Turk -ey -ish -oman *or*
  Turcoman
turkey -s
turmeric
turmoil
turn -ed -ing -er -ery; *not*
  tern (bird)
turnip
turpentine, turps
turpitude

turquoise
turret - ed
turtl/e - er - ing
  (TER TIR TOR)

TUS

Tuscan - y
tush - ery
tusk - ed - er - y
tusser *or* tussore *or* tussah
  (silk)
tussle - ed - ing
tussock - y
  (TUES)

TUT

tut - tut!
tutel/age - ar - ary
tutor - ial - ially; *but* tuition
tutti (*lt*)
tutti - frutti (*lt*)
tutty
tutu (*F*)
  (TEUT)

TUW

tuwhit - tuwhoo!
  (TWO TOO)

TUX

tuxedo - s *or* - es
  (TOX TUC)

TUY

tuyere *or* twyer
  (TOI TOY TUI)

TWA

twaddl/e - ed - ing - er - y
twain
twang - ed - ing
twankay
'twas, *for* it was
tway - blade
  (TUA)

TWE

tweak - ed - ing - er
twee, *for* sweet
tweed - y - ier - iest - iness
'tween, *for* between
tween/y - ies
tweet (bird - song)
tweezers
twel/ve (12) - fth - fthly
 - vefold
twent/y (20) - ieth - yfold

'twere, *for* it were
twerp *or* twirp

TWI-TWO

twic/e - er
twiddl/e - ed - ing - er
twig - ged - ging - gy - gier
 - giest - giness
twilight
twill - ed
'twill, *for* it will
twin - ned - ning - ship
twin/e - ed - ing - ingly
twing/e - ed - ing
twinkl/e - ed - ing
twirl - ed - ing
twirp *or* twerp
twist - ed - ing - er - able
twit - ted - ting - tingly
twitch - ed - ing
twitter - ed - ing
'twixt, *for* betwixt
two (2); *not* to, too
  (TUI)

TYC-TYN

tycoon
tying (tie)
tyke
tyler *or* tiler
tymp - an
tympan/um - a - ic (ear - drum,
  space over door, etc.); *not*
  timp - (orchestral drum)
Tynwald
  (TI)

TYP

typ/e - ed - ing - ist - al
typewrit/e - ing - ten - er
typhoid
typho/on - nic
typhus
typical - ly - alness; *but*
  atypical (not typical)
typif/y - ies - ied - ying - ier
 - ication
typist
typograph/y - ic - ical - ically
typolog/y - ic - ical - ically - ist
typonom/y - ic - ical - ically - ist
  (TIP)

TYR

tyran/t -ny -nical -nically -ous
  -ously
tyrannicide
tyrannis/e -ed -ing (z)
tyre *or* tire (on wheel)
tyro *or* tiro -s
Tyrol -ese -ean
Tyrrhen/e -ian
  (TIR)

TZ

Tzigane
  (TSI)

U

U-UK

U -boat, *for* Unterseeboot
  (*Ger*)
U -bolt, U -turn, etc.
ubiety
ubiquit/y -ous -ously
udder
udomet/er (rain -gauge) -ry;
  not eudiometer (gas)
ufo, *for* unidentified flying
  object
uforia? *No*, euphoria
ugli (fruit) -s
ugly -ier -iest -iness -ies
ukulele
  (EU HU YU)

UL

ulcer -ous -ously -ate -ated
  -ating -ation
ullage
uln/a -ae -ar
Ulster
ult, *for* ultimo
ulterior
ultima -te -tely
ultimat/um -ums *or* -a
ultimo (last month)
ultra -*, *prefix meaning*
  beyond, etc.
ultramarine
ultra vires (*L*)
ultrasonic -s

ululat/e -ed -ing -ion
  (EUL HUL YUL)

UM

umbel -late -liferous
umber -ed
umbilic/us -al -ate -ation
umbles
umbo -nal -nic -nate
umbr/a -ae -al
umbrage -ous
umbrella -'d *or* -ed
umpir/e -ed -ing
umpteen -th
umu (*NZ*)
  (HUM)

UN*

un -*, *a prefix which reverses
  the meaning of the rest of
  the word; it is sometimes
  interchangeable with* in -,
  e.g. unequal, inequality

UN*A UN*B

unanim/ous -ously -ity
unbeknown -st

UN*C

uncial
uncle
unco (*Sc*)
uncouth -ly -ness
unct/ion -uous -uously
  -uousness
  (HUNK HUNC UNK UNS)

UN*DE

under
under -*, *used as a prefix*
undergo -ing -ne; *but*
  underwent
under/lay -laid -laying (*see*
  lay)
under/lie -lay -lying -lain (*see*
  lie)
underling
underneath
underrat/e -ed -ing
understand -stood -standing
under/write -wrote -written
  -writer

---

* If the word you wish to spell is not in this list, omit the prefix
and look for the rest of the word.

UN*DI-UN*DU
undid (did undo)
undies, *for* underwear
undine
undo - ing - ne - er; *but* undid
undulat/e - ed - ing - ion - ory
UN*E
unearth - ed - ing
unerring - ly
(UNI)
UN*G
ungain/ly - lier - liest - liness
ungual
unguent
ungul/a - ae - ate
(HUNG)
UNI*
uni-*, *prefix meaning* one
unicameral
unicorn
uniform - ed - ing - ly - ity
unif/y - ied - ying - ier - ication
unilateral - ly
union - ism - ist - istic
uniparous - ly
uniplanar
unique - ly - ness
unison
unit - ary - ian
unit/e - ed - ing - ive
univalent
univers/e - al - ally - ality
universalis/e - ed - ing
 - ation (z)
universit/y - ies
(UNE)
UN*K
unkempt
unknit - ted - ting
unknot - ted - ting
(HUNK UNC)
UN*L-UN*W
unless
unmistakabl/e - y
unparalleled
unrul/y - iness
unt/ie - ied - ying

until *or* till
untilled (not ploughed)
unto
unuch? *No*, eunuch
unutterabl/e - y
unwield/y - ily - iness
(HUN)
UP
up - per - permost - ish - ishly
 - ishness - ward
up-*, *used as a prefix*
upanishad
upas - tree
upbraid (reproach) - ed - ing
up - end - ed - ing
upheaval
uphill
uphold - ing - er; *but* upheld
upholster - ed - ing - y - er
upon
upright - ly - ness
uproar - ious - iously
 - iousness
uprush
upset - ting - ter
upshot
upside - s - down
upsilon (*Gr*)
upstage
upstairs
upstart
upstroke
uptake
(EUP)
URA
uraem/ia - ic
uran/ium - ic - ous
Uran/us - ian
(EUR)
URB
urban - ise - ised - ising
 - isation (z)
urban/e - ely - ity
(HERB)
URC
urchin
(HERC IRK)

* If the word you wish to spell is not in this list, omit the prefix
and look for the rest of the word.

URD
Urdu
(ERRED HER HUR)
URE
urea
uret/er - itis
urethr/a - al - itis - otomy
uretic
(EUR EWER YOUR)
URG-URI
urg/e - ed - ing
urgen/t - tly - cy
uric
urim and thummim
urin/e - al - ary - ous - ate - ated
- ating - ation
(EUR)
URL
(EARL HURL)
URM
(ERM HERM)
URN
urn (vase); *not* earn, erne
(HERN)
URO
urolog/y - ist
(EURO)
URS
ursine
Ursul/a - ine
(ERS HEAR HIRS)
URT
urtic/aria - ate - ation
(HURT)
US
us/age - ance
us/e - ed - ing - er
use/ful - fully - fulness
useless - ly - ness
usher - ette - ed - ing
usquebaugh *or* whisky
(*Sc*)(*Ir*, whiskey)
usual - ly - ness
usufruct - uary
usurp - ed - ing - er - ation
usur/y - ious - iously
- iousness - er
(EUS HUS)
UT
utensil

uter/us - i - ine
utilitarian - ism
utilit/y - ies
utilis/e - ed - ing - able - ation
- er (z)
utmost
Utopia - n - nism
utric/le - ular
utter - ed - ing - ance - most
utu (NZ)
(EUT HUT YOU)
UV
uvul/a - ar
(EUPH OV YOU)
UX
uxorious - ly - ness

V
V-VAI
v, *for* versus
vacan/t - tly - cy
vacat/e - ed - ing - ion; *not*
vocation (calling)
vaccinat/e (inoculate) - ed
- ing - ion
vaccine
vacillat/e (waver) - ed - ing
- ion
vacuole
vacu/ity - ous - ously
- ousness
vacu/um - ums *or* - a
vade - mecum (*L*)
vagabond - age - ism - ish
vagar/y - ies
vagin/a - al - ate - itis
vagran/t - tly - cy
vague - ly - ness
vain (conceited, etc.) - ly; *but*
vanity; *not* vane, vein
(VE)
VAL
valance (short curtain)
vale (valley); *not* veil (cover)
valedict/ory - ion
valen/t - ce - cy (chemistry)
valentine
valerian
valet - ed - ing
valetudinar/y - ian

259

valgus
Valhalla
valiant - ly
valid - ly - ity
validat/e - ed - ion
valkyrie - s
valley - s
vallum (L)
valoris/e - ed - ing - ation (z)
val/our - orous - orously
valse (waltz)
valu/e - ed - ing - er - able - ably
  - ation
valueless - ly - ness
valv/e - ed - ar - ular - ate
  - eless
  (VEL VOL)

VAM
vamoos/e - ed - ing
vamp - ed - ing - er
vampir/e - ic - ism

VAN
van
van, for vanguard, advantage
vanad/ium - ate - ic - ous
vandal - ism
vandyke
vane (weathercock, etc.); not
  vain, vein
vanguard
vanilla
vanish - ed - ing
vanit/y - ies; but vain
vanquish - ed - ing - er - able
vantage, for advantage
  (FAN THAN VEN)

VAP
vapid - ly - ness - ity
vap/our - orous - ouring
vaporis/e - ed - ing - ation (z)

VAR
vari/able - ably - ability; but
  vary
vari/ant - ation - ous - ously
  - ousness
varicella
varicocele
varicoloured
varicos/e - ed - ity
variegat/e - ed - ing - ion

variet/y - ies
variform
variol/a - ic - ous
variometer
variorum
varlet
varnish - ed - ing
varve
var/y - ies - ied - ying; but see
  variable, etc.
  (VER VIR VOR)

VAS-VAX
vas - al - ectomy
vascular - ly - ity
vascul/um - ose
vase
vaseline
vassal - age
vast - er - est - ly - ness
vat - ful
Vatican - ism - ist
vaticinat/e - ed - ing - ion - or
vaudeville
vault - ed - ing
vaunt - ed - ing
vaxinate? No, vaccinate
  (VE VI)

VEA-VEI
veal
vector - ial
ved/a - anta - ic
vedette
veer - ed - ing - ingly
veget/able - ation - al - ality
vegetarian - ism
vehemen/t - tly - ce
vehic/le - ular
veil (cover) - ed - ing; not vale
vein (blood - tube, etc.) - ed
  - ing; not vain, vane
  (VA)

VEL
veld
velleity
vellum
velociped/e - ist
velocit/y - ies
velours
vel/um - ar
velvet - y - een

(VAL VOL)

VEN

venal (bribable) -ly -ity; *not*
 venial
ven/ation -ous
vend -ed -ing -or -ible -ibility
vendace
vendetta
veneer
venera/ble -te -ted -ting -tion
 -tor
venere/al -ally
venge/ance -ful -fully
 -fulness
Ven/ice -etian
venial (pardonable) -ly -ity;
 not venal
venison
venom -ed -ous -ously
 -ousness
vent -ed -ing
ventil
ventilat/e -ed -ing -ion -ive
 -or
ventral -ly
ventric/le -ular -ulous
ventriloqu/y -ism -ist -istic
 -ial
ventriloquis/e -ed -ing (z)
ventur/e -ed -ing -er
venturesome -ly -ness
venue
Venus -ian; *not* venous
 (VAN VERN)

VERA-VERD

veraci/ty (truth) -ous -ously;
 not voracity
veranda(h)
verb -al -ally -iage
verbalis/e -ed -ing -ation (z)
verbatim
verbena
verbos/e -ely -ity
verd/ant -antly -ancy -ure
verderer
verdict
verdigris
verditer
 (VAR VIR VOR)

VERG

verg/e -ed -ing
verger -ship
 (VERJ VIRG)

VERI

veridic/al -ally -ous
verif/y -ies -ied -ying -ication
verily
verisimilitude
verit/y -ies -able -ably
 (VARI VERY VIRI)

VERJ

verjuic/e -ed
 (VERG VIRG)

VERM

vermeil
vermi/an -cular -culate
 -culation
vermi/form -fuge -vorous
 -cide
vermicelli
vermiculite
vermilion
vermin -ous -ously
vermouth
 (FERM FIRM)

VERN

vernacular -ly -ism -ity
vernacularis/e -ed -ing
 -ation (z)
vernal -ly
vernier
 (FER FUR)

VERO

Veron/a -ese
veronica
 (FERO FERR VIRO)

VERR

verruc/a -al -ose -ous -iform
 (VIR FER)

VERS

versant
versatil/e -ely -ity
vers/e -ed -ify -ified -ifying
 -ification
versic/le -ular
version -al
vers libre (*F*)
verso
verst (*Russ*)

261

versus (*L*)
(AVER)

VERT
vertebr/a - ae - al - ally - ate
 - ated - ation
vert/ex - ices
vertical - ly - ity
vertig/o - inous - inously
(VIRT)

VERV
vervain
verve
vervet (monkey)

VERY
ver/y - ily
(VARI VERI VIRI)

VES
vesic/a - al - ate - ated - otomy
vesic/le - ular - ulous - ulation
vesper - s - tine
vesp/ine - iform - iary
vessel - ful
vest - ed - ing
vesta
vestal - ly
vestibul/e - ar - ate
vestig/e - ial - ially
vestment
vestr/y - ies
vestur/e - ed - ing - er
Vesuvi/us - an
(VAS VICI VIS VOCI)

VET-VEX
vet - ted - ting , *for* veterinary
 surgeon *or* check
vetch - y - ling
veteran (old hand)
veterinar/y (animal diseases)
 - ian
veto - es - ed - ing
vex - ed - ing - ingly - edly
vexati/on - ous - ously
 - ousness
(VAT VIT)

VIA
via (*L*)
viab/le - ly - ility

viaduct
vial (small vessel); *not* vile
 (bad) *or* viol (music)
viands
viaticum
(VIO)

VIB
vibrant - ly
vibrat/e - ed - ing - ion - or - ory
vibrato (*It*)
viburnum
(FIB)

VICA
vicar - age - ate - ial
vicaria (textile)
vicarious - ly - ness
(VAC)

VICE
vic/e (evil) - ious - iously
 - iousness
vice *or* vise (grip)
vice - *, *prefix meaning* next
 in rank to
vicegerent; *not* viceregent
vicennial (20 years) - ly
vice/roy - alty - regal
vice versa (*L*)

VICH-VICU
Vichy water
vicin/ity - ities - age
vicious - ly - ness
vicissitud/e - inous
vicount? *No*, viscount
victim - ise, - ised - ising
 - isation (z)
victor - y - ies - ious - iously
Victoria - n
victual - led - ling - er; *not* vital
vicuña (*Sp*)

VID-VIK
vide (*L*, see)
videlicet (*L*) *or* viz (namely)
video - *, *prefix meaning* see
vie, vied, vying
Vienn/a - ese
view - ed - ing - er - y - less
vigil - ant - antly - ance

* If the word you wish to spell is not in this list, omit the prefix
and look for the rest of the word.

vigilante
vignett/e -er -ist
vigoroso (*It*)
vigour -less
vigor/ous -ously -ousness
viking

VIL

vil/e (bad) -ely -est -eness;
  not vial, viol
vilif/y -ies -ied -ying -ication
villa -dom
villag/e -er
villain -y -ies -ous -ously
villein (serf) -age
  (VEL)

VIN

vinaigrette
vindic/able -ably -ability
vindicat/e -ed -ing -ion -or
  -ive -ory
vindictive
vine -ry -yard
vinegar -y -ish
vin/y -ous -osity -ometer -yl
vin ordinaire (*F*)
vint/age -ager -ner
  (VEN)

VIOL

viol (music); *not* vial *or* vile
viol/a -ist
violin -ist
violoncell/o -os -ist; *or* cello
viol/et -a (flowers)
violat/e -ed -ing -ion -or
violen/t -tly -ce
  (VIA)

VIP

v.i.p., *for* very important
  person
viper -ish -ine -ous -oid

VIR

virago (fierce woman) -s; *not*
  farrago (medley)
virgate
Virgil -ian
virgin -ity -al -ally
virginals (music)
Virginia -n
Virg/o -an
virid/ian -ity -escent

-escence
viril/e -ly -ity
viro/logy -logist -us; *but* virus
virtu -oso -osos
virtual -ly
virtu/e -ous -ously
virulen/t -tly -ce
virus -es
  (VAR VER VOR)

VIS

visa, visa'd *or* vised
visag/e -ed
vis -à -vis (*F*)
viscer/a -al
viscerat/e -ed -ing -ion; *also*
  evisc-
viscid -ity
visc/ose -ous -ously -osity
viscount -ess
vise *or* vice (grip)
visib/le -ly -ility
vision -ary -ariness -al
visit -ed -ing -ation -or -ant
visor *or* vizard
vista -'d
visual -ly -ity
visualis/e -ed -ing -ation (z)
  (THIS VES VIC VIZ)

VIT

vital -ly -ity -ism -ist
vitalis/e -ed -ing -ation (z)
vitamin
vitiat/e -ed -ing -ion -or
viticultur/e -al -ist
vitreous
vitrif/y -ied -ying -action
vitriol -ic -ically
vittles? *No*, victuals
vituperat/e -ed -ing -ion -or
vituperative -ly -ness

VIV-VIZ

viva, *for* viva voce (*L*)
vivace (*It*)
vivac/ity -ious -iously
vivari/um
vive! (*F*)
vivid -ly -ness
vivif/y -ies -ied -ying -ication
vivipar/ous -ously -ousness
vivisect -ed -ing -ion -or

vixen -ish
vizard *or* visor
viz, *for* videlicet (*L*)

VOC-VOG

vocab/le - ulary - ularies
vocal - ism - ist
vocalis/e - ed - ing - ation (z)
vocative
vocation - al - ally; *not*
  vacation (holiday)
vocifer/ate - ated - ating - ation
  - ant
vocifer/ous - ously - ousness
vodka
voe (*Shetland*)
vogue
  (VA)

VOI

voic/e - ed - ing - eless
void - ed - ing - ly - able - ance
voile
  (VIO VOY)

VOL

volatil/e - ity - eness
volatilis/e - ed - ing - ation (z)
vol - au - vent (*F*)
volcan/o - oes - ic - ically; *but*
  vulcanism
vole
volet
volition - al - ally - ary
volley - s - ed - ing - er
volt - age - aic - ameter
volte - face (*F*)
volub/le - ly - ility
volum/e - etric - etrical
  - etrically
volumin/ous - ously - ousness
voluntar/y - ies - ily - iness
volunteer - ed - ing
voluptu/ary - aries - ous - ously
  - ousness
volut/e - ion
  (VAL VEL)

VOM-VOO

vomit - ed - ing - ory - ive
voodoo - ism - ist

VOR

vorac/ity (appetite) - ious
  - iously; *not* veracity (truth)

vort/ex - ices *or* exes - ical
  - ically - icular
vortic/ism - ist
  (VAR VER VIR)

VOT

votar/y - ies
vot/e - ed - ing - er - able
votive

VOU

vouch - ed - ing - er
vouchsaf/e - ed - ing
voussoir

VOW

vow - ed - ing; *also* avow
vowel - led

VOY

voyag/e - ed - ing - er
voyeur
  (VOI)

VUL

vulcan/ism - ist - icity; *but*
  volcano
vulcanite
vulcanis/e - ed - ing - ation (z)
vulgar - ly - ity - ian
vularis/e - ed - ing - ation (z)
vulgate
vulner/able - ably - ability
vulpine
vultur/e - ine - ish - ous
vulv/a - ar - ate - iform - itis
  (VOL)

W

*Some English (but not
Scottish, Irish or Welsh)
spellers may need to be
reminded of the difference
in pronunciation between* W
and Wh.

WAD

wad - ed - ding
waddl/e - ed - ing - ingly
waddy (*Aus*)
wad/e - ed - ing - er - able; *not*
  weighed (heaviness)
wadi (*Arab*)
  (WOD)

WAF

wafer - ed - ing

waffl/e -ed -ing
waft -ed -ing
WAG
wag -ged -ging -ger -gish
  -gishly -gishness -gery
wag/e -es -ed -ing
wager -ed -ing
wagga (*Aus*)
waggl/e -ed -ing -y -iness
waggon *or* wagon -er -ette
wagon -lit (*F*)
WAH
wahine (*NZ*)
WAI
waiata (*NZ*)
waif -s
wail (lament) -ed -ing; *also*
  bewail; *not* whale
wain (waggon); *not* wane
  (decline)
wainscot -ed -ing
waist (middle) -ed; *not* waste
  (squander)
wait -ed -ing -er -ress; *also*
  await
waiv/e (forgo) -ed -ing -er;
  not wave
  (WAY WEI WHEY)
WAK
wak/e -ing -ed *or* woke,
  woken; *also* awake
waken -ed -ing; *also* awaken
  (WHA)
WAL
Wales; *but* whales
walk -ed -ing -er
wall -ed -ing -er
wall -ey/e -ed
wallah (*Hind*)
wallab/y -ies
wallaroo (*Aus*)
wallet
Walloon
wallop -ed -ing -er
wallow -ed -ing -er
walnut
Walpurgis -night
walrus -es
waltz -es -ed -ing -er
  (WHA)

WAM
wampum
  (WOM)
WAN
wan (pale) -ly -ness; *not* won,
  one
wand
wander (roam) -ed -ing -ingly
  -er; *not* wonder
wanderlust (*Ger*)
wanderoo (monkey)
wandoo (*Aus*, tree)
wane (decrease) -ed -ing; *not*
  wain (waggon)
wangl/e -ed -ing -er
want -ed -ing
wanton -ed -ing -ly -ness
WAP
wapentake
wapiti
wappenshaw (*Sc*)
  (WHOP)
WAR
war -red -ring -fare -like
warbl/e -ed -ing -er
ward -ed -ing -ship
warden
ward/er -ress
wardrobe
ware! (beware!)
ware -s (goods) -e house;
  not wear
warlock
warm -er -est -ed -ing -ly -th
  -ness
warn -ed -ing -ingly; *not*
  worn (wear)
warp -ed -ing
warrant -ed -ing -y -ies
warren
warrigal (*Aus*)
warrior
wart -y -ier -iest -iness
war/y -ier -iest -ily -iness
  (WHAR WHOR WOR)
WAS
was, wasn't
wash -ed -ing -er -able -ably
  -ability; *also* awash
wash -stand

265

wash/y -ier -iest -ily -iness
wasp -y -ish -ishly -ishness
wassail
wast/e -ed -ing -er -age; *not*
  waist (middle)
wasteful -ly -ness
wastrel
  (WAIS)

WAT

watch -ed -ing -er -ful -fully
  -fulness
water -ed -ing -y -iness
watt -age -meter
wattl/e -ed
  (WHAT WOT)

WAV WAX

wav/e -ed -ing -let -less; *not*
  waive (forgo)
wav/y -ier -iest -ily -iness
waver -ed -ing -ingly -er
wax -ed -ing -en -y -ier -iest
  -ily -iness

WAY

way -faring -farer; *also*
  away; *not* weigh
  (heaviness)
wayla/y -id -ying
wayward -ly -ness
wayzgoose
  (WAI WEI WHEY)

WE WEA

we, we're (we are), we've
  (we have), we'd (we had,
  would)
weak -er -est -ly -ness -ling
  -ish
weaken -ed -ing
weal (flesh-wound); *not*
  wheel
weald -en; *not* wield (hold
  and use)
wealth -y -ier -iest -ily -iness
wean -ed -ing -er -ling
weapon
wear (dress) -ing -er; *but*
  wore, worn; *not* ere, where
wear/y -ier -iest -ily -iness
wearisome -ly -ness
weasel
weather -ed -ing; *not* wether

(sheep), whether (if)
weav/e -ing -er; *but* wove,
  woven; *not* we've
  (WEE WHEA WHEE WIE)

WEB WED

web -bed -bing
wed -ded -ding -lock
we'd, *for* we would, we had
wedg/e -ed -ing
Wedgwood pottery
Wednesday

WEE

wee -er -est
weed -ed -ing -er
week (7 days) -ly -lies; *not*
  weak (not strong)
weep -ing -er; *but* wept
weevil -led -y
  (WEA WEI WHEA WHEE
  WIE)

WEI

weigh -ed -ing (heaviness);
  not way
weight -y -ier -iest -ily
  -iness; *not* wait (pause)
weir (dam); *not* we're
weird -er -est -ly -ness -ie
  (WEA WEE WHEA WHEE
  WIE)

WEL

welcom/e -ed -ing -eness
weld -ed -ing -er -able
welfare
welkin
well -ed -ing
we'll, *for* we will *or* we shall
Wellington -s -ia
Welsh
welsh -ed -ing -er
welt -ed -ing
welter -ed -ing
welth? *No,* wealth
  (WHEL)

WEN

wen
wench -es -ing -er
wend -ed (*or* went) -ing
Wensleydale
Wensday? *No,* Wednesday
went (did go)

WEP
wept (did weep)
wepon? *No*, weapon

WER
were (was); *not* where
  position
weren't, *for* were not
we're, *for* we are; *not* weir
  (dam)
werewolf
  (WEI WHER WHIR WOR
  WUR)

WES WET
Wesley -an -anism
west -ward -ing -erly -erlies
  -ering
western -er
westernis/e -ed -ing -ation
  (z)
wet -ter -test -ted -ting
  -ness -ly -tish; *not* whet
  (sharpen)
wether (sheep); *not* weather,
  whether
  (WHE)

WHA
whack -ed -ing -er
whal/e -ing -er; *not* wail
  (lament)
whang -ed -ing
whar/f -fs *or* -ves -fage
  -finger -fy
what -ever -soever
whaup (*Sc*)
  (WA)

WHEA
wheal (*Cornish*, mine)
wheat -en
wheatear
  (WEA WEE WHEE WIE)

WHEE
wheedl/e -ed -ing -ingly
wheel -ed -ing -er -wright
  -less
wheelbarrow
wheez/e -ed -ing -y -ier -iest
  -ily -iness
  (WEA WEE WHEA WIE)

WHEL
whelk
whelm -ed -ing; *also*
  overwhelm
whelp -ed -ing
  (WEL)

WHEN
when -ever -soever
whence
  (WEN)

WHER
where (position) -ever
  -soever; *not* were
where -about -abouts -at -by
  -fore -from -in -into -of -on
  -out -through -to -under
  -unto -upon -with -withal
wherr/y -ies
  (WER WHIR)

WHET
whet (sharpen) -ted -ting;
  not wet
whether (if); *not* weather,
  wether

WHEY
whey (milk product); *not*
  way, weigh

WHIC-WHIP
which -ever -soever; *not*
  witch
whiff -ed -ing
whiffl/e -ed -ing
whig (political party) -gish;
  not wig (hair)
whil/e -ed -ing -st -om; *also*
  awhile; *not* wile (trick)
whim -sy -sies -sical -sically
  -sicality
whimbrel
whimper -ed -ing -ingly -er
whin -stone
whin/e -ed -ing -ingly -er;
  not wine (drink)
whinn/y -ied -ying
whip -ed -ing -er -py -piness
whippet
whippoorwill
  (WI)

WHIR
whir(r) -red -ring

267

whirl -ed -ing
whirligig
(WER WUR)
WHIS
whisk -ed -ing
whisker -ed -y
whisk/y -ies (Sc),
whiskey -s (Ir)
whisper -ed -ing -ingly
whist
whistl/e -ed -ing -er
(WIS)
WHIT
whit (particle); not wit
whit/e -er -est -ely -eness
whiten -ed -ing -er
white-eyed
white-thorn
white-thorn
white-throat
whitewash -ed -ing
whither (to where) -soever
whit/ish -y
whiting
whitlow
Whitsun
whittl/e -ed -ing -er
(WIT)
WHIZ
whiz(z) -zed -zing
(WIS WIZ)
WHO
who -ever -soever
whom -ever -soever
whose (belonging to whom)
who's, for who is
whoa! (stop!); not woe
whodun(n)it
whol/e -ly -eness; not hole,
holy, holiness
wholehearted -ly -ness
wholesale -r
wholesome
whoop -ed -ing -er
whoopee
whop -ped -ping -per
whor/e -ed -ing -edom -ish
whorl -ed
whortleberry -ies
(HOO)

WHY
why -ever
(WI WY)
WIC WID
wich? No, which
wick
wicked -er -est -ly -ness
wicker -ed
wicket
widdershins
wid/e -er -est -ely -th -ish
widen -ed -ing
wi(d)geon
widgie (Aus)
widow -er -ed -ing
width
WIE
wield -ed -ing
(WEA WEE WHEA WHEE
WHY)
WIF
wife -ly -like -less; but wives
(WHIF)
WIG
wig -ged -ging -less
wiggl/e -ed -ing -y
wigwam
(WHIG)
WIL
wild -er -est -ly -ness
wildebeest
wilderness -es
wile (trick); not while
wilful -ly -ness
wilga (Aus)
will -ed -ing -ingly -ingness
will-o'-the -wisp
willow -ed -ing -y
willy-nilly
willy-will/y -ies (Aus)
wilt -ed -ing
wil/y -ier -iest -ily -iness
WIM
wimmin? No, women
wimpl/e -ed -ing
(WHIM)
WIN
win -ning -ningly -ner; but
won
winc/e -ed -ing

268

wincey - ette
winch - ed - ing
wind (air) - y - ier - iest - ily
 - iness - ed
wind (turn) - ing - er; *but*
 wound
windlass
window - ed - less
Windsor
wine (drink); *not* whine
 (snivel)
wing - ed - ing
wing/e (*Aus*) - ed - eing
wink - ed - ing - er
winkl/e - ed - ing - er
winnow - ed - ing - er
winsome - ly - ness
winter - ed - ing
wintr/y - iness
 (WHIN WYN)

WIP
wip/e - ed - ing - er
 (WHIP)

WIR
wir/e - ed - ing - y - ier - iest
 - iness
wireless
 (WHIR WER WOR WUR)

WIS
wisdom
wis/e - er - est - ely
wiseacre
wish - ed - ing - er
wishful - ly - ness
wishy - wash/y - iness
wisp - y
wistaria *or* wisteria
wistful - ly - ness
 (WHIS WIZ)

WIT
wit - ty - tier - tiest - tily - tiness
witless - ly - ness
wit - ted - ting
witticism
witan *or* witenagemot
witch - ed - ing - ery - craft;
 also bewitch
witchetty grub (*Aus*)
with
withal

withdraw - n - ing - al
wither (shrivel) - ed - ing
 - ingly; *not* whither
withers
withhold - ing; withheld
within
without
withstand
with/y - ies
witness - es - ed - ing
 (WHIT)

WIV
wivern *or* wyvern
wives (wife)
 (WITH)

WIZ
wizard - ry - ries
wizen - ed
 (WHIZ WIS)

WOA-WOL
woad
wobbl/e - ed - ing - er - y
wodge
woe - ful - fully - fulness
woebegone
wok/e - en; *also* awok/e - n;
 but wake
wold
wol/f - ves - fed - fing - fish
wolfram
wolverine
 (WHO)

WOM
woman - ly - liness - like - ish
 - ishly
womanis/e - ed - ing - er (z)
women
womb
wombat
 (WAM WHOM)

WON
won (did win); *not* one (1),
 wan (pale)
wonce? *No,* once
wonder - ed - ing - ingly - ment
wonderful - ly - ness
wondrous - ly - ness
wonga - wonga (*Aus*)
wonk/y - ier - iest - ily - iness
wont (custom, habit) - ed

won't, *for* will not
(ONE WAN)

WOO

woo - ed - ing - ingly - er
wood - ed - y - ier - iest - iness
wooden - ly - ness
wood - bine - pecker - wind
  - worm, etc.
woof *or* weft
wool - len - ly - lier - liest
  - liness
woollies
woomera (*Aus*)
(WO-)

WOR

word - ed - ing - y - ier - iest - ily
  - iness
wore (did wear)
work - ed - ing - er - able - ably
  - ableness
world - ly - lier - liest - liness
  - ling
worm - ed - ing - y - iness
wormwood
worn (wear)
worr/y - ied - ying - yingly - ier
wors/e - en - ened - ening
worship - ped - ping - per
worshipful - ly - ness
worst - ed - ing
worsted (woollen yarn)
wort
worth - less - lessly - lessness
worth/y - ies - ier - iest - ily
  - iness
(WAR WHOR WUR)

WOS

(WAS)

WOT

wot (know)
(WAT WHAT)

WOU-WOW

would (will); *not* wood
  (timber)
would - be
wouldn't, *for* would not
wound - ed - ing
wound (did wind)
wov/e (did weave) - en
wow

wowser (*Aus*)
(WHO WOO)

WRA

wrack (seaweed, etc.); *not*
  rack
wraith
wrangl/e - ed - ing - er
wrap - ped - ping - per - page
wrasse
wrath (anger); *not* wroth
  (angry)
(RA RHA)

WRE

wreak (avenge) - ed - ing; *not*
  reek
wreath - e - ed - ing
wreck - ed - ing - er - age
wren
wrench - ed - ing
wrest (twist) - ed - ing; *not*
  rest
wrestl/e - ed - ing - er
wretch - es - ed - edly - edness
(RE RHE)

WRI

wriggl/e - ed - ing - er
wright (shipwright, play-,
  wheel-, etc.)
wring (twist) - ing - er; *but*
  wrung; *not* ring
wrinkl/e - ed - ing
wrist - let
writ
writ/e - ing - ten - er; *but*
  wrote; *not* right, rite
writh/e - ed - ing - en
(RHI RI RY)

WRO-WRY

wrong - ed - ing - ful - fully
  - fulness - ly
wrongdo/er - ing
wrongous (*Sc*, legal)
wrote (did write); *not* rote
wroth (angry); *not* wrath
  (anger)
wrought
wrung (did wring); *not* rung
wry - er - est - ly - ness
(RHO RO)

WU
wurley (*Aus*)
(WER WHIR)
WY
wyandotte
wych *or* witch - elm, - hazel, etc.
wynd (*Sc*, alley); *not* wind
wyvern *or* wivern
(WHY WI)

X
Initial x *is normally pronounced as* z, *but see also* ex.

XA-XY
xanth/eine - ate - ic - ous - ophyll
xebec
xeno/gamy - philia - phobia - phobic
xenon
xero/graphy - graphic - graphically
xerophilous
xi (*Gr* letter x)
xiphoid
Xmas, *for* Christmas
X-ray - ed - ing
xylem
xylocarp - ous
xylograph/y - ic
xylonite
xylophone
xyster

Y
YA
yabber (*Aus*)
yacht - ed - ing - sman
yaffle
yah!
yahoo - s
yak
yakka *or* yacker (*Aus*)
yam
yammer - ed - ing
yank - ed - ing
Yank - ee
yap - ped - ping - per

yarborough
yard - age - arm
yarn - ed - ing - er
yarran (*Aus*)
yarrow
yashmak
yate (*Aus*)
yaw - ed - ing
yawl
yawn - ed - ing - ingly
yaws (disease); *not* yours
(IA)
YC
yclept (named)
YE
ye (you)
yea (yes)
yean - ed - ing - ling
year - ly - ling
yearn - ed - ing - ingly
yeast - y - iness
yell - ed - ing
yellow - er - est - ed - ing - ly - ness
yelp - ed - ing
yen
yeom/an - en - anry
yes - man
yester/day - night - morn - eve
yet
yeti
yew (tree); *not* you, hue
YI
Yid - dish
yield - ed - ing - ingly - er
YO
yob; yobbo - es
yodel - led - ling - ler
yog/a - i - is - ism
yoghourt; yogurt
yoicks!
yoke (shoulder - piece)
yokel
yolk (egg - yellow)
yon - der
yore (old times); *not* your
york - ed - ing - er
York - shire - ist
yot? *No*, yacht
you, you'd (you would), you'll

(you will), you're (you are),
  you've (you have)
young - er - est - ster
your (belonging to you); *not*
  you're
yours (*not* your's)
yoursel/f - ves
youth - ful - fully - fulness
yowl - ed - ing
yo - yo - s
  (AEO EO IO)

YU
yucca
Yugoslav - ia - ian
yule - tide
  (EU HU U YEW YOU)

Z

ZA
zan/y - ies
Zanzibar - i
zariba *or* zareba
  (SA XA)

ZE
zeal - ot - ous - ously
zebr/a - ine
zebu
zemindar (*Hind*)
zemstvo(*Russ*)
zenana (*Hind*)
zenith - al
zeolite
zephyr
zeppelin
zero
zest
zeugma - tic
  (SE XE)

ZI
zigzag - ged - ging
zin/c - ked - king - ky
zinco/graph - graphy - graphic
  - type
zinnia
Zion - ism - ist
zip - ped - ping - per
zircon - ium - ic - ate
zither - n - nist
  (PSY SI SY XY ZY)

ZO
zodiac - al
zoetrope
zoic
zoll (*Ger*, customs) - verein
zombie
zon/e - ed - ing - al - ally
zoo, *for* zoological garden
zoo -*, *prefix meaning* animal
zoolite
zo/ology - ologist - ological
zoomorph - ic - ism
zoophyt/e - ic
zoom - ed - ing
Zoroast/er - rian - rianism
zouave (*F*)
  (SO)

ZU
zucchetto (*It*)
Zulu
  (SOO SOU SU ZOO)

ZY
zygodactyl -ous
zygomorphous
zygospore
zygoma -ta -tic
zygo/sis -te
zymo/sis -tic
  (SI SY XY ZI)

* If the word you wish to spell is not in this list, omit the prefix
and look for the rest of the word.

Common Word-endings

This list ignores etymological niceties; its purpose is to help the unsure speller.

Word-ending	Examples	Comments
-a	1 Paula, signora	feminine
	2 data, lepidoptera	plural
-able,-ably, -ability	agreeable, movable	see Guidelines 6
-ac	cardiac, maniac	'belonging to'
-aceous	herbaceous, farinaceous	'of the nature of'
-acious	gracious, capacious	'inclined to'
-acity	capacity, sagacity	see -ity, -acious
-acy	accuracy, piracy	see -ate 2, -cracy
-ade	blockade, renegade	
-ae	hominidae, antennae	plural
-age	peerage, baggage	'belonging to'
-aire	commissionaire, legionnaire	French form of -ary
-al	municipal, principal	see -ally, -ical, -le
-algia	neuralgia, nostalgia	'pain'
-alia	regalia, paraphernalia	'things associated with'
-ally	principally, comically	never -aly; see -ially
-an	Mexican, Roman	see also -ian
-ana	Victoriana, railwayana	'relics'
-ance	ignorance, riddance	also-ant, -ancy, -ence-nce, -ns
-ancy	vacancy, infancy	also-ant, -ance, -ence
-ant	vacant, ignorant	also-ance, -ancy, -ent
-ar	bursar, beggar	also-er, -or
-arch -archy	monarch, anarchy	'rule'
-ary	unwary, seminary	see -ery, -ory -ry
-at	secretariat, proletariat	a form of -ate 3
-ate	1 dictate, oscillate	action
	2 accurate, obstinate	description
	3 syndicate, episcopate	office, function; see -at
	4 sulphate, carbonate	chemistry; see -ide
-atic	erratic, asthmatic	'liable to'; see -ic endings
-atile	volatile, fluviatile	denoting quality; see -ile
-ation	alteration, starvation	see -tion, -ion
-ble, -bility	portable, audible	see Guidelines 6
-ch	sandwich, detach	but see-tch
-cide, -cidal	homicide, suicide	'kill'
-cle	tentacle, particle	'little'; see. -le,-icle
-cracy, -crat, -cratic	democracy, autocracy	'rule', see -acy
-cycle	bicycle, tricycle	not -icle
-dom	freedom, kingdom	'state of'

-drome	hippodrome, aerodrome	'course'
-ean	European, Herculean	'belonging to'
-eau	bureau, tableau	plural adds -s or -x
-ectomy	hystorectomy	medical, 'cutting out'; also -otomy
-ed	needed, denied,	in the past; also -ened
-ee	payee, addressee	'recipient'
-een, -eenth	thirteen sixteen	
-eer	auctioneer, volunteer	see also -ier
-en, -ened, -ening	moisten, deepen	
-ence, -ent	reverence, impudence	see Guidelines 7
-ency, -ent	potency, valency	see Guidelines 7
-er	1 baker, officer	agent, but see -or; -eur
	2 smaller, higher	comparison
-ery	bakery, snobbery	see -er, -ary, -ory, -ry
-es	roses, wishes	plural; see Guidelines 1
-escent	fluorescent, obsolescent	'tending to be'
-ese	Portuguese, Chinese	
-esque	picturesque, burlesque	'resembling'
-ess	lioness, hostess	feminine ending
-est	fastest, truest	'most'
-et	bullet, sonnet	'little'; see also -ette
-etic	pathetic, emetic	see -ic
-ette	cigarette, marionette	'little'; see also -et
-etto	falsetto, allegretto	'somewhat', Italian
-eur	restaurateur, voyeur	French form of -er
-faction, -factory	satisfaction,	see -fy, -fication
-fer, -ferous	conifer, rotifer	but see -vorous
-fic	pacific, scientific	see -fy, -fication
-fication	pacification, identification	see -fy, -fic
-fold	tenfold, manifold	'times'
-form	uniform, cruciform	'arrangement'
-ful, -fuls	1 cup, spoonful	see Guidelines 8
-ful, -fully	2 hopeful, faithful	see Guidelines 8
-fy, -fying, -fied	satisfy, beautify	see -faction, -fication
-graph, -graphy	photograph, geography	also with -er, -ic, -ical, -ically
-gue	vague, rogue	silent -ue, except in ague, argue see also -logue
-hood	manhood, hardihood	'state of being'
-ia	1 Asia, Georgia	territories
	2 mania, militia	see also -algia, -alia
	3 dahlia, mammalia	groups, families
-ial, -ially	official, editorial	see -al, -tial, -ly
-ian	Aberdonian, Dickensian	see also -ician, -ean
-ible, -ibly, ibility	legible, visible	see Guidelines 6
-ic	1 sulphuric, oxalic	chemistry
	2 alcoholic, meteoric	also -fic, -atic, -etic, -otic
-ic, -ical	magic, critic	
-ician	magician, physician	see also -an, -ision, -tion
-icle	vehicle, icicle	also -cle; not cycle, -ical
-ide	1 iodide, carbide	chemistry
	2 divide, collide	see also -ision, -cide
-ie	birdie, doggie	playful variant of -y
-ier	cashier, bombardier	but see -eer
-ile, -ility	senile, agile	see also -atile
-ily	busily, merrily	see also -ly; -phily
-ine	1 divine, feminine	
	2 chlorine, fluorine	chemistry

274

-ing	going, coming	see Guidelines 3 and 4
-ion	companion, accordion	see -ian, -sion, -tion
-ior	superior, exterior	comparison; see -er 2
-iour	behaviour, saviour	-ior in American use
-ious	bilious, curious	see -ous
-ise	surprise, advertise	see -ize and Introduction 8
-ish	1 English, Scottish	'belonging to'
	2 girlish, goodish	
-ision	division, precision	see also -ician, -tion
-ism, -ist, -istic	tourism, Darwinism	
-ite	1 Israelite, Luddite	'member, follower'
	2 graphite, cordite	
-itis	arthritis, phlebitis	'inflammation'
-ity, -ities	unity, electricity	also -acity, -osity
-ium	1 medium, tedium	
	2 sodium, iridium	chemistry
-ive, -ively, -ivity	captive, extensive	
-ize, -ization	baptize, moralize	see -ise, -yse and Introduction 8
-le	handle, principle	also -able, -cle, -icle; but see al
-less, -lessly, -lessness	careless, merciless	'without'
-let	tablet, hamlet,	'little'
-like	ladylike, sportsmanlike	
-ling	duckling, underling	'little'
-logue	dialogue, catalogue	'word'; -log in American use
-logy, -logical	biology, analogy	'word'
-loquy	soliloquy, obloquy	'speech'
-ly	sincerely, totally	also -ably, -ally, -fully, -ially, -ily, -orily, -phily
-ment	payment, acknowledgment	
-meter, metric	barometer, kilometer	-tre in French use
-nce	convince, enhance	also -ance, -ence,
-nse	expense, expanse	
-ness	goodness, business	
-ock	bullock, paddock	
-oid	rhomboid, mongoloid	'resembling'
-oma	fibroma, sarcoma	'a growth'
-oon	balloon, buffoon	
-or	1 doctor, motor,	but see -er
-or, -ority	2 minor, major	see also -ior
-orama, -oramic	panorama, cyclorama	'view'
-ory, -ories	1 directory, dormitory	see -ary -ery -ry
-ory, -orily	2 satisfactory, cursory	see -ary, -ory
-ose	1 glucose, cellulose	chemistry
-ose, osity	2 verbose, bellicose	see also -ity
-osis, -otic	hypnosis, sclerosis	medical
-otic	chaotic, exotic	see -atic -etic
-our	honour, candour	-or in American use
-ous	porous, resinous	also -ious, -acious, -ferous
-phil(e) -phily, -philous	Anglophil, toxophily	'fond of'
-phobe, -phobia, -phobic	Anglophobe, agoraphobia	'hatred of'
-polis, -politan	metropolis, cosmopolis	'city'
-que	oblique, opaque	-ue not sounded
-quy	soliloquy, obloquy	
-rhoea	diarrhoea, logorrhoea	'flow'
-rix	testatrix, executrix	legal; feminine of -or
-ry	yeomanry, pedantry	but see -ary, -ery -ory
-s	dogs, guys,	plural; see Guidelines 1
-sect	dissect, intersect	'cut'
-ship	scholarship, partnership	

275

-sion	tension, confusion	see -ion, -tion, -ision, -ician
-spect	inspect, prospect	**'look'**
-tch	batch, etch, itch	see -ch
-th	1 eighth, eightieth	order
	2 growth, strength	
-tial	martial, partial	see -al, -ial
-tic	cosmetic, lunatic	see -ic, -atic, -etic, -otic, -ytic
-tion	ambition, motion	see -ion, -sion
-tomy	osteotomy, phlebotomy	medical, 'cut'; also -ectomy
-tude	magnitude, solitude	
-ule, -ular	nodule, capsule,	'little'
-ure	portraiture, legislature	
-ute, -ution	absolute, institute	
-vore, -vorous	carnivore, herbivore	'feeding'; not -fer, -ferous
-ward	upward, backward	
-ways	sideways, lengthways	but see -wise
-wise	lengthwise, otherwise	but see -ways
-y	1 piggy, Tommy	'little'; see -ie
	2 greedy, stony	but see -ie, -ily
-yse, -ysis, -ytic	paralyse, analyse	but see -ise

A book for everyone who has to put pen to paper or paper to typewriter.

This book is essential for all uncertain spellers who want a quick way of finding out how a word should be spelt. The author has devised a unique and simple system which quickly guides a mis-speller to the correct spelling of a word and its derivatives.

The vocabulary equals that of a medium-sized dictionary. It includes words in everyday use which have not yet found their way into many dictionaries, some common American spellings, foreign words and phrases in common use and also some words that are used mainly in Australia and New Zealand.

Cover design by David Cox Studios
TEACH YOURSELF BOOKS/HODDER AND STOUGHTON

Published in USA by David McKay Company, Inc.

ISBN 0 340

UNITED KINGDOM